INSIDI

MASS

HELP US KEEP THIS GUIDE UP TO DATE

We would love to hear from you concerning your experiences with this guide and how you feel it could be improved and kept up to date. Please send your comments and suggestions to:

editorial@GlobePequot.com

Thanks for your input, and happy travels!

INSIDERS' GUIDE® TO
MASSACHUSETTS

FIRST EDITION

MARIA OLIA

INSIDERS' GUIDE

GUILFORD, CONNECTICUT
AN IMPRINT OF GLOBE PEQUOT PRESS

All the information in this guidebook is subject to change. We recommend that you call ahead to obtain current information before traveling.

To buy books in quantity for corporate use or incentives, call **(800) 962–0973** or e-mail **premiums@GlobePequot.com**.

INSIDERS' GUIDE ®

Editor: Kevin Sirois
Project Editor: Lynn Zelem
Layout: Joanna Beyer
Text Design: Sheryl Kober
Maps: Alena Joy Pearce © Morris Book Publishing, LLC

ISBN 978-0-7627-8645-9

Printed in the United States of America
10 9 8 7 6 5 4 3 2 1

CONTENTS

CONTENTS

CONTENTS

ABOUT THE AUTHOR

Maria Olia is a freelance travel and parenting writer. Her work has appeared in dozens of newspapers and magazines including the *Boston Globe* and *Working Mother*. She has also written *Day Trips New England* for Globe Pequot Press. Maria has called Massachusetts home for the last three decades. She lives in Newton with her husband and is the mother of three grown sons and a teenage daughter. When not writing, she can be found going for long walks or frequenting her favorite Boston museums and restaurants.

ACKNOWLEDGMENTS

The love and support of my husband Masoud and my children, Bijan, Kian, Cameron, and Leda, made this book possible. They deserve my heartfelt thanks for accompanying me on endless excursions throughout the state and then allowing me time to disappear into my garret office to write it all down. Thanks also to my parents, Robert and Josephine Dascanio, for a childhood of wonderful travel memories.

INTRODUCTION

Welcome to Massachusetts.

There may be no better place to experience American history than here, where the Pilgrims landed to create the settlement known as Plymouth Colony, where Boston patriots Sam Adams, Paul Revere, and John Hancock launched the American Revolution; where a host of intellectual and literary lights, including Ralph Waldo Emerson, flourished in Concord.

The Bay State, so named for its Atlantic gulf formed by the flexed arm of Cape Cod, has quite a lot to offer visitors. Besides the well-known historic sites of Boston, Massachusetts is very much a destination for appreciating the outdoors in every season. Across the state, from the densely forested Berkshire Hills to the lush Pioneer Valley to the tip of Cape Cod, there are breathtaking hiking and biking trails, mountains for skiing, and pristine ocean beaches for relaxing.

Located in the center of New England, Massachusetts is not only the region's geographic heart, but also in many ways its cultural heart. You'll discover a dizzying array of art, music, and theater from one end of the state to the other. There's high art at Boston's Museum of Fine Art and at the Isabella Stewart Gardner Museum. In North Adams, MASS MoCA galleries are full of exciting, provocative works. The Boston Symphony performs at Boston's Symphony Hall, and in the summer classical music lovers follow the orchestra to Tanglewood in the Berkshires. The theater scene is centered in Boston and Cambridge (and the Berkshires in the summer), but theatrical richness can also be found throughout the state in places as far-flung as Watertown, Stoneham, and Cape Cod.

Massachusetts is steeped in history and tradition but is surprisingly modern. In 2004 the state was one of the first in the nation to legalize same-sex marriage. And the state's pioneering state-mandated universal health care plan legislation of 2006 was the model for the federal 2010 Affordable Care Act. Massachusetts's progressive attitudes are no doubt energized by its college and university communities and keep the state at the crossroads of the country's intellectual and moral conversation.

Massachusetts is home at the table, too. Boston is the hub of the state's food scene, from celebrated kitchens and hip watering holes to quirky neighborhood bistros. But you can find great dining experiences just about anywhere you look in the state these days, from ethnic eateries in Cambridge (and Somerville, too), to the locavore-focused Berkshires, to superb seafood including chowders, lobster rolls, and baskets of whole-belly fried clams all along the coast.

Geographically, it is not a large state. But nearly 400 eventful years have left their mark here. Visiting Massachusetts will breathe life into those dusty elementary school history lessons. Discover, too, the endlessly fascinating Massachusetts of the present, its geographic diversity and cultural richness. Take the time to experience it in person. You'll see.

HOW TO USE THIS BOOK

This book is not only a handy on-the-ground guide to Massachusetts for the independent traveler, but with its tons of listings on everything from restaurants, entertainment, and shopping to health clubs, hiking trails, and even farmers' markets, it is also an invaluable tool for local residents or those contemplating moving to the state.

The format is organized in such a way that it leaves virtually no travel stone unturned.

While including all the expected vacation sites, such as the Freedom Trail and Cape Cod beaches, this book also mixes in a good number of lesser-known destinations. Such places as the home of architect Walter Gropius in Lincoln and Lowell's Boat House in Amesbury, as well as wonderful and unexpected "hidden treasures" like the Berkshires's Bash Bish Falls and Rockport's Paper House, are worth going out of the way to visit and can make your vacation an adventure.

The Area Overview chapter provides context for your trip, with sections on the state's landscape, cuisine, people, and the arts. The Getting Here/Getting Around chapter provides the nuts-and-bolts details you need to begin planning your visit to Massachusetts—everything from navigating your way through Logan Airport to an overview of the Massachusetts highway system to a rundown of the state's excellent public transit options, including the MBTA (or "T") subway and commuter rail lines. The History chapter makes for good pre-trip reading and presents a broad survey of Massachusetts's rich history, highlighting must-see sites and explaining why they are important.

This book is organized to make it as easy as possible to find what you are looking for and plan your perfect trip. The main part of the book is divided into seven chapters that correspond to a Massachusetts region: **Boston & Greater Boston, Merrimack Valley & North Shore, Southeast Massachusetts & South Shore, Cape Cod & The Islands, Worcester County, Pioneer Valley,** and **The Berkshires.** Within each regional chapter there is an overview of the area along with an easy-to-read map, which is followed by main sections devoted to describing Attractions, Activities & Events, Shopping, Accommodations, and Restaurants. At the end of each chapter there is also a detailed Day Trip itinerary that takes you from stop to stop with simple route directions accompanied by an easy-to-use bullet map with details of the most interesting places to visit along the way.

Throughout the book are **Insiders' Tips** (indicated by an ℹ️), which give you some tidbits gleaned from locals on things you might not otherwise have known about; sidebars, which condense practical information and basic facts into an easy-to-read list; and **Close-ups,** which spotlight things worth spending more time on.

You'll also find listings accompanied by the ✳ symbol—these are our top picks for attractions, restaurants, accommodations, and everything in between that you shouldn't miss while you're in the area. You want the best this region has to offer? Go with our **Insiders' Choice.**

Those who are relocating to Massachusetts—welcome! Check out the blue-tabbed pages at the back of the book, where you will find the **Living Here** appendix. It offers sections on relocation, education, child care, health care, and media. It provides quick answers to common questions.

ACCOMMODATIONS PRICE CODE

The price categories below are for two people in a standard double room during the week and in high season, excluding taxes, service charges, and fees for extra amenities.

$ . . . . **Less than $100**
$$ . . . . **$100 to $150**
$$$ . . . . **$150 to $200**
$$$$ . . . . **More than $200**

RESTAURANT PRICE CODE

Prices at restaurants are difficult to categorize, except in very broad terms, because so much depends on what you order. As a guide, the following price code corresponds to an average main course per person without drinks or a tip.

$ . . . . **Less than $10**
$$ . . . . **$10 to $20**
$$$ . . . . **$20 to $30**
$$$$ . . . . **More than $30**

AREA OVERVIEW

Practically every corner of Massachusetts has some historic site of national significance. Whether you're visiting for the first time or have lived here all your life, head
to Boston first and walk the Freedom Trail, which takes in 16 historic sites that trace
the country's path to independence for an introduction to what Massachusetts is all
about. Enjoy, too, Boston's world-class museums, mind-boggling array of restaurants,
and sizzling nightlife. North of the city, the Revolutionary War battle sites at Lexington
and Concord, bewitching Salem, the fishing port of Gloucester, and the shipbuilding
village of Essex all make for memorable exploring. Then move farther afield, where the
thickly settled South Shore offers a string of pretty harbor towns and a window on the
real history of the first Thanksgiving in Plymouth. In the center of the state, Worcester
typically gets short shrift by travelers but is home to several fine museums. Also in the
center of the state and defined by the great Connecticut River that bisects its heart, the
Pioneer Valley is home to the college towns of Amherst, Holyoke, and Northampton,
where young minds meet academic tradition and political and social ideas of all kinds
are welcome. Lying to the west, the Berkshire Hills are where you'll find serene natural
beauty and cultural richness—and they serve as the summer home of the Boston Symphony. And after so much history and activity, head to Cape Cod for miles and miles of
stunning beaches—and to relax in the present.

GEOGRAPHY

Massachusetts is located in the northeastern part of the US. New Hampshire and Vermont are to the north; Connecticut and Rhode Island are to the south, with New York to the west and the Atlantic Ocean to the east. Massachusetts is the 7th smallest state, just 113 miles long and 180 miles wide. Massachusetts's relatively compact size works to your advantage and the state's excellent transportation system makes it easy to get around. But there are so many things to see and do in the state that it may take awhile to get through them!

Within its tight borders, Massachusetts's terrain is diverse and gradually changes from a low coastal plain on the eastern seacoast, to rolling hills in the central Pioneer Valley, to the north–south spine of the Taconic Range (usually referred to as the Berkshire Hills) in the west. The highest point in the state is Mount Greylock at 3,491 feet, on the border with New York. The state has 1,500 miles of Atlantic coastline from Newbury-port in the north near New Hampshire to the hook-shaped peninsula of Cape Cod and on to New Bedford in the southwest part of

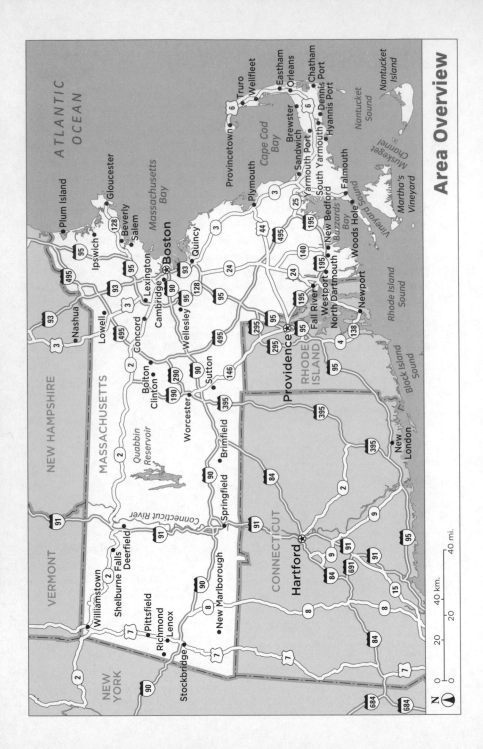

Area Overview

the state near Rhode Island, as well as the islands of Martha's Vineyard and Nantucket. Major rivers include the Charles, which flows roughly northeast from its beginning in Hopkinton to Boston, and the Connecticut (the longest in the state), which courses north–south through the Pioneer Valley in the western part of the state.

PEOPLE

Massachusetts residents are known to be reserved—even standoffish. Massachusetts residents are buttoned up, both literally and otherwise. Some say it's the cold winters. Others blame it on blue laws. Even today the state manages to retain (and enforce) laws that regulate alcohol sales and shopping on holidays that hark back to the Commonwealth's Puritan roots. But give Bay Staters a try; if you stop and ask for directions, they want to be helpful—just don't expect a lot of small talk.

As you would expect from a state with some of the country's best universities, Massachusetts residents tend to be well educated. And while the "Massachusetts liberal" is an archetype, and used by some as a political slur, there is some truth to the image. The current Massachusetts delegation to Washington is all Democratic.

The native Massachusetts character is made more complex by the state's diversity. Whites account for 84 percent of the population, blacks 8 percent, and the percentage of Asians and Latinos is increasing. In terms of ethnicity, Massachusetts has forever been altered by the influx of immigrants from Ireland in the mid-1800s. Irish roots still prevail here. More than 25 percent of Bay Staters have some Irish ancestry, more than any other background. Other ethnic groups that predominate include Italians, French/French Canadians, and Portuguese.

THE ARTS

Just as America's sense of history started in Massachusetts, so too the country's development of the arts. Many of the towering individuals who played fundamental roles in creating the country's early cultural landscape were from Massachusetts.

The list of important literary figures from Massachusetts is long indeed. In Cambridge, poet and Harvard professor Henry Wadsworth Longfellow wrote narrative story poems like *Paul Revere's Ride* and the *Song of Hiawatha* that helped create American myth.

Some 50 years after the Revolution, Concord was the epicenter of transcendentalism, the country's first uniquely American intellectual movement, led by writers Ralph Waldo Emerson, Henry David Thoreau, and Nathaniel Hawthorne. You can visit the homes of several notable female writers who resided in the state, including Louisa May Alcott's Orchard House, the Emily Dickinson Homestead in Amherst, and Edith Wharton's The Mount in Lenox. Today the Massachusetts literary tradition continues. Because Massachusetts is a world center for higher education, there is a steady stream of academic publishing going on. Massachusetts counts among its resident writers David McCullough, Doris Kearns Goodwin, and Dennis Lehane, as well as numerous others.

Boston is the region's largest and most cosmopolitan city and is the center of cultural life not just for the state, but also for New England. In terms of the quality and quantity of its theatrical productions, musical offerings, and dance performances, few cities in America can match Boston when it comes to the arts. The Boston stage accommodates both the traditional and the avant-garde, including alternative plays, revivals, and contemporary drama. Boston has an impressive number of orchestras, including the world-renowned Boston Symphony Orchestra—as well as many chamber groups, historic instrument ensembles, and choral groups. In Boston the resident ballet and opera companies, the Boston Ballet and the Boston Lyric Opera, are vibrant and forward-thinking institutions and anything but staid. The performing arts scene is further augmented by traveling Broadway shows and visiting music concerts. Thanks to the city's large student population, you'll also find cutting-edge music with a pulse that can be felt in bars, club, and lounges all over the city. In the summer the theater and music scene shifts focus to the Berkshires and the Boston Symphony at Tanglewood, the Jacob's Pillow Dance Festival, and the Williamstown Theater Festival.

For more than a century, Massachusetts has produced and been home to countless artists. Among the Massachusetts-based artists to look for in museums across the state are 19th-century portraitist John Singer Sargent, landscape artist Winslow Homer, sculptor Daniel Chester French, and illustrator Norman Rockwell. The state is home to several distinguished museums. You'll find prized collections from ancient to contemporary at Boston's Museum of Fine Arts, which since 1876 has played a major part in the life of the city. Among the state's many specialty art museums are the Isabella Stewart Gardner Museum in Boston, the Museum of Russian Icons in Clinton, the Clark Museum in Williamstown, the Daniel Chester French Museum in Stockbridge, and the Norman Rockwell Museum, also in

Stockbridge. You'll find, too, a plethora of art galleries and artisan studios throughout the state, but especially in Boston, the Berkshires, and Cape Cod, where you can purchase the work of talented area artisans and artists as unique gifts or for your own collection.

OUTDOOR ACTIVITIES

Massachusetts is an outdoor activity paradise throughout four very distinct seasons. Although it is the country's third most densely populated state, you never have to look far for a patch of park or grassy green because Massachusetts is chock-full of open space and recreational areas.

With miles of ocean coastline, lakes, pond, and rivers, the state offers numerous opportunities for sailing, kayaking, canoeing, rafting, and more. If you enjoy the beach, Cape Cod, Martha's Vineyard, and Nantucket offer a wonderful variety of water sports, starting, of course, with the fine-sand beaches for swimming.

Many city and town parks have mixed-use walking/hiking/biking trails. The state's Department of Conservation and Recreation maintains 3,000 miles of walking trails and 145 miles of paved biking trails through its network of parks. Other big players in state land conservation and recreation are Massachusetts Audubon, with more than 50 sanctuaries, and the Trustees of Reservations, with more than 100 properties. A portion of the Appalachian Trail passes through Massachusetts, entering at the state's border with Connecticut in the southern Berkshires and running along the state's highest peaks before exiting into Vermont. These are good times for bikers. Massachusetts abounds with hundreds of miles of paths designed for biking—and there are more every year.

Major trails include the Cape Cod Rail Trail from Dennis to Wellfleet and the Minuteman Bikeway from Cambridge to Bedford.

Camping enthusiasts will have no problem finding a place to pitch a tent or park an RV. The Department of Conservation and Recreation maintains more than two dozen drive-in campgrounds throughout the state including yurt camping on the Boston Harbor Islands, cabin camping on the Mohawk Trail, and tent/RV camping at Horseneck Beach in Westport.

All Massachusetts kids grow up learning to ice-skate, usually by pushing along a stack of upturned milk crates at their town rink. The state Department of Conservation and Recreation maintains the state's network of indoor ice rinks and offers public skating hours throughout the winter. Boston's Frog Pond is the state's most well-known outdoor refrigerated ice-skating rink. But outdoor ice-skating rinks are scattered throughout the state. In the heart of winter, you can also skate outdoors on any of the state's open, natural ponds. Double-check, though, that the ice is safe—and strong enough to support your triple toe-loop jumps.

The best downhill-ski areas are located in the Berkshires in the western part of the state. Jiminy Peak and Ski Butternut have vertical drops of 1,000 feet and all the services you would expect of a professional ski resort. Cross-country skiing is increasingly popular and is as close as the Weston Ski Track or, if you have your own equipment, your local golf course.

As for golf, you can tee off at scores of public and semiprivate courses—they're scattered throughout the state like lost golf balls. The Cape alone has more than 50 courses.

Tens of thousands of sports enthusiasts from across the country—indeed, from around the world—flock to the state every year to attend as participants or spectators such major events as the Boston Marathon, the Pan Mass Bike Challenge, and the Charles Regatta.

CUISINE

There is great food to be had in Massachusetts. In the past decade, the state has upped its culinary credentials with a new generation of young chefs. The hard part for diners is making a decision. Among your choices: celebrity-chef-backed restaurants, waterfront seafood houses, ethnic mom-and-pops of all types, and neighborhood spots that allow you to have a good meal any day of the week. Throughout the state restaurants big and small, inexpensive and pricey, take care to use fresh produce and meats from local farms and farmers' markets and especially the sea.

Seafood is most associated with Bay State cuisine and the fish dishes here tend to be outstanding. The most common fish on Massachusetts menus is cod. Whether fried or broiled, cod is reliably excellent. Sometimes in tourist areas you'll see the term "scrod." Scrod is cod, too; the word is an acronym for "small cod received on dock." Oysters are always local and they are usually served raw on the half shell—and they are superb. The best come from the towns of Wellfleet, Duxbury, and Chatham. Clams are native to Massachusetts as well and are usually served fried or in creamy clam chowder. Lobster is another native Massachusetts food. Bet you didn't know that Massachusetts is the second largest harvester of lobster in the country (after Maine, of course). Enjoy lobster rolls, lobster bisque, or steamed whole boiled lobster. Lobster in any form is a culinary delight and a must-do culinary experience while you are in the state.

The most appealing dining trends of late include a proliferation of eateries that serve sophisticated comfort food along with craft cocktails and serious beer lists. Places like Strip-T's in Watertown, Nudel in Lenox, Hungry Mother in Cambridge, and State Road in Martha's Vineyard are so good that diners travel from miles around to eat there.

i **Boston's restaurant weeks are a twice-annual (March and August) opportunity to sample dinner in some of the best restaurants—at budget-friendly prices. Choose from among 200 restaurants offering prix-fixe menus at lunch and dinner, including Ming Tsai's Blue Ginger in Wellesley and Abe & Louie's in the Back Bay. Restaurant-week specials are offered in addition to the restaurant's regular fare and don't include beverage, tax, or tip. For more info visit bostonusa.com/visit/restaurantweek.**

WITH CHILDREN

Massachusetts offers a host of attractions historic and new, as well as beaches and parks that make the state a natural for a family vacation. It's little wonder that kids of all ages come to know and love Massachusetts—and come back to the state to attend college. The most popular destinations for family vacations in Massachusetts include Boston and Cape Cod, but in general the entire state has lots to offer families. You'll find places that are specifically geared to children under the Kidstuff heading in each chapter.

i **The Massachusetts Office of Travel and Tourism (10 Park Plaza, Ste. 4510, Boston, MA 02116; 617-973-8500; massvacation.com) has an excellent website that offers a wealth of Massachusetts travel information as well as discounts from its travel partners.**

Throughout the state, you'll have no problem finding child-friendly hotels and restaurants that go out of their way to make kids feel welcome. The vast majority of Massachusetts hotels permit kids to stay in their parent's room for free and many restaurants offer children's menus. And of course almost all attractions offer reduced admission for children and students.

WHEN TO GO

The draw of Boston's big-city attractions, ocean beaches, and ski mountains makes Massachusetts busy virtually year-round. Statewide, the largest number of visitors come during the summer, which brings beachgoers and family vacationers and the busiest schedule of all-around tourist fun. Fall is popular with leaf peepers, who come to see the spectacular fall foliage, though you might want to avoid the first week in September in Boston, as the city experiences its annual student invasion when the college kids return to campus. In the winter there's good skiing to be had throughout the state. As well, there's something to be said for snow-covered beach walks or after-dinner drinks by the fire in the bar of a Boston hotel. Also, in January and February low hotel prices (even at high-end hotels) are easy to come by and crowds are fewer. In some years it seems that spring is just one long good-bye to winter. March and April are known by Bay Staters as mud season. Visiting Massachusetts in May can be best of all, offering near-perfect weather and low hotel rates.

What you've heard is true: The weather in Massachusetts is famously fickle. Variations from day to day and even hour to hour can be enormous. Certainly a windswept nor'easter or winter blizzard will add undeniable drama to your visit. And even the most stoic Bay Stater occasionally complains about the weather. Winters can be "wicked cold" and snowy, too. The average seasonal snowfall ranges from 30 inches on the Cape, to 40 inches in Boston, to 60 inches in Worcester. From December through February temperatures generally average just above 32 degrees and are often lower—pack boots and a warm coat and you'll fare well. Spring is the state's shortest season. It's often rainy, damp, and wildly unpredictable—with snow sometimes in April. In summer coastal Massachusetts can be quite hot and oppressively humid, but generally it's pleasantly warm with highs in the manageable mid-80s in July and August. Inland, particularly in the Berkshires, cool summer nights are the norm. Fall weather is typically lovely with days that are often warm, with crisp cool nights, even into late October.

GETTING HERE, GETTING AROUND

Accessible by air, car, bus, rail, and even ferry, Massachusetts is easy to get to and you can choose from several forms of transportation to reach every corner of the state once you arrive. Many Massachusetts cities, towns, and attractions are close together and are near major highways or are located in the western part of the state where public transportation options are limited, so getting around by car is a great way to travel—with one exception. Unless you absolutely have to, don't even think about driving in Boston. The streets are narrow, many are one-way, and parking is next to impossible and expensive. Boston is a compact city and walking really is the best way to get around and experience its neighborhoods. Otherwise, the state's public-transport system, the MBTA (Massachusetts Bay Transportation Authority; mbta.com), includes not only the Boston subway and bus system, better known as the "T," but also commuter ferries that service South Shore towns, such as Quincy and Hingham, as well as a vast commuter rail system that includes such areas as Newburyport, Worcester, and Plymouth that are far outside the city.

GETTING HERE

Airports

LOGAN INTERNATIONAL AIRPORT (BOS)
1 Harborside Dr.
Boston, MA 02128
(800) 235-6426
massport.com/logan-airport
Boston's Logan International Airport is the main gateway to the entire region. The airport itself is located across Boston Harbor, just 3 miles northeast of the city. It's generally a 15-minute ride on the T (Silver or Blue line) or the T water ferry and, depending on your destination, about the same by taxi to downtown.

Logan is served by most major US airlines; low-cost carriers Southwest, AirTran, and JetBlue; regional carrier Cape Air, serving Martha's Vineyard and Nantucket; and many international airlines, including British Air, Virgin Atlantic, Air France, KLM, Air Canada, and Japan Airlines. Each of Logan's four terminals (A, B, C, and E) is connected to the others and to central parking via (relatively short) walkways or the free Logan Airport Shuttle. Terminal E handles international arrivals and departures (along with AirTran and Southwest). Logan's terminals are vintage mid-20th-century Jet Age design—with lots of glass and steel and polished concrete—but have been fully renovated several times over the years and have generally aged well. With completion of a 2008 modernization project, Terminal E evokes sleek 1960s glamour while Terminal A's 2005 upgrade earned it the country's first LEED-certified airport terminal designation.

If you have time to kill, Logan touts a variety of services. To unwind, sit by the big windows in one of the airport rocking chairs where you can marvel at the takeoffs and landings. Within Logan's vast commercial space are dozens of shops and eateries including several outposts of Boston favorite Legal Sea Foods. Families will want to check out the "Kidport," airport-themed play space located in Terminals A and C where kids can romp and let off steam. But perhaps Logan's most appreciated amenity is free Wi-Fi, which is available throughout the facility.

Secondary airports to Logan include New Hampshire's Manchester Airport (MHT; 603-624-6556; flymanchester.com), which is a one-hour drive to the north, and T. F. Green Airport (PVD; 401-737-4000; pvdairport.com), located just outside Providence, Rhode Island, and just one hour to the south of Boston. Both airports are serviced by major carriers as well as low-cost airlines. Bradley International Airport (BDL) in Windsor Locks, Connecticut (860-292-2000; bradleyairport .com), and Albany International Airport (ALH) in New York (518-242-2200; albanyairport .com) are both a one-hour drive from the Berkshires and are convenient for destinations in the western part of the state.

Accommodations

Logan has two airport hotels that are good options to start your vacation if you have an early flight, or at the end of your trip if you have a late flight back. The 600-room Hilton Boston Logan Airport (1 Hotel Dr., Boston, MA 02128; 617-568-6700; hilton.com) has a direct connection to Logan's Terminals A and E via an enclosed sky bridge. The 270-room Harborside Hyatt (101 Harborside, Boston, MA 02128; 617-568-1234; harborside.hyatt .com) is located farther away on the airport's property but has the advantage of a gorgeous waterfront location. Both hotels have their own free 24-hour shuttle service to the airport and both hotels offer park-and-fly packages where you can leave your car after staying for just one night.

Parking

Parking at Logan is ample and convenient with an assortment of lots including hourly, daily, extended stay, and premium guaranteed options. All the garages except the economy lot (which is serviced by the free Logan Airport Shuttle) are within walking distance or connected to the terminals. Hybrid/alternative vehicles enjoy priority parking close to the terminals. There is also a free cell phone waiting lot at Hotel Drive and Service Road available for drivers to wait for arriving passengers until they get the "I've landed" phone call.

Ground Travel

Because of Logan's proximity to Boston, getting to and from the airport is relatively easy. The least expensive and often quickest way into the city is to take the T (mbta.com). You can take the free Silver line T bus (SL1) from any of the terminals to connect to South Station in the Back Bay. Or take the free Logan Airport Shuttle to the Airport T station and connect to the Blue line to downtown. For a novel way into Boston, hop on the MBTA Harbor Express (F2) year-round (covered), scheduled water taxi service from the Logan Dock for a 10-minute ride across the harbor to Long Wharf. On-call water taxi service options include City Water Taxi (617-422-0392; citywatertaxi.com) and Rowes Wharf Water Taxi (617-406-8584; roweswharf watertransport.com). Boston Logan Super Shuttle (617-567-8900; bostonloganairport shuttle.com) provides door-to-door shared van service and works especially well if you are traveling with a group of four or more. No reservations are required to get from Logan to your destination, but they are required for your return trip to the airport. Of course, taxicabs are plentiful, as are hotel shuttle buses—check to see if yours is one of them. If you are planning extensive travel outside of Boston, you may be picking up your rental car from Logan. On the arrivals level of each terminal (usually near the baggage carousel), there is either a rental car counter (sometimes several) and/or a rental company courtesy telephone.

Travel Information & Resources

Massachusetts Department of Transportation
10 Park Plaza
Boston, MA 02116
(857) 368-4636
massdot.state.ma.us

Massachusetts Registry of Motor Vehicles
630 Washington St.
Boston, MA 02111
(617) 351-4500
massrmv.com

Other Airports

BARNSTABLE MUNICIPAL AIRPORT (HYA)
480 Barnstable Rd.
Hyannis, MA 02601
(508) 775-2020
barnstable-airport.com/airport

Located just a mile outside downtown Hyannis and universally called Hyannis Airport, this is the main airport for the Cape. In 2011 the airport unveiled its spiffy new 35,000-square-foot passenger terminal. Cape Air (508-771-6944; flycapeair.com) is the airport's principal tenant, flying to Boston, Martha's Vineyard, and Nantucket and seasonally to White Plains, New York. Other airlines that operate scheduled service from here are Nantucket Airlines (508-228-6234; nantucket airlines.com) and Island Air (508-228-7575; islandair.net) to Nantucket.

NANTUCKET MEMORIAL AIRPORT (ACK)
14 Airport Rd.
Nantucket, MA 02554
(508) 325-5300
nantucketairport.com

This small island airport is actually the second busiest in the state after Boston's Logan International Airport. Numerous airlines fly regularly scheduled service to and from Nantucket, including Cape Air (508-771-6944; flycapeair.com), Nantucket Airlines (508-228-6234; nantucketairlines.com), and Island Air (508-228-7575; islandair.net). You can fly into JFK on Delta (800-221-1212; delta.com) and to Newark, New Jersey, on United (800-864-8331; united.com). Seasonally, JetBlue (800-538-2583; jetblue.com) flies from Nantucket to both Boston and JFK. The Nantucket Regional Transit Authority (NRTA) Wave bus (508-228-7025; nrtawave.com) has a dedicated Airport route during the summer season that runs to town; otherwise you'll need to take a cab.

GETTING AROUND

Highways

In New England, and especially in Massachusetts, it seems that all roads connect to Boston. Despite the nightmarish congestion on I-93 and Route 128 near Boston, the state has quite a few scenic drives (notably Route 2 in Concord and Route 127 from Gloucester to Rockport) just outside the city. Massachusetts has several state highways that pass through hilly, dense forest, open farmland, and historic villages, and along the coast. When—if—time permits, it's worth venturing off the road well-traveled to enjoy some of the scenery of the state's country roads.

If you plan to travel between December and March, be advised that winter weather can make roads icy or snowy. Occasionally car travel on state roads is banned during and shortly after a storm, but in general Massachusetts roads are well maintained in the winter, and even after a major storm, side streets and highways are cleared fairly quickly.

i Many locals use E-ZPass, a computerized system for paying toll roads, tunnels, and bridges via a transponder on the car's windshield. Along with being able to save time by using the dedicated E-ZPass lanes, you are charged a lower fare than the cash toll. New transponders are provided to residents at no cost. Visit a Registry of Motor Vehicles location or sign up at massdot.state.ma.us.

I-90

Stretching just over 3,020 miles from Boston to Seattle, I-90 is the longest interstate highway in the country. This is its easternmost portion, connecting with the New York Thruway at West Stockbridge and ending in Boston at Logan Airport. Called the Massachusetts Turnpike and referred to as the "Mass Pike," this is a toll road along its entire 138-mile length in the state. The Mass Pike is the state's major east–west route connecting Springfield, Worcester, and Boston. The towns of Natick, Framingham, and Westboro are popular Boston bedroom communities. For commuters, the trip to and from Boston along the Mass Pike is generally thought to be easier than the one from the North Shore or South Shore. Anticipate weekday rush hour delays, though, at exit 14-15 (I-95/Route 128) and at exit 18 (Allston-Brighton-Cambridge).

i A welcome addition to the Mass Pike in recent years has been the service-plaza weekend farmers' markets, selling homegrown produce and made-in-Massachusetts products, such as maple syrup, honey, and goat cheese. The outdoor markets are open from May through October, Friday through Sunday.

I-95

The main north–south highway along the East Coast, I-95 runs almost the state's entire length, connecting Massachusetts to highways in Rhode Island in the south and New Hampshire in the north. The quiet part of I-95 is the 12-mile southern 6-lane section from Attleboro to Route 495 and Foxboro. I-95 between Route 128 and I-495 in both directions bears considerable commuter traffic from Sharon and Canton during the weekdays as well as weekend traffic related to events at Gillette Stadium in Foxboro. At Canton I-95 becomes Route 128 (see below) and heads north for 45 miles as it encircles Boston to Peabody. To confuse you, this part of I-95 is also designated Route 128, but mercifully dual I-95/Route 128 signs are posted along the highway. At Newton the highway expands to eight lanes (it's still not enough), passing Waltham, Lexington, Burlington, and Reading. At Peabody I-95 separates from Route 128 (which goes on to Gloucester) and becomes I-95 again as it heads north for 25 miles until exit 59 and the town of Salisbury near the New Hampshire state line.

I-91

In the western part of the state I-91 is the major road that passes through the Pioneer Valley, linking the region to Connecticut in the south and Vermont (and eventually Canada) in the north. In Massachusetts I-91 begins in Longmeadow and travels 55 miles (parallel to the Connecticut River), connecting the cities of Springfield, Northampton, and Greenfield. I-91 is mostly a rural interstate, and except for the area around Springfield, the highway is largely without traffic and congestion.

I-93

I-93 is a north–south highway that extends north to Canada and south to the Cape and is one of only two interstates that enter Boston directly (the other is the Mass Pike). From the South Shore, the I-93/Southeast Expressway morning and rush hour commute ranges from inconvenient to catastrophic and is generally recognized as the worst in the region.

In Massachusetts I-93 is just under 50 miles in length. From the south, I-93 originates in Canton and runs east through Randolph to Braintree at exit 7, which is known locally as the "Braintree split." From Braintree I-93 interchanges with Route 3 south, the major route from Boston to the Cape. Heading north, the 12-mile portion of I-93 from Braintree to exit 18 in Boston (it's signed as both US 1 and MA 3) is known as the Southeast Expressway. As I-93 reaches Boston it becomes a tunnel—the Central Artery—passing beneath the city to reemerge near the TD Garden before crossing the Zakim Bridge, a 10-lane cable-stayed span across the Charles River. Curving north, the fastest section of I-93 passes Medford, Stoneham, and Methuen, where it continues into New Hampshire.

i I-93 has two designated carpool lanes. These high-occupancy vehicle (HOV) lanes require two passengers during rush hour travel times in the morning and evening. South of the city is a 6-mile HOV stretch between Dorchester and Quincy. North of the city is a 2-mile HOV lane between Medford and the Zakim Bridge.

I-495

Constructed in the 1960s and 1970s, I-495 is a parallel beltway to Route 128, a 120-mile highway that forms the outer edge of Boston's suburbs, about 30 miles west of the city. I-495 links eight major expressways from I-195 at its beginning in Wareham near the Cape to Route 90 (the Mass Pike) at Hopkinton in the west to I-95 at its northern end in Newburyport. The expression "greater Boston area" usually refers to cities and towns located within the area bounded by

I-495. The I-495 region has seen tremendous growth in recent years and the 6-lane highway can't always keep up—expect weekday commuting bottlenecks at the Mass Pike interchange in Hopkinton and at Route 9 in Southboro.

Route 128

Although the idea of a beltway to circumnavigate Boston was conceived as early as the 1920s and the road itself was largely built in the 1950s, Route 128 is synonymous with the state's high-tech industry. By the 1980s several notable Massachusetts-based companies had established suburban office parks within the Route 128 beltway, including Digital and Raytheon. Today you'll often hear the term Route 128 used as a metonym to refer to Boston's inner suburbs, especially when describing real estate.

Skirting Boston from 11 miles outside the city, Route 128 is a 57-mile stretch of highway that for 45 miles is also I-95 (see above). Officially, the southern end of Route 128 begins in Canton, although most locals consider the 7-mile section of I-93 from Canton to the Braintree split part of Route 128 as well. As Route 128 heads to its end point in Gloucester, it has 18 numbered interchanges that intersect with all major approaches to the city, including Route 9 (exit 19A Newton/Wellesley), I-90 (exit 25 Weston), Route 2 (exit 29 Concord Turnpike), Route 3 (exit 32A Burlington), and I-93 (exit 33A Reading). As many as 200,000 cars per day travel along Route 128 and even though it is mostly an 8-lane highway, gridlock is not uncommon, especially during the morning and evening rush hours.

Other Major Roads

Route 2

Rural Route 2 is truly a path through history. Beginning at the New York border in Williamstown and crossing the northern part of the state for 142 miles from west to east, Route 2 ends in Boston at Boston Common and the start of the Freedom Trail. The first portion of Route 2 travels 65 miles from Williamstown to Orange and is famously known as the Mohawk Trail. It is one of the country's great scenic byways, and makes for an exceptional fall foliage driving tour. The next segment, the 45 miles from Orange to the town of Harvard, crosses the heart of the Commonwealth's apple-growing region and is known as the Johnny Appleseed Trail. The eastern segment of Route 2 includes Concord and Lexington and incorporates Revolutionary battlefields, literary sights, and farm stands along the way. The end of Route 2 and Boston is reached via Cambridge by crossing the Charles River at the Longfellow Bridge.

Route 6

Of the three roads that roughly traverse the length of the Cape from east to west, Route 6 is the main thoroughfare. In Massachusetts, Route 6 begins in Fall River near the Rhode Island border and follows 54 miles of the coast through New Bedford until it reaches the Sagamore Bridge, where it crosses the Cape Cod Canal. From this point, Route 6 is also known as the Mid-Cape Highway. It begins as a 4-lane highway for 30 miles until Dennis, where it becomes a narrow 2-lane road. The 12 mile stretch of Route 6 from Dennis to Orleans is sadly also known as Suicide Alley because of the high number of head-on collisions that have occurred here over the years. Consequently, this road requires headlight use during the day. From the Orleans rotary, the final 18 miles are a slow go (but are tremendously scenic) following the contour of Cape Cod Bay through Eastham, Wellfleet, and Truro and on to lively Provincetown.

Public Transportation

MASSACHUSETTS BAY TRANSPORTATION AUTHORITY (MBTA)
(617) 222-3200
mbta.com
With roots dating back to 1897, the Massachusetts Bay Transportation Authority, or MBTA, is one of the country's oldest and largest transit agencies. The MBTA runs the subways, buses, ferries, and commuter rail in Boston and the suburbs. The MBTA is best known for Boston's subway system, called the "T." Other than walking, the T is the easiest and most efficient way to get around the city.

The T lines are referred to by color: Green, Red, Blue, and Orange. There is also a Silver line that is a quasi-bus/light rail route. The Purple line refers to the MBTA commuter rail system. The entire T system operates from 5:30 a.m. to 12:30 a.m., 7 days a week (Boston is not New York). Whatever the distance, the T fare is $2 using a CharlieCard or $2.50 using a CharlieTicket or cash on board. Bus travel is far-reaching, but much slower than the T. Bus fares are $1.50 using a CharlieCard or $2 using a CharlieTicket or cash on board. Commuter rail fares and commuter ferries cost more and are sold on an individual basis depending on the distance you travel.

If you plan to use the T a lot while you're in Boston, you might want to do what commuters do: get a CharlieCard, which is a plastic, rechargeable stored-value fare card that's cheaper and way faster to use than a CharlieTicket—you just touch it to the target on a fare gate inside the T station or fare box inside the subway or bus. You can pick up CharlieCards at main subway stations or at various retail outlets. Load the card with value using cash or a credit or debit card and you're good to go.

The T has kept up with smart-phone technology. For online information on the entire system that's always up-to-the-minute, including service alerts, visit mbta.com.

Trains

AMTRAK
(800) USA-RAIL (872-7245)
amtrak.com
Amtrak offers daily service to Boston from New York, Washington, DC, and Chicago. In Boston, Amtrak trains arrive at historic South Station (700 Atlantic Ave.; south-station.net) a turn-of-the-20th-century Beaux Arts masterpiece that offers a marketplace of shops and restaurants and is conveniently located in the center of downtown and connects with the T and commuter rail lines.

Much of Massachusetts is also accessible by train. Amtrak has a fairly extensive system of routes that criss-cross the state basically following the same east–west route of the Mass Pike (I-90), the north–south path of Route 128 that rings Boston, and the north–south route of I-91 in the western part of the state. The Northeast Regional is the most frequent Amtrak train route that departs out of South Station, making stops in New York City and Washington, DC. Amtrak also runs the high-speed Acela Express train, which is popular with business travelers, between Boston's South Station and New York City's Penn Station several times a day.

Buses

Massachusetts is well serviced by a network of national and regional buses. Bus travel is now newly popular, thanks to Megabus (877-462-6342; megabus.com) and BoltBus (877-265-8287; boltbus.com) and their fleet of cheap, comfortable and Wi-Fi-enabled buses. Quite a few buses travel daily between Boston and New York City, and a growing number of buses travel between Boston and other cities scattered up and down the East Coast. By the way, the cool factor of BoltBus and Megabus may be high, but they are both subsidiaries of traditional long-haul bus lines; BoltBus is part of Greyhound and Megabus is part of Coach USA.

GREYHOUND
(800) 231-2222
greyhound.com
Greyhound buses connect just about the entire country with Boston. They pull in at the South Station Transportation Center (700 Atlantic Ave.), which also connects to Amtrak and the MBTA T and commuter rail lines.

Local Bus Service
PETER PAN
(800) 343-9999
peterpanbus.com
Peter Pan Bus Lines principally serves western Massachusetts and Connecticut. Peter Pan operates out of South Station in Boston and its own terminal in Springfield. Peter Pan is a lifeline of sorts for area college students, with frequent service between the University of Massachusetts Amherst and Boston.

PLYMOUTH & BROCKTON LINE
(508) 746-0378
p-b.com
This bus line principally covers southeastern Massachusetts, including local service on the South Shore and the Cape. Plymouth & Brockton's frequent (and as early as 4 a.m.) daily service between Hyannis and Boston is the commuting method of choice for many Cape Cod residents who would rather leave the driving to someone else.

HISTORY

Church steeples, country villages, and winding country roads? Check. Wooden sailing ships and lighthouses? You bet. Revolutionary War sites? In spades. Massachusetts residents revel in their state's history and revere their past. Although relatively small, Massachusetts has had a disproportionate impact on the country's history. There's modern American culture, too, of course, but the focus always returns to history. Throughout Massachusetts you'll find countless museums, preserved homes, and heritage trails. It's a place to connect with America's roots.

PRECOLONIAL PERIOD

Long before the European settlers arrived, the land that would eventually become Massachusetts belonged to several Native American tribes, including the Wampanoag in the southeast and the Massachusetts people in the area around present-day Boston. The earliest encounters between the Natives and Europeans may have occurred as early as the 15th century, when men in boats from Portugal, France, England, and Ireland came across the Atlantic to fish the waters off the North American coast. The first European explorers known to map and trade in the region include France's Samuel de Champlain in 1604 and Great Britain's Henry Hudson in 1609.

The first permanent European settlement in Massachusetts was the English colony established in present-day Plymouth. The settlement was really the result of happenstance. In September 1620 a group of 102 colonists (later known as Pilgrims) crossed the Atlantic from England on the *Mayflower* to create a new settlement north of the already established colony in Jamestown, Virginia. Blown off course by storms, the *Mayflower* reached land 66 days later and anchored off the tip of Cape Cod near present-day Provincetown. It was November and winter was setting in. After a number of scouting expeditions over the course of several weeks, the colonists decided to establish the new settlement, "New Plimoth," on the abandoned remains of a Native village west of the bay. Serious problems soon emerged at the small English outpost, including starvation and disease—half the colonists did not survive that first winter.

Early relations with the Native Wampanoag tribe were tenuous but cooperative. Chief Massasoit viewed the settlers as valuable trading partners and as possible allies against rival tribes. Under the leadership of William Bradford, the Pilgrims understood that their survival depended on cooperation with the Wampanoag. Massasoit shared Wampanoag techniques for planting and fishing with the Pilgrims. The original harvest festival that has since become known as the first Thanksgiving likely took place in October 1621 and was celebrated by the Pilgrims along with Massasoit and 90 of his men and consisted of fish, deer, geese, and ducks. Turkey? Maybe.

Although Plymouth was the first permanent settlement in the region, it was the Puritan establishment of the Massachusetts Bay Colony that shaped the state. In 1630 a group of 800 English settlers, mostly Puritans escaping religious and political persecution, were led by John Winthrop to the peninsula called Shawmut by the Massachusetts tribe. They established "a shining city on a hill" and named the city Boston in honor of the port of Boston in the county of Lincolnshire in England, the hometown of several of the Puritan leaders.

The Puritans created a conservative Christian society based on a strict theocratic ideal that valued industriousness and personal virtue. Dissension was not tolerated within the community. In 1658 laws were passed to allow the execution of Quakers. In 1659 the celebration of Christmas was banned. But the Puritans did value education. They established the first public school, Boston Latin, in 1635, and the first college, Harvard, was founded in 1636 with the purpose of training future clergy. By the 1650s nearly 20,000 settlers had arrived in Boston from Britain and the city thrived as an orderly and prosperous port in shipbuilding and the trade of fur, fish, and lumber.

However, colonial expansion throughout the region displaced Native tribes. King Philip was the English name for Massasoit's son Metacomet and relations came to a bloody head with the Native uprising known as King Philip's War in 1675–1676. Both sides suffered greatly, several colonial frontier settlements were decimated, most notably Springfield, and the region's Native population was greatly reduced.

COLONIAL PERIOD & THE BIRTH OF A NATION

In the aftermath of King Philip's War, the Massachusetts Bay Colony was increasingly independent-minded. The colony refused to abide by the Navigation Acts that required trade only with the British. In the meantime, the British were not pleased with the Puritan leadership's religious intolerance. Evidence of rising tension could be found throughout the colony as early as 1684, when England revoked the Massachusetts Bay Colony charter and ended the colony's right to pick its own governor. King's Church, an Anglican congregation, was established in Boston in 1686 and Massachusetts was, for the first time, open to settlement by non-Puritans. In 1692 the Salem witch trials took place and 20 were executed—the backlash against the trials signaled the end of Puritan rule in New England.

As religious fervor waned during the early 1700s, it was replaced with political fervor. The legacy of Puritan rule in Massachusetts was the Congregational churches that dotted the landscape and were the center of New England village life. Each New England town offered residents a measure of self-government that included a popularly elected colonial council and court, juries made up of local citizens, and the right to hold open town meetings.

To finance the massive debts incurred from their victory in the 1756–1763 French and Indian War, the British enacted a series of unpopular tax levies throughout the colonies, including the 1765 Stamp Act, which placed a direct tax on all newspapers and legal documents. In protest, Patriots organized throughout the continent in groups known as the Sons of Liberty. In Boston, among their members they counted John Hancock, Dr. Joseph Warren, Paul Revere, John Adams, and Sam Adams. Their motto became "No taxation without representation" because the colonies had no representation in the British Parliament.

It was a tumultuous time. In Boston, to protest the Stamp Act, the colonists clashed in the streets and ransacked the homes of Loyalist officials. By 1768 the British occupied Boston. On March 5, 1770, a motley mob of colonists taunted a small group of British soldiers, which fired upon the crowd, resulting in five civilian deaths. Somewhat erroneously referred to as the "Boston Massacre," the event greatly galvanized the colonists' cause.

The boiling independence movement could not be contained. On December 7, 1773, at Boston's Old South Meeting House, an impassioned speech by Sam Adams led to the fearless dumping of 342 chests of tea from three British ships into Boston Harbor.

Sensing the upcoming war, Massachusetts citizens organized existing town militias to increase their numbers and to form Minutemen companies—pledged to be ready at a "minute's" notice. They didn't have to wait long. On the evening of April 18, 1775, Paul Revere rode to Lexington to warn Samuel Adams and John Hancock that the British regulars were coming to arrest them. The next day the "shot heard 'round the world" was fired in Concord and the colonists succeeded in routing the British army. On June 17, 1775, the first major battle of the Revolutionary War was fought at Bunker Hill and although the British won the fight, they took a major hit from the scrappy colonists.

George Washington, a veteran of the French and Indian War, was appointed commander in chief by the Continental Congress in Philadelphia and arrived in Boston in July 1775. Washington fortified Dorchester Heights with canons brought from Fort Ticonderoga in New York. On March 17, 1775, British troops ended their occupation of Boston and the colonists reclaimed the city. The theater of battle shifted from Boston to New York and the Mid-Atlantic, but it wasn't too much longer before the Declaration of Independence was read from the steps of Boston's Old State House.

Hack Holidays

Hack holidays are alive and well in Massachusetts. Public employees in Suffolk County (including Boston) celebrate two legal holidays connected with the Revolutionary War. Bunker Hill Day is celebrated on June 17 to honor the 1775 Battle of Bunker Hill. Evacuation Day commemorates the day in 1776 when British troops ended their occupation of Boston. Evacuation Day is sometimes referred to as the "High Hack" holiday. It's celebrated on March 17, which not so coincidentally is also St. Patrick's Day.

A SEAFARING HERITAGE

Much of Massachusetts's early economic development came from the sea. Fishing and boat-building provided a living; after the Revolutionary War, whaling and the maritime trade made people rich. The waters off Massachusetts were a nest of privateering activity during the Revolutionary War, disrupting British trade and capturing British reinforcements and supplies. After the war, Boston and Salem's fleet of "Yankee clipper" schooners were ideal for the long journey to the emerging (and very profitable) trade markets of the Far East.

The whaling industry also flourished in Massachusetts during the mid-19th century. Whale oil was used for lamps and to make candles, and whalebone was used in such items as corsets and umbrellas. It was a lucrative business and vast fortunes were made in whaling, particularly in New Bedford and Nantucket.

PIONEERING THE INDUSTRIAL REVOLUTION

Massachusetts had a leading role in the Industrial Revolution, which in the space of 100 years, between 1820 and 1920, transformed life in the region. Advancements in the harnessing of waterpower and later steam engines enabled cotton manufacturing to be moved from home workshops to factories. Lowell was America's first planned industrial city. Sturdy brick mill buildings lined the Merrimack River, row homes were built for the workers (local farm girls, then a steady influx of immigrants largely from Ireland and Canada), and a town of around 20,000 people in 1800 grew steadily into a city of 110,000 at its peak in the early 1900s. Besides the activity in Lowell, the growth of the textile industry saw the construction of huge weaving mills in cities throughout the state, including Holyoke, Chicopee, and Lawrence.

But times were changing almost too rapidly. The Blackstone Canal was built to link farmers in central Massachusetts with markets in Providence. The 45-mile course was constructed largely by immigrant Irish labor and built quickly over the span of three years. Initially successful when it opened in 1828, by 1848 it was rendered obsolete by the arrival of the railroad.

ROLE IN THE CIVIL WAR

In the early decades of the 19th century, Massachusetts was a center of progressivism. The leaders of the transcendentalist literary movement—Ralph Waldo Emerson, Henry David Thoreau, Nathaniel Hawthorne, and Louisa May Alcott—all lived in Concord and were neighbors to one another.

Boston was also a hotbed of abolition activity during the Civil War. Prominent politician Charles Sumner and the *Liberator* newspaper editor William Lloyd Garrison took on the charge to challenge the young nation's indifference toward slavery. The 54th Massachusetts Regiment, the first documented African-American regiment formed in the North, came from Boston. The regiment's story was recounted in the 1989 film *Glory*.

POWER SHIFT: BOSTON BRAHMINS & IRISH IMMIGRANTS IN THE 19TH CENTURY

In the years following the Civil War, the state turned its attention toward manufacturing, which continued apace until the Great Depression dealt the deathblow and the state began the slow process of diversifying its economy. Boston's merchant-prince and industrialist ruling class, the so-called Brahmins, were behind the city's expansion into the Back Bay and established many of the city's great cultural and philanthropic institutions, including Massachusetts General Hospital, Boston's Museum of Science, and the Boston Symphony. Drawn by factory jobs, European immigrants poured into the region from Ireland, Italy, Canada, Portugal, Germany, Poland, and Russia, arriving in Boston and then fanning out to such cities as Lowell, Worcester, and Springfield. Urban immigration in the late 19th century was keenly felt in Boston, which experienced a population increase of 150 percent from 1860 to 1890.

Such growth and new prosperity brought another kind of social change: the idea that America was the "land of opportunity," which gave way to machine-era ward politics and such colorful figures as Mayor John F. Fitzgerald (President Kennedy's grandfather) and four-time Boston mayor James Michael Curley.

THE 20TH CENTURY & BEYOND

In Boston the traumatic 1970s reached a low point in 1974 with violent clashes over court-ordered busing to desegregate the public schools. The late 20th century also brought the first wave of urbanization to the city with showplace office towers springing up downtown and the widespread expansion of the city's hospitals and college campuses,

which helped to create the anchor institutions that remain a major economic force to this day. Ongoing, never-ending urban renewal programs, most notably the "Big Dig" in Boston and the growth of service and high-tech and biotech industries within the Route 495 belt, have boosted the economy throughout the state.

Massachusetts is home to some significant sports history. Basketball was invented in Springfield in 1891, volleyball in Holyoke in 1895. Massachusetts is home to each of New England's professional sports teams— and residents don't mind sharing with sports fans from the rest of the region. The 2000s were a remarkable decade for New England's professional sports teams. In 2004 an 86-year-old curse was exorcised when the Boston Red Sox did the unthinkable and finally won the World Series for the first time since 1918. The Red Sox then stunned everyone and did it again in 2007. In football the New England Patriots won an amazing three Super Bowl championships in the four years from 2002 to 2005. And in 2008 the Celtics captured their 17th NBA title, the first since 1986 and the glory days of Larry Bird. Even the Bruins stepped it up and won the Stanley Cup during the 2010–2011 season. Bay Staters love their sports—and they never tire of a downtown Boston duck boat parade.

BOSTON & GREATER BOSTON

Boston is the best of both worlds, a vibrant cosmopolitan city that's also very traditional. Founded in 1620 by Puritan colonists from England, Boston is one of America's oldest cities. A walk in any direction reveals the shrines of the American Revolution shoulder-to-shoulder with modern office buildings joined most recently by a visionary revitalization of the waterfront.

There is no denying that Boston is history proud. But it is also a center of culture with unparalleled museums, world-class music, dance, and theater, as well as standout shopping. And as home to more than 50 colleges and universities in addition to several world-renowned hospitals, Boston can rightfully stake a claim as an intellectual and medical capital.

More than ever before, one of the great pleasures of visiting Boston is the dining (and drinking) scene. For downtown dynamism, try the Seaport District, which offers a profusion of chef-driven restaurants that highlight fresh, local ingredients. For laid-back glamour, consider drinks or late-night dining in the trendy South End.

Across the Charles River, Cambridge is a separate city, and in many senses a world apart from Boston. Anchored by Harvard and MIT, the "People's Republic of Cambridge" is a bustling student enclave of bookstores, ethnic eateries, art-house cinemas, and bars.

The number of side-trip-worthy attractions just outside of Boston is truly astonishing. It's a good thing that Boston's subway system—called the "T"—links many of the suburbs to downtown. Tree-shaded Brookline is an affluent streetcar suburb with a large Jewish community (lots of good bagel shops and delis here) and is the childhood home of John F. Kennedy. Next door, Newton is a patch of low-key restaurants, independent shops, and abundant green space that allows residents to enjoy the benefits of village living within just a few minutes of the city.

As the T stretches north from the city, Somerville is undergoing gentrification in Davis Square, where Tufts University students and hipsters mix with townies at quirky watering holes and ethnic restaurants. Medford, Everett, and Revere are all within trolley-stop distance of downtown, offering plentiful recreational activities: hike at Middlesex Reservation in Medford, rock-climb in Everett, and swim in the ocean at Revere Beach. Though even farther north, Stoneham has a fine small zoo.

Within the Route 128 belt north and west of the city, Watertown, Waltham, Arlington, and Belmont are each just minutes from Boston (and from each other), offering entertainment, restaurants, and specialty shopping within vibrant and walkable downtown districts. To the south, football and soccer fans routinely trek the 20 miles from downtown (via Dedham and some very fancy strip malls) to visit Foxboro's singular attraction—Gillette Stadium.

ATTRACTIONS

Historic Sites & Landmarks

✳BEACON HILL
Along Mount Vernon and Charles Streets
Boston, MA 02114
The area located behind the Massachusetts State House was named for one of Boston's tallest peaks, the site of a beacon light as far back as the 1600s. Beacon Hill was (and still is) the home of Boston's old-money elite. Preserving the neighborhood's residential origins is a group of elegant early 19th-century brick federal-style townhomes around Louisburg (pronounced "Lewisburg") Square—it is one of the city's most exclusive addresses (US Secretary of State John Kerry's home is No. 19). Be sure to find your way over to pretty, cobblestoned Acorn Street, a narrow servant's alley, "just two cows wide" that is said to be the city's most photographed byway. As you wander you won't have to search hard to find quirky shops, antiques stores, and exceptional bistro dining.

CHINATOWN
Beach and Hudson Streets
Boston, MA 02111
A true urban Chinatown, a traditional Paifang Gate marks the ceremonial entrance to Boston's Chinatown. Located between Downtown Crossing and the South End, since the 1870s the neighborhood has been the first Boston address for generations of Chinese immigrants. On weekends especially, the neighborhood explodes with the sights and sounds of the unfamiliar. Find intriguing goods in the mom-and-pop grocery stores and follow your nose to the nearest noodle or dumpling shop and indulge.

CITGO SIGN
660 Beacon St., Kenmore Square
Boston, MA 02215
The double-sided 60-foot-by-60-foot red, white and blue CITGO sign is a landmark of the Boston skyline. The sign is located on top of the Boston University Bookstore Building but you can't buy gas here, so don't even try. For Boston Marathon runners, the sign is known as the one-mile-to-go mark. The illuminated red triangle with its dancing lights is beloved by Red Sox fans, who can see it from Fenway over the left field wall; when the Red Sox hit a home run in that direction, you'll C-IT-GO.

✳FENWAY PARK
4 Yawkey Way, Fenway
Boston, MA 02115
(617) 226-6666
redsoxmlb.com
It has been said that the true religion of New Englanders is the Red Sox. So it follows, then, that Fenway Park is hallowed ground. Opened in 1912, Fenway is the oldest ballpark in the major leagues. This is urban baseball at its finest; the park is wedged within several blocks of the city's densely crowded Kenmore neighborhood, resulting in several field idiosyncrasies that make it a "hitter's park," including scarce foul territory and the fabled "Green Monster," a 37-foot-high left field wall that turns fly balls into singles. And although the halcyon days of the 2004 and 2007 World Series winning seasons seem long ago, loyal Red Sox fans still pack the park regardless of the team's record. Seeing a Red Sox game at Fenway Park is one of Boston's ultimate tourist experiences. And although it is difficult to get Red Sox tickets, it's no longer impossible. Check online or in person at the Gate D box office.

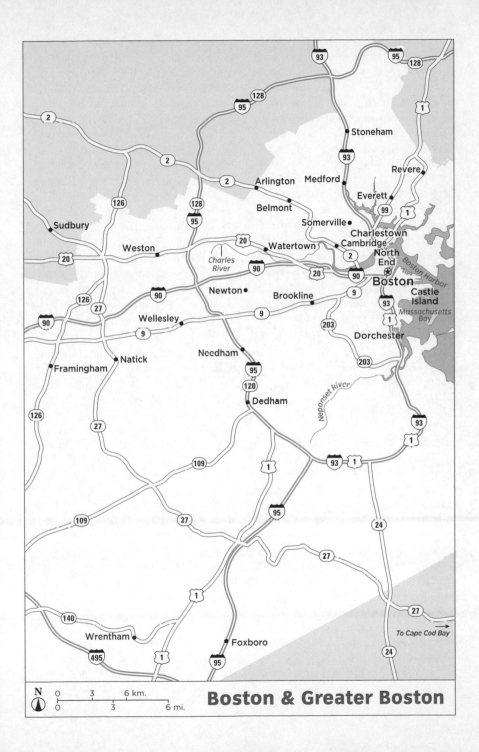

Boston & Greater Boston

If you can't experience a Red Sox game, the next best option is to take a guided tour of Fenway Park. Tours are offered year-round, 7 days a week. Get a behind-the-scenes look at the stadium (including the press boxes and sometimes the locker rooms and warning track) by guides who are well versed in Red Sox lore.

i The Red Sox offer a limited supply of same-day tickets for nearly every home game (often standing-room or bleacher seats). Game-day tickets are sold at Fenway Park's Gate E two hours before first pitch. Get there early, though, really early. The line officially forms five hours before the game and ticket sales are limited to one per person.

＊HARVARD UNIVERSITY
Harvard Information Center
1350 Massachusetts Ave.
Cambridge, MA 02138
(617) 495-1573
harvard.edu/visitors
Cambridge and Harvard are inextricably linked. America's oldest university and one of the world's most prestigious, Harvard was modeled after Cambridge University in England. Today, Harvard still adheres to the purpose of its 1650 charter for "the advancement of all good literature, arts and sciences." Harvard Yard is the oldest part of the campus, a rarefied enclave of stately, ivy-covered 18th- and 19th-century buildings where tree-shaded walkways criss-cross manicured green lawns. Enter under the arch at Johnston Gate on Mass Avenue, considered the main entrance to the university. Follow the path toward University Hall, where Daniel Chester French's iconic

statue of John Harvard presides over all from his bronze seat in Harvard Yard that is inscribed, "John Harvard, Founder, 1638" and has been dubbed "The Statue of Three Lies." Despite what the inscription says, Harvard was founded in 1636, John Harvard was not a founder, but an early benefactor of the college, and as there are no known paintings of John Harvard, French used student Sherman Hoar as a model. The university offers a free, one-hour student-led, history-focused tour of the campus daily; check the website for exact times. If you prefer to tour the campus on your own, pick up a map at the visitor center or download the university's mobile or audio tour. The information center is closed Sun and has limited hours in the summer and during university holidays.

i The best way to get to Charlestown from Boston is to take the MBTA Inner Harbor Ferry (F4) from Long Wharf near the aquarium to the Charlestown Navy Yard. Enjoy fantastic views of Boston and the comings and goings on the harbor during the 15-minute cruise—and at just $3 each way, it is one of Boston's best travel bargains.

JOHN F. KENNEDY NATIONAL HISTORIC SITE
83 Beals St.
Brookline, MA 02446
(617) 566-7937
nps.gov/jofi
On May 29, 1917, John Fitzgerald Kennedy was born in the master bedroom of a modest 2½-story home on a quiet residential street in Brookline, Massachusetts. Now at this National Historic Site park rangers take small groups of visitors on guided tours

of the home. Early in the tour, visitors of a "certain age" will be asked where they were when President Kennedy was assassinated. On the first floor, you will see the dining room set for company and the living room, where the piano has pride of place. Upstairs you will peek in the nursery, the master bedroom (with two single beds!), a guest room, and the home's only bathroom. The best is last—the early 1920s kitchen is the home's historically most accurate room complete with a soapstone sink, enamel stove, and icebox. Apparently the kitchen was the domain of the family's cook, but you will hear an audio recording by Mrs. Kennedy recounting how the family would eat warmed-over baked beans with brown bread for Sunday supper—very Boston.

JOHN HANCOCK TOWER
200 Clarendon St., Back Bay
Boston, MA 02116
(617) 572-6420

Boston's tallest building, the 60-story John Hancock Tower is a beloved landmark of the city skyline. But it wasn't always so. Built in 1976 and designed by I. M. Pei and Partners, the striking blue-tinged glass skyscraper was initially plagued by engineering flaws that caused the giant 500-pound plate-glass windows to fall out—65 in all—crashing to the sidewalk below. Each of the 10,000-plus windows were reengineered and replaced and for years Bostonians dubbed the boarded-up building the "Plywood Palace." Now the John Hancock Tower stands proudly, an example of ambitious architectural design worthy of appreciation. The building's observatory has been closed to the public since September 11, 2001, but another view is worth checking out: Note the reflection of Trinity Church in the John Hancock Tower's

mirrored windows—an elegant juxtaposition of Boston old and new.

i Since 1950—long before smart phones—Bostonians have relied on the lights from the beacon at the top of the Old John Hancock Building (200 Berkeley St.) and a little poem as a quick prognosticator of the weather. Steady blue, clear view. Flashing blue, clouds due. Steady red, rain ahead. Flashing red, snow instead. (Although during baseball season flashing red means that the Red Sox game has been called for rain.)

LONGFELLOW HOUSE–WASHINGTON HEADQUARTERS NATIONAL HISTORIC SITE
105 Brattle St.
Cambridge, MA 02138
(617) 876-4491
nps.gov/long

Set back on Brattle Street, this glorious yellow clapboard Georgian-style mansion sure has stories to tell. Henry Wadsworth Longfellow and his wife, Frances Appleton, were given the home in 1843 as a wedding gift from her father. Longfellow lived here until his death, writing his most famous verses, including *Paul Revere's Ride* and *The Song of Hiawatha* from his study overlooking the Charles River. Longfellow wasn't the home's first illustrious resident. Taking command of the Continental army, George Washington made this house his headquarters during the Siege of Boston from July 1775 to March 1776. The home's official name has only recently been changed to reflect Washington's occupancy of the house. Longfellow, who in his 1845 poem "To a Child" wrote "Once, ah, once, within these walls, One whom memory oft

⊙ Close-up

Freedom Trail, Boston

Walk in the footsteps of Revolutionary War heroes and get a crash course on Boston's storied past. The **Freedom Trail** is a 2.5-mile brick (sometimes red-painted) path along the sidewalks of downtown Boston and connects the dots of some of the most important events that shaped American history. Armed with a map, you'll find all the destinations within strolling range; visit Faneuil Hall, which provided Bostonians a forum for the boiling independence movement; stand at the site of the Boston Massacre, which further stirred up anti-British sentiment; and take a peek inside Paul Revere's tiny wood home.

The National Park Service and Freedom Trail Foundation are the big players (and cooperative partners) of the trail. The Freedom Trail is free, but the three museum sites, Old South Meeting House, the Old State House, and the Paul Revere House, charge a small admission fee.

You can easily follow your own itinerary; all 16 sites have excellent signage and/or have guides on hand to answer questions. Pick up a map from either the **National Park Service Visitor Center** (First floor, Faneuil Hall; 617-242-5642; nps.gov/bos) or from the **Boston Common Visitor Center** (148 Tremont St.), or download one from the Freedom Trail Foundation site (thefreedomtrail.org).

Boston Common. *Bordered by Park, Tremont, Beacon, and Charles Streets.* The country's oldest park, the Common was established in 1634 as a "trayning field" for militia and for "the feeding of Cattell." The Common is ever-evolving; cows have been prohibited since 1830. Today there is no shortage of things to do, with walking paths, softball fields, and ice-skating in the winter and a wading pool in the summer at Frog Pond.

Massachusetts State House. *Corner of Beacon and Park Streets; (617) 727-3676.* The golden dome of the State House dominates not only the Beacon Hill neighborhood but also the Boston skyline. Designed by Charles Bulfinch in 1798, it is a wonderful example of federal-style architecture. Excellent free tours are offered Mon through Fri 10 a.m. to 3 p.m. by civic-minded docents.

Park Street Church. *1 Park St.; parkstreet.org.* Built of dignified red brick with a majestic white wood steeple, this 1809 church is the New England ideal. On July 4, 1829, William Lloyd Garrison delivered his first major antislavery speech here.

Granary Burying Ground. *Park and Tremont Streets.* Located next to Park Street Church and consecrated in 1660, this graveyard has notable residents including Revolutionary War patriots Samuel Adams, Paul Revere, and John Hancock.

King's Chapel. *School and Park Streets; kings-chapel.org.* Established in 1686 as the first Anglican church in New England, this stone building was designed by renowned colonial architect Peter Harrison. The outside may be austere, but the interior is airy with white Corinthian columns, individual box pews, and elegant lighting.

King's Chapel Burying Ground. *Tremont Street.* Adjacent to King's Chapel, this is Boston's oldest burying ground, dating from 1630. It's a small graveyard but it contains several notable gravesites including those of William Dawes, who rode with Paul Revere to warn of the British invasion, and Elizabeth Pain, her gravestone—with the large letter "A"—is said to be Nathaniel Hawthorne's inspiration for *The Scarlet Letter*.

Benjamin Franklin statue and the site of the first public school. *45 School St.* The colorful sidewalk mosaic mimics a needlework sampler and marks the original site of Boston Latin, the country's first public school. Boston Latin's most famous dropout is Benjamin Franklin, who was born nearby.

Old Corner Bookstore. *285 Washington St.* This 1712 gambrel-roofed building is one of the oldest in the city. From 1832 to 1865 it was the headquarters for Ticknor & Fields, which published *Atlantic Monthly* and the writings of many of the transcendentalists, including Longfellow and Thoreau. This one is a walk-by, unless you're craving a burrito—the space is now occupied by a Chipotle.

Old State House. *206 Washington St.; (617) 720-1713; bostonhistory.org.* Dating from 1713, this high-Georgian-style building was the seat of colonial government and is the oldest public building in Boston. The 7-foot gold lion and unicorn statues are symbols of the British monarchy. They are replicas; the originals were torn down and burned in a bonfire shortly after the signing of the Declaration of Independence.

Old South Meeting House. *310 Washington St.; oldsouthmeetinghouse.org.* Built in 1729, this Puritan meetinghouse was the largest building in colonial Boston and was the frequent location of impassioned speeches against British rule. On December 16, 1773, Old South was ground zero for the events that led to the Boston Tea Party and the dumping of 342 chests of tea into Boston Harbor.

Site of the Boston Massacre. *206 Washington St.* A simple circle of cobblestones marks the site where on March 5, 1770, a mob of angry Bostonians, frustrated by nearly two years of British occupation, taunted (they threw snowballs) the British soldiers on duty in front of the Old State House. Five civilians died and the "massacre" then became a rallying point for the colonists.

Faneuil Hall and Quincy Market. *Congress and North Streets; (617) 242-5675; nps .ogv/bost.* A marketplace and meeting hall since 1742, Faneuil Hall (rhymes with "Daniel") earned the nickname "the cradle of liberty" because it was here that Revolutionary leaders such as Samuel Adams waged the oratory battle against the British. Adjacent Quincy Market was once the city's wholesale food warehouse; 1970s urban renewal transformed the area into a celebrated festival marketplace for dining and shopping.

Old North Church. *193 Salem St., North End; (617) 523-6676; oldnorth.com.* Built in 1723, this is Boston's oldest church building. As immortalized by Longfellow's poem *Paul Revere's Ride*, "one if by land, two if by sea" lanterns were hung in its steeple to signal the movement of British troops.

Paul Revere House. *19 North Sq., North End; (617) 523-2338; paulreverehouse.org.* Dating from 1680, this modest Tudor clapboard is the oldest house in Boston. Silversmith and patriot Paul Revere along with his family (he had eight children with each of two wives!) lived here for nearly 30 years.

Bunker Hill Monument. *Monument Square, Charlestown; (617) 242-5641; nps .gov/bost/historyculture/bhm.htm.* A granite obelisk commemorates the site of the Battle of Bunker Hill, the first major battle of the war on June 17, 1775. It was a Pyrrhic victory for the British, who suffered heavy casualties while the colonists, although outnumbered two-to-one, proved themselves worthy fighters.

USS *Constitution*. *Charlestown Navy Yard, Charlestown; (617) 242-5670; nsp.gov/ historyculture/ussconst.htm.* Launched in 1797, this is the oldest commissioned warship afloat in the world. The USS *Constitution* earned its nickname "Old Ironsides" during the War of 1812 off of the Barbary Coast when shots from the British ship HMS *Guerriere* appeared to bounce off the strong oak hull.

recalls, The Father of his Country, dwelt," likely would have approved. The grounds are open daily year-round, dawn to dusk. The home is open seasonally June through Oct, Wed through Sun, by guided tour only. Check website for exact times.

i If eye-opening architectural design catches your interest, spend some time armed with a camera checking out the modernist gems by I. M. Pei, Eero Saarinen, and Frank Gehry on MIT's campus (pick up a map from the Visitors Center, Building 7, 77 Massachusetts Ave.).

✳MOUNT AUBURN CEMETERY
580 Mount Auburn St.
Cambridge, MA 02138
(617) 547-7105
mountauburn.org
This cemetery is an otherworldly jewel that is much more than a final resting place. Founded in 1831 and covering more than 175 acres, this designated National Historic Landmark was inspired by the landscape style of Père Lachaise Cemetery in Paris. You can pay your respects to the earthly remains of many 18th- and 19th-century Boston notables including Charles Bulfinch, Henry Wadsworth Longfellow, Isabella Stewart Gardner, Winslow Homer, Fanny Farmer, and Asa Gray. Walk along the winding paths bordered by majestic trees and gardens and note the intricate headstones and grand crypts popular in Victorian Boston. Climb the 95 steps of Washington Tower for a terrific panoramic view of Boston and Cambridge. A map is available at the front entrance gate, or you can download a walking tour and cemetery plot locations to your smart phone. There are also regularly scheduled

historic tours and bird walks. Mount Auburn is a birding hot spot—turns out that Mount Auburn's abundant green space provides a wonderful refuge for birds as well.

✳NORTH END
Hanover Street
Boston, MA 02113
This tiny waterfront neighborhood has always led a colorful existence. Since its founding in the 1630s, Boston's North End has been home to colonial artisans such as Paul Revere, slaves, and most recently Italian immigrants. Hordes follow the faded redbrick path of the Freedom Trail to visit the Old North Church and the Paul Revere House. But there's an authentic residential feeling to the tidy streets where you can stop for a gelato, sip a cappuccino at a *caffè*, or enter the most homey trattoria and get a truly memorable meal of pasta and Chianti.

i Before there was Julia, there was Fanny Farmer. Her first book, *The Boston Cooking School Cook Book,* was published in 1896 and was a seminal work, revolutionizing modern cooking by standardizing measurements—no more "a handful of this," "a teacup of that." Her subsequent books and the cooking school that she later founded made her a household name for more than a century.

✳TRINITY CHURCH
26 Clarendon St., Back Bay
Boston, MA 02116
(617) 536-0944
trinitychurchboston.org
Considered to be Henry Hobson Richardson's masterwork, Trinity Church stands majestic in the heart of Copley Square. An army of

craftsmen toiled from 1872 to 1877 to realize the bold Romanesque revival design, which features a modified Greek-cross plan, impressive stonework, and a massive central tower. The huge weight of the building is supported by 4,500 pilings underneath the building on landfill—quite an engineering feat for the time. The interior of the church is no less spectacular. John LaFarge, William Morris, and Edward Burne-Jones were commissioned to do the stained-glass windows; LaFarge also painted the brilliant murals. One or more guided tours are offered every day (check for hours) that highlight the church's architecture, history, and art. Self-guided maps are also available.

i The elegant, asymmetrical 10-lane cable-stayed bridge that spans the Charles River at North Station is Boston's northern gateway. A signature project of the Big Dig, the bridge became an instant icon when it was completed in 2002. It is officially named the Leonard P. Zakim Bunker Hill Memorial Bridge to honor the work of the late local civil rights leader Lenny Zakim and to commemorate the Battle of Bunker Hill. Most locals call it "the Zakim" and Charlestown residents call it the "Bunker Hill Bridge."

Museums

DANFORTH MUSEUM OF ART
123 Union Ave.
Framingham, MA 01702
(508) 620-0050
danforthmuseum.org
Located in the town of Framingham, 30 miles west of Boston, the Danforth is a small gem of an art museum that specializes in mostly American art from the 19th and 20th centuries. Highlights of the permanent collection include a portrait by painter Gilbert Stuart, a James McNeil Whistler work, and several sculptures by Harlem Renaissance artist (and Framingham resident) Meta Warrick Fuller. There is also an emphasis on new work by living artists. The Danforth also offers an extensive program of art workshops and classes for children (from preschoolers through the teen years) and adults. Closed Mon and Tues.

✳HARVARD ART MUSEUMS
485 Broadway
Cambridge, MA 02138
(617) 495-9400
harvardartmuseums.org
For an intimate look at an outstanding collection of great art, Harvard's Sackler Museum building provides an ideal (if temporary) setting. Noteworthy works by Renoir, Monet, and Van Gogh, a Rembrandt, and a Titian are arranged in altogether fascinating ways. The "Re-View" exhibition focuses on highlights of the museum's wide-ranging holdings, including pieces from its American, Asian, and Islamist collections. Meanwhile, across the street, the Fogg Museum's Quincy Street building undergoes a Renzo Piano–designed expansion and renovation that is scheduled for completion in early 2014 and will ultimately reunite Harvard's art museums under one roof. The museum is closed Sun and Mon.

✳HARVARD MUSEUM OF NATURAL HISTORY
26 Oxford St.
Cambridge, MA 02138
(617) 495-3045
hmnh.harvard.edu
Fans of the *Night at the Museum* movies will be totally engaged at the Harvard Museum

of Natural History, where the exhibits track the natural world from anthropology to zoology. Located on the grounds of Harvard University, the museum has beginnings that can be traced back to 1859 with the founding of the Museum of Comparative Zoology by explorer and scientist Louis Agassiz. It is the most visited tourist attraction at Harvard, and as a research center, it is still used by many different people, from scientists to college students to artists. Kids explore the renovated Great Mammal Hall and ooh and aah over massive whale and dinosaur fossils. For adults, especially those with an interest in gardening, visiting the Glass Flowers collection is a must. The more than 3,000 scientifically accurate glass models of 847 plant species were made by father and son German glassmakers Leopold and Rudolf Blaschka at their Dresden workshop between 1886 and 1936. They were commissioned at the time for use as a biological teaching and research aid. Today the delicate glass replicas of blossoms and fruits are regarded as extraordinary works of art.

✳INSTITUTE OF CONTEMPORARY ART
100 Northern Ave., Seaport District
Boston, MA 02210
(617) 478-3100
icaboston.org
The Institute of Contemporary Art is architecturally impressive; the glass and steel building overlooking Boston Harbor highlights space, light, and the water, and is widely regarded as a work of modern art itself. In the permanent collection, which includes art from the late 20th century to the present, seek out Cornelia Parker's *Hanging Fire,* where the burnt, charred wood remains of a suspected arson fire are suspended by wires from the ceiling. You'll also find Thomas

Hirschhorn's *Wood Chain (Pisa Tower),* and every visit to the ICA should include time with Paul Chan's *1st Light,* a digital image projected onto the floor. The ICA also hosts ever-changing exhibits on individual artists from all over the world. Past shows have included Anish Kapoor, Tara Donovan, and Mark Bradford. Lately the ICA has increased its after-hours programming of edgy dance, music, and film performances, attracting art-scene crowds.

✳ISABELLA STEWART GARDNER
  MUSEUM
280 The Fenway
Boston, MA 02115
(617) 566-1401
gardnermuseum.org
Modeled after a 15th-century Venetian palazzo complete with a magnificent flower-filled interior courtyard, the Isabella Stewart Gardner Museum makes you feel like you're being transported to Italy. This is one of the preeminent small art museums in the US with a high quality collection of old masters paintings. Socialite Isabella Stewart Gardner was one of Victorian Boston's most fascinating personalities. The wife of Boston Brahmin Jack Lowell Gardner, she was known for her eccentricities; she famously wore a white headscarf inscribed with "Oh you Red Sox!" to a performance of the Boston Symphony. After her husband's death, Gardner designed an opulent home in Boston's Fenway neighborhood to house the treasures she and her husband had collected on their travels. After the museum's completion in 1903, Gardner herself planned the exhibition galleries, and today the paintings are arranged exactly as they were during her lifetime. You'll also find little in the way of signage—the museum still preserves the ambience of Gardner's private

home. Titian's *Rape of Europa* is one of the most important paintings of any art museum in New England and is a must-see. It was a favorite of Gardner's as well; she chose to have a piece of her ball-gown fabric (from the Paris House of Worth) displayed beneath it. After paying your respects to Isabella—John Singer Sargent's *Portrait of Isabella Stewart Gardner* shows "Mrs. Jack" in her prime—allow time to seek out the museum's other notable works, including a pencil drawing by Michelangelo, *The Colonna Pieta,* Rembrandt's *Self-Portrait, Aged 23,* and Botticelli's *The Story of Lucretia.* In 2012 the museum completed a Renzo Piano expansion: a modern glass annex to house Calderwood Hall, a 300-seat performance space, and Cafe G, where the seasonal menu choices are inspired by the museum and its collections. Important note: The museum is closed Tues.

**✳JOHN F. KENNEDY PRESIDENTIAL
  LIBRARY & MUSEUM
Columbia Point
Dorchester, MA 02125
(617) 514-1600
jfklibrary.org**
Located on the Boston campus of the University of Massachusetts, the library traces the political career of the 35th president, John F. Kennedy, Boston's beloved native son. Overlooking Dorchester Bay, the soaring I. M. Pei–designed building with its glass atrium and white triangular concrete tower evokes a sailboat and Kennedy's lifelong love of the sea. The introductory film—a memoir of Kennedy's early life—is narrated by Kennedy himself. There is a replica of Kennedy's Oval Office and another of the Kennedy-Nixon debate TV set. Several exhibits are dedicated to pivotal events during the 1,000 days of the Kennedy presidency: space exploration,

the Cuban missile crisis, the formation of the Peace Corps, and the civil rights movement. In the atrium library there's a significant section of the Berlin Wall on display, a reminder of JFK's *"Ich bin ein Berliner"* speech of June 26, 1963. The easiest way to reach the library is to take the T (Red line to JFK/UMASS); a free shuttle bus provides service between the station and the library.

**LARZ ANDERSON AUTO MUSEUM
15 Newton St.
Brookline, MA 02445
(617) 522-6547
larzanderson.org**
This museum is a car buff's delight. Located on the grounds of the former Anderson estate, now Brookline's largest public park, this is one of America's oldest car collections. Larz and Isabel Anderson were a prominent and wealthy family at the turn of the last century who amassed an outstanding collection of early motorcars. Among the nearly two dozen cars on permanent display in the estate's 19th-century carriage house are the 1899 Winton Runabout, which began the collection, a 1907 Fiat, and a 1937 Packard Limo. The museum itself is open year-round Tues through Sun and some Mon holidays. From May through Oct the museum also sponsors Sunday lawn events; past themes have included Studebaker Day, Tutto Italiano, and Micro Mini Car Day. The sloping hill offers great views of the Boston skyline.

**MASSACHUSETTS GENERAL HOSPITAL
  MUSEUM OF MEDICAL HISTORY AND
  INNOVATION
2 N. Grove St., West End
Boston, MA 02114
(617) 724-8009
massgeneral.org**

Founded in 1811, MGH has always been regarded as one of the country's top hospitals. In celebration of its recent 200th birthday, MGH opened a brand-new museum showcasing the hospital's medical history and its role in medical advances through the years. The modern, 2-story building itself is a stunner: a slim glass structure clad in copper and topped by a steel pergola. The first-floor permanent exhibits have a modern cabinet-of-curiosities aura—there's an 1845 surgical kit (including a saw used for amputations) and a 19th-century traveling apothecary kit with glass bottles filled with powders and potions as well as exhibits on MGH's latest medical innovations, such as an infant incubator for use in developing countries that features readily available components such as automobile headlights. The second floor houses community meeting rooms and temporary exhibit space. Up a flight of stairs, the lush rooftop garden features flowering trees, benches, and a patio that offer visitors and patients respite (nature can be medicine, too), with views of Beacon Hill. The museum is free and open to the public Mon through Fri.

i Visit the Ether Dome, MGH's original operating theater, where on October 16, 1846, inhaled ether used as an anesthetic during surgery was first publicly demonstrated. The tiered amphitheater and skylight have been restored to their 19th-century appearance. Other relics on display include the 2,500-year-old Egyptian mummy Padihershef, an anatomical teaching skeleton, and exhibits of early surgical tools. The Ether Dome is located on the fourth floor of the Bulfinch Building and is open to the public daily from 9 a.m. to 8 p.m. (unless the room is being used for a medical lecture).

MIT MUSEUM
265 Massachusetts Ave.
Cambridge, MA 02139
(617) 253-5927
mit.edu/museum
Art and science converge at the MIT Museum. The exhibit "Gestural Engineering: The Sculpture of Arthur Ganson" features ingenious kinetic machines—really sculptural art in motion. Before there was Siri, there was Kismet; you can visit early MIT artificial intelligence prototypes at "Robots and Beyond." Be sure to see some of MIT's holographic images. The museum has the largest and most comprehensive hologram collection in the world and there is always a selection of pieces on display. How you see the work depends on your movement and position. Fascinating.

MUSEUM OF AFRICAN AMERICAN
HISTORY
46 Joy St., Beacon Hill
Boston, MA 02108
(617) 725-0022
afroammuseum.org
Starting in the early 1800s the north slope of Beacon Hill was home to an established community of free blacks. Tucked into a dead-end street on Beacon Hill sits the Museum of African American History. The museum includes the Abiel Smith School, established in 1834 as the first public school for black children. Next door visit the restored 1806 African Meeting House, which was a place of worship, a community center, and a gathering place where charismatic Frederick Douglass was a frequent speaker and the New England Anti-Slavery Society was founded in the basement by William Lloyd Garrison. The African Meeting House became known as the "Black Faneuil

Hall" and Boston became the center of the abolitionist movement. The museum is closed Sun.

i The National Park Service offers free, daily guided tours of the 14 sites of the Black Heritage Trail from June through September (meet at the NPS Faneuil Hall Visitor Center) and maps for those interested in doing a self-guided walk of the trail on their own.

*MUSEUM OF FINE ARTS
465 Huntington Ave., Fenway
Boston, MA 02115
(617) 267-9300
mfa.org
The Museum of Fine Arts houses an internationally renowned collection of more than 450,000 works representing nearly all the world's cultures throughout the ages. Come visit the recently renovated (and highly acclaimed) Art of the Americas Wing. The museum's painting and sculpture galleries make up one of the world's finest collections of American art. It's a broadly chronological journey from the exhibits of ancient and Native American works on the lower level to the collection of iconic Revolutionary War–era paintings, including John Singleton Copley's portrait of Paul Revere and Thomas Sully's mythic *Passage of the Delaware* on the first floor. Also on display here are important collections of American decorative arts, including a Revere Sons of Liberty silver bowl. Among the museum's best-known and best-loved works, *The Daughters of Edward Darley Boit* by John Singer Sargent is the centerpiece of the second-floor galleries. Finally, works by 20th-century artists including Edward Hopper, Georgia O'Keeffe, and

Andrew Wyeth are found on the third floor. And should you have more time, the rest of the MFA is pretty impressive, too. Of the antiquities in "The Art of the Ancient World," the most notable collection is the Egyptian artifacts, including jewelry, sculpture, and burial sarcophagi (museum-speak for mummies). The MFA's extraordinary French Impressionist collection is not to be missed, and you may want to linger in the newly refreshed European Gallery with its fine collection of 16th- and 17th-century paintings from Italy, France, Spain, and Flanders displayed against a backdrop of rich red damask-covered walls. If you are hungry, you are a little bit captive at this end of Huntington Avenue. Thankfully, there are several good dining options within the museum. For a quick pick-me-up, Taste Cafe (located near the main gift shop) offers coffee, wine, and choices that include quiche and cheese plates with fruit. The New American Cafe overlooking the buzzing atrium courtyard features salads, sandwiches, soups, and desserts. Get away from the crowds entirely at Bravo, the MFA's fine dining restaurant, open for lunch daily and dinner Wed through Fri. There is also a self-serve cafeteria on the museum's lower level. Special events and exhibits including concerts, lectures, and film screenings keep locals coming back time and time again.

The MFA gift shop is one of the best in Boston, selling wonderful and stylish reproductions of museum jewelry and decorative art items (porcelain bowls, paintings, sculptures, antique coins). You might also appreciate the high-end collection of Boston souvenirs and Red Sox gift items. The book selection is also superb with a wide-ranging array of art-inspired books and travel guides about Boston and New England. And you don't need to pay admission to the museum to visit the gift shop.

ℹ You cannot see this museum in one visit. If you don't have to do Boston in a day, you might want to visit the MFA over two days. General admission includes a free repeat visit within 10 days—take advantage! Those with little time should take a guided tour (either the general collection guided tour, gallery-specific tours, or, for those with a short attention span, the "3 in 30 Minutes" tour).

✳MUSEUM OF SCIENCE
Science Park, West End
Boston, MA 02114
(617) 723-2500
mos.org
At the Museum of Science there are loads of dazzling (and painlessly educational) hands-on exhibits geared to everyone from pre-schoolers to post-grads. Kids of all ages are awestruck by the dinosaur exhibit; there's a fair share of fossils and massive life-size models. Budding engineers can test their creative reasoning skills by building a model wind-powered sailing vessel. And teens and adults can interact with area experts about scientific issues in the headlines at "Behind the Scenes"; recent topics have included climate change and biodiversity. This place is so vast (there are more than 500 exhibits) that a single visit just touches the surface of its offerings. The museum also hosts such traveling shows as the recent "Harry Potter: The Exhibition." Buy a combination ticket that includes the exhibit halls, an IMAX movie at the Omni Theatre, and a planetarium or laser show and you could hunker down for an entire day.

✳NEW ENGLAND HOLOCAUST MEMORIAL
Carmen Park at Congress and Union Streets, Government Center
Boston, MA 02129
(617) 457-8755
nehm.org
While not an official part of the Freedom Trail, the New England Holocaust Memorial is located along it and encourages visitors to think about the consequences of having freedom taken away. It is a sobering experience. At the memorial, located just a couple blocks from Faneuil Hall, visitors walk along a granite path through six 54-foot-high glass and steel columns that represent the main Nazi death camps; each is etched with 1 million ID numbers symbolizing the 6 million who died. Smoke continuously rises from metal grates beneath each tower; in the evening the towers are illuminated. Together the subject matter and the design of the site conspire to evoke a powerful reaction regardless of visitors' religious or ethnic background.

✳SPELLMAN MUSEUM OF STAMPS AND POSTAL HISTORY
235 Wellesley St.
Weston, MA 02493
(781) 768-8367
spellman.org
An obvious must-stop for stamp hobbyists, this museum has a lot to offer almost anyone with even a passing interest in history, the arts, sports, or other cultures. The museum was opened in 1963 on the campus of Regis College with the stamp collection of Cardinal Spellman, former Archbishop of New York, and over the years has expanded to include more than 2 million stamps. On permanent display is a collection of philatelic

rarities, including the world's first postage stamp, a British 1840 Penny Black, and the first American stamp, which bears the image of Benjamin Franklin and dates from 1847. Prior special exhibits have included "Delivering the Mail," "Art with Stamps and the Mail," and stamps commemorating the 50th anniversary of John F. Kennedy's inauguration. With their colorful images and real-life stories, even in the age of e-mail, postage stamps have a lot of appeal for kids. For families there are scavenger hunts, design-a-stamp materials, and puzzles. Best of all, kids get a free packet of stamps to begin their own collection. Be sure to stop at the museum shop, where you can pick up stamps on almost any theme—a thoughtful gift. The museum is open Thurs through Sun with additional days during school vacation weeks and summer.

Parks & Beaches

✴THE ARNOLD ARBORETUM
125 The Arborway
Boston, MA 02130
(617) 524-1718
arboretum.harvard.edu
Set incongruously in the middle of the city, this living museum of trees, shrubs, and herbaceous plants is a research arm of Harvard University. It encompasses 265 acres of beautifully wooded and landscaped grounds with more than 2 miles of paved walkways throughout that make it easy to meander. And walk you will—cars are prohibited from the grounds (if you drive, you'll need to park on the Arborway, outside the main gate). Worth a visit any time of year, the arboretum is most popular from Apr through Oct. Deliciously fragrant lilac bushes are true harbingers of spring and are the arboretum's most famous collection—the lilac bushes here are

among the country's oldest. Summer highlights include flowering trees, shrubs and vines such as dogwoods, hydrangeas, and clematis. In autumn, as you would expect from a New England institution dedicated to the study of trees, the fall foliage display is stunning. Even winter is lovely with the stark outline of the trees against the winter sky and a clear vista of Boston from the overlook at Peters Hill. Be sure to stop at the Hunnewell Visitor Center to pick up a walking map and brochures. Self-guided tours can be downloaded to your smart phone or you can take a guided tour. General guided tours take palce on weekends from Apr through Nov and a variety of themed tours are scheduled every season. Classes and workshops for adults and children are also offered year-round.

✴BOSTON HARBOR ISLANDS NATIONAL PARK
Long Wharf, Waterfront
Boston, MA 02110
(617) 223-8666
bostonharborislands.org
Take to the sea! Comprising 34 islands scattered across Boston Harbor, this national park is a treasure hidden in plain sight. Georges Island, just 7 miles and a 30-minute ferry ride from downtown Boston, is the park's main island and its transportation hub. The focal point of Georges Island is historic Fort Warren, a Civil War–era stronghold where visitors can explore the bunkers and tunnels (bring a flashlight) and take in fine panoramic views of Boston. National Park Service rangers lead free tours and will regale you with tales of the "Lady in Black." Swimming is not permitted on Georges Island, but it is a wonderful spot to walk along the shore enjoying the scent of beach

roses and skipping stones. There are open fields for throwing a Frisbee or flying a kite. Bring your provisions for lunch—there are lots of grills and tables under shady trees, making the island a popular spot for group/extended-family barbecues. There is also an outpost of Summer Shack (open Fri through Sun) offering good-value boxed lunches and a la carte selections including lobster rolls, chowder, salads, burgers, and hot dogs. For swimming, take the free shuttle ferry over to Spectacle Island, which has a lifeguarded beach, changing facilities, and another Summer Shack (weekends only). To reach Georges Island take the Harbor Express Ferry from Boston's Long Wharf. Bonus: The outbound ferry is narrated, so you will learn a bit of the harbor and island history on the way. Ferries generally operate from early May through Columbus Day weekend; check website for departure times.

i Perched at the tip of Little Brewster Island is Boston Light, America's oldest lighthouse, established in 1716. The only way to access the lighthouse is to sign up for the three-hour Boston Light Cruise Tour, offered June through September by the Boston Harbor Island Alliance (islandalliance.org). Tours include a National Park Service ranger–guided cruise to the island and an opportunity to climb the 76 steps of the lighthouse for an up-close view of the Fresnel lens.

CASTLE ISLAND PARK
William J. Day Boulevard, South Boston
Boston, MA 02127
(617) 727-5290
mass.gov/dcr/parks/metroboston/castle.htm

Castle Island is sheltered from the city's hubbub, an outpost of spectacular views, Revolutionary history, and open space. No longer an island, this waterfront park is part of South Boston (yes, the Southie of Hollywood movies: *Good Will Hunting, The Departed,* and *The Town*) and is connected to the mainland by a causeway where locals push strollers, play catch with their kids, and bring the old folks out to sit on the benches. The main feature of the island is Fort Independence, a granite Civil War–era fortress that replaced Castle William, a British 1701 fort. Free tours are offered Thurs and weekends from Memorial Day through Columbus Day. Walk along the 2-mile loop around Pleasure Bay, enjoy the sea breeze, and watch the planes take off and land at Logan (best plane-spotting views are on the eastern side of Fort Independence).

GARDEN IN THE WOODS
180 Hemenway Rd.
Framingham, MA 01701
(508) 877-7630
newfs.org/visit/Garden-in-the-Woods

Garden in the Woods is the headquarters and the principal botanic display gardens of the New England Wildflower Society. This Eden of woodlands is located on 45 acres with both natural and cultivated gardens, showcasing more than 1,700 kinds of plants. In the spring hundreds of native flowers are in bloom among the forest of trees. In the summer the meadows teem with a rich variety of wildflowers. For families, a walk along the trails through the forest and across the small brook past the pond and across the bog is a delight of fairy-like flora and fauna. A guided tour is offered each day (and included with admission) and the garden shop is a tremendous resource with exceptional native plants for sale. Open Tues through Sun and holiday Mon, Apr through Oct.

MASSACHUSETTS HORTICULTURAL SOCIETY AT THE ELM BANK RESERVATION
900 Washington St.
Wellesley, MA 02482
(617) 933-4900
masshort.org

Once a private estate along the Charles River, this 19th-century mansion and 36 adjoining acres are now the headquarters of the Massachusetts Horticultural Society. You can explore several themed gardens including the Bressingham Garden, which looks as if it were transplanted from an English country estate with a lush lawn and flowering perennials. There's a formal 1926 Italianate garden, originally designed by Frederick Law Olmstead. But perhaps the most popular space is "Weezie's Garden" for children. As interactive as a playground, this garden offers kids the chance to climb the tree house, visit the koi (Japanese carp) found on Tortoise Island, or experience the scents from the herb garden. If you want some fauna to go with your flora, keep an eye out for deer and wild turkeys to appear amid the open fields near the forest clearing and waterfowl along the Charles River. And lots of classes and workshops are scheduled throughout the year that will help turn your brown thumb green. Open daily dawn to dusk; admission by donation.

✳THE PUBLIC GARDEN AND THE SWAN BOATS
Bordered by Arlington, Beacon, Charles, and Boylston Streets, Back Bay
Boston, MA 02116
(617) 635-4505
cityofboston.gov/parks

BOSTON SWAN BOATS
swanboats.com
(617) 522-1966

Located in the heart of downtown, the Public Garden is a pristine urban oasis of formal flower gardens, established in 1837 as the country's first botanical garden. Meandering walkways lined with trees shading benches, fountains, and sculptures lead to the grassy banks of a lagoon, the park's focal point. It's a charming spot, populated by the Swan Boats (each can seat up to 20 people) and some very well-fed ducks.

REVERE BEACH
Revere Beach Boulevard
Revere, MA 02151
reverebeach.com

For a quick beach escape from the city, head north to Revere Beach. Established in 1895, this is the oldest public beach in the country. In its heyday during the early 1900s, Bostonians would flock to Revere Beach to enjoy ocean breezes, amusement rides, and dance pavilions. After its near demise in the 1970s, Revere Beach has been revitalized by the city of Revere and the Metropolitan District Commission, and the water and sand have never looked better. Take a nice long walk (the beach is 2 miles) on the wide, white-sand beach and enjoy the Atlantic surf and great people-watching. The beach is free and accessible by I (Revere Beach stop on the Blue line) or by car—there's plenty of free parking. Afterward, head over to Kelly's Roast Beef; the beach-side stand is a local institution.

WELLESLEY COLLEGE GREENHOUSES
106 Central St.
Wellesley, MA 02481
(781) 283-3094
wellesley.edu/wcbg

Even in the middle of winter, it feels like a warm summer day at the Wellesley College Botanic Gardens. The 13 interconnected greenhouses feature more than 1,000 varieties of exotic plants from around the world, including tropicals, orchids, and cacti. The greenhouses are a research and teaching resource for Wellesley College that along with the Botanic Garden and Arboretum are free and open daily to the public.

Wildlife & Zoos

*FRANKLIN PARK ZOO
1 Franklin Park Rd.
Dorchester, MA 02121
(617) 541-LIONS
zoonewengland.org
If you are tired of crowded, tourist-filled Boston sites, take an excursion to the Franklin Park Zoo. Located in the city's Dorchester neighborhood, this is one of the city's least busy attractions—even on a warm summer day. Established in 1912, it is one of the country's oldest zoos. It's a medium-size park with all the kids' favorite big zoo animals, including giraffes, tigers, and lions. There's a nice mix of shady trees, open space, and wide pathways connecting the exhibit areas, making this a perfect choice for even the stroller set. Among the highlights for families are Franklin Farm, a petting zoo with chickens, cows, goats, bunnies, and sheep. But the 3-acre Tropical Forest is the zoo's centerpiece, an indoor pavilion that is home to ocelots, tapirs, and crocodiles and free-flight birds that coexist. The real stars of the exhibit are the zoo's 8 lowland gorillas. At the glass viewing stations, kids love to stand face-to-face with the gorillas and watch them monkey around.

*NEW ENGLAND AQUARIUM AND NEW ENGLAND AQUARIUM WHALE WATCHES
Central Wharf, Waterfront
Boston, MA 02110
(617) 973-5200
neaq.org
The biggest "wow" attraction at the New England Aquarium is its 4-story glass, circular Giant Ocean Tank (GOT), which houses a re-created Caribbean coral reef that is the home to more than 600 animals, including sharks, stingrays, and barracudas. Look for Myrtle the sea turtle, who is easily GOT's most famous resident and is said to be more than 80 years old. The biggest school of fish in the tank are the "look-downs"—ask one of the many friendly aquarium volunteers stationed around the tank to point them out. The aquarium also has a huge Penguin Pool with nearly 70 animated and very cute penguins. Try to catch a training session at the Marine Mammal Center, which educates visitors about seals' agility and intelligence as much as it entertains. GOT is undergoing a $17 million transformation (scheduled to be completed in the summer of 2013), which will keep the aquarium on the cutting edge of marine science. But don't fret: Even while the aquarium is under construction, the museum will be open and there is still plenty to see and explore. The adjacent IMAX Theater shows 3-D movies several times a day. Arrive early on weekends and during the summer to beat the crush. Your best bet is to buy your tickets online in advance; otherwise the wait to enter can be 2–3 hours. If you are ready for a high-seas adventure of your own, head out with aquarium naturalists on the *Voyager III* for a memorable whale-watching experience. Thousands of whales

(finback, humpback, and right) feed at Stellwagen Bank Marine Sanctuary, 30 miles off the coast. Be sure to wear something warm (it's often cold on the water, even in summer) and bring binoculars. Trips run for 3 to 4 hours, so budget a good chunk of the day for this trip.

STONE ZOO
149 Pond St.
Stoneham, MA 02180
(781) 438-5100
zoonewengland.org
Kids can't get enough of animals? Then head north to Zoo New England's other zoo, Stone Zoo. Brother bears Smoky and Bubba are the zoo's star attraction and are fun to watch. The zoo volunteers stationed here are used to answering questions from kids about sibling rivalry. Don't miss the Sierra Madre exhibit, with its cougars and jaguars, and the Barnyard attracts kids of all ages with friendly goats and sheep.

Wineries & Breweries

✳HARPOON BREWERY
306 Northern Ave., Seaport District
Boston, MA 02110
(617) 574-9551
harpoonbrewery.com
Located on the downtown waterfront, Harpoon Brewery is the largest specialty brewer in New England. Its flagship beer is the Harpoon IPA; its UFO Hefeweizen is popular as well. Pay a visit to this fun brewery for factory tours that consist of a cat-walk visit of the plant and the highlight of sampling green beer straight from a tank. Tours take place daily, cost $5, and include several tastings. Check the website for times. Get there early—they often sell out.

✳SAMUEL ADAMS BREWERY
30 Germania St., Jamaica Plain
Boston, MA 02130
(617) 368-5080
samueladams.com
Sam Adams is the granddaddy of the American craft beer movement and Boston is known the world over for great beer because of it. In 1984 sixth-generation brewer Jim Koch made the first batch of Sam Adams Boston lager in his kitchen. The Jamaica Plain brewery isn't much bigger than an industrial kitchen; this facility is used for making the company's interesting and still groundbreaking specialty beers and R & D (you may very well see Jim Koch among the brew kettles). On your 45-minute tour you will see the entire brewery process from start to finish and (more important) sample beers with names like Old Fezziwig Ale and Porch Rocker at the conclusion of the tour. Tours are offered Mon through Sat (check hours in advance), and be sure to get there early; the tours are free (a $2 local charity donation is requested) but fill up quickly, especially on Fri and Sat. Closed Sun.

ℹ Sam Adams Boston Lager is named after the patriot (and part-time brewer and beer aficionado) Sam Adams. The picture on the company's label is drawn from the Sam Adams statue that stands in front of Faneuil Hall (only happier).

ACTIVITIES & EVENTS

Arts Venues

ARSENAL CENTER FOR THE ARTS
321 Arsenal St.
Watertown, MA 02472
(617) 923-0100
arsenalarts.org
Established as a military arsenal in 1816 that served the US Army for 150 years, the Arsenal Center for the Arts has been restructured to house several community arts organizations in multiple performance areas, including gallery and studio space, classrooms, and a 380-seat theater. Its resident theater company, New Rep, is among the area's best. Recent productions have included Mamet's *Race* and Truman Capote's *Holiday Memories* and the Tony award–winning play *Amadeus*.

BANK OF AMERICA PAVILION
290 Northern Ave., Seaport District
Boston, MA 02210
(617) 728-1600
bankofamericapavilion.net
The opportunity to enjoy live music under the stars draws large crowds to this 5,000-seat open-air amphitheater along the waterfront in downtown Boston. Stevie Wonder, Norah Jones, Bonnie Raitt, Maroon 5, and Santana are just a few of the headliners who have performed here. The season runs from June through Sept and concertgoers can choose from three seating arrangements: table seats, reserved seats (both under cover), or the lawn—which is strictly BYOB—bring your own blanket!

BERKLEE PERFORMANCE CENTER
136 Massachusetts Ave., Back Bay
Boston, MA 02115
(617) 747-2261
berklee.edu/bpc
This 1,215-seat theater is the main stage of the Berklee School of Music, the country's largest independent college of contemporary (jazz, rock, and pop) music. During the academic year, Berklee offers hundreds of public concerts by both student and professional groups that range from vocal showcases to jazz combos and world music ensembles. Most concerts are low cost—less than the price of a movie ticket.

BOSTON CENTER FOR THE ARTS
539 Tremont St., South End
Boston, MA 02116
(617) 426-5000
bcaonline.org
The Boston Center for the Arts is perhaps the most vibrant center of performance in the city, with several enthusiastic young companies exploring innovative drama, poetry, dance, and music within several buildings in a campus-like setting. Along with several galleries there are 4 stages including the Calderwood Pavilion, a spin-off project of the nearby Huntington Theater. **The Beehive** (see p. 54) shares space here; go early for a preperformance drink.

BOSTON OPERA HOUSE
539 Washington St., Downtown
Boston, MA 02111
(617) 259-3400
bostonoperahouse.com
Built in 1928 and extensively refurbished, the wine-red and gold Boston Opera House with its double grand staircase lobby and magnificent crystal chandeliers is not just a night

out but also a whole experience. The Boston Ballet calls this home and it's a popular stage for touring Broadway shows.

☀BOSTON PUBLIC LIBRARY
700 Boylston St., Back Bay
Boston, MA 02116
(617) 536-5400
bpl.org

Founded in 1852, the Boston Public Library was the first free lending library in the country. Located on Copley Square, the main branch library was designed by the architecture firm of McKim, Mead, and White and completed in 1895, and is a fine example of Italian Renaissance revival architecture. The library's great bronze doors are the work of Daniel Chester French. Ascend the sweeping marble double staircase to Bates Hall, the library's main reading room, with its extraordinary barrel-vaulted ceiling and rows upon rows of oak tables and green study lamps that inspire students and readers alike. To really appreciate the space, walk through (along the side so as not to disturb those studying) or take a break and borrow the newspaper from the nearby research delivery desk. On the third floor a series of allegorical murals, including *Triumph of Religion* by John Singer Sargent, are not to be missed (and are quite unlike his portrait work). The library's interior Italian courtyard is a hidden treasure featuring a bubbling center fountain and tables under the arches— pick up sandwiches and drinks from the library's Map Room Cafe and pretend you are in Europe. A free hourlong guided tour of the library is offered daily; check website for time.

BOSTON UNIVERSITY THEATER
264 Huntington Ave.
Boston, MA 02115
(617) 266-0800
huntingtontheatre.org

Dating from 1925, this 900-seat theater is splendid, with plush blue velvet seating, gold leaf moldings, and Hamlet's "To hold as t'were the mirror up to nature" carved above the proscenium arch. The theater is owned by Boston University (although it's actually practically on Northeastern's campus) and used as workspace by its drama students, but the theater is mostly used by the Huntington Theater as its principal performance space.

CALDERWOOD HALL AT THE ISABELLA STEWART GARDNER MUSEUM
280 The Fenway
Boston, MA 02115
(617) 566-1401
gardnermuseum.org

Music has been a vital part of the Gardner Museum since its 1903 opening that featured a concert by members of the Boston Symphony Orchestra. Experience concerts in the intimate setting of the state-of-the-art Calderwood Hall, part of the 2012 Renzo Piano renovation and expansion project of the Isabella Stewart Gardner Museum. Three balcony levels of front-row seating surround all four sides of a central performance stage. The Sunday concert series provides a platform for internationally acclaimed classical musicians and emerging artists at critical moments in their careers. The museum also sponsors an ongoing jazz and contemporary concert series.

THE CENTER FOR THE ARTS (TCAN)
14 Summer St.
Natick, MA 01760
(508) 647-0097
natickarts.org
Community theater, dance performance, art and photography gallery exhibits, and children's classes jam the schedule at this renovated 1875 fire station on the Natick town green. The 290-seat theater books local as well as national acts. Previous headline performers have included saxophonist David Sanborn, singer Livingston Taylor, and the Second City comedy troupe.

*COOLIDGE CORNER THEATER
290 Harvard St.
Brookline, MA 02215
(617) 734-2500
coolidge.org
Located in Brookline, this 1933 Art Deco theater is one of the Boston area's most beloved independent movie houses, devoted to bigger indie films, foreign films, and midnight cult shows. The crowd is low-key, parking is easy, and the concessions are better than average (they sell beer and wine, too). The theater offers more than a dozen regular programs including movies for moms and babies, kids' Saturday morning shows, benefit screenings, film festivals, and ballet and opera in cinema.

HATCH MEMORIAL SHELL
46 David G. Mugar Way, Beacon Hill
Boston, MA 02108
(617) 626-4970
mass.gov/dcr
This outdoor amphitheater located on the Charles River Esplanade is most well-known as the location for the July 4 Boston Pops Esplanade Orchestra Fireworks Spectacular but it is also host to pop and jazz music concerts, film screenings, and festival events all summer long. Best of all, all Hatch Shell events are free.

*JORDAN HALL
290 Huntington Ave.
Boston, MA 02115
(617) 585-1100
necmusic.edu/jordan-hall
During the academic year, the New England Conservatory sponsors nearly 100 student and faculty performances of incredible quality—most of which are free and open to the public. Classical music is often on the program but jazz, drama, dance, and interdisciplinary works make appearances on the schedule as well. Jordan Hall is a lovely theater, both acoustically and visually, and is also used for local professional chamber ensemble concerts.

*SANDERS THEATRE
Harvard University
45 Quincy St.
Cambridge, MA 02138
(617) 496-4595
fas.harvard.edu/~memhall/sanders.html
Located in Harvard's Memorial Hall, this fabulously ornate theater is an atmospheric backdrop for a wide range of performances, including undergraduate choirs and orchestral groups as well as professional classical music ensembles, such as Boston Baroque and the Boston Chamber Music Society. Sanders's best-known annual event is the Christmas Revels, a joyous celebration of midwinter solstice traditions from around the world woven together through song, dance, and storytelling. Revels's signature piece, "The Lord of the Dance" (a variation of the Quaker hymn "Simple Gifts") takes place

just before intermission and has the audience joining hands with the cast dancing through the aisles.

SCHUBERT THEATER
265 Tremont St., Theater District
Boston, MA 02116
(617) 482-9393
wangcenter.org

Nicknamed the "Little Princess," this wonderfully intimate and elegant theater has hosted many luminaries over its 100-plus years. Great performers of the past who have graced its stage include Sir John Gielgud, John Barrymore, and Richard Burton. Today the Schubert hosts touring Broadway shows (*Jersey Boys* has had quite a run here) and is the home of the Boston Lyric Opera.

SOMERVILLE THEATRE (AND MUSEUM OF BAD ART)
55 Davis Sq.
Somerville, MA 02144
(617) 625-5700
feitheatres.com/somerville-theatre

This independent movie house shows first-run films in 5 smallish theaters—almost like a private screening room, but with good sight lines. Draws here include low ticket prices and a concession stand that offers Richardson's ice cream by the scoop, and this is one of the few area theaters to offer alcohol. Be sure to check out the brilliantly droll (and free) Museum of Bad Art downstairs before or after the show.

✳SYMPHONY HALL
301 Massachusetts Ave., Fenway
Boston, MA 02115
(617) 266-1492
bso.org

The modest exterior of Boston's Symphony Hall conceals a highly regarded acoustical concert hall where the best of the international classical music scene perform. Designed by McKim, Mead, and White in 1900, the hall has superior acoustics that come in part from the structure's long, tall, and narrow shape. The interior has little ornamentation except the gold leaf proscenium arch above the stage. Beethoven's name is inscribed on the plaque in the center of the arch—the rest of the plaques remain blank because he was the only composer the original trustees agreed deserved the honor. Symphony Hall is mostly known as the home of the Boston Symphony and Boston Pops. The Handel & Haydn Society presents its concerts here as well, and Symphony Hall is a popular spot for the Celebrity Series. Take a guided tour and experience Symphony Hall in a whole new way. Tours are offered Wed at 4 p.m. and Sat at 2 p.m. throughout the season; check online for dates.

WANG THEATER
270 Tremont St., Theater District
Boston, MA 02116
(617) 482-9393
citicenter.org/theatres/wang

Opened in 1925 as a movie theater, the Wang was designed in the grand movie palace tradition. In the early 1990s its elegant murals, gilded moldings, and 4-story lobby were restored to their original glory. With nearly 3,600 seats, this is one of the largest theaters in the city. The Wang is also the largest stage in Boston, and the theater of choice for big production touring shows like Alvin Ailey American Dance Theater and musicals like *Miss Saigon* and *Peter Pan*.

Cruises

✳BOSTON HARBOR CRUISES
1 Long Wharf, Waterfront
Boston, MA 02110
(617) 227-4321
bostonharborcruises.com

From May through October, Boston Harbor Cruises offers several historic 90-minute round-trip narrated tours that take you past the landmarks along Boston Harbor. Other options include lunch and sunset cruises and themed cruises that travel to the USS *Constitution*, the Boston Tea Party Ships & Museum, or the lighthouses in Boston Harbor. Thrill-seeking teens might enjoy *Codzilla*, a wave-jumper powerboat ride in the harbor. Boston Harbor Cruises also runs several daily 90-minute fast ferries to Provincetown during the summer season—hands down the best way to do a day trip to the Cape from Boston.

CHARLES RIVERBOAT COMPANY
100 Cambridgeside Place
Cambridge, MA 02141
(617) 225-0894
charlesriverboat.com

Boston fronts water on two sides: along the Boston Harbor and the Charles River. A 60-minute cruise on the Charles River is a pleasant way to get oriented to the city while enjoying a live narrative about the sights along the river. The cruise passes by Beacon Hill, the Esplanade, Fenway, Boston University, MIT, and Harvard. The awning-ed boats are basic with big windows and room for everybody to enjoy the view. Snacks and drinks are available on board for purchase. The season runs from May through Oct. From June through Aug there is also a daily sunset cruise.

COME SAIL AWAY NOW
Pier 6, 8th St.
Charlestown, MA 02129
(617) 828-9005
comesailawaynow.com

Savor stunning views of Boston's skyline on the *Tupelo Honey,* a 31-foot replica of a 1904 Friendship sloop. You'll also pass tugboats, freighters, and cruise ships—a reminder that Boston Harbor is very much a working port. During the summer season (June–Aug), cruises leave port several times a week for scheduled public tours; check website for departure times. Private charter sails are also available.

✳NEW ENGLAND AQUARIUM WHALE WATCH
Central Wharf
Boston, MA 02110
(617) 973-5200
neaq.org

Seeing a whale up-close is an experience you won't soon forget. Naturalist-led whale watches aboard the New England Aquarium's *Voyager III* help support the aquarium's whale research efforts. The round trip to the whales' feeding ground at the Stellwagen Bank Marine Sanctuary typically takes 3–4 hours. The season typically runs from Apr through Oct, with departures daily. Advance booking is advised.

Festivals & Annual Events

BERKLEE BEANTOWN JAZZ FESTIVAL
Columbus Avenue (between Burke Street and Massachusetts Avenue), South End
beantownjazz.com

Held on the last Saturday of September, this free outdoor music festival celebrates the sounds of jazz in all its forms including blues,

Latin, and pop. The lineup typically includes big names and up-and-comers along with faculty and student musicians from the Berklee College of Music. Spread out over a 6-block area of the South End, spectators soak up the sounds and dance in the street. It's a quite sight in staid Boston.

*BOSTON HARBORFEST
Venues throughout the city
Boston, MA
bostonharborfest.com
There is no better place to be on the Fourth of July than Boston. The city celebrates Independence Day not for just one day, but with an entire week packed with activities and events that include colonial reenactments, military band concerts, and Chowderfest, the chance to decide for yourself who has the best chowder in Boston. Principal locations are City Hall Plaza, the Harborfront, and Faneuil Hall Marketplace, and most events are free.

*BOSTON MARATHON
Copley Square, Back Bay
Boston, MA 02116
(617) 236-1652
baa.org
The Boston Marathon is second to none. One of the world's most prestigious running events, taking place every year since 1897, this is also the world's oldest annual marathon. An elite field of world-class marathoners along with 20,000 ordinary runners (as if running 26.2 miles is ever "ordinary") takes off from the town of Hopkinton on a course that takes the athletes through Ashland, Framingham, Natick, Wellesley, Newton, and Brookline before finishing next to the Boston Public Library in Copley Square. The race is held on the third Monday of April, Patriots'

Day (a legal Massachusetts holiday), which may help explain why half a million fans line the streets—everyone has the day off.

*BOSTON POPS FIREWORKS SPECTACULAR
Along the Esplanade, Beacon Hill
Boston, MA
july4th.org
The Boston Pops Fireworks Spectacular is really two events in one. Pack a blanket and picnic and head to the Hatch Shell for a free concert featuring Keith Lockhart and the Boston Pops Esplanade Orchestra along with a big-name guest artist (recent years have featured Jennifer Hudson, Aerosmith, and Rascal Flatts). Other highlights include a rousing patriotic sing-along and Tchaikovsky's 1812 Overture accompanied by fireworks, live howitzer cannons, and lots of confetti. Immediately after the concert, the main fireworks show lights up the sky over the Charles River.

i The Boston Pops performs a full-scale dress rehearsal "preview" concert of the Fourth of July show on July 3 beginning at 8:30 p.m. (gates open at 4 p.m.). There aren't any fireworks, but it is a lot less crowded.

*FIRST NIGHT BOSTON
Venues throughout the city
Boston, MA 02108
(617) 542-1399
firstnight.org
Started in Boston in 1976, First Night Boston is the country's original New Year's festival of arts and culture and has become a model for similar celebrations worldwide. Each December 31, as many as 1 million revelers crowd Boston to ring in the New

Year at this alcohol-free and family-friendly event. With 1,000 participating artists and 200 events at 40 locations throughout the city, there really is something for everyone. Highlights include the ice sculptures in Copley Square and the Boston Common and the Grand Procession followed by the family fireworks on the Boston Common at 7 p.m. Join the crowds as the city becomes a virtual pedestrian mall and walk toward Boston Harbor, where at midnight you'll be wowed by another impressive fireworks display. Be sure to bundle up for frigid weather and don't forget warm socks!

HEAD OF THE CHARLES REGATTA
Boston and Cambridge
hocr.org
The world's largest 2-day rowing regatta draws a field of some 9,000 athletes and a crush of 300,000 cheering spectators to the banks of the Charles River. It's a prestigious race and a competitive field with rowers from high school, college, and club teams from the US and nearly 30 countries. But the weekend is as much a giant party as it is a race meet. Stake out your viewing spot at any one of the six bridges that cross the Charles along the 5-kilometer course. No matter where you watch the action, the Head of the Charles is a spectacle—the races take place during the third weekend of October, which coincides with the peak of Boston's fall foliage.

Fishing

JAMAICA POND
507 Jamaica Way, Jamaica Pond
Boston, MA 02130
cityofboston.gov/parks/emerald/
Jamaica_Pond.asp

The largest body of freshwater in Boston (it covers 68 acres), Jamaica Pond is stocked heavily in spring and fall and is very good for largemouth bass, perch, pickerel, and brook and rainbow trout (and sometimes salmon). Jamaica Pond also offers sailboat and rowboat rentals; rowboat rentals are discounted 50 percent if you show your fishing license.

LT. JOHN J. MCCORKLE FISHING PIER
Day Boulevard Castle Island, South
Boston
Boston, MA 02127
For saltwater fishing, McCorkle Pier at Castle Island in South Boston is a well-known spot. Drop a line off the long concrete pier and try your luck; common catches are mackerel, striped bass, bluefish, and herring. Located at the entrance of the Inner Harbor, the pier offers the bonus of watching the harbor traffic and the planes take off from and land at Logan.

Golf

NEWTON COMMONWEALTH
212 Kenrick St.
Newton, MA 02458
(617) 630-1971
sterlinggolf.com/newton
Donald Ross designed this 18-hole, par 70 public course in the early 1920s. It's still a challenging layout; the tree-lined course is known particularly for its hills, short greens, and narrow fairways.

WILLIAM J. DEVINE GOLF COURSE AT
   FRANKLIN PARK
1 Circuit Dr., Dorchester
Boston, MA 02121
(617) 265-4084
cityofbostongolf.com

This historic golf course was established in 1896 and is the second oldest public course in the US. The course is part of Franklin Park, one of the baubles in Frederick Law Olmstead's Emerald Necklace, the chain of parks throughout the city. Donald Ross did the redesign in 1922, expanding the course to 18 holes, and Franklin Park (as it's known locally) still has an old-school feel with rolling terrain, wide fairways, and mature trees—with the sights and the sounds of the city nearby. It's open year-round (weather permitting), so if you want to play in February and there is no snow on the ground, the course will be all yours.

Health & Wellness

DEDHAM HEALTH AND ATHLETIC COMPLEX

200 Providence Hwy.
Dedham, MA 02026
(781) 326-2900
dedhamhealth.com

Fitness nuts, families, and grandmas all feel at home at this health club. There's plenty of shiny equipment to go around so you don't have to worry about waiting for a treadmill. Membership includes free personal training sessions and access to a weekly schedule of 70 classes that are actually fun, including Zumba, Aquafit, and Body Flow (a combination of Pilates, yoga, and tai chi). Drop in at the open gym for basketball or check out the boxing studio, and when you're done, head to one of the 2 indoor pools. If you have little ones, take advantage of child care or enroll the older kids in a class while you work out: They can start swim lessons at 6 months (with your participation); school-age kids can take karate or rock climbing lessons. During the summer the outdoor heated swimming/

wave pool with water slides will keep everyone in the family happy.

KARMA YOGA STUDIO

1120 Massachusetts Ave.
Cambridge, MA 02138
(617) 547-9642
karmayogastudio.com

This Cambridge studio is Zen-like, a light-filled oasis of serenity offering a variety of classes with an emphasis on the spiritual side of yoga as much as the physical. Vinyasa is the main tradition, but all major styles of yoga are available. Small class sizes and a professional group of teachers and wellness practitioners attract a loyal crowd. You can work up a sweat, too—there is a fully equipped fitness space here as well. After class enjoy a cup of herbal tea in the cafe.

MAYYIM HAYYIM LIVING WATERS COMMUNITY MIKVEH

1838 Washington St.
Newton, MA 02466
(617) 244-1836
mayyimhayyim.org

Founded by author Anita Diamant (*The Red Tent*), this modern take on the centuries-old Jewish *mikvah* (ritual bath) tradition is a welcoming space for the Jewish community (both women and men) to celebrate life changes, such as marriage, bar/bat mitzvahs, birthdays, divorce, or conversion to Judaism.

MOUNT AUBURN CLUB

57 Coolidge Ave.
Watertown, MA 02472
(617) 923-2255
mountauburnclub.com

The 11 indoor/outdoor tennis courts reign supreme here, and the club keeps members occupied by offering private lessons, group clinics, and kids' tennis programming along with free play. And while tennis may be the star, there are other reasons to join: a huge cardio room with 40 machines, free-weight rooms, a spin studio, an indoor pool, and a full schedule of 90 group-fitness classes a week that range from boot-camp-style conditioning to yoga for everyone. While the Mount Auburn offers a cafe and spa services, it is still more of a friendly gym than a "country club" setup.

SPA AT THE MANDARIN ORIENTAL HOTEL
766 Boylston St., Back Bay
Boston, MA 02199
(617) 535-8820
mandarinoriental.com/boston/
luxury-spa

Once you are ensconced inside this fabulously luxurious spa at the Mandarin Oriental Hotel, you may never want to leave. The spa is lovely, with marble floors, bamboo accents, fabrics in calming beiges and golds, and well-appointed locker rooms. Give yourself time to enjoy the spa's amenities before or after your treatment; experience the steam room, vitality pool (hot tub), and shower room with choices like cool mist and tropical rain. The Mandarin offers an extensive roster of spa treatments: massages, body wraps and scrubs, facials, and manicures and pedicures. Whatever you choose, you'll experience lavish service. Not ready to return to the real world just yet? Linger at the Spa Cafe with a salad and freshly squeezed juice.

TOGETHER IN MOTION
1 Broadway
Arlington, MA 02474
(781) 643-1377
togetherinmotion.com

There really is something for everyone at this family gym and exercise studio. Among the classes for adults are Zumba, yoga, self-defense, and a dodgeball league. Drop-in play for kids is offered every day in a padded gym with tunnels, balls, and not-too-high climbing structures. Parents love that the play area can be observed in the lounge—and there's free Wi-Fi access. School-age kids can choose from classes like yoga and martial arts. Commitment phobic? There are no membership fees—you pay by the class or with a punch card.

Hiking, Biking & Walking

CHARLES RIVER BIKE PATH
Boston to Newton
massbike.org

The 23-mile looping Charles River bike path starts at the Museum of Science (park in the museum's garage or at the Cambridgeside Galleria) and runs along both sides of the Charles River through Watertown and Waltham and as far as Newton. Download a route map from massbike.org and look for the granite pillars with the blue heron to lead the way.

CHARLES RIVER ESPLANADE
Along the Charles River, Beacon Hill
Boston, MA 02108
esplanadeassociation.org

This 3.5-mile grassy, shady promenade along the banks of the Charles River is one of the city's jewels, a link in the chain of parks called the Emerald Necklace. The Esplanade runs parallel to the Charles River from the Museum of Science to the Boston University Bridge and is equipped with paths for walking, running, and cycling. There are also tennis courts, fields for baseball/softball and soccer, and a terrific playground for the little ones. This stretch of the Charles is also the location of **Community Boating** (see p. 59) and the **Hatch Shell** (see p. 59), where the Boston Pops Esplanade Orchestra plays its Fourth of July concert. There isn't any dedicated parking; access is from any of the 8 footbridges that cross Storrow Drive. Also, you certainly don't want to be walking here after dark, except for an organized event.

MIDDLESEX FELLS RESERVATION
68 S. Border Rd.
Medford, MA 02155
(781) 662-2340
mass.gov/dcr/parks/metroboston/fells
.htm
fells.org

Just 10 miles north of Boston, the Fells is a rocky, hilly 2,500-acre parcel that offers a wilderness experience for all levels of outdoorsiness, from rugged backwoods types to weekend dabblers. The reservation spans several towns, including Malden, Medford, Stoneham, Melrose, and Winchester. The 1-mile Long Pond Trail takes just an hour and is a good choice for first-timers. Experienced hikers will want to take on the Skyline Trail, which has nearly 7 miles of woodland terrain and great views of the Boston skyline from the Wright Observation Tower. Among the other park diversions, some of the trails are designated for mountain biking, there are boat rentals at Spot Pond in Stoneham, and the 10-acre Sheepfold area is a popular meet-up place for local dogs and their owners.

i On Sundays from spring through fall, the 2-mile stretch of Cambridge's Memorial Drive between Western Avenue and Mount Auburn Street is closed to vehicular traffic and open for everyone to walk, run, and bike. It's all about healthy recreation!

Ice Skating

✳BOSTON COMMON FROG POND
84 Beacon St., Beacon Hill
Boston, MA 02108
(617) 635-2120
bostonfrogpond.com

Ice-skating on Frog Pond in the Boston Common is one of the city's most picturesque winter activities—it's a scene straight from Currier & Ives. There are skate rentals, lockers, restrooms, and a concession stand. In the evening, enjoy the crisp night air and skating under the stars (all very romantic). But be prepared for throngs on the weekends, especially around the holidays.

CHARLES HOTEL ICE SKATING RINK
One Bennett St.
Cambridge, MA 02138
(617) 864-1200
charleshotel.com

For wintery charm, there is nothing more enjoyable than ice-skating on an outdoor rink in the city. Every winter the Charles Hotel converts its outdoor plaza to an ice-skating rink that is open to the public. At 3,000 square feet, it's a small oval and uncrowded compared to nearby Kendall Square. Here, the ice is kept in very good shape.

COMMUNITY ICE SKATING @KENDALL SQUARE
300 Athenaeum St.
Cambridge, MA 02142
(617) 492-0941
kendallsquare.org/play/details/
community-ice-skating

Strap on some ice skates for a few turns at this charming outdoor oval in Cambridge's Kendall Square neighborhood. The facility offers skate rentals and lessons and daily public skating. When you need a rest, grab a cup of hot cocoa from the snack bar. Après skate, there are lots of restaurants nearby including Aceituna Cafe and Redbones Rib Shack.

MASSACHUSETTS PUBLIC SKATING RINKS
Multiple locations
(617) 727-4708
mass.gov/dcr/recreate/skating.htm
Massachusetts has an extensive network of municipal indoor skating rinks—this is New England, after all. The Department of Conservation and Recreation's website lists locations, hours, admission fees, and availability of skate rentals. Children and adult learn-to-skate programs are offered at many of the rinks. (Or you can just hang onto the wall.)

Kidstuff

ARTBEAT
212A Massachusetts Ave.
Arlington, MA 02474
artbeatonline.com
It is easy for kids to be inspired at Artbeat. This is one of the area's largest walk-in art studios specializing in helping kids and teens create their own high-quality art projects. Typical drop-in projects include children-of-the-world dolls, sticky sand art, paintable papier-mâché sculptures, or rolled beeswax candles. The patient staff provides free instruction; projects are suitable for children over age 5, and most take just about an hour to complete. Parent or caregiver involvement is requested for young kids; for children over age 8, you have a drop-off option (and maybe can get a quick cup of coffee!). Artbeat also offers scheduled art classes (some for adults), vacation art camps, and birthday party packages.

ARTESANI PLAYGROUND AND SPRAY PARK
1255 Soldiers Field Rd.
Brighton, MA 02135
(617) 626-4973
mass.gov/dcr/recreate/pools.htm
The Charles River is the idyllic setting of this playground and spray park. Chase your tot from the swings to the merry-go-round at the playground. Then visit the spray park, where the highlight for most kids is the antenna-like sprinklers in the wading pool. Always crowded with frolicking kids, the park has plenty of lifeguards to keep it all under control.

✳BOSTON CHILDREN'S MUSEUM
308 Congress St., Seaport District
Boston, MA 02110
(617) 426-6500
bostonkids.org
Children's museums aren't just about play. That's abundantly evident at the Boston Children's Museum, which aims to inspire creativity and a lifelong love of learning for children ages 2–10. Located on Boston's waterfront, the museum's centerpiece is the 3-story New Balance Climb structure with its wavy carpeted platforms artistically suspended in the air with cables (and netting). In addition to the dozens of fabulous galleries, including "Science Playground," with its giant bubbles, and "The Common," where kids and parents can play chess with giant game pieces, the Children's Museum features exceptional multicultural exhibits including a re-created 100-year-old Japanese house and "Boston Black," where kids can shop at Pico Duarte Market and do a little salsa dancing at the Cape Verdean cafe. The museum is a terrific resource for parents of young children; classes in art and movement and talks by

area experts for parents on child-related topics are sponsored here, too.

5W!TS PATRIOTS PLACE
202 Patriot Place
Foxboro, MA 02035
(508) 698-1600
5-wits.com

Part scavenger hunt, part physical challenge, these themed interactive reality experiences are like stepping into an adventure movie. A guide/actor takes you through either the Espionage or the 20,000 Leagues adventure, where successfully navigating the game requires teamwork, puzzle-solving, and physical skill. At Espionage kids can put their sleuthing skills to work by cracking a safe, dodging lasers, and defusing a bomb. At 20,000 Leagues you'll board a Victorian-era submarine where hidden latches and secret doors are opened only when you figure out the musical code and reconfigure the gears in the engine room. Both adventures are totally G-rated (although the dark room and special-effect lighting may be mildly scary to very young kids); the activities are suitable for children ages 7 and over, and your kids will probably complete the tasks better than you!

✳FROG POND
84 Beacon St., Beacon Hill
Boston, MA 02108
(617) 635-2120
bostonfrogpond.com

In the winter it's a famed ice-skating rink but in the summer, Frog Pond transforms into a wading pool. Since it's only 6 inches deep, it's a great spot for little kids to splash around and cool off. It's generally open to coincide with the Boston public school calendar, daily from the end of June through

Labor Day. Nearby the well-equipped Tadpole Playground attracts kids with its colorful climbing apparatus. A recent addition to the Common, the Frog Pond carousel is of 1947 vintage and features a menagerie of animals in addition to horses. It operates from mid-April through October and the hours vary (best to check ahead if you don't want to disappoint the kids!).

FULL MOON RESTAURANT
344 Huron Ave.
Cambridge, MA 02138
(617) 354-6699
fullmoonrestaurant.com

Parents, you need a break today—and we are not talking fast food. If fine dining is one of your all-time favorite activities and you have a baby or toddler in tow, this restaurant (located just a little more than a mile from Harvard Square) is almost too good to be true. There's a play space with a train table, buckets of toys, and pretend kitchen. Kids dine happily on dishes like cheddar quesadillas, mac and cheese, and "green eggs and ham," all served with carrot sticks and fruit. Parents can kick back and relax while enjoying sophisticated American bistro fare—including salmon with greens and ginger lime dressing, grilled sirloin with blue cheese butter, arugula salad and french fries, or seafood stew in lemongrass coconut broth with rice noodles. For dessert, order chocolate pudding cake all around. Open daily for dinner, Mon through Fri for lunch and Sat and Sun for brunch.

PUPPET SHOWPLACE THEATER
32 Station St.
Brookline, MA 02445
(617) 731-6400
puppetshowplace.org

This puppet theater has been entertaining Boston-area children for more than 30 years. Both traditional fairy tales like Aesop's Fables and *The Gingerbread Man*, along with more contemporary stories like *The Day It Snowed Tortillas*, are presented. The performances are always delightfully staged by master puppeteers who use hand puppets, rod puppets, and marionettes to tell the story. Different shows are presented each week, with an extended schedule during Massachusetts's school vacation weeks. Most performances are suitable for children ages 3–6 (and over) and are timed for 45 minutes or so—just right for short attention spans.

WHEELOCK FAMILY THEATRE
Wheelock College
200 The Riverway, Fenway
Boston, MA 02215
(617) 879-2300
wheelock.edu/wft
If you want to introduce your kids to family theater at its finest, look no further. The Wheelock Family Theatre is a professional equity company on the campus of Wheelock College that features award-winning theater for young people. Past kid-pleasing productions have included *Seussical the Musical, Charlie and the Chocolate Factory*, and *Pippi Longstocking*. Wheelock Family Theatre also offers school-year, summer, and vacation theater workshops for kids. Among its famous young "graduates" is Academy Award–winning actor Matt Damon.

Nightlife

✳**BEEHIVE**
541 Tremont St., South End
Boston, MA 02116
(617) 423-0069
beehiveboston.com

Dimly lit and artfully chaotic, this glamorous restaurant/jazz club/bar in the tradition of a Paris *caveau* seems to make the dining and drinking experience larger than everyday life. Toast your companions with a champagne cocktail and enjoy a profusion of expertly prepared variations on ethnic cuisine using fresh, local ingredients. Combine small plates like silky chicken liver mousse brûlée and crisp lamb phyllo rolls for a tapas-style feast. Patrons span all ages, but are mostly in their thirties and early forties and appreciate the cross-cultural diversity of the nightly live jazz. No cover.

BULL MCCABE'S
366A Somerville Ave.
Somerville, MA 02143
(617) 440-6045
bullmccabesboston.com
Come as you are for a burger, a beer, and the ballgame. It's a devoted, mostly local crowd that meets at this Irish bar for its laid-back friendliness. There's Guinness and Smithwick's on tap and traditional Irish fare like sirloin tips, shepherd's pie, and fish and chips to accompany the drink. The evenings of local, live music are very well attended.

HAVANA CLUB
288 Green St.
Cambridge, MA 02138
(617) 312-5550
havanaclubsalsa.com
Put on your dancing shoes and salsa the night away at the Havana Club, which takes place on Friday and Saturday nights at the Greek American Political Club in Central Square. Salsa novices come for a dance lesson from 9 to 10 p.m. before the crowd (300 dancers a night is fairly typical) turns

out. Lessons are free and are included as part of the cover charge, and there's a cash bar. When you are ready to try out your skills on the dance floor, you'll find a friendly, mixed crowd of young and old from all corners of the globe who come together to have a good time dancing—it is all very Cambridge.

HOUSE OF BLUES
15 Lansdowne St., Fenway
Boston, MA 02215
(888) 693-2583
houseofblues.com/boston
Despite its name, the House of Blues extends well beyond the blues genre and stages shows of just about every kind, including accomplished regional rockers like the Tedeschi Trucks Band and Grace Potter and the Nocturnals. With a good sound setup, unobstructed sight lines, and affordable general admission ticket prices, this is the best midsize club in the city. The club is located next to Fenway, so shows on game days are consistently packed.

MIDDLESEX LOUNGE
315 Massachusetts Ave.
Cambridge, MA 02139
(617) 868-6739
middlesexlounge.com
Jammed nightly with a diverse crowd of Harvard Business School students and twenty-something night owls, Middlesex is the perfect balance between a comfy local bar and a hipster hangout with creative cocktails and interesting takes on bar food, such as 10 tiny tacos and jerk chicken sticks. The setting is minimalist and features low moveable benches and a DJ who spins some of the best music around—old-school funk and '90s hip-hop.

STORYVILLE
90 Exeter St., Back Bay
Boston MA 02166
(617) 236-1134
storyvilleboston.com
Located in the basement of the Copley Square Hotel, this nightclub hot spot calls to mind the 1920s and '30s with rich red velvet, Art Deco crystal chandeliers, and photos of jazz greats. It's an under-forty crowd of mostly young professionals and international students who nibble on eclectic small plates like fried oysters and kimchee while sipping a tangerine fizz as the dance floor throbs with Top 40 sounds. Open Wed through Sat evening; there's a dress code but no cover charge.

✳WALLY'S CAFE
427 Massachusetts Ave., South End
Boston, MA 02118
(617) 424-1408
wallyscafe.com
This is as close to a down-and-dirty jazz club as Boston gets. Since 1947 this tiny jazz haunt has hosted amateurs and the area's best professional musicians alike in a close-knit atmosphere. Open 365 days a year, the club holds traditional jams on Sat and Sun at 6 p.m.; gigs start at 9 p.m. and go until 1 a.m. There isn't a cover charge, but there is a one-drink minimum.

Performing Arts

✳BOSTON BALLET
19 Clarendon St., South End
Boston, MA 02116
(617) 695-6955
bostonballet.org
Boston's resident professional ballet company, directed by Mikko Nissinen, continues to expand its repertoire and performs a wide

variety of classical (*Swan Lake* and *Coppélia*) and contemporary works (Jerome Robbins's *Fancy Free*) that take place Oct through May at the restored Opera House. The center-piece of the company's season is always its Christmastime production of the *Nutcracker*, which in 2012 premiered with all-new sets and costumes.

＊BOSTON BAROQUE
10 Guest St.
Boston, MA 02135
(617) 987-8600
bostonbaroque.org
This preeminent period-instrument ensem-ble and chorus, under the direction of Martin Pearlman, celebrates the music of 17th- and 18th-century composers includ-ing Handel, Haydn, Vivaldi, and Bach. Con-certs are held at Harvard's Sanders Theatre, New England Conservatory's Jordan Hall, and other local venues. Recent-season artis-tic highlights include a semi-staged pro-duction of *Orfeo ed Euridice* and Haydn's *Creation*. The orchestra's signature event is its annual Gala New Year's Eve Concert at Harvard's Sanders Theatre.

＊BOSTON LYRIC OPERA
11 Avenue de Lafayette
Boston, MA 02111
(617) 542-6772
blo.org
The Boston Lyric Opera is New England's largest opera company, staging 4 operas a year between Nov and May. Three works each season represent a mix of traditional favorites, such as *Don Giovanni* and *The Barber of Seville*, and lesser-known works, such as Dvorak's *Rusalka* and contemporary composer John Musto's *The Inspector*. For the past few seasons a fourth "Opera Annex,"

site-specific production has been performed in "found" space, such as the John F. Ken-nedy Library and the Park Plaza Castle, in an effort to make opera more accessible to college students and the under-40 audience (it's been hugely successful). Fear not about language—although BLO operas are always performed in their original language, all per-formances have English subtitles projected on screens above the stage.

＊BOSTON SYMPHONY AND BOSTON
POPS
301 Massachusetts Ave., Fenway
Boston, MA 02115
(617) 266-1492
bso.org
Considered one of the world's best sym-phony orchestras, the BSO performs at incomparable Symphony Hall from Sept through May. Without a conductor since Maestro Levine's departure in 2011, Andris Nelsons was named the BSO's Music Direc-tor designate, to begin with the 2014–2015 concert season. In the meantime, the BSO's impressive schedule of concerts will con-tinue to feature many of the world's most celebrated guest artists, including Yo-Yo Ma, Anne-Sophie Mutter, and Emanuel Ax. The BSO's repertoire is wide-ranging: from crowd-pleasing Mozart and Beethoven to contemporary classics by Schoenberg and newly commissioned works by Harbison. The Boston Pops, conducted by Keith Lock-hart since 1995, is composed of members of the Boston Symphony performing concerts of light classics, jazz, popular music, and film music. In December the Pops (and Santa) take over Symphony Hall to perform a con-cert series of holiday favorites.

*HANDEL & HAYDN SOCIETY
300 Massachusetts Ave., Fenway
Boston, MA 02115
(617) 266-3605
handelandhaydn.org

Founded in 1815, Boston's Handel & Haydn Society is said to be the oldest continuously performing music ensemble in the country. Headed by Harry Christophers, the group presents performances featuring historic instruments and plays in the stylistic standard of earlier eras. Handel & Haydn's main performance venue is Boston's Symphony Hall but they also use New England Conservatory's Jordan Hall and Harvard's Sanders Theatre. The Society is credited with the US premiere of Handel's *Messiah* in 1818, which it has performed annually since 1854. It's a highlight of the Christmas performance season in Boston and always sells out.

Rock Climbing

HAMMOND POND RESERVATION
Hammond Pond Parkway
Newton, MA 02467
(617) 333-7404
mass.gov/dcr/parks/metroboston/
hammond.htm

Well-known within the rock-climbing community, the rock croppings at Hammond Park are located practically in the shadow of the Chestnut Hill Shopping Plaza and are especially popular for those just starting outdoor bouldering and rope climbing.

METRO ROCK
69 Norman St.
Everett, MA 02149
(617) 387-7625
metrorock.com

A haven for serious climbers, this public climbing gym is home to the state's tallest indoor rock wall (45 feet) and more than 17,000 square feet of climbing surface with more than 30 lead routes. In New England this is as close as it gets to climbing outdoors! "Learn the ropes" of climbing here; expert instruction is available for climbers of all abilities, interests, and ages. For parents, consider this: If your kids are climbing the walls in the winter, this may be the place for them. Day pass, punch card, and monthly membership plans are available. An additional location is in Newburyport.

Skiing

WESTON SKI TRACK
200 Park Rd.
Weston, MA 02493
(781) 891-6575
skiboston.com

Experience the quiet beauty of cross-country skiing and snowshoeing. Just outside of Boston on the Newton and Weston town line, the Weston Ski Track has 15 kilometers of groomed, natural trails and snowmaking on a 2.5-kilometer looping track that ensures consistent cross-country throughout the winter. Weston Ski rents both cross-country skis and snowshoes and offers an introductory lesson that is perfect for first-timers.

Spectator Sports

AGGANIS ARENA
Boston University, Kenmore
925 Commonwealth Ave.
Boston, MA 02215
(617) 358-7000
bu.edu/agganis

College sports tickets are an entertainment bargain. Agganis is the home of Boston University's impressive hockey program—you may just catch a college player before he or she hits the "big time." Besides Terrier sporting events, this arena also hosts rock concerts (the Dropkick Murphys and Smashing Pumpkins have played here recently), and touring shows like Cirque du Soleil and *Sesame Street Live*.

GILLETTE STADIUM
1 Patriot Place
Foxboro, MA 02035
(508) 543-8200
gillettestadium.com

Home to the New England Patriots and the New England Revolution (Major League Soccer), Gillette Stadium is a 68,000-seat state-of-the-art outdoor stadium loaded with amenities including theater-style seating, unobstructed views, and 2 massive HDTV screens at each end zone. Gillette is located 20 miles southwest of Boston, but it is in the middle of nowhere. Pre- and postgame gridlock on Route 1 and surrounding roads is legendary and the parking fee on football game days is $40 (ouch!). Taking the MBTA (mbta.com) football train from Boston or Providence may be a convenient, less expensive, and greener option.

TD GARDEN
100 Legends Way, West End
Boston, MA 02114
(617) 624-1000
tdgarden.com

The TD Garden opened in 1995, replacing the beloved 1928 Boston Garden. It has had several name changes since its construction, and they can call it whatever they want, but for Bostonians it will forever be "The Gah-Din." The state-of-the-art arena is the home of the NBA Celtics and the NHL Bruins. And when U2, Bruce Springsteen, and Taylor Swift come to town, they routinely fill all 20,000

seats. If you have seats on one of the higher levels, bring binoculars.

i A highlight of the winter sports season, every February Boston University, Boston College, Harvard, and Northeastern University face off in the Beanpot Hockey Tournament (beanpothockey.com) at the TD Garden for ice hockey bragging rights.

Theater

AMERICAN REPERTORY THEATER
64 Brattle St.
Cambridge, MA 02138
amrep.org

Associated with Harvard, A.R.T. (say each letter) specializes in new works, rethought revivals, and collaborations. A.R.T. always has something good to offer, recently staging *Johnny Baseball*, a Red Sox musical, and *Beowulf—A Thousand Years of Baggage*. Every Saturday night A.R.T.'s nearby Club Oberon (2 Arrow St., Cambridge) is transformed into a 1970s Studio 54–like setting for *The Donkey Show*, a disco version of *A Midsummer Night's Dream*.

✻HUNTINGTON THEATRE COMPANY
264 Huntington Ave., Fenway
Boston, MA 02115
(617) 266-0800
huntingtontheatre.org

For more than 30 years, this acclaimed regional theater company has staged revivals of classic plays like *Our Town* and *All My Sons* and works by contemporary playwrights like August Wilson (*Ma Rainey's Black Bottom*), David Lindsay Abaire (*Good People*), and Yasmina Reza (*God of Carnage*). Look for the occasional musical, such as 2011's *Candide* and 2009's *Pirates! (Or, Gilbert & Sullivan*

Plunder'd). Most performances take place at the Boston University Theater; smaller shows are staged at the Boston Center for the Arts.

LYRIC STAGE COMPANY
140 Clarendon St., Back Bay
Boston, MA 02116
(617) 437-7172
lyricstage.com
At this cozy 240-seat theater located in the Boston YWCA building, you can see premieres (such as the highly successful *Curse of the Bambino*), contemporary works like *Stones in His Pockets,* and excellent revivals like *The Mikado,* often with a modern spin.

STONEHAM THEATRE
395 Main St.
Stoneham, MA 02180
(781) 279-2200
stonehamtheatre.org
One of the region's most highly respected professional repertory companies, the theater performs 8 classic and contemporary plays during its season, which typically runs from Sept through May. Well-known pieces such as *Thoroughly Modern Millie* and *Double Indemnity* mix with more offbeat fare, such as *Lumber Jacks in Love.*

Water Sports

BOSTON HARBOR BOAT RENTALS
70 E. India Row, Waterfront
Boston, MA 02110
(617) 240-2900
bostonharborboatrentals.com
Be your own captain and rent a powerboat on Boston Harbor for just a few hours or a day at prices that are affordable for families or a group of friends. Conveniently located near the New England Aquarium, the operation has a fleet of 5 boats ranging from 12 to 25 feet long. For novice (and not so novice) boaters, free behind-the-wheel instruction is offered with explicit guidance on how to drive the boat, good seamanship, and the best places (islands and dockside restaurants) to anchor for lunch.

✳CHARLES RIVER CANOE & KAYAK
1071 Soldiers Field Rd.
Brighton, MA 02134
(617) 965-5110
paddleboston.com
Enjoy a leisurely paddle along the Charles River to gain a new perspective of Boston. Charles River Canoe & Kayak offers hourly rentals of canoes, kayaks, and the latest water sport craze: stand-up paddleboards. The kiosk on Soldiers Field Road in Boston's Allston/Brighton neighborhood has the greatest visibility of the 5 rental locations; the Kendall Square location has the advantage of being close to public transportation—the Kendall/MIT T station on the Red line. Each location offers rentals and lessons; each location (except Natick) offers guided tours. Among the offerings are barbecue kayak tours from Allston/Brighton or Kendall Square, kayak ecotours from Nahanton Woods, and skyline tours from Kendall Square. The start of the canoe season is highly dependent on the severity of winter, but it generally begins sometime in May and lasts through Columbus Day weekend. For information on additional area locations, check out their website.

✳COMMUNITY BOATING
21 David Mugar Way, Beacon Hill
Boston, MA 02114
(617) 523-1038
community-boating.org

If you like the feel of the wind at your back, this is the place. This full-service public sailing school (the oldest and largest in the country) caters to every level of sailor (especially captain kids), teaching introductory to competitive sailing. The boathouse is located on the Esplanade, next to the Charles Street footbridge. The Charles River is a terrific sailing basin—flat water, little current, and plenty of wind. If you are an experienced sailor, club membership allows access to the fleet; for occasional sailors, a sailboat pass is inexpensive and will get you out on the water for the day.

COMMUNITY ROWING
20 Nonantum Rd.
Boston, MA 02135
(617) 923-7557
communityrowing.org
On the banks of the Charles River, Community Rowing's stunning new boathouse has garnered multiple design awards since opening in 2008. It has also greatly increased the visibility of the sport in the Boston area. Community Rowing offers recreational and competitive opportunities for rowers of all ages and skill levels in single-person (sculling) boats and 8-person (sweep) boats.

SHOPPING

Antiques

CAMBRIDGE ANTIQUE MARKET
201 Monsignor O'Brien Hwy.
Cambridge, MA 02141
(617) 868-9655
marketantique.com
Housed in a 5-story building, this antiques market features 100 dealers that sell everything from antiques to junk. Sifting through the stalls can be challenging, but there are

finds to be had—typewriters, prints, records, vintage bikes, and an entire floor dedicated to antique furniture. The market has its own parking lot, which is a big plus in Cambridge. Open Tues through Sun.

RESTORATION RESOURCES
1946 Washington St., South End
Boston, MA 02118
restorationresources.com
Architectural salvage is what recycling is all about. Anyone who owns an old house or wants to add character to a newer home will love browsing this sprawling space that stocks hundreds of one-of-a-kind pieces including mantels, claw-foot tubs, garden statuary, leaded stained-glass windows, doors of every type, and smaller items like antique crystal door knobs. Open Tues through Sat and Mon by appointment.

Artisan Market

✳SOWA MARKET
460 Harrison Ave., South End
Boston, MA 02118
(800) 403-8305
sowaopenmarket.com
Activist artists first coined the name SoWa, or South of Washington Street, in the early 2000s. What began as a small community effort to bring vitality to the South End by showcasing local businesses, artists, and craftspeople has blossomed into New England's biggest and most beloved weekly market. The collection of artistic goods ranges from handmade jigsaw puzzles to screen-printed T's and letterpress stationery. The farmers' market and local food vendors add color to the proceedings. SoWa is also the city's best weekend gathering of food trucks. Participating vendors include Boston Speed Dog, Lobsta Love,

and Roxy's Gourmet Grilled Cheese, among others. It's increasingly popular with tourists, but locals love it because it's still authentic, thankfully.

Beauty

MINILUXE
296 Newbury St., Back Bay
Boston, MA 02115
(857) 362-7444
miniluxe.com
Spotlessly clean and fuss-free, Miniluxe stores are popping up all over the Boston area. By the time the nail technician has scrubbed, filed, buffed, and rubbed, you will feel totally pampered. Polish generally stays chip free for a week (sometimes longer). Check out the company website for information on additional area locations.

Books

*BRATTLE BOOK SHOP
9 West St., Downtown
Boston, MA 02111
(617) 542-0210
brattlebookshop.com
Located in a 3-story brick building on a side street in Downtown Crossing, this antiquarian bookshop is a bibliophile's paradise. Dating from 1825, this is one of the oldest bookshops in the country. You may recognize owner Ken Gloss, who is often in the store; he is a frequent guest appraiser on the PBS series *Antiques Roadshow*. The inventory of 250,000 volumes includes a superb collection of used, first-edition, and rare books. For an unbeatable book deal, be sure to check out the $1, $3, and $5 used books on the outdoor racks in the alley next to the store.

BROOKLINE BOOKSMITH
279 Harvard St.
Brookline, MA 02445
(617) 566-6660
brooklinebooksmith.com
Long established and well regarded, this independent bookstore in Brookline's Coolidge Corner allows community spirit to thrive. You can sense it in the staff recommendation notes interspersed between the stacks and in the enthusiasm behind the store's writers and readers series, which hosts more than 200 events a year. The stock is wide-ranging: from best-selling fiction and nonfiction to local interest as well as used books (in the basement) and children's books, plus cards, gifts, and stationery.

CURIOUS GEORGE BOOKSTORE
One JFK St.
Cambridge, MA 02138
(617) 547-4500
thecuriousgeorgestore.com
Find all things related to Curious George, everyone's favorite mischievous monkey from the children's book and PBS television series, at this delightful shop. The store also carries books of all kinds for all ages including picture books, early readers, and chapter books and a wide selection of toys that heavily favor creative and open-ended play. There's an exceptionally cozy reading nook, and to the delight of young fans, George himself often makes store appearances.

HARVARD BOOKSTORE
1256 Massachusetts Ave.
Cambridge, MA 02138
(617) 661-1515
harvard.com

Directly across the street from Harvard, this independent bookstore is totally committed to books and their patrons. The shelves are chock-full of national best sellers as well as classic and contemporary literature, and the staff is beyond helpful in making recommendations. The store has countless readings and book signings by locally and nationally known authors—often from the Harvard academic community. Head to the basement for great deals on remainders and gently used volumes. Come also to see the book-making machine Paige M. Gutenborg in action. The on-demand press instantly prints any one of 5 million titles or self-published manuscripts. Pretty neat.

HARVARD COOP
1400 Massachusetts Ave.
Cambridge, MA 02138
(617) 499-2000
thecoop.com

Crimson pride is on display at this ultimate showcase of Harvard paraphernalia. You can find Harvard logoed everything at this sprawling 4-level bookstore complex, from key chains to teddy bears to clothing (T-shirts, sweatshirts, rugby shirts) in every size and style. "The Coop" (rhymes with scoop) was founded in 1882 by students as a cooperative to buy school supplies and books (along with firewood and coal to keep their rooms warm!). The Coop is the official bookstore of Harvard and it is still a cooperative (faculty, students, and staff receive a yearly rebate) and is open to the public.

*NEW ENGLAND MOBILE BOOK FAIR
82 Needham St.
Newton, MA 02461
(617) 964-7440
nebookfair.com

Don't let the name fool you; there's nothing mobile about New England's largest independent bookstore. Open for more than 50 years in a quirky, rambling warehouse in a Newton commercial/business district, the Book Fair is beloved by bibliophiles near and far. The store's haphazard layout lends itself to browsing. There are more than a million books in stock, mostly organized by publisher, a throwback to the days when the store catered to librarians and other bookstores that would come here for their inventory. Everything is always discounted at least 20 percent off of publisher's list. Special strengths of the Book Fair are its children's, travel, and cookbook departments. And the Book Fair's frequent author events are among the best in the area.

PORTER SQUARE BOOKS
25 White St.
Cambridge, MA 02140
(617) 491-2220
portersquarebooks.com

This independent bookstore is one of the best literary destinations in the Boston/Cambridge area. A calendar full of book events and a cafe that does a perfect latte make this a great place to meet friends, relax, and browse. The store isn't tremendously big, but the shelves are fully stocked with not only the latest best sellers, but also books you've never heard of, but should. The very knowledgeable, and even friendly staff will help you navigate it all.

*SCHOENHOF'S
76A Mount Auburn St.
Cambridge, MA 02138
(617) 547-8855
schoenhofs.com

This is the largest foreign bookstore in the country and a mecca for foreign-language learners, language teachers, and international expats. They stock a large selection of language guides, dictionaries, and novels in dozens of languages as varied as Chinese, Farsi, and Russian. Their Spanish, French, Italian, and German departments are phenomenal. The children's section has language-learning materials, picture books, and Harry Potter translated into a dozen languages. The store also sponsors book events, conversation groups, and language-specific book clubs. Closed Sun.

TRIDENT BOOKSELLERS & CAFE
338 Newbury St., Back Bay
Boston, MA 02115
(617) 267-8688
tridentbookscafe.com
Located at the "low rent" end of Newbury Street, this bookstore/cafe is one of Boston's best-loved independent bookstores. Recently expanded—the store took over the building's second floor—it has increased its offerings to include more new releases and a larger children's book department. The store is a popular gathering space for locals and visitors, but it's a little frenetic; the cafe serves eclectic eats (with inexpensive tabs) and is always packed. The store offers free Wi-Fi, lots of author events (author signings, trivia nights), and long hours (it's open daily until midnight).

Crafts Stores

✳FABRIC SHOWPLACE
86 Coolidge Ave.
Watertown, MA 02472
(617) 926-2888
fabricshowplace.net
This family-owned company is a one-stop shop for drapery, upholstery, and accent fabrics. The showroom is warehouse-like but stocked floor to ceiling with beautiful woven prints, silks, and sheers—all deeply discounted. It can be overwhelming, so plan to spend lots of time browsing. They also do excellent upholstery and custom drapery work.

Farmers' Markets & Pick Your Own

✳BOSTON COPLEY SQUARE FARMERS' MARKET
Along Boylston, Dartmouth, and St. James Streets, Back Bay
Boston, MA 02116
massfarmersmarkets.org
This charming and enticing European-style food market delights foodies and chefs who come to peruse the stalls selling some of the region's choicest vegetables, fruits, breads, flowers, and prepared take home meals. You'll be amazed at the variety and quality. Star buys include homemade toaster pastries from the Danish Pastry House, cranberry lavender lemonade from the Herb Lyceum, goat cheese from Crystal Brook Farm, baguettes from Iggy's bread, and hummus chicken wraps from Seta's. Open mid-May through just before Thanksgiving, Tues and Fri 11 a.m. to 6 p.m.

HAYMARKET
Along Blackstone Street, Government Center
Boston, MA 02109
Scruffy and chaotic, Haymarket offers dirt-cheap fruits and vegetables ($1 a pound is a common price) alongside a slice of local life. Located between Faneuil Hall and the North End, this historic open-air market has operated here since the 1830s. Good things to know: It's open Fri and Sat (year-round) from dawn to dusk, it's cash only, and don't touch the produce (or else the vendor will yell at you).

LAND'S SAKE FARM

90 Wellesley St.

Weston, MA 02493

(781) 893-1162

landssake.org

This is a charming, not-for-profit, pick-your-own farm that features locally grown, pesticide- and chemical-free fruits and vegetables. Don't miss the farm stand, which is stocked with the farm's own organic produce, maple syrup, and honey.

✳VOLANTE FARMS

292 Forest St.

Needham, MA 02492

(781) 444-2351

volantefarms.com

Avid gardeners have been coming to Volante's greenhouses for years for the impressive selection of perennials, annuals, and shrubs. Now expanded, the farm stand proffers dozens of varieties of Volante's own fresh fruit and vegetables straight from the fields just outside, along with locally made cheese, fresh-baked breads, and baked goods. Volante's house-made soups, sandwiches, and prepared entrees make it all too convenient to bring home a delicious, ready-made dinner. And on a warm summer evening the take-out ice cream window sees nonstop action.

Fashion & Shoes

BOBBY FROM BOSTON

19 Thayer St., South End

Boston, MA 02118

(617) 423-9299

What's old is new. This expertly stocked vintage shop for gents touts an eclectic and refined collection of tweed jackets, wool vests, bow ties, and cuff links. A small room is dedicated to women's vintage as well. Prices are downright reasonable. Closed Mon.

E. A. DAVIS

579 Washington St.

Wellesley, MA 02482

(781) 235-0668

eadavisshop.com

Filled with pastels and tailored designs, E. A. Davis is a Wellesley institution selling women's, men's, and children's clothing. From Palm Beach bright shifts by Lily Pulitzer, to menswear by country-club favorite Peter Millar and Barbour wax-finished coats for the entire family, the fashions at E. A. Davis are synonymous with quality and good taste.

FORTY WINKS

56 JFK St.

Cambridge, MA 02138

(617) 492-9100

shopfortywinks.com

Find a well-curated selection of upscale silky and lacy things by Chantelle, Eberjay, and Huit at this pretty lingerie boutique in Harvard Square. You can also pick up basics, shape wear, and cozy cotton pajamas. This is a great place for an expert bra fitting; the staff are welcoming and knowledgeable.

LOUIS

60 Northern Ave., Seaport District

Boston, MA 02210

(617) 262-6100

louisboston.com

Pronounced "Louie's," this Boston mainstay since the late 1800s has been the city's benchmark for sophisticated department store shopping. Recently relocated to a modern waterfront space in the burgeoning Seaport District, the store buzzes with excitement displaying fashion for men and women by some of the design world's most promising talents, including Marni and Proenza Schouler. Not to be overlooked are the cosmetics department and lots of edgy and funky must-haves in the accessories department. Even if you don't buy anything, patronize the store's excellent top-floor restaurant, Sam's, for lunch, dinner, or drinks with a view.

SALMAGUNDI
765 Centre St.
Jamaica Plain, MA 02130
(617) 522-5047
salmagundiboston.com

This ultra-hip shop sells high-quality hats for men and women, ranging from bowlers to newsboy caps to cloches and fascinators. The store stocks as many as 9,000 hats; many of the designs are custom-made and exclusive to Salmagundi. Women's hats often feature intricate feather work, detailed ribbon trims, and vintage elements like veiling. Men's fur-felt fedoras have an elegant satin lining, and the straw Panamas sport stylish striped bands. Most of the inventory hovers between $200 and $400, but the store also stocks less expensive styles.

VOWS BRIDAL OUTLET
130 Galen St.
Watertown, MA 02472
(617) 923-7587
bridepower.com

Few stores in Boston have received as much publicity recently as Vows, the high-end bridal discount outlet now featured on TLC's *I Found the Gown*. Expect discounts from 50 percent to 80 percent on samples and close-outs of last year's collections from such designers as Vera Wang, Carolina Herrera, and many more. Eager-to-please staffers are on hand to help you find your dream dress from the vast selection of breathtaking ball gowns, demure lace numbers, and sculptural fit and flare silhouettes. Visit the website to make an appointment in advance or come on Saturday when it is walk-in only.

Gifts

ABODEON
1731 Massachusetts Ave.
Cambridge, MA 02138
(617) 497-0137
abodeon.com

When you want to get a truly original gift for your best friend or a statement furniture piece for your home, this well-edited collection of home accents, furnishings, and gifts hits the mark. You'll find modern, artful design that might range from whimsical lab-glass salt and pepper mice shakers to a vintage George Nelson sofa.

Grocery

*RUSSO'S
560 Pleasant St.
Watertown, MA 02472
(617) 923-1500
russos.com

This is one of the Boston area's best all-in-one, affordable produce markets. Although it is mostly non-organic, you'll find a huge variety of fruit and vegetables and all kinds of specialty ingredients. International cuisines are extremely well represented with Italian, Asian, Latin American, and Middle East foodstuffs at a fraction of the usual cost. There are top-of-the-line cheeses from New England and around the world, a gourmet delicatessen counter, loads of irresistible nibbles like olives and nuts, fragrant cut flowers, house-baked breads and bakery items, and prepared take-home dinners including every working mom's secret weapon: rotisserie chicken.

Home

MACHINE AGE
645 Summer St., Seaport District
Boston, MA 02110
(617) 464-0099
machine-age.com
This showroom gem in the Seaport District is well-known to savvy collectors and local interior designers for its large collection of midcentury furniture pieces and quirky selection of accessories in near-perfect condition. You might find a 1960s original Eames lounge chair and ottoman or a Lucite dining table by Vladimir Kagan. Prices are high, but the store makes for great browsing.

Jewelry

*SHREVE, CRUMP & LOW
39 Newbury St., Back Bay
Boston, MA 02116
(617) 267-9100
shrevecrumpandlow.com
In business since 1796, Shreve's is a Boston institution for its breathtaking selection of jewelry. Its prohibitive prices match its old-money image. But the store is also a gold mine for visitors with lots of well-priced Boston-themed gifts under $100 including Swan Boat Christmas ornaments, silver-plate Paul Revere bowls, and the store's signature Gurgling Cod pitcher.

Kids' Fashion & Toys

*IRVING'S TOYS AND CARD SHOP
371 Harvard St.
Brookline, MA 02446
(617) 566-9327
If a film crew were scouting for an old-school neighborhood toy store, this would be it. In business since 1939, this venerable toy store has been loved by generations of Brookline schoolchildren. The tiny shop with the red and white striped awning is a wonderland stocked with an assortment of toys and novelties: cap guns, fake mustaches, board games, jump ropes, and yo-yos. Store owner Ethel Weiss is 98 years young and still has a way with kids, presiding over the candy counter every afternoon when the children from Devo (Devotion Elementary School, where John F. Kennedy was a student from kindergarten through 3rd grade) troop in after school to buy Mallo Cups, Swedish Fish, and jawbreakers with their allowance money.

LESTER HARRY'S
115 Newbury St., Back Bay
Boston, MA 02116
(617) 927-5400
lesterharrys.com
Grandparent alert! The gorgeous, pricey clothing at this children's boutique is unusual enough to be special, but not weird. Lester Harry's stocks infant to size 14 clothing for girls and boys, including styles by Petit Bateau, Lili Gaufrette, and the Milly Mini line. You'll also discover unusual gifts not found in the average toy store, such as wood ride-ons and handmade fabric mobiles.

STELLABELLA TOYS
1360 Cambridge St.
Cambridge, MA 02139
(617) 491-6290
stellabellatoys.com
This local toy store chainlet is the go-to place for the latest fun, creative, and unique toys. Find well-made fantasy play costumes, first baby dolls, European-made wooden vehicles, nifty craft and science kits, and every sort of manipulative to encourage open-ended play. Thanks to in-store programming that includes art, music, and story time, Stellabella has become a gathering place for area families looking to make new friends. Additional locations in Somerville, Burlington, and Dedham.

Malls

FANEUIL HALL MARKETPLACE AND QUINCY MARKET
Bordered by Congress, North, Clinton, Commercial, and Chatham Streets
Boston, MA 02109
(617) 523-1300
faneuilhallmarketplace.com
When Faneuil Hall was developed in the mid-1970s, the concept of an urban waterfront festival marketplace was visionary and inspired similar projects throughout the country. The marketplace is actually 4 locations. **Faneuil Hall** is the 1742 marketplace and meeting hall (see p. 29). Quincy Market is a bustling food court. Some of the best bets here include Kilvert & Forbes Bake Shop, Steve's Greek Cuisine, and Bay State Chowda. Nearly 75 shops, several restaurants, and dozens of pushcart vendors are located in the North and South Market buildings. Many stores are franchises of national chains like Ann Taylor, Coach, and

Urban Outfitter. Of special interest are local/regional brands, including Boston Pewter Company, Boston Campus Gear, Orvis, and Irish Eyes.

WRENTHAM PREMIUM OUTLETS
One Premium Outlets Blvd.
Wrentham, MA 02093
(508) 384-0600
premiumoutlets.com/wrentham
Although it's designed like a quaint New England village, this outdoor outlet center is anything but small with 170 mostly high-end outlet stores, including Coach, Hanna Andersson, 7 for All Mankind, Kate Spade, Penguin, Restoration Hardware, Williams-Sonoma, and Wedgewood/Waterford. Located just 35 miles from Boston, this is also the region's largest outlet center. Wrentham is so popular with shopping-focused international tourism groups that the public address announcements are made in Chinese, Spanish, and Portuguese.

> **i** If you are a AAA member, stop by the Wrentham Mall office and show your membership card for a valuable coupon book.

Pet Care

JEANA'S DIRTY DOG SALON
298 Concord Ave.
Cambridge, MA 02138
(617) 868-5377
jeanasdirtydog.com
This quaint neighborhood dog boutique and salon offers wonderfully personal service including comprehensive grooming (including shampoo and brush-out) along with add-on spa services like remoisturizing, defleaing, preventive dental care, and

blueberry facials. The boutique stocks high-end collars and premium (but practical) treats. Special cat-only days are scheduled each month. Book well in advance.

Specialty Foods

*ATHAN'S BAKERY
1621 Beacon St.
Brookline, MA 02446
(617) 734-7028
athansbakery.com
This sunny European bakery is an established neighborhood favorite in Brookline for its plentiful seating, free Wi-Fi, excellent coffee (served in real cups), and delectable pastries. The traditional Black Forest and tiramisu pastries are outstanding, but the real stars of this bakery are the baklava—there are more than a dozen types of Greek phyllo pastries, redolent of honey and cloves. Athan's also has beautifully packaged gift baskets ready to go, filled with chocolates, cookies, and other treats perfect for hostess gift-giving.

*CLEAR FLOUR BREAD
178 Thorndike St.
Brookline, MA 02466
(617) 737-0060
clearflourbread.com
This small-scale artisanal bread bakery looks to France and Italy for inspiration to produce its repertoire of loaves. Everything from the *pain au chocolat* to morning buns, baguettes, and focaccia is top-notch. Try the dense, nourishing buckwheat walnut loaf, a crunchy powerhouse of whole grains. Just add some butter for satisfying proof that the simplest things are often the best.

FORMAGGIO KITCHEN CAMBRIDGE
244 Huron Ave.
Cambridge, MA 02138
(617) 354-4750

FORMAGGIO KITCHEN SOUTH END
268 Shawmut Ave.
Boston, MA 02118
(617) 350-6996
formaggiokitchen.com
Whether you want a soft brie de Meaux, a crumbly Stilton, or a farmhouse clothbound Vermont cheddar, you can find your choice of cheese here. Not sure what you want? The staff encourages tasting of the more than 200 varieties, which they cut fresh from the wheel. The Cambridge store has been in business for more than 30 years; ask for a walk-through of its subterranean cave, where cheese is allowed to age and ripen—it was one of the first in the country. Both stores also stock all kinds of specialty goods including house-made charcuterie (try the duck breast pastrami), fresh pastas, gourmet sandwiches, prepared dinners, and desserts along with fine wine and craft beer. Also check out their schedule of cooking classes, demonstrations, and in-store events.

*KUPEL'S
421 Harvard St.
Brookline, MA 02446
(617) 566-9528
kupelsbakery.com
The Sunday morning line out the door pretty much says it all. Opened in 1978, Kupel's prides itself on producing bagels that have a balance between chewy and doughy. They offer more than 2 dozen varieties of bagels, lots of cream cheese choices, and several smoked fish options, too. There's also an extensive bakery selection including challah

bread and bubkas and strudels. It's takeout only with no seating and kosher, too, so it's closed Friday afternoon and all day Saturday.

☀MARIA'S PASTRY
46 Cross St., North End
Boston, MA 02113
(617) 523-1196
mariaspastry.com
This simple, unpretentious shop is a destination for those looking for the finest cannoli in the North End. Here, the light, crisp shells are filled to order with a not-too-sweet mixture of ricotta. Another pastry associated with Maria's is *sfogliatelle,* a flaky shell-shaped pastry filled with orange-scented ricotta. Unlike at the better-known North End pastry shops (Mike's and Modern), there's never a line here. But because there are just a few seats inside and out, your best bet is to take your pastry and coffee to the cafe table at North End Park (at New Sudbury and North Street) across the street.

☀PARTY FAVORS
1356 Beacon St.
Brookline, MA 02446
(617) 566-3330
partyfavorsbrookline.com
This beloved Brookline party supply store is packed to the brim with coordinated invitations, paper tableware, balloons, and favors. Party Favors is also a great resource for custom-designed special-occasion cakes in any size. The cakes are dense with a true buttercream frosting. Flavor-wise, cake choices include chocolate, gold, white, carrot, mocha, and lemon, to name just a few. Also in high demand here are cupcakes and personalized sugar cookies with elaborate icing art.

☀TAZA CHOCOLATE
561 Windsor St.
Somerville, MA 02143
(617) 284-2232
tazachocolate.com
Wonderful aromas emanate from this chocolate factory located in Somerville, just a few miles from downtown Boston. Taza specializes in producing stone-ground organic chocolate—intense taste with a rustic texture. The factory store stocks the brand's entire line of chocolate bars, Mexican-style hot chocolate discs, and chocolate-covered nuts and nibs at a discount. You can watch the chocolate-making operation from the big glass windows in the store or, better yet, join one of the scheduled hourlong tours that take place Wed through Sun (no golden ticket required, but make reservations online, in advance).

Sporting Goods

☀MARATHON SPORTS
671 Boylston St., Back Bay
Boston, MA 02116
(617) 267-4774
marathonsports.com
Whether you are a recreational walker, an amateur running enthusiast, or an elite competitor, Marathon Sports has the serious athletic footwear you need. Marathon's "shoe wall" has all the best athletic brands including Saucony, New Balance, Asics, Brooks, and Nike. The friendly staff (runners all) are experienced in gait analysis. Come with an open mind; you don't choose the brand or the color—it's all about finding the absolute perfect-fitting sneakers for you. For additional area location information, check out their website.

*NEW BALANCE FACTORY STORE
40 Life St.
Boston, MA 02135
(617) 779-7429
newbalance.com

Buying local at its best, New Balance is the only sneaker manufacturer still making shoes in the US, with several factories in New England. The Massachusetts-based athletic footwear company offers marked-down sneakers from past seasons and discontinued models at this factory store in Brighton, next to its company headquarters. You'll also find New Balance athletic clothing and running accessories, all at a hefty discount.

ACCOMMODATIONS

Inns & Bed-and-Breakfasts

CLARENDON SQUARE INN $$$
198 W. Brookline St., South End
Boston, MA 02118
(617) 536-2229
clarendonsquare.com

The Clarendon Square Inn offers guests a genuine brownstone experience in the leafy and lovely South End. Located in a meticulously restored 1860s townhouse, the inn spoils guests with luxury including limestone bathrooms, high-count linens, and a bountiful European-style continental breakfast. There are only 3 rooms to go around, which makes this an ideal choice for a romantic hideaway weekend in the city.

*COLLEGE CLUB OF BOSTON $$
44 Commonwealth Ave., Back Bay
Boston, MA 02116
(617) 536-9510
thecollegeclubofboston.com

In a historic 1860 townhouse just 1 block from the Public Garden, the College Club

of Boston, the country's first social club for college-educated women, welcomes visitors (both men and women) to their bed-and-breakfast accommodations. The 11 high-ceiling rooms are each individually decorated—inspired and named in honor of a college; the Smith College room features the school's colors in its soft yellow walls and blue toile fabric; the Connecticut College room has Currier & Ives prints on the wall and is painted taupe in honor of the school's mascot. Double rooms have a private bath; single rooms share a bath in the hallway with one other single room. Rates include free Wi-Fi and continental breakfast.

INN AT ST. BOTOLPH $$$
99 St. Botolph St., Back Bay
Boston, MA 02116
(617) 236-8099
innatstbotolph.com

Think of the Inn at St. Botolph as an urban refuge. This 16-room inn's architectural features (such as a turret and working fireplaces) and understated contemporary decor (steel four-poster beds, high-end fabrics, 42-inch TVs, and rainforest shower heads in the bathrooms) enchant romancing couples and business travelers alike. Rates include continental breakfast and free Wi-Fi, which, combined with the terrific Back Bay location within walking distance of some of the city's hippest bars, restaurants, galleries, and shops, make this a top moderate accommodation choice.

LONGFELLOW'S WAYSIDE INN $$
72 Wayside Inn Rd.
Sudbury, MA 01776
(978) 443-1776
wayside.org

Set back on the old Boston Post Road in the quiet town of Sudbury, this classic stagecoach inn has been welcoming "man and beast" since 1716. Originally named the Red House Tavern, the inn was renamed the Wayside Inn in honor of Henry Wadsworth Longfellow's book of poems, *Tales of a Wayside Inn,* which includes his most well-known work, *Paul Revere's Ride.* The 9 guest rooms, or "bed chambers," are exactly what one would expect—and want—in a colonial inn with sloped wide-plank floors, simple white bedspreads, and period and reproduction antiques; each has a private bath. Rates include a full breakfast at the inn's restaurant. Bonus, too, that this is a nonprofit historic site, so room rates are low. Leave time to wander the Wayside Historic District, which is on the National Register of Historic Places and encompasses 125 acres of woodland, fields, and trails and includes an operating historic grist mill and a 1-room schoolhouse that are open for tours (limited days and hours; check ahead).

SAMUEL SEWALL INN   **$$$**
143 St. Paul St.
Brookline, MA 02446
(617) 713-0213
samuelsewallinn.com
This gracious Victorian home is discreetly located on a residential street in the leafy "streetcar" suburb of Brookline and is a perfect romantic hideaway. Each of the 14 guest rooms (5 are suites) has a private bath and is individually decorated in rich, warm colors with antique beds and wood floors overlaid with Persian area rugs. Enjoy the included buffet breakfast each morning in the dining room or retreat to the delightful, secluded outdoor garden patio in good weather. Boston's attractions are just a short trolley ride away (it's a 3-minute walk to the T) and the inn offers on-site parking (for a fee).

Hotels & Motels

✳BOSTON HARBOR HOTEL   **$$$$**
70 Rowes Wharf, Waterfront
Boston, MA 02110
(617) 439-7000
bhh.com
If you are looking for both luxury and location, you have arrived. And once you are ensconced inside the Boston Harbor Hotel, you may have no inclination to leave. The expansive lobby's floor-to-ceiling windows let you take in the grandeur of Boston Harbor and landscaped terraces overlook the lively marina. Each of the hotel's 224 rooms and suites comes with a view of either the water or the city skyline and is sumptuously appointed in a subtle nautical chic style, while the decadent spa and indoor pool set a new standard for urban sophistication and refined service. The hotel's Meritage restaurant is among the city's best, well-known for its deep wine list and New American cuisine. Find more casual waterfront dining (and a terrific afternoon daily tea) at Rowe's Wharf Sea Grille.

CHARLES HOTEL   **$$$$**
1 Bennett St.
Cambridge, MA 02138
(617) 864-1200
charleshotel.com
The Charles Hotel is Cambridge's most luxurious hotel, it enjoys a prime location just a block from Harvard's campus, and it has the tweedy and faculty-lounge vibe that perfectly fits its erudite surroundings. The simplicity of geometric Shaker quilts and light cherrywood furniture and rooms done in shades of taupe and soft green give the rooms a warm, tranquil feel. The 249-room hotel has a full-service spa, but it doesn't have a fitness center (guests enjoy

free admission to the next-door Wellbridge Fitness Club).

You'll have several dining options without ever having to step outside. For dining choose among casual locavore fare at Henrietta's Table, dress up to visit elegant Rialto, one of the area's best Italian restaurants, or relax over an evening cocktail and live jazz at Regattabar. In the summer, a lively farmers' market sets up in the hotel's plaza; in the winter the area becomes an ice rink.

COLONNADE $$$
120 Huntington Ave., Back Bay
Boston, MA 02116
(617) 424-7000
colonnadehotel.com

This popular hotel has an excellent location opposite the Prudential Center with Newbury Street just a short stroll away. The building may look generic from the outside, but inside, the rooms are spacious and smartly appointed with pillow-top mattresses, blond woods, a chocolate brown and taupe palette, and marble baths with rain showers. All bathrooms come with a complimentary rubber ducky—a Colonnade signature touch. The hotel has an excellent fitness center and an outdoor pool that over the years has become the place for urban poolside lounging. The seasonal 11th-floor rooftop pool attracts a good-looking crowd of locals and visitors alike for cocktails and city (and other) views. The generally excellent Brasserie JO offers all-day dining.

HOTEL COMMONWEALTH $$$$
500 Commonwealth, Kenmore Square
Boston, MA 02215
(617) 933-5000
hotelcommonwealth.com

This luxurious Kenmore Square hotel has consistently made it onto *Travel + Leisure's* World's Best Large City Hotels list. Positioned just steps from Fenway Park, the hotel is both superbly stylish and known for its impeccable service (it's the accommodation of choice for baseball teams and baseball industry bigwigs). The rooms are spacious, decorated in muted tones, and large enough to hold a generous work area. Both of the hotel's on-site restaurants, authentic French brasserie Eastern Standard and boisterous Island Creek Oyster Bar, offer no-fail dining experiences.

HOTEL 140 $$
140 Clarendon St., Back Bay
Boston, MA 02116
(617) 585-560
hotel140.com

Located around the corner from Copley Square, this is one of Boston's best low-price hotel choices. Several floors of Boston's original 1929 YWCA building have been converted to make this hip hotel, which shares space with the Lyric Stage Company. Rooms are compact with contemporary furnishings and each room comes with a neat, tidily arranged bathroom (not all have tub/shower combinations; some have just a shower).

✳KENDALL HOTEL $$
350 Main St.
Cambridge, MA 02142
(617) 577-1300
kendallhotel.com

Located in a renovated firehouse and just blocks from the T and the campus of MIT, this small hotel has paid attention to every detail, combining fresh, modern decor with New England artisan craft touches. Most striking are the auction-worthy American antiques (fire trucks and Dalmatians predominate) in the lobby. The homey touches extend to each of the 77 guest rooms, which feature cozy quilt-covered beds and bathrooms with subway tiles and pedestal sinks. Rates include full American breakfast buffet and hosted wine receptions Mon through Thurs evenings.

✳LENOX HOTEL $$$
61 Exeter St., Back Bay
Boston, MA 02116
(617) 536-5300
lenoxhotel.com
Housed in a beautiful Beaux Art building from 1900, the Lenox has an elegant boutique-like style. High-ceiling guest rooms present a handsome decor of warm taupes and golds with marble baths, while corner rooms have working fireplaces. The rates are somewhat less expensive than at other Boston hotels offering the same degree of personable service and chicness. City Table and City Bar impress, offering comfort food with a twist, and Sólás will meet your Boston Irish pub drinking needs.

OMNI PARKER HOUSE $$$
60 School St., Downtown
Boston, MA 02108
(617) 227-8600
omniparkerhouse.com
The Parker House is Boston's most historic hotel, having been a hub of activity and legends since it opened its doors in 1855. In its early years the hotel served as the meeting place for the Saturday Club—literary luminaries Emerson, Thoreau, Hawthorne, Longfellow, and Harvard scientists (and adversaries) Louis Agassiz and Asa Gray and other assorted intellectuals. Conveniently located just steps from the Freedom Trail and close to the statehouse, today the Parker House counts corporate executives, political lobbyists, and getaway travelers among its clients. The hotel's original ornate parlor-style walnut-paneled lobby with its elaborate plaster molding, fireplaces, and high ceilings is still in place. The 551 idiosyncratic guest rooms run the gamut from single rooms suitable for one to grand suites and have recently been refreshed with cherrywood furniture, rich color schemes, and high-count linens. The hotel's restaurant, Parker's, has a storied history as well. Boston cream pie (which is a cake) and fluffy Parker House rolls were invented here. At the end of the day, take in the dark mahogany and leather at the Last Hurrah Bar (a reference to 4-time Boston mayor James Michael Curley), which features (what else?) a vast selection of single-malt whiskeys.

SEAPORT HOTEL $$$
1 Seaport Ln., Seaport District
Boston, MA 02210
(617) 385-4000
seaportboston.com
There's plenty of hustle and bustle weekdays at this 426-room waterfront hotel, which serves mainly conventioneers attending functions at the next-door Seaport Boston World Trade Center. The location is also excellent for vacationers—within walking distance of both the Institute of Contemporary Art and the Boston Children's Museum. On weekends when the area is relatively quiet, leisure travelers can take advantage of huge room savings and enjoy all the extras—the indoor heated pool and fitness center—on a shoestring. Guest rooms have simple but pleasing modern decor and free Wi-Fi. The Seaport has received several "green" awards in recognition of its energy

and water conservation and reduction in waste output (guests can participate in the in-room recycling program) along with other environmentally friendly initiatives—such as an on-site organic garden and a rooftop bee apiary that supply the hotel's Aura restaurant and Tamo bar, and complimentary bike rentals for guests.

Hostels

HOSTELLING INTERNATIONAL $
19 Stuart St., Theater District
Boston, MA 02116
(617) 536-9455
bostonhostel.org

Hostels are not just for scruffy backpacker types. No matter your age, you can save a lot by staying at a hostel. Located in the Theater District, Boston's LEED-certified 480-bed hostel opened its doors in 2012. By hostelling standards, this one is downright plush: bright and airy with a minimalist European design aesthetic (think IKEA); single-sex dorm rooms with bunk beds; male/female rooms; and private rooms with bath. Rates include linens, towels, locker, free Wi-Fi, complimentary continental breakfast, and no curfew. The hostel also sponsors activities, events, and excursions to help you explore the city and at the same time meet people from around the world.

Camping

BOSTON HARBOR ISLANDS $
Bumpkin, Grape, Lovells, and Peddocks Islands
Boston, MA
(617) 223-8666
bostonharborislands.org

Experience urban camping at its finest. The only camping opportunity available within the city limits is located on the islands in the middle of Boston Harbor. The National Park Service maintains campgrounds on 4 of the Boston Harbor Islands: Bumpkin, Grape, Lovells, and Peddocks Islands. This is rustic camping (without flush toilets or showers) and from tents and sleeping bags to food and water, you bring everything you need in with you and out when you leave. You'll take a park passenger ferry and then a shuttle boat to get to your campsite. Pack light! Sites come with a picnic table and grill. Camping season is late June through Labor Day weekend. Each island has just 6 to 10 campsites; advance reservations are a must.

RESTAURANTS

American

OAK LONG BAR + KITCHEN AT
THE COPLEY PLAZA HOTEL $$–$$$
138 St. James Ave.
Boston, MA 02116
(617) 585-7222
oaklongbarkitchen.com

In celebration of 100 years of history, the storied Oak Bar and Oak Dining Room at the Copley Plaza Hotel underwent a total renovation in 2012 and is once again one of the city's hot spots to gather for drinking and dining. The dramatic wood paneling and coffered ceiling have been retained but the room has been opened up and a dramatic 80-foot copper-top bar has been installed along with new Waterford crystal chandeliers, marble-top tables, and tufted leather bar stools and red leather chairs. Stuffy it is not. The menu features all-day dining from 6:30 a.m. to 1 a.m. with an emphasis on New American fare made with local ingredients (much coming from the Copley Plaza

Farmers' Market across the street)—and the bar still makes the best martini in town.

*UNION OYSTER HOUSE $$
41 Union St., Government Center
Boston, MA 02108
(617) 227-2750
unionoysterhouse.com

The cozy, low-ceiling warren of rooms dates from 1716 and reeks of history. Operating as a restaurant since 1826, the Union Oyster House was a favorite haunt of both Daniel Webster and John F. Kennedy, so it is probably good enough for you. Some guidance? Wait for a seat at the ancient soapstone and oak raw bar in the front window for freshly shucked oysters to have along with a Sam Adams Colonial Ale (brewed exclusively for the Union Oyster House). The thick and creamy clam chowder, arguably one of the best in Boston, is another solid choice.

Asian (Eclectic)

*BLUE GINGER $$-$$$
583 Washington St.
Wellesley, MA 02482
(781) 283-5790
ming.com

Opened in 1998, celebrity chef Ming Tsai's much-lauded pan-Asian establishment still ranks among the top restaurants in the Boston area. Dishes like sake-miso marinated sablefish and garlic–black pepper lobster with lemongrass fried rice continue to draw crowds. Asian-style appetizers in the lounge, such as the popular Ming's Bings (a kind of burger/dumpling), and a lunch menu that offers several ramen and noodle dishes at a lower price point are attracting a younger crowd. Ming is often in the house, and because of a recent expansion and interior-design makeover of the Wellesley space, it's no surprise that Blue Ginger still feels fresh.

EAST BY NORTHEAST $$-$$$
1128 Cambridge St.
Cambridge, MA 02139
(617) 876-0286
exnecambridge.com

The cuisine at this casual Inman Square spot is Chinese by way of New England and everything is made in house—including the dumpling wrappers and noodles. The menu is big on pig but also heavy on vegetarian offerings and seasonally driven flavors. It's a tapas-style menu; craft your meal by ordering several dishes for the table. Must-orders include the scallion pancakes with roasted chile sauce, pork belly on fluffy mantou buns with pickled vegetables, and the short-rice noodles with delicata squash, local greens, and sweet bean sauce. It's all very reasonably priced, so you can afford to visit on a regular basis. The everyday prix fixe—5 courses from the regular menu—is one of the area's best dining deals. Open for dinner Tues through Sat, brunch only on Sun, and closed Mon.

GOURMET DUMPLING HOUSE $$
52 Beach St., Chinatown
Boston, MA 02111
(617) 338-6223
gourmetdumpling.com

All sorts of Beijing-style soup dumplings, fried dumplings, and pillowy steamed buns are the main draw at this Chinatown favorite. Be sure to order the scallion pancakes, too—they are exceptional, both crispy and chewy at the same time. The menu has a host of classic Chinese entrees to try—not just the Kung Pao chicken–type stuff, but more authentic dishes like shredded pork with bitter melon and a super-spicy Szechuan-style whole fish soup. By Chinatown standards, Gourmet Dumpling House is a medium-size restaurant, and a line is always to be expected. Order well and you'll be glad you went.

Breakfast & Lunch

THE FRIENDLY TOAST $
1 Kendall Sq.
Cambridge, MA 02139
(617) 621-1200
thefriendlytoast.net
Eclectic is the word at this funky hipster cafe in Cambridge's Kendall Square neighborhood. The decor is '50s retro kitsch: Formica tables with stainless steel trim, vinyl booths, mismatched melamine plates. The pumpkin pancakes are legendary for brunch paired with a mimosa or Bloody Mary. For lunch and dinner, the mostly sandwich menu leans nostalgic with dishes like a BLT, an 8-ounce burger on a kaiser roll, and several types of grilled cheese sandwiches.

Burgers & Sandwich Shops

✳MR. BARTLEY'S BURGER COTTAGE $
1246 Massachusetts Ave.
Cambridge, MA 02138
(617) 354-6559
mrbartley.com
Located practically in the shadow of Harvard Yard, this Cambridge joint is worth seeking out for its seemingly endless menu of reasonably priced, creatively topped 7-ounce hamburgers. The fun menu names its burgers after local and national newsmakers: the iPhone, made with Boursin cheese, grilled mushrooms, and onions, is of the moment, while the People's Republic of Cambridge, topped with coleslaw and Russian dressing,

never seems to go out of style. Order a heap of fried onion rings on the side and leave room for a frappe (what New Englanders call milk shakes). Cash only and they are closed Sun.

SAUS $
33 Union St., Government Center
Boston, MA 02108
(617) 248-8835
eatfrites.com
Around the corner from Faneuil Hall, Saus is a sandwich shop/cafe that has it all: fantastic Belgian-style (thick, house-cut) french fries with your choice of a dozen homemade mayonnaise- and ketchup-based sauces along with an impressive menu of northern European street food: Dutch *frikandellenn* (a kind of hot dog/sausage), chicken sate pockets, Liege-style waffles with Nutella or lemon cream. Add a terrific beer list for one of Boston's most unique and fun (and relatively inexpensive) dining experiences.

i Take to the streets on two wheels. Boston's bike share program, Hubway (thehubway.com), lets you pick up a bike at one of its more than 100 stations in Boston and the nearby suburbs and return it to a location near your destination.

Cafes & Coffeehouses

FLOUR BAKERY & CAFE $
12 Farnsworth St., Seaport District
Boston, MA 02110
(617) 338-4333
flourbakery.com
Financial district office workers, Fort Point loft-dwellers, and stroller-pushing tourists visiting the nearby Children's Museum adore

this spot for wonderful breakfast pastries and coffee, quick gourmet lunches, and indulgent, home-style dinners. The soup and half-sandwich combo (perhaps the spicy minestrone and the roast chicken sandwich with avocado and jicama) is the way to go here—especially as it means you'll have room for dessert. Chef Joanne Chang's sticky buns are legendary; they were featured on an episode of *Throwdown with Bobby Flay*—and won. Among the other sweet offerings that put this bakery over the top: impossibly flaky croissants, a decadent triple chocolate mousse cake, and hand-formed tarts bursting with seasonal, local fruit. Additional locations in the South End, Cambridge, and the Back Bay.

L. A. BURDICK $
52 Brattle St.
Cambridge, MA 02138
(617) 491-4340
burdickchocolate.com
Tempting European cakes and handmade artisan chocolates are served in these inviting Harvard Square and Back Bay cafes, but the setting could just as well be the Left Bank of the Seine. For a sweet indulgence, you must try the hot chocolate, which is so thick that it coats the inside of your demitasse cup. It comes in dark, milk, and white and is absolutely habit forming. Calories be damned. An additional location is at 220 Clarendon St., Boston, MA 02116 (617-303-0113).

3 LITTLE FIGS $
278 Highland Ave.
Somerville, MA 02130
(617) 623-3447
3littlefigs.com

At this cafe, as cute as a button as any cafe is bound to be, you'll find a variety of fresh-baked homespun pastries and breakfast sandwiches in exotic flavors that skew Greek. Among the offerings: lavender biscuits, lemon doughnut muffins, and a tasty Greek breakfast sandwich of scrambled eggs with feta and prosciutto on a brioche roll. The baristas are skilled and the counter service is cheerful—smitten regulars can't think of a better destination for breakfast or an afternoon pick-me-up. Closed Mon.

Eclectic

STRIP-T'S $$–$$$
95 School St.
Watertown, MA 02472
(617) 923-4330
stripts.com
Chef Tim Maslow (formerly of New York's Momofuku Ssam Bar) has returned home and taken over the family restaurant, Strip-T's. Sophisticated but not serious, this small eatery is worth knowing for eclectic and memorable, seasonal cuisine that is relaxed enough to enjoy at any time. In the spirit of Strip-T's days as a sandwich shop, the lunch menu offers dishes like a soft-shell clam po' boy, a turkey Reuben with house everything, and a kim(chee) cheesesteak sub. Dinner is even more interesting; appetizer choices include grilled romaine lettuce with oxtail and a poached egg and charred Spanish octopus, while mains have included buttermilk fried chicken with dirty rice and a burger with smoked miso and lemon aioli. Prices are high for the suburbs, but it's an outstanding value for the quality.

French

CLIO $$$$
Eliot Hotel
370A Commonwealth Ave., Kenmore
Square
Boston, MA 02215
(617) 536-7200
cliorestaurant.com

The recent redesign at Clio's, a tawny-colored enclave with luxurious touches just blocks from Fenway, is even better than the original. Award-winning Chef Ken Oringer (James Beard 2001 Best Chef: Northeast) does a very nontraditional, whimsy-touched, mostly French menu. Examples include the black licorice–roasted Muscovy duck and the sweet butter–basted Maine lobster with chanterelles and fava beans. Desserts are modern: a cylindrical chocolate coulant with a warm coconut center, topped with cocoa nib ice cream. The staff is extremely well informed and the wine list is superb, with selections deriving from the best vintages of France, Italy, Spain, and California. But know that Clio is an elegant gustatory experience and may not be for everyone, so be sure to dress up and know proper etiquette.

DEUXAVE $$$
371 Commonwealth Ave.
Boston, MA 02115
(617) 517-5915
deuxave.com

Sitting at the intersection of Comm and Mass Ave., Deuxave (pronounced "Dooh-aaahve") is a contemporary restaurant located in a Back Bay brownstone where Chef-Owner Chris Coombs's kitchen turns out elegant plates of well-priced French-inspired fare made with local ingredients. For the main course consider Deuxave's defining dish, the spiced Long Island duck breast accompanied by lentils and prunes stuffed with foie gras. This is not the place to beg off dessert—the menu is small but wonderfully creative with dishes like PB & J, a salted peanut butter mousse with Concord grape jam and sorbet. There's a savvy wine list and the staff is meticulously trained.

GASLIGHT BRASSERIE $$–$$$
560 Harrison Ave., South End
Boston, MA 02118
(617) 422-0224
gaslight560.com

Nearly every night of the week, this bustling brasserie in the heart of the hip South End is full of joie de vivre from neighborhood regulars and couples on dates. It's a handsome space with an old-fashioned feel (etched glass, subway tiles, rustic wood beams) to enjoy the flavors of Paris in classic dishes like steak frites with béarnaise sauce, duck confit with cherries, and pan-roasted bass with ratatouille. There's an outstanding wine list, too, with unique by-the-glass opportunities. The weekend prix-fixe brunch is stellar—choice of several entrees, coffee, and juice, available for a pittance (currently $9.95) all day Saturday and before noon on Sunday.

Ice Cream

CHRISTINA'S $
1255 Cambridge St.
Cambridge, MA 02139
(617) 492-7021
christinasicecream.com

Ask Cambridge locals for an ice cream recommendation and chances are good they'll point you to this Inman Square institution, nearly equidistant between Harvard and MIT. This is premium, homemade ice cream made on the premises and the flavors are downright mind-blowing. The Mexican chocolate is lush and deeply flavored with a spicy kick. There's a fiercely addictive coffee Oreo and refreshingly tart sorbets, such as cranberry and ginger Kaffir lime and pomegranate lemon.

J. P. LICKS $
659 Centre St., Jamaica Plain
Boston, MA 02130
(617) 524-6740
jplicks.com
Bringing together homemade ice cream and innovative flavors, J. P. Licks is one of New England's most beloved local ice cream chains. Corporate headquarters, ice cream production, and an ice cream shop are all housed in this building in Boston's Jamaica Plain neighborhood (hence the "J.P."). Some of J.P. Licks's favorite regular flavors include Oreo cake batter and a spot-on sweet cream that tastes freshly churned just minutes ago (because it probably was). Seasonal flavors, such as pumpkin custard in the fall and Raspberry Lime Rickey in the summer, rotate in on a monthly basis. For over-the-top indulgence, get an ice cream sundae smothered in homemade hot fudge or bring back home or to the office one of their ridiculously good handpacked ice cream cakes. For information on other area locations, check out their website.

Italian

ANTICO FORNO $$–$$$
93 Salem St., North End
Boston, MA 02113
(617) 423-6363
anticofornoboston.com
Families, relaxed urbanites, and tourists converge at this North End gem for simple, savory dishes done well. It's a warm and welcoming space, thanks to its appealing brick and beam decor. Begin your meal with the smartly seasoned antipasti of meats,

cheeses, and marinated vegetables. The pizza is a must-order; it's exquisitely charred in the wood-burning oven, resulting in an authentic Neapolitan pie. *Antico forno* means "ancient oven" and it lends a smoky flavor to several baked entrees including the homemade gnocchi topped with tomato sauce and fresh mozzarella and the roasted half chicken with herbs, roasted potatoes, and green beans. The pleasant service, nice wines by the glass, and reasonable tabs make this a winning choice.

IL CASALE $$$
50 Leonard St.
Belmont, MA 02478
(617) 209-4942
ilcasalebelmont.com
It's worth a special trip to Belmont (an easy 15-minute jaunt from Boston) for some of the area's best Italian cuisine. The exposed brick, dim lighting, and warm wood panels add to the cozy Old World ambience of this one-time firehouse. Chef-Owner (and Belmont native) Dante de Magistris is a master of his craft, offering superb sfizi (love the pork meatballs!) and rustic-chic dishes like gnocchi with porcini *crema* and roasted peppers and grilled lamb chops with smoked eggplant and farro salad. Don't skip dessert; here they are both homespun and indulgent: a slice of chocolate *semifreddo* with hazelnut *anglaise* or an *affogato* of vanilla gelato with a double espresso.

Japanese

DOUZO $$$$
131 Dartmouth St., South End
Boston, MA 02116
(617) 859-8886
douzosushi.com
Located in the Back Bay, Douzo has a decidedly trendy and upscale vibe that sets it apart

from Boston's other sushi restaurants. Begin your meal with miso soup or some pickled vegetables as a prelude to the wide variety of beautifully crafted sushi and sashimi (tuna, salmon, yellowtail, fluke, shrimp, and more) that are the centerpiece of this restaurant's menu. Among the specialty rolls, the star is the Torch roll, made with avocado and cucumber wrapped in seared yellowtail. For the timid, there are cooked entrees, including a flaky and tender black cod with miso. The budget-minded may want to come between noon and 3 p.m., when the best deal is the lunch set, an ultra-generous portion of the chef's-choice sushi.

Mediterranean

✳OLEANA   **$$$$**
134 Hampshire St.
Cambridge, MA 02139
(617) 661-0505
oleanarestaurant.com

Chef Ana Sortun has quite a following. Oleana, located in Inman Square, is a little off Cambridge's beaten path and yet this Mediterranean/Middle East restaurant remains one of the area's toughest reservation scores. It's a local favorite for celebratory dinners as well as for meeting friends; so many options make this a great choice for vegetarians and meat-eaters alike. The cuisine is a mixture of mostly Greek, Turkish, and Lebanese specialties utilizing hyperlocal flavors and farm-fresh ingredients—many from Sudbury's Siena Farms, owned by Sortun's husband, Chris Kurth. You could easily make a meal of meze, which are absolutely luscious: tamarind glazed beef and smoky eggplant with pine nuts, rose-scented quail with barberries, spinach falafel with tahini and beets, and whipped feta with red pepper. Leave room for dessert and order the Baked Alaska—it's

made with coconut ice cream and passion-fruit caramel and it is a showstopper.

Pizza

PICCO   **$$**
513 Tremont St., South End
Boston, MA 02116
(617) 927-0066
piccorestaurant.com

Pizza and ice cream are two staples that Bostonians have serious opinions on, and Picco (which stands for Pizza and Ice Cream Company) manages to please everyone with its paper-thin charred-crust pizza and creative toppings like sausage, ricotta, and red onion or an Alsatian version with crème fraîche, bacon, and gruyère. Salads, such as the excellent warm spinach salad with bacon, white beans, and goat cheese, and a few pastas, such as spaghetti puttanesca, round out the menu. Either American craft beer or a bottle of wine will go well with your meal, but be sure to save room for dessert; the homemade dark chocolate ice cream is particularly indulgent. Can't decide? Then order a 3–ice cream sampler and (maybe) share.

PIZZERIA REGINA   **$$**
11½ Thacher St., North End
Boston, MA 02113
(617) 227-0765
reginapizzeria.com

The setting is totally no-frills and the service is often rushed, but Pizzeria Regina gets props because it captures so well the essence of the bygone North End era. Established in 1926, this is the chain's flagship and original location. The pies that come out of the ancient brick oven are some of the best thin-crust pizza Boston has to offer. Pizza-lovers have been known to grow misty-eyed as they describe the experience of eating the pizza Margherita, while the sausage cacciatore pizza has its own share of fans and is equally delicious. The place is always filled to capacity, so if you know what's good for you, don't come on a weekend night or just before or after a Garden event.

Pubs & Taverns

GRAFTON STREET PUB & GRILL $$
1230 Massachusetts Ave.
Cambridge, MA 02138
(617) 497-0400
graftonstreetcambridge.com
Named for the pedestrian thoroughfare in Dublin, Grafton Street offers a place for tourists and those affiliated with Harvard to duck in for amped-up bar food, such as lobster macaroni and cheese, beef short rib pot roast, and fish tacos with local hake and smoked chile aioli. If the sun is shining, have your meal at the lovely front sidewalk patio. Flying solo? That's what the bar is for.

PARK RESTAURANT & BAR $$
59 JFK St.
Cambridge, MA 02138
(617) 491-9851
parkcambridge.com
This large subterranean restaurant/tavern is an ideal spot for almost any occasion: to unwind after a long workday, a casual date night, or a boisterous dinner with a group of old friends. A huge U-shaped bar takes center stage, and there are several rooms including a classroom space with vertical slat-back school chairs and a chalkboard, and a semiprivate living room space with a fireplace, leather sofas, wing chairs, and cases filled with antique books and oddities like a vintage Singer sewing machine. The bar serves plenty of craft beer and killer mixed drinks (try the gin-based Lavender

Moon). And the food? Enjoy a diverse menu that includes crispy mussels with preserved lemon, a roasted half chicken, and a great burger.

PUBLICK HOUSE $$
1648 Beacon St.
Brookline, MA 02445
(617) 277-2880
eatgoodfooddrinkbetterbeer.com
This atmospheric Belgian-inspired brasserie is a Boston mainstay for a low-key evening. It features a Eurocentric beer menu with almost 40 taps and more than 100 specialty bottles that represent a full range of beer choices including rich triple-fermented Belgians, traditional English ales, and a solid selection of New England craft beers. The menu features buckets of mussels served with paper cones of thick-cut Belgian-style fries, generous charcuterie and cheese boards, and a renowned mac and five-cheese sauce that arrives sizzling in a cast-iron pan.

Seafood

ISLAND CREEK OYSTER BAR $$$
Hotel Commonwealth
500 Commonwealth Ave., Kenmore Square
Boston, MA 02215
(617) 532-5300
islandcreekoysterbar.com
This sleek, smart bar located in Kenmore Square's Hotel Commonwealth is always buzzing with flocks of foodies and Sox fans. Oyster obsessives wax rhapsodic about Island Creek's quality and the innumerable varieties of plump, briny bivalves. This is sea-to-table dining at its best—the restaurant is part owned by the founder of Massachusetts-based Island Creek Oyster Farm. The

menu is rounded out by dishes like oyster sliders, lobster roe noodles, and marinated skirt steak with salsa verde. Expect to wait (especially on game days), but you can sit at the 25-seat bar with a hand-swizzled cocktail.

LEGAL HARBORSIDE $$$
270 Northern Ave., Seaport District
Boston, MA 02210
(617) 477-2900
legalseafoods.com
Established in 1950, Boston's best-known seafood restaurant is still one of the city's best. Located in Boston's Seaport District and opened in 2011, this sprawling (it's 23,000 feet with 700 seats) trilevel restaurant has great harbor views and is the local chain's flagship location. On the third floor, the after-work bar scene hops with business types having drinks with raw-bar selections before being spirited away to the second-floor fine dining room for such dishes as smoked lobster with roasted cauliflower and bourbon honey butter or filet mignon with Alaska king crab. The casual first floor is more light-hearted with a fish market, a lively bar, picnic tables, and patio seating. The menu features fresh-as-can-be seafood and New England standards, such as Legal's legendary clam chowder, along with Mediterranean and Asian flavors in shareable plates, such as white clam pizza with pancetta and arugula and braised short rib tacos with hoisin barbecue sauce. Families will appreciate the kids' menu; it's way better than average, with choices including fresh cod sticks, a half lobster (taken out of the shell), or fish-shaped cheese ravioli with tomato sauce. And even when it is crazy busy (as it is most of the time), you'll find that service is better than good. See their website for additional locations.

YANKEE LOBSTER COMPANY $$
300 Northern Ave., Seaport District
Boston, MA 02210
(617) 345-9799
yankeelobstercompany.com
You're practically as close to the source as you can be without getting wet at this no-fuss (think picnic tables and paper plates) lobster wholesaler a block from the waterfront. The menu is mostly New England–style seafood simply prepared—either broiled or fried—at bargain prices. Order a boiled lobster dinner if you want to wrestle the beast. Or go for the lobster roll, straightforward lobster goodness: a quarter pound of fresh claw and knuckle meat, with a touch of mayonnaise, piled high in a lightly toasted roll.

Senegalese

TERANGA $$
1746 Washington St.
Boston, MA 02118
(617) 266-0003
terangaboston.com
Who knew that Senegal cuisine is so wonderful? Senegal cuisine reflects a melting pot of cultures including native African traditions, early French and Portuguese colonists, and more recent Vietnamese immigrants. Appetizer choices include *nems,* Vietnamese spring rolls, or wonderful little pan-fried fish cakes served with cilantro and garlic sauce. For entrees you can go conservative with lemon-marinated grilled chicken or be adventurous and sample the bold flavors of *thiébou djeun,* Senegal's national dish, a tomato-based stew that features an herb-stuffed fish, cassava, eggplant, and pumpkin over rice. Alcohol is available (not always the case, as most Senegal spots are Muslim). There's a high-end feel to the intimate dining room with its exposed brick walls, low

lighting, burnished wood tables, and patterned-gourd art pieces. You'll find welcoming service and a staff that enjoys sharing with diners an amazing cultural experience.

Southern

HUNGRY MOTHER   **$$**
233 Cardinal Medeiros Ave.
Cambridge, MA 02141
(617) 499-0090
hungrymothercambridge.com
A hip, clean-lined interior and authentic southern theme distinguish this appealing restaurant. The menu is traditional southern Sunday supper with a twist: fried green tomatoes and lobster remoulade, Wagyu beef brisket with creamed corn, cast-iron chicken with grits and braised greens, catfish in brown butter with cauliflower and rice. All of which is fittingly complemented by a bourbon-heavy cocktail program. On most nights there are just a few dessert choices, but all are stellar. You can't go wrong with country kitchen sweets like peach cream pie or red velvet cake. Open Tues through Sun, dinner only.

Spanish

TORO   **$$–$$$**
1704 Washington St., South End
Boston, MA 02118
(617) 536-4300
toro-restaurant.com
Open and noisy, this place captures the feel of old Madrid, everyone drinking and snacking on small plates with *mucho animacion*. This Ken Oringer/Jamie Bissonnette operation does tapas brilliantly well. There are many gems on the menu—the grilled corn with Cotija cheese is considered one of the iconic dishes of the Boston food scene and

is a must-order. The roasted bone marrow with oxtail marmalade and a citrus radish salad is another dish you should order. The deceptively simple menu is enhanced by an all-Spanish wine list and superb cocktails. Toro famously doesn't take reservations (and 2-hour weekend-night waits are not uncommon). The secret to getting a table? Come for lunch and come with friends. It's not nearly as crowded and if you are a party of 6 or more, they will take a reservation.

Steak House

ABE & LOUIE'S   **$$$$**
793 Boylston St., Back Bay
Boston, MA 02116
(617) 536-6300
abeandlouies.com
This clubby space with its classic dark-wood trim, brass fixtures, white tableclothed tables, and crowded bar is Boston's high-end shrine to steak. The portions are exceedingly generous in that old-school way with favorites that include a massive cold shellfish tower and the signature bone-in aged filet mignon. If any room remains, there's a host of desserts to try, including a chocolate soufflé with raspberry sauce and a house-made key lime pie.

Vegetarian

CLOVER FOOD LAB   **$**
7 Holyoke St.
Cambridge, MA 02138
cloverfoodlab.com
What started as a food truck is now a popular Harvard Square fast-food restaurant serving simple, wholesome, and affordable vegetarian cuisine. The menu features composed salads like beet, mint, and feta, a chickpea fritter sandwich, an egg and eggplant

sandwich, and fantastic rosemary french fries. The bright white dining room and open kitchen concept offers lots of open space and a communal table that more often than not is populated by an interesting assortment of Cambridge characters.

DAY TRIP IN BOSTON

Explore where Boston first began. If you have only one day in Boston, this itinerary is a terrific introduction to the city. For a one-day visit concentrate on downtown Boston and the waterfront. This is a walking tour and the sites are clustered closely together so that you can get the most out of your day. You'll wander through streets that are as old as any in Boston—the cobblestones are a testament to the old colonial town and to those who long ago bravely paved America's path to freedom.

If you want to have any chance of seeing everything on this itinerary, you'll need to get an early start. Have breakfast on Beacon Hill, located near Boston Common and the beginning of the Freedom Trail.

Pick up a tray and wait in line cafeteria style at the **Paramount** (44 Charles St., Beacon Hill; 617-720-1152; paramountboston .com), where breakfasts like caramel banana french toast and Western omelets are made to order. If you prefer a smaller breakfast, grab an authentic croissant and perfect latte from the French bakery **Cafe Vanille** (70 Charles St., Beacon Hill; 617-523-9200; frenchmemories.com) just down the street. Before heading across the Common, take a peek at quaint **Acorn Street.** Walk north on Charles Street for 1 block, and make a right on Mount Vernon. Walk 2 blocks and make a right on West Cedar Street and take the first left onto Acorn Street.

To get a sense of what Boston is all about, nothing tops walking the **Freedom Trail.** Exploring each of the 16 historic sites would take the better part of a day with time for little else, so consider taking the excellent 90-minute "Walk into History" tour offered by the 18th-century costumed guides of the Freedom Trail Foundation (Boston Common Visitor Center; thefreedomtrail.org). From Beacon Hill, cross Boston Common to the Boston Visitor Center on Tremont Street. Map in hand, you can easily walk the Freedom Trail on your own, but the Freedom Trail Foundation tour is both entertaining and informative and covers a lot of ground—11 sites—in a short amount of time.

Faneuil Hall Marketplace makes a logical stopping point for lunch. You could duck into the food court, but there are better possibilities. The **Union Oyster House** (41 Union St., Government Center; 617-227-2750; unionoysterhouse.com) is a historic dining opportunity not to be missed. Established in 1826, it is Boston's oldest restaurant. The best seats in the house are at the curved raw bar in the front window—be sure to order some clam chowder. To get there from Faneuil Hall, walk 1 block north along Congress Street and make a right on North Street and the first left on Union Street. Or for a more contemporary lunch option, walk over to the North End and **Neptune Oyster** (63 Salem St.; 617-742-3474; neptuneoyster.com) for what many consider the best raw-bar oysters in the city. To get to Neptune from Faneuil Hall, walk north along Congress Street for 2 blocks, make a right on Hanover Street, walk 2 blocks, make a left on Cross Street, and take the first right onto Salem Street.

Whether you have chosen to eat at Neptune Oyster or the Union Oyster House for lunch, follow the red painted line of

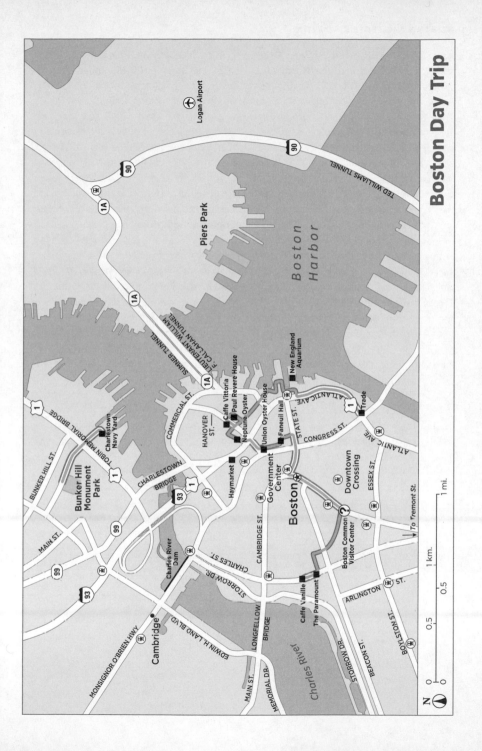

Boston Day Trip

Logan Airport

Piers Park

Boston Harbor

TED WILLIAMS TUNNEL

SUMNER TUNNEL

LIEUTENANT WILLIAM F. CALLAHAN TUNNEL

Caffe Vittoria
Paul Revere House
Neptune Oyster
Union Oyster House
Faneuil Hall
New England Aquarium

HANOVER ST.

COMMERCIAL ST.

Charlestown Navy Yard

Trade

ATLANTIC AVE

STATE ST.

CONGRESS ST.

ATLANTIC AVE.

Haymarket

Government Center

Boston

Downtown Crossing

ESSEX ST.

CHARLESTOWN

BRIDGE

CAMBRIDGE ST.

BUNKER HILL ST.

Bunker Hill Monument Park

TOBIN MEMORIAL BRIDGE

Boston Common Visitor Center

To Tremont St.

MAIN ST.

Charles River Dam

CHARLES ST.

STORROW DR.

ST.

ARLINGTON

Cambridge

Caffe Vanille
The Paramount

MONSIGNOR O'BRIEN HWY

MAIN ST.

MEMORIAL DR.

EDWIN H. LAND BLVD.

LONGFELLOW BRIDGE

STORROW DR.

Charles River

BEACON ST.

BOYLSTON ST.

N

0   0.5   1 km.
0   0.5   1 mi.

the Freedom Trail down Hanover Street as it continues on into the **North End.** Boston's North End is known as the city's Italian enclave, but in colonial times this was Paul Revere's neighborhood. Visit **Paul Revere's house** (19 North Sq., North End; 617-523-2338; paulreverehouse.org) and discover fascinating details about the American patriot who looms large in so much of Boston's history. Follow Hanover Street and make a right on Richmond Street and a left on North Street.

Now would be a good time to rest your legs and have a midafternoon snack. Head back down Hanover Street, where you can enjoy espresso, cannoli, or gelato (or all three!) at **Caffe Vittoria** (290–296 Hanover St.; 617-227-7606; vittoriacaffe.com), which has held forth from this spot since 1929.

End the afternoon on the water. It's a pleasant 10-minute stroll along the harbor and through Christopher Columbus Park to Long Wharf to pick up the Inner Harbor T ferry (mbta.com) for a ride across Boston Harbor to the Charlestown Navy Yard and a tour of **"Old Ironsides,"** the 215-year-old Navy ship the USS *Constitution*.

The Freedom Trail continues to its final stop, the **Bunker Hill Monument** (Monument Square, Charlestown; 617-242-5641; nps.gov/bost/historyculture/bhm.htm). If you climb the stairs (294!) and look out, you'll have views of Boston and Cambridge that even most locals haven't discovered. Return to the Charlestown Navy Yard and hop back on the ferry to Long Wharf. Take a small detour and walk over to the next dock, Central Wharf, which is the home of the **New England Aquarium** (617-973-5200; neaq .org), and spend a few minutes watching the antics of the aquarium's Atlantic harbor seals in their outdoor exhibit space. After a day of exploring Boston's colonial history, it's worth remembering that Boston has a proud heritage as a world seaport and over the centuries has acquired a taste for the exotic. Walk ½ mile more down Atlantic Avenue and finish the day with dinner and drinks at stylish **Trade** (540 Atlantic Ave.; 617-451-1234; trade-boston.com), where the menu roams the globe with dishes like steamed mussels with curry and spicy aioli, baked stuffed lobster with saffron cream, and a burger with pancetta and Vermont cheddar.

MERRIMACK VALLEY & NORTH SHORE

North of Boston encompasses both the historic Merrimack Valley outside the city and the towns that extend along the curve of coast northward to the New Hampshire border.

Just 20 miles northwest of Boston, the quaint, quintessentially white-clapboard New England towns of Lexington and Concord saw some of the first military action of the American Revolution. Lexington's Battle Green and Concord's Old North Bridge at the Minute Man National Historic Park are the principal sites for the events that took place on April 19, 1775. For fans of American literature, Concord has additional appeal. By the 19th century, Concord was the center of the transcendentalist movement and home to some of New England's greatest writers. For visitors the town has a seemingly endless supply of historic literary house museums to explore: Ralph Waldo Emerson's house, Nathaniel Hawthorne's Wayside, Henry David Thoreau's Walden Pond, and Louisa May Alcott's Orchard House. To the north, roughly follow the Concord River to the industrial city of Lowell. In a town renowned as the "City of Spindles," the mill build ings that line the banks of the Merrimack River make up the Lowell National Historic Park and attest to the city's role in the shift from farm to factory in America's Industrial Revolution.

The Salem witch trials of 1692 made Salem famous—notorious in fact—but Salem is much more than witches. Salem's Maritime National Historic site tells the story of the city's development as a major seaport and the Peabody Essex Museum houses an impressive collection of art and other spoils from the far reaches of the globe.

Forty miles north of Boston, the city of Gloucester and the towns of Manchester-by-the-Sea, Essex and Rockport make up the Cape Ann peninsula, which is sometimes referred to as the "Other Cape." Gloucester is a legendary fishing port with family-friendly beaches. Manchester-by-the-Sea's Singing Beach is perfect for a sunset stroll. Essex is famed for its antique shops, tidal flats, and fried clams while Rockport's Bearskin Neck shops and restaurants are a good destination if you are feeling spendy. Beyond Cape Ann, stretching almost to the New Hampshire border, the towns of Ipswich, Newburyport and Plum Island are comparatively remote with extensive unspoiled shoreline that attracts nature lovers to enjoy serene beaches and the blissful solitude of wildlife sanctuaries.

ATTRACTIONS

Historic Sites & Landmarks

✳GLOUCESTER FISHERMAN'S MEMORIAL
Stacy Boulevard
Gloucester, MA
The iconic Gloucester Fisherman's Memorial, an 8-foot bronze statue of a fisherman looking out over the harbor, pays tribute to the town fishermen who have lost their lives at sea. Nearby, bronze markers list more than 5,000 names; you'll find the names of the 6-member crew of the *Andrea Gail,* the subject of the book and movie *The Perfect Storm,* listed under 1991.

i If you grew up eating frozen fish sticks, the Gloucester Fisherman's Memorial will look very familiar. The image of the man at the wheel has been used as a logo for Gloucester-based frozen seafood company Gorton's since the 1960s.

GREAT HOUSE AT CASTLE HILL
290 Argilla Rd.
Ipswich, MA 01938
(978) 356-4351
thetrustees.org
Perched on the highest hill in Ipswich with a wide lawn that slopes to the sea, the Great House at Castle Hill was built as a summer retreat by Richard T. Crane, a 19th-century plumbing-supply baron. The 59-room family home was built in the English country manor style in 1928. The estate itself comprises 2,100 acres and includes **Crane Beach** (see p. 96) and the **Inn at Castle Hill** (see p. 109). Guided tours of the home as well as a popular landscape tour are offered May through Oct; check website for days and times. Other

events are scheduled throughout the year, most notably a summer Thursday evening picnic concert series and a Christmas open house, when the estate is dressed up in its finest greenery for the season.

GROPIUS HOUSE
68 Baker Bridge Rd.
Lincoln, MA 01773
(781) 259-8098
historicnewengland.org
German-born Walter Gropius, the founder of the Bauhaus design movement, moved to America to teach at Harvard. Built in 1938, his modest family home in Lincoln became a living laboratory for his then-revolutionary ideas of home design. The home is integrated with its wooded surroundings combining traditional New England materials like brick, clapboard, and fieldstone with industrial design elements like plate glass and chrome. The furniture throughout is original, much of it designed by Marcel Breuer. Guides, well informed in architecture, take small groups on a tour of the house on the hour. Open June through Oct 15, Wed through Sun 11 a.m. to 5 p.m.; Oct 16 through May, Sat and Sun 11 a.m. to 5 p.m.

✳HOUSE OF THE SEVEN GABLES
115 Derby St.
Salem, MA 01970
(978) 744-0991
7gables.org
"Half-way down a by-street of one of our New England towns, stands a rusty wooden house, with seven acutely peaked gables facing towards various points of the compass, and a huge, clustered chimney in the midst." As immortalized in Nathaniel Hawthorne's spine-tingling novel *The House of Seven Gables,* there's nothing staged about

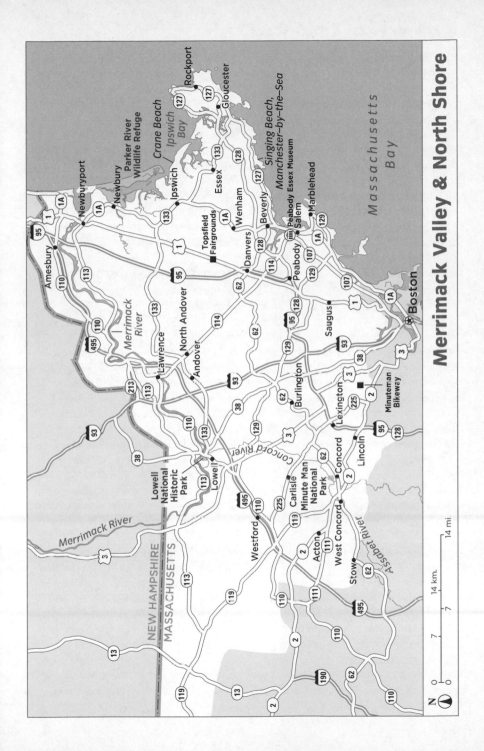

Merrimack Valley & North Shore

the spookiness of this house. Overlooking Salem Harbor, this rambling 1668 mansion was well-known to Hawthorne; at one time it belonged to his cousin Susannah Ingersoll. Tours of the house are by guided tour; save some time before or after to admire the neatness of the seaside parterre garden featuring colonial-era plants.

*LEXINGTON GREEN AND LEXINGTON HISTORICAL SOCIETY SITES
13 Depot Sq.
Lexington, MA 02420
(781) 862-1703
lexingtonhistory.org

The event that is popularly known as the Battle of Lexington was the first organized armed resistance by the colonial militia against the British, but it is perhaps more accurately described as a skirmish. In the early morning hours of April 19, 1775, Paul Revere's "midnight ride" brought him to the Hancock-Clarke House (36 Hancock St.) to warn Patriots John Hancock and Sam Adams that British troops were approaching to seize the colonists' supply of munitions in Concord. Nearby, at Buckman Tavern (1 Bedford St.), some 75 Lexington militia gathered under the command of Captain John Parker. The colonial militia assembled on Lexington Common in the face of 700 advancing British troops. Shots rang out, fire was exchanged, and 8 rebels died in the ensuing clash. The British continued their march to the neighboring town of Concord, where they met unexpected resistance and returned to Lexington late in the day to regroup at Munroe Tavern (1332 Massachusetts Ave.), just outside the center of town, before continuing the march back to Charlestown. Each of Lexington's historic home sites—the Hancock-Clarke House, Buckman Tavern, and

Munroe Tavern—is open to the public and offers guided tours daily; check website for hours and admission fees.

i Chat up the costumed Lexington Historical Society guides who can be found milling about Lexington Common (Massachusetts Avenue and Bedford Street). The guides are well informed about the events that led to the Battle of Lexington and are entertaining as well; some guides refuse to admit that they aren't in 1775!

*LOWELL NATIONAL HISTORIC PARK
246 Market St.
Lowell, MA 01852
(978) 970-5000
nps.gov/lowe

The advent of water-powered factory mills along the Merrimack River catapulted a young agricultural US into the Industrial Age. The first Lowell cotton mill opened in 1823 and by the 1850s nearly 40 brick mill factory buildings operated here. The Lowell National Historic Park is urban with buildings spread over several blocks in downtown Lowell. Start at the visitor center (246 Market St.) to get maps and plan your day. Check out the schedule of free ranger-led walking and trolley tours offered daily. You can also buy tickets for the ranger-led canal cruise tours. The Boott Cotton Mills Museum (115 John St.) is the park's principal attraction, where the sound of 88 cloth-weaving looms is deafening (earplugs are provided). In the museum gift shop you can buy a souvenir dishtowel made from the fabric produced here. You can also visit a worker boardinghouse (40 French St.) and hear stories from one-time "Mill Girls" and immigrant workers to get a sense of what it was like to work in the factories. In the summer be sure to take the canal cruise. The ingenuity of the 6-mile system of waterways that made possible the operation of the mills is fascinating.

LOWELL'S BOAT SHOP
459 Main St.
Amesbury, MA 01913
(978) 834-0050
lowellsboatshop.com
Established in 1793, this is the country's oldest boat-building shop. Boating enthusiasts and those who appreciate woodwork will not want to skip this working museum, which continues to make handcrafted wooden rowing fishing dories that were once the mainstay of the New England fishing industry. Visitors can drop in to view the boat builders at work, or sign up for a museum membership and you can try your hand at rowing a Lowell skiff on the Merrimack River just outside the shop's door. Open Tues through Fri 11 a.m. to 4 p.m. and weekends by appointment.

*MINUTE MAN NATIONAL HISTORIC PARK
Minute Man Visitor Center
250 N. Great Rd.
Lincoln, MA 01773
(978) 369-6993
nps.gov/mima
The Minute Man National Historic Park is located in the towns of Lincoln, Concord, and Lexington. The Minute Man Visitor Center should be your first stop, where you can pick up a free map, check the day's schedule of events, and consider taking a ranger-led tour. Don't miss the 25-minute multimedia presentation *The Road to Revolution,* which brings to life the events that took place in Lexington and Concord on April 19, 1775.

From the visitor center, walk some or part of the Battle Road, which follows the path the British soldiers took on their march from Boston to Lexington and Concord. Along the way, about ½ mile from the visitor center, is the site where Paul Revere was captured by a British patrol (and then questioned and released). Continue along the Battle Road by foot or by car along Route 2A to Concord and the Old North Bridge. It was here that more than 400 colonial soldiers gathered and for the first time were able to oust the British in what would become the first major battle of the Revolutionary War. Be sure to walk across the Old North Bridge (it is a replica) to visit the 1875 Minute Man statue sculpted by Concord native Daniel Chester French. At the base are inscribed the stirring words from the first stanza of Ralph Waldo Emerson's "Concord Hymn": "By the rude bridge that arched the flood, / Their flag to April breeze unfurled, / Here once the embattled farmers stood, / And fired the shot heard 'round the world."

NEW ENGLAND QUILT MUSEUM
18 Shattuck St.
Lowell, MA 01852
(978) 452-4208
nequiltmuseum.org
If you are nimble with a thimble, you will love this museum. Just a short walk from the Lowell National Historic Park, this museum is devoted to quilts as both craft and art. The main gallery displays a rotating selection of the museum's permanent collection of 400+ pieces representing both traditional and contemporary quilt-making. Among the museum's holdings are early-American indigo quilts, late 19th-century Amish geometrics, and dazzling modern collage wall hangings. Recent themed shows have

included "African-American Quilts Today" and "Campaigns and Commemoratives: Quilts for Presidents." The museum shop is a terrific resource and features gifts, quilting supplies, and consigned one-of-a-kind finished quilts. The museum also offers workshops and quilting classes for adults and children. Open Tues through Sat 10 a.m. to 4 p.m., and Sun May through Oct noon to 4 p.m.

*OLD MANSE
269 Monument St.
Concord, MA 01742
(978) 369-3909
oldmanse.org
On the banks of the Concord River, within sight of the Old North Bridge, this 1770 parsonage belonged to William Emerson, who witnessed the battle of April 19, 1775, as it unfolded nearby. His grandson Ralph Waldo Emerson lived here for a short time and drafted *Nature* from the study. The house was later rented to Nathaniel Hawthorne and his bride, Sophia. Highlights of the guided tour include the windowpane love poems etched in the glass by the newlyweds. Closed Mon; check website for tour times.

*PAPER HOUSE
52 Pigeon Hill St.
Rockport, MA 01966
paperhouserockport.com
A New England house made almost entirely of newspaper that has stood for more than 90 years is an attraction worth seeing. This 2-room summer cottage once belonged to Elis Stenman, a mechanical engineer and amateur inventor. Stenman built the home between 1922 and 1942 using more than 100,000 newspapers to construct the walls and furniture. His 20-year DIY project

is remarkably well preserved—you can still see the headlines through the varnish. Open daily spring through fall. The house is usually unattended, but there is a lockbox honor system for admission.

RALPH WALDO EMERSON HOUSE
28 Cambridge Turnpike
Concord, MA 01742
(978) 369-2236
Philosopher and poet Ralph Waldo Emerson was at the center of the transcendentalist movement; he established himself in Concord and lived in this clapboard foursquare home with his family from 1835 until his death in 1882. It was in this house that he wrote most of his work, including the essay "Self-Reliance," and hosted a stream of distinguished guests. The home is still owned by the Emerson family and except for the contents of his study, which are housed across the street at the Concord Museum, and his library of books, which is at Harvard, much of the furniture and artifacts are original. Open mid-April through mid-October, Thurs through Sat 10:30 a.m. to 4:30 p.m., Sun and holiday Mondays 1 to 4:30 p.m.

REBECCA NURSE HOMESTEAD
149 Pine St.
Danvers, MA 01923
(978) 774-8799
rebeccanurse.org
For an account of the Salem witch trials without the hocus-pocus, head to Danvers. Many of the events associated with the 1692 Salem witch trials occurred here when the town, located 5 miles north of Salem, was known as Salem Village. Rebecca Nurse, a mother and grandmother, and respected member of the community, was one of the first to

be accused and hanged for witchcraft. The interior of her family's 1678 saltbox home is authentic to the period. Guided tours of the homestead focus on myths and misconceptions relating to the trials. Open mid-June through Oct 31.

✳SALEM MARITIME HISTORIC DISTRICT
193 Derby St.
Salem, MA 01970
(978) 740-1650
nps.gov/sama

Tea, rum, molasses, spices, and fish—at the height of trade with the Far East, between the end of the Revolutionary War and the War of 1812, as many as 200 cargo ships were seen daily in Salem Harbor. This harborside park includes 9 historic buildings and 3 wharves that tell the tale of Salem's rich maritime history. At the visitor center see the orientation film and pick up maps and brochures for a self-guided visit or check the schedule for free ranger-led tours. Moored at Derby Wharf, the handsomest vessel in all of Salem Harbor is the *Friendship,* a wood replica of a 1797 three-mast square-rigged "East Indiaman" merchant ship. In the summer the boat is open for self-guided tours; during the rest of the year visits are restricted to those who take the ranger-led guided tour. In the early part of the 19th century, trade in pepper with the island of Sumatra made Salem the center of the world's spice trade. Peruse the shelves at the West India Goods Store (164 Derby St.) for whole and ground spices from around the world to add some oomph to your cooking. The shop also sells Salem-related souvenirs, penny candy, and period trinkets.

✳SALEM WITCH TRIALS MEMORIAL
Liberty Street
Salem, MA 01970

Salem's tribute to victims of the witchcraft hysteria was dedicated in 1992 and is located behind the Peabody Essex Museum. The small, shady park is surrounded by a low stone wall with 20 rough-hewn granite benches, each inscribed with the name and execution date of a victim. It's a peaceful and contemplative place to consider the consequences of intolerance and justice gone awry.

i Originally known by its Native American name Naumkeag, the area was renamed in 1629 as Salem, a derivative of the Arabic word *salaam* and the Hebrew word *shalom,* both meaning "peace." Historical irony, that.

✳SLEEPY HOLLOW CEMETERY
Bedford Street
Concord, MA 01742
(978) 318-3233

The natural landscape design of Sleepy Hollow, a cemetery founded in 1855, reflects the transcendental aesthetic with curving paths that follow the contours of the hilly woodland. Concord's literary luminaries—Henry David Thoreau, Nathaniel Hawthorne, Ralph Waldo Emerson, and Louisa May Alcott—are buried in the section known as Authors' Ridge. It's a serene spot beneath tall trees. Thoreau's grave is a sentimental favorite; admirers often leave small tributes: acorns, pinecones, and pencils (his family owned a pencil factory).

THE WAYSIDE
455 Lexington Rd.
Concord, MA 01742
(978) 318-7863
nps.gov/mima

The Wayside is three centuries old and is also known as the "Authors' House." Louisa May Alcott lived here with her family as a young girl; she and her sisters would perform their "theatricals" in the barn. When the Alcott family moved to Orchard House across the street, they sold the house to Nathaniel Hawthorne, who enlarged it by adding a study tower, where he wrote his later works. In the 20th century, Harriett Lothrop, author of the *Five Little Peppers* children's book series (under the pen name Margaret Sidney), lived here. The Wayside is part of the Minute Man Historical Park, and visits to the home are by ranger-led guided tour. Open mid-April through October, Tues through Sun; check website for hours.

Museums

AMERICAN TEXTILE HISTORY MUSEUM
491 Dutton St.
Lowell, MA 01854
(978) 441-0400
athm.org

From spinning wheels to Lowell's power mills to the latest high-tech fabrics, this museum chronicles the history of textiles in America. Located in a renovated mill building, the collection includes clothing, fabric fragments, and examples of the machines used to make them. The museum is newly affiliated with the Smithsonian Institution and temporary exhibitions like the recent "Suited for Space" are usually noteworthy. The museum is open Wed through Sun; closed Mon and Tues.

CAPE ANN MUSEUM
27 Pleasant St.
Gloucester, MA 01930
(978) 283-0455
capeannmuseum.org

The luminous seascape paintings of native son Fitz Henry Lane are at the core of this museum. Other notable collections include the maritime gallery, which features painstakingly accurate ship models and tools used in the local fishing industry. Closed Mon and during Feb.

✳CONCORD MUSEUM
58 Cambridge Turnpike
Concord, MA 01742
(978) 369-9763
concordmuseum.org

Henry James once referred to Concord as the "biggest little place in America." Visit the Concord Museum and you will understand why. Located in the center of town, the museum is a terrific place to begin a visit to Concord. The museum has an esteemed collection of artifacts relating to Concord's role in early American history and 19th-century literature, including the contents of Emerson's study and the desk where Thoreau penned *Walden*. The museum's prized possession is one of the lanterns that was hung in the belfry of Boston's Old North Church on the night of Paul Revere's midnight ride.

DECORDOVA SCULPTURE PARK AND MUSEUM
51 Sandy Pond Rd.
Lincoln, MA 01773
(781) 259-8355
decordova.org

Art and nature—the DeCordova Sculpture Park and Museum offers visitors the best of both worlds: a museum of contemporary art and a showstopping sculpture garden. Light pours in through the floor-to-ceiling windows of the museum's galleries, which feature rotating exhibits of international-caliber artists as well as a growing permanent collection. The highlight of the museum campus is the Sculpture Park, where the easy looping walking path through the grounds and woods of the property provides a soft-edge setting for some 60 large-scale contemporary works. Rest on one of the benches and contemplate the scene or bring a blanket—picnicking is encouraged. Bring a camera, too—there are lots of fun photo ops among the sculptures. Closed Mon (except some holidays).

ESSEX SHIPBUILDING MUSEUM
66 Main St.
Essex, MA 01929
(978) 768-7541
essexshipbuildingmuseum.org
From the 1800s through the 1950s, Essex was a village of shipwrights. At one time most of Gloucester's 2-mast wood fishing schooner fleet was "Essex built." Inside the workshop, on the grounds of the former Story Shipyard, you can take classes in traditional wooden boat-building and watch the carpenter/volunteers work on restoration throughout the year. Open mid-May through October, Wed through Sun.

✳ORCHARD HOUSE
399 Lexington Rd.
Concord, MA 01742
(978) 369-5778
louisamayalcott.org
Louisa May Alcott's most well-known work, *Little Women,* has been a beloved first novel for generations of young American girls.

Alcott lived in this unpretentious brown clapboard house with her parents and sisters between 1858 and 1877. She wrote and set *Little Women* at Orchard House and used her family as the fictionalized characters in the book. Now a museum, the house has been faithfully and lovingly cared for through the years. Look for Alcott's writing desk (it's little more than a shelf) between the windows in her bedroom. Guided tours are the only way to see the house. Don't hesitate to ask questions—the museum guides are passionate about the lives of the Alcott family and their place in American literary history.

✳PEABODY ESSEX MUSEUM
161 Essex St.
Salem, MA 01970
(978) 745-9500
pem.org
Boston is not the only city in Massachusetts with a world-class museum. Founded in 1799, the Peabody Essex Museum is considered the oldest continuously operating museum in the country. PEM underwent an impressive expansion in 2003; the museum's sweeping light-filled central atrium space evokes both ships and the sea. The museum is a treasure trove of artifacts, ship models, and paintings that tell the story of Salem's golden age of maritime trade with the Far East, Africa, and Oceania. Recent blockbuster temporary exhibitions have included "Ansel Adams: At the Water's Edge" and "The Emperor's Private Paradise: Treasures from the Forbidden City." Be sure to visit Yin Yu Tang, a 2-story, 200-year-old home that was transported lock, stock, and barrel from China. Free family events, usually involving storytelling and drop-in workshops, are organized on weekends and school holidays. The museum is set to get even bigger when new galleries

open in 2017. Open Tues through Sun (and some holiday Mondays).

WHISTLER HOUSE MUSEUM OF ART
243 Worthen St.
Lowell, MA 01852
(978) 452-7641
whistlerhouse.org

"I shall be born when and where I want, and I do not choose to be born in Lowell." The artist James McNeil Whistler may not have been proud of his birthplace, but Lowell is tremendously proud of Whistler. This simple 1823 clapboard house is where Whistler was born and is now the home of the Lowell Art Association. The museum's small permanent collection focuses on late 19th- and 20th-century artists from New England. Among the more familiar artists represented are Frank Weston Benson and William Morris Hunt. Although the museum does not own a Whistler painting, it does have a very nice collection of his etchings. The Parker Gallery behind the house expands the museum's exhibit space with juried members' shows, so there are always new discoveries to be made.

Parks & Beaches

APPLETON FARMS GRASS RIDES
219 Country Rd.
Ipswich, MA 01982
(978) 356-5728
thetrustees.org

Happy trails. Appleton Farms dates from 1636 and is one of the oldest working farms in the country. Appleton Farms offers 6 miles of marked, rolling hiking trails that are popular with casual hikers and those who enjoy solitude. The rides—grass carriage paths originally designed for horse-drawn

vehicles—take you through woods and meet like the spokes of a wheel at the Roundpoint, a clearing marked by a 9-foot granite pinnacle. Farmstead cheese, butter, and yogurt—all made with milk from the farm's own herd of grass-fed cows—are available at the farm stand.

✳CRANE BEACH
Argilla Road
Ipswich, MA 01938
(978) 356-4354
thetrustees.org/pages/294_crane_beach.cfm

This spectacular 4-mile stretch of wide-open white sandy shoreline is by far the most popular beach on the North Shore. Administered by the Trustees of Reservations, Crane has plenty of parking (there's a fee in season), restrooms, outside showers, and a snack bar. Crane Beach is also a wildlife refuge offering visitors a unique environment for a hike along the shore with more than 5 miles of trails that meander in and out of dunes (wear shoes appropriate for walking in soft sand). Crane Beach is also a nesting site for the piping plover; in summer visitors have a good opportunity to see this endangered species.

> **i** Crane Beach is notorious for its greenhead flies. The pesky greenhead thrives in Ipswich's coastal salt marsh environment and delivers a painful bite. During the peak days of greenhead season (typically in mid-July), signs advising beachgoers are posted at the entry gate and online. Heed the warnings. These bugs are big and they are out for blood!

*DRUMLIN FARM (MASSACHUSETTS
    AUDUBON HEADQUARTERS)
208 S. Great Rd.
Lincoln, MA 01773
(781) 259-2200
massaudubon.org/drumlin

Drumlin Farm is the headquarters of the Massachusetts Audubon Society, a working farm and a wildlife sanctuary. In the farmyard there are several barns where you can visit the sheep, pigs, chickens, and cows. Drop-in seasonal farm activities include maple sugaring in the winter and sheep shearing in the spring. The skunks, owls, hawks, and foxes that live at the sanctuary are here because they have been injured or orphaned and can't return to the wild. Easy hiking trails through woods and cultivated fields are a wonderful way for families to explore nature together. End your visit with a hayride, available in the spring, summer, and fall. The gift shop stocks everything avian including feeders, binoculars, and high end nature-themed gift items. And be sure to stop by the farm stand for Drumlin-grown vegetables, berries, eggs, and wool products. Drumlin Farm summer camp programs for preschoolers through early teens get high marks for the variety of hands-on nature activities and enthusiastic staff. Closed Mon (except some holidays).

GOOD HARBOR BEACH
Thatcher Road
Gloucester, MA 01930

There is always plenty of blanket space but come early (or late afternoon) to claim your parking spot in the public lot (there's a fee in season) before it fills up at this beautiful dune-backed mile-long stretch of white-sand beach. It's a barrier beach, and at high tide there are just-right waves for Boogie Board surfing. At low tide walk across the revealed sandbar to explore nearby Salt Island. Amenities include restrooms, outdoor showers, and a concession stand.

HALIBUT POINT STATE PARK
Gott Avenue
Rockport, MA 01966
(978) 546-2997
mass.gov/dcr/parks/northeast/halb.htm

Good things do come in small packages, and this relatively short ocean ramble (just over 1 mile) offers quite the reward: views of Crane Beach in Ipswich, New Hampshire's Isles of Shoals, and Maine's Mount Agamenticus. At what was once a granite quarry, you can soak in the scenery by sitting on the large, flat boulders that line this part of the coast. At low tide the crashing waves leave behind salty tidal pools in the rocks that teem with snails and horseshoe crabs. Halibut Point is also a great spot to view seabirds like loons and grebes and if you are lucky, sometimes seals.

JOPPA FLATS SANCTUARY
    (MASSACHUSETTS AUDUBON)
1 Plum Island Turnpike
Newburyport, MA 01950
(978) 462-9998
massaudubon.org

Experienced birders know that their life list can be expanded without any great effort by a trek to Joppa Flats because the sanctuary is a stopover for migratory birds along the Atlantic flyway. Located at the mouth of the Merrimack River where it spills into the Atlantic Ocean, Joppa Flats also supports a healthy population of native shorebirds, such as plovers and sandpipers. Budding naturalists can learn about birds and coastal ecosystems through hands-on activities at the Education Center, such as helping collect and identify freshwater specimens and observing the seals and birds native to the area. Open Tues through Sun and Mon holidays.

PARKER RIVER NATIONAL WILDLIFE REFUGE
6 Plum Island Turnpike
Newburyport, MA 01950
(978) 465-5753
fws.gov/northeast/parkerriver
Named for the wild beach plums that still grow here, this 11-mile barrier island is located off the coasts of Newburyport, Newbury, and Ipswich. The island is connected to the mainland by a causeway and is home to both the Parker River National Wildlife Refuge and Massachusetts Audubon's **Joppa Flats Sanctuary** (see p. 97). Nearly 300 species of migratory birds and waterfowl visit Plum Island seasonally. Hone your observation skills and take one of the free naturalist-guided tours that leave from the visitor center. The beaches within the refuge are open to the public. And although there are few beach amenities (no food concessions or showers), most visitors are content to soak up the tranquil beauty. Know, too, that birds have priority—the beaches are closed during piping plover nesting season.

SINGING BEACH
119 Beach St.
Manchester-by-the-Sea, MA 01944
(978) 526-7276
manchester.ma.us/pages/manchester
ma_recreation/singingbeach
What Singing Beach lacks in access—unless you have a magic resident beach sticker, parking is extremely limited—it more than makes up in sheer beauty. This

is one of the most desirable beaches in New England, with a ½-mile swath of fine sand and sparkling-clean water. This beach really is musical—take off your flip-flops and when you walk across the wet sand it squeaks! Note: In season, a walk-on beach fee is collected (children ages 12 and under are free).

> **i** The Singing Beach lot is for residents only Friday through Sunday and fills up early the other days of the week. There is some metered parking in Manchester but it has a 2-hour limit. On weekends your best bet is to park and pay at the commuter rail lot run by the Boy Scouts or better yet, consider taking the Rockport commuter line to Manchester-by-the-Sea and follow everyone else to the beach.

WALDEN POND
915 Walden St.
Concord, MA 01742
(978) 369-3252
mass.gov/dcr/parks/walden
"I went to the woods because I wanted to lived deliberately, to front only the essential facts of life." Thoreau built his 1-room cabin next to Walden Pond on land that at the time was owned by his friend Ralph Waldo Emerson. Thoreau's 2-year experiment in solitary living served as the basis for *Walden*, published in 1854. There is a replica of the cabin next to the parking lot. If you are looking for peace and tranquility, walk the 2-mile trail that circumnavigates the pond. But come early in the summer; the pond is part of a state park and is a popular swimming destination.

WINGAERSHEEK BEACH
Gloucester, MA 01930
Situated between the Annisquam River and Ipswich Bay, Wing Beach has soft white sand, mild water (in the 70s), and few waves, making it a good pick for families. When the tide recedes (as much as a mile), timid toddlers can splash about and bigger kids will love exploring the teeming tide pools left behind. Families will appreciate the beach amenities here: close parking (there's a fee in season), a concession stand, restrooms, and outdoor showers.

Wildlife & Zoos

THE BUTTERFLY PLACE
120 Tyngsboro Rd.
Westford, MA 01886
(978) 392-0955
butterflyplace-ma.com
Walking along the flower-lined paths in the greenhouse atrium here can transform even the coldest New England winter day into a magical summer escape. In this lush tropical setting, hundreds of butterflies float and flit about the lantanas and purple coneflowers. Color charts help with identification and a guide is always on hand along the path to point out the butterflies that may be camouflaged underneath a leaf. Bring a camera and wear brightly colored clothing—you never know if a butterfly might land on you.

WOLF HOLLOW
114 Essex Rd.
Ipswich, MA 01938
(978) 356-0216
wolfhollowipswich.org
Since 1990 Wolf Hollow has been dedicated to the preservation of wolves and the education of the general public to dispel wolf-related myths. During a 1-hour structured presentation, you'll get to meet several of these canines and observe wolf-pack behavior (which has much in common with human families) in action. Each session ends with a group howl—sometimes the pack answers back! Apr through Nov presentations are given on Sat and Sun; Dec through Mar presentations are on Sun only; check website for time.

ACTIVITIES & EVENTS

Arts Venues

NORTH SHORE MUSIC THEATER
62 Dunham Rd.
Beverly, MA 01915
(978) 232-7200
nsmt.org
The North Shore Music Theater is popular for its slick, professional productions of musicals. The 1,750-seat in-the-round theater is an intimate space to enjoy *Cats* and *The Sound of Music* along with an annual production of *A Christmas Carol*. A children's theater series with small-scale productions, such as *Snow White* and *Charlotte's Web*, is staged as well.

PAUL E. TSONGAS CENTER AT UMASS LOWELL
300 Martin L. King Jr. Way
Lowell, MA 01852
(978) 934-5760
tsongascenter.com
The Tsongas Center is home ice for UMass Lowell ice hockey and programs everything from business conventions to local high school graduations in an adaptable space that ranges from 6,500 to 7,800 seats. Shows include major rock and pop acts as well as touring family shows, such as the Harlem Globetrotters and *Scooby Doo Live*.

Cruises

CAPE ANN WHALE WATCH
415 Main St.
Gloucester, MA 01930
(800) 877-5110
seethewhales.com

Seeing a whale up close and personal is an awe-inspiring experience. Humpbacks, finbacks, minkes—they all spend the summer feeding in the waters of the Stellwagen Bank Marine Sanctuary off the coast. Cape Ann Whale Watch operates May through Oct, sending out 2 cruises daily during the high season (July and Aug) from Gloucester Harbor. A naturalist accompanies each trip to identify the species and explain whale behavior and feeding habits—many of the whales are old friends to the crew and are named and tracked.

ESSEX RIVER CRUISES
35 Dodge St.
Essex, MA 01929
(978) 768-6981
essexcruises.com

If you are eco-minded, take a narrated cruise aboard the *Essex River Queen,* a covered pontoon boat. As it wends along the wildlife-rich coastal Essex River estuary, scan the skies for peregrine falcons and the banks for osprey nests. Cruises are offered daily May through Oct; check ahead to confirm departure time.

Festivals & Annual Events

HAUNTED HAPPENINGS
Venues throughout the city
Salem, MA 01970
hauntedhappenings.org

Salem, also known as "Witch City," celebrates the holiday right with an entire month of events. The Haunted Happenings festival includes a parade, costumed ball, carnival midway, children's fair, and haunting-themed tours at many of the city's historic sites (with extended evening hours). It all culminates on Halloween night when Salem becomes the center of the Halloween universe with throngs of costumed revelers partying in the streets with fireworks over the harbor.

LOWELL FOLK FESTIVAL
Venues throughout downtown
Lowell, MA 01852
(978) 970-5000
lowellfolkfestival.org

Tap your toes to zydeco, klezmer, polka, mariachi, and the blues at the country's largest free folk festival, which is held on 6 outdoor stages the last full weekend in July. The festival's food offerings are another highlight, reflecting Lowell's cultural diversity with dishes from Liberia, Laos, Greece, and more.

✳ROCKPORT CHAMBER MUSIC
 FESTIVAL
37 Main St.
Rockport, MA 01966
(978) 546-7391
rcmf.org

It's hard to find a more gorgeous setting for music than the Shalin Liu Performance Center, perched on the edge of the Atlantic. A 2-story "window to the sea" serves as the backdrop for concerts in this intimate, 330-seat chamber recital hall. The smartly programmed festival takes place in June and July and typically features more than 20 concerts. Past guest artists have included pianist Leon Fleisher, violinist Anne Akiko Meyers, and the Grammy-winning Parker String Quartet.

TOPSFIELD FAIR
207 Boston St.
Topsfield, MA 01983
(978) 887-5000
topsfieldfair.org
Sleepy Topsfield is home to New England's oldest county fair, a North Shore autumn tradition since 1818. For 10 days in early October, you'll find prize livestock in the 4-H barn, mutant pumpkins, and a giant midway.

Fishing

TUNA HUNTER
75 Essex Ave.
Gloucester, MA 01930
(978) 546-7992
tunahunter.com
Giant tuna weighing more than 300 pounds are not uncommon on the Gloucester docks. Tuna Hunter charters offers half-or full-day deepwater angling fishing trips in search of tuna and striped bass.

Health & Wellness

LATITUDE SPORTS CLUB
194 Newbury St.
Peabody, MA 01960
(978) 536-0777
latitudesportsclubs.com
With its 5 locations, convenience is a huge part of this family-owned North Shore fitness chain's appeal. The abundance of strength and cardio equipment at each location means there's no waiting for a machine and each club features a full schedule of dance, yoga, Zumba, and spin classes. The Peabody location has the most amenities, including an indoor pool, indoor tennis courts, indoor track, regulation basketball court, and a climbing wall. See the website for additional locations.

MAISON ESTHETIQUE
94 High St.
Danvers, MA 01923
(978) 777-7278
malsonesthetique.net
Set in a plush Victorian, this spa is an intimate retreat. Think overstuffed sofas and a fireplace in the lounge, European-style treatment rooms, and a grotto-like hot-tub space. Facials are the spa's specialty, though they also offer a range of other wonderful services including manicures and pedicures as well as nonsurgical medical procedures like Botox and laser treatments. For your first experience, try the seasonal-fruit body peel and massage and you'll float out the door, ready to face the world again.

Hiking, Biking & Walking

THE MINUTEMAN BIKEWAY
End points are at South Street in Bedford and the Alewife T station in Cambridge
minutemanbikeway.org
Turn up the foot power. The flat, 11-mile paved Minuteman Bikeway is an off-road trail that is separate from traffic and follows the old Boston and Maine Railroad line through the picturesque towns of Bedford, Lexington, Arlington, and Cambridge. Keep in mind that it is one of the country's most used bike paths and can be busy with strollers and runners.

Kidstuff

BAREFOOT BOOKS
89 Thoreau St.
Concord, MA 01742
(978) 369-1770
barefootbooks.com
Barefoot Books is an independent children's publisher, and this fabulously fun shop is

devoted to the company's charming collection of storybooks. Spend an hour here with your kids and you will leave with loads of books. The well-rounded selection is geared toward preschoolers through beginning readers and favors international and multicultural stories like *Up and Down the Andes* and retellings of classic kids' favorites like *The Twelve Dancing Princesses*. The store holds daily story times (sometime twice daily) and offers free drop-in art and yoga classes. There is also a paint-your-own pottery studio.

THE DISCOVERY MUSEUMS
177 Main St.
Acton, MA 01720
(978) 264-4200
discoverymuseums.org
The Discovery Museums in Acton has a two-museums-in-one format. The pretty Victorian house is the site of the Children's Discovery Museum, which is all about play and geared toward very young children. Here, at Bessie's Diner, preschoolers delight in pretending to make and serve meals to their parents or pull and set a lobster trap at the outdoor ship play space. Older siblings will enjoy the next-door Science Museum, which focuses on interactive science and nature exhibits. A favorite is the SoundLab, where kids can pretend to be an audio engineer and have fun mixing sounds. Closed Mon (although the museum is generally open on holiday Mondays).

IMAJINETHAT
354 Merrimack St.
Lawrence, MA 01843
(978) 682-5338
imajinethat.com
For an educational slant to your preschooler's indoor play, Imajinethat can't be beat.

Located in a historic mill building in revitalized downtown Lawrence, this is one of the area's largest indoor play spaces and features a dinosaur climbing structure, bouncy house, play grocery store, arts and crafts area, and infant and toddler area. Staff-led storytelling and music activities are scheduled throughout the week and the cafe stocks healthy snack options, such as fruit cups, salads, juice, and yogurt. Imajinethat also offers parent workshops and themed birthday packages.

*KIMBALL FARM
400 Littleton Rd.
Westford, MA 01886
(978) 486-3891
kimballfarm.com
Minigolf, bumper boats, and ice cream—fun-seeking families have been flocking to Kimball Farms for generations, and for good reason. The two challenging 18-hole minigolf courses are attractively landscaped with water features and flowering plants. Other fun family activity options include a driving range, batting cages, a bumper boat pond, and a petting zoo. After all that playtime, finish up with Kimball's famous homemade ice cream. The Kimball Special has 3 softball-size scoops of ice cream and a choice of toppings. Double dare someone in your family to finish it. The season generally runs Apr through Oct.

THE WENHAM MUSEUM
132 Main St.
Wenham, MA 01984
(978) 468-2377
wenhammuseum.org
Step back in time at the Wenham Museum, which celebrates the treasures of childhood in New England from the 17th century to

today. The exhibits include an extensive collection of dolls, a room full of operating model trains, and a fine collection of 19th- and 20th-century toys including toy soldiers, dollhouses, and mechanical toys. In the Family Discovery Room kids can dress in colonial costumes, play with puppets, and build with blocks. Bring the grandparents; this is a wonderful museum for intergenerational fun. Closed Mon.

Nightlife

CAPE ANN BREWING COMPANY
11 Rogers St.
Gloucester, MA 01930
(978) 282-7399
capeannbrewing.com
This Gloucester brewpub is a magnet for those seeking good food and company—not to mention great beer. There is a varied selection of 6 to 8 house-brewed ales on tap, including the well-known Fisherman's Brew lager and seasonal offerings. The menu is expansive, including everything from fresh fish cakes to sirloin tips to linguine with seafood. Come on Tuesday and Saturday nights for live music.

VIC'S BOATHOUSE
86 Wharf St.
Salem, MA 01970
(978) 745-3400
vicsboathouse.com
The liveliest happy hour on the North Shore may be at this Salem waterfront hangout where everyone seems to know everyone else's name. Come more than once, and the bartenders will know your name, too. Vic's is part of the Victoria Station restaurant; it offers a full bar with craft brews and a traditional pub menu with a few modern twists like flatbread pizzas and turkey burger sliders. There's live music 3 nights a week and

karaoke and open-mic nights the rest of the week. In warm weather the patio or the dock is the perfect excuse for an après-dinner drink (or two).

Skiing & Snow Tubing

AMESBURY SPORTS PARK
12 South Hunt Rd.
Amesbury, MA 01913
(978) 388-5788
goslide.com
Get tubular! Amesbury Sports Park has a fast hill, snowmaking, and 2 rope tow lifts that make it easy to enjoy fun in the snow. Although you can go snow tubing in jeans, soggy pants are not fun—snow pants (and waterproof gloves) are a good idea.

GREAT BROOK SKI TOURING CENTER
AT GREAT BROOK FARM STATE PARK
1018 Lowell Rd.
Carlisle, MA 01741
(978) 369-7486
greatbrookski.com
Enjoy the rustic beauty of cross-country skiing at Great Brook. The 10 miles of machine-groomed trails meander through rolling farmland and quiet woods. Cross-country ski and snowshoe rentals are available. The rustic lodge is a converted barn where you can sit by a wood stove and sip hot cocoa or soup after your trek. There is night skiing "under the lights" on Tuesday and Thursday evening, when a 1-mile trail loop is lit by lanterns. Enchanting.

NASHOBA VALLEY SKI AREA AND
SNOW TUBING PARK
79 Powers Rd.
Westford, MA 01886
(978) 692-3033
skinashoba.com

Nashoba Valley is well-known as a family-oriented, learn-to-ski mountain. There are 7 trails that are serviced by 4 chairlifts, a terrain park for snowboarders, and a separate snow tubing area. There are lessons for kids as young as age 3 and even race lessons for the more advanced skier. Nashoba's snow tubing park is the largest in New England, with 18 lanes and 4 tow lifts, so there is hardly ever a wait to get to the top of the hill.

Spectator Sports

LOWELL SPINNERS AT EDWARD LELACHEUR PARK
450 Aiken St.
Lowell, MA 01854
(978) 459-1674
lowellspinners.com

Tickets to Red Sox games can be hard to come by, but it is easy to score tickets to the Lowell Spinners, a Red Sox Minor League A affiliate. Located on the banks of the Merrimack River, LeLacheur is a newer, small park (just 5,000 seats) with an appealing old-time feel. Activities are geared toward families, with lots of entertainment between innings and promotions throughout the season including a very popular annual bobble-head giveaway. You might even catch a future pro-baseball star—Jonathan Papelbon, Jacoby Ellsbury, and Clay Buchholz each did a stint here before making it to the big leagues.

> **i** The Lowell Spinners' 2003 bobblehead doll of native son and Beat Generation author Jack Kerouac earned it a spot in the National Baseball Hall of Fame in Cooperstown, New York.

Water Sports

NORTH SHORE KAYAK OUTDOOR CENTER
9 Tuna Wharf
Rockport, MA 01966
(978) 546-5050
northshorekayak.com

This outfitter specializes in guided sea kayak tours for all levels of paddlers. First-timers can enjoy a fine day in the harbor with a short, 2-hour guided paddle to Straitsmouth Island and an up-close view of the lighthouse. Seasoned paddlers can sign on for the 3½-hour round-trip Thacher Island tour, which allows time to go ashore and climb the island's twin lighthouses.

SOUTH BRIDGE BOAT HOUSE
496 Main St.
Concord, MA 01966
(978) 369-9438
canoeconcord.com

As your canoe slices through the calm waters of the Concord River, it's easy to imagine how this waterway inspired Emerson, Hawthorne, and Thoreau. South Bridge rents a variety of canoes and kayaks and will make sure you know the rudiments before you set out. It's a leisurely paddle by the Old Manse to reach the Old North Bridge of "shot heard 'round the world" fame. Open mid-April through Oct, hours change seasonally; call in advance.

SHOPPING

Antiques

ANDREW SPINDLER ANTIQUES
163 Main St.
Essex, MA 01929
(978) 768-6045
spindlerantiques.com

A converted 18th-century barn with a modern gallery feel is the setting for this collection of antiques and art. The stylish and eclectic collection includes big-ticket furniture as well as smaller accents such as silver, mercury glass, lighting, and white ironstone. It is a collection of the highest order, most of which "reads" modern and works well in today's homes. Closed Tues.

Art

ROCKY NECK ART COLONY
53 Rocky Neck Ave.
Gloucester, MA 01930
(978) 282-0917
rockyneckartcolony.org

Rocky Neck is a slender spit of land that juts out into Gloucester Harbor. With its pretty cove, weathered fishing shacks, and ever-changing light, the "Neck" has attracted artists for more than 150 years. Fitz Henry Lane, Winslow Homer, Childe Hassan, and Edward Hopper are only a handful of painters with ties to the area. Today, Rocky Neck has dozens of galleries and studios. Much of the art scene revolves around the Rocky Neck Gallery (53 Rocky Neck Ave.; 978-282-0917), a juried cooperative of 30 local artists featuring original art and fine crafts. The Rocky Neck season is generally Memorial Day through Labor Day; in the off-season check with individual galleries for hours.

Beauty

PLUM ISLAND SOAP COMPANY
205 Northern Blvd.
Newburyport, MA 01950
(978) 465-0238
plumislandsoap.com

Handmade soap is one of life's little luxuries. The Plum Island Soap Company makes its all-natural and handcrafted small-batch soap and skincare products on the premises of this quaint shop on Plum Island. All the ingredients are pronounceable and the products—like the green mud soap scented with ylang-ylang oil and lavender—smell nice, look pretty, and nourish your skin. Service is very one-on-one and the shop stocks the company's entire line, including lip balms, body scrubs for women, and their best-selling Man-Can just for the guys: Fisherman's scrub soap, Spicy shave gel, Bay Rum moisturizer, and more packed in a nifty gallon paint can.

Books

ANDOVER BOOKSTORE
89R Main St.
Andover, MA 01810
(978) 475-0143
hugobookstores.com

Buy your books from the second oldest bookstore in America. This 2-story bookshop dating from 1809 has a wonderfully atmospheric feel with books and chairs scattered throughout. In the winter, patrons are encouraged to curl up in a wing chair by the fire with their finds. The store is an active bookseller; events include author talks, weekly children's story time, and fiber-arts classes for kids and adults. Its book and wine club is a novel combination.

CONCORD BOOKSHOP
65 Main St.
Concord, MA 01742
(978) 369-2405
concordbookshop.com

Concord has a strong literary heritage and this is reflected in the Concord bookshop's choice of titles (lots of local-interest and children's books), its author events, and the knowledge of the staff. Located on Main Street, with pretty window displays (one window changing weekly is always dedicated to a community partner or event like the Concord Orchestra or the elementary school geography bee), the store is popular with locals and tourists alike.

JABBERWOCKY BOOK SHOP
50 Water St.
Newburyport, MA 01950
(978) 465-9359
jabberwockybookshop.com

Housed in a 2-story renovated mill building with soaring timbered ceilings, the largest independent bookstore on the North Shore has an extraordinary range of titles and has been a fixture in the Newburyport community for more than 40 years. The store hosts many author events (often featuring local authors) and is one of the principal sponsors of the annual Newburyport Literary Festival. You'll find the staff is unfailingly helpful and genuinely excited about the stock. Be sure to check out the deeply discounted "once-read" books in the Green Room.

Farmers' Markets & Pick Your Own

HONEY POT HILL ORCHARDS
144 Sudbury Rd.
Stow, MA 01775
(978) 562-5666
honeypothill.com

Acres and acres of apples—over 200 acres. Honey Pot Hill is an especially scenic farm that has been an apple-picking destination for generations of New Englanders. Take a hayride through the scenic orchards, where you'll typically find 12 varieties of apples during the u-pick season. Be sure to stop by the Appleshop, which is well stocked with

caramel apples, cider donuts, and apple pies. The kids will want to visit the "three little pigs" in the barn and will beg to be allowed to get lost in Honey Pot Hill's awesome privet hedge mazes. The Honeypot season begins with the blueberry u-pick crop in June and the farm stand is open through Christmas selling apples and Christmas trees. Cash only.

SMOLAK FARMS
315 S. Bradford St.
North Andover, MA 01845
(978) 682-6332
smolakfarms.com

Take your pick: In the summer Smolak Farms has pick-your-own strawberries, blueberries, peaches, and plums. Return in the fall, when Smolak offers a good mix of old, antique, and modern apples for picking. In the fall there's a festival atmosphere with weekend hayrides and a barn where kids can say hello to the farm animals. The Smolak bakery is famous for its apple cider donuts and delectable fruit pies. Local favorite Treadwell's ice cream is sold at the ice cream stand—cones along with hand-packed quarts, to go with that pie. Open spring through Dec; hours change seasonally; check website for hours.

WILSON FARM
10 Pleasant St.
Lexington, MA 02421
(781) 862-3900
wilsonfarm.com

Much more than a farm stand, family-owned Wilson's is an 8,500-square-foot showcase barn that offers one-stop shopping year-round. In the summer, the vegetables here are better than fresh off the truck—they're from the 30 acres of farmland out back (or Wilson's 500 additional acres in New Hampshire). The daily selection of prepared foods feature the absolute best of the season—including homemade soups, entrees, and desserts. CSA (community-supported agriculture) shares are available for produce, fish, and flowers, so you have an excuse to come back weekly. Besides the farm-fresh eggs, milk, cheese, and groceries, you can pick up nursery plants for your own garden.

Fashion & Shoes

BOBBLES & LACE
92 Washington St.
Marblehead, MA 01945
(781) 631-0190
bobblesandlace.com
These North Shore boutiques cater to the modern, young fashionista with lots of options at not-crazy prices. The emphasis is on basics, be it a sheer lace blouse or a slim knit skirt with an exposed zipper, that mix well with items already in your closet. Then pull it all together with eye-catching accessories like a beaded bib-style necklace or a funky gold-studded wristlet. Check the website for additional locations.

FRENCH + ITALIAN
129 Washington St.
Marblehead, MA 01945
(781) 639-5129
frenchitalian.com
Browse these racks for covetable pieces that exude European flair, including superb Italian wool pullovers, fete-ready dresses, impeccable silk blouses, and lots of scarves. Everything is timeless, with a touch of edge. Closed Sun and Mon.

Gifts

THE PAPER MERMAID
57 Main St.
Rockport, MA 01966
(978) 546-3553
papermermaid.com
This adorable shop is brimming with eye-catching gifts like brightly colored bags and candles and delicate Japanese paper earrings, not to mention one-of-a-kind greeting cards (the very best kind) and an array of stationery and gift wrap in a staggering variety of colors and textures. Particularly nice, too, is the selection of toys, books, and games for kids, including Automoblox vintage wood toy cars.

THE PEWTER SHOP
16 Bearskin Neck
Rockport, MA 01966
(978) 546-2105
rockport-pewter.com
Located on Bearskin Neck, this nearly eight-decade-old shop sells mostly American-made pewter products, some of which are handcrafted by local artisans. You can get anything from a sand-dollar necklace to colonial candlesticks and a lobster-claw bottle opener; the Christmas tree ornaments are very popular souvenirs.

Specialty Foods

✳A+J KING ARTISAN BAKERS
48 Central St.
Salem, MA 01970
(978) 744-4881
ajkingbakery.com
This Paris-by-way-of-Salem bakery/cafe satisfies locals and visitors with its traditional, handmade baguettes and buttery sugared brioche. Among the specialty offerings is a

MERRIMACK VALLEY & NORTH SHORE

gorgeous brown butter cake and a super-aromatic semolina apricot fennel bread. There is a delicious assortment of skillfully crafted sandwiches, too. The Vietnamese ham sandwich, for instance, is perfection: smoked ham with pickled vegetables, cilantro, and house-made mayo on a ciabatta roll. Get there early on weekends; they often sell out of baked goods before noon.

✳HARBOR SWEETS
85 Leavitt St.
Salem, MA 01970
(978) 745-7648
harborsweets.com
The bewitching aroma of rich chocolate is intoxicating at this small redbrick factory. This artisan New England chocolate maker has been churning out confections since 1973 and is best known for its iconic Sweet Sloops, a sailboat-shaped butter crunch covered in white chocolate with a dark chocolate hull. Public tours are given Tues and Thurs at 11 a.m. The store stocks a full array of Harbor Sweets chocolates and all visitors are offered a full-size chocolate sample. Closed Sun.

ACCOMMODATIONS

Inns & Bed-and-Breakfasts

BLUE, THE INN ON THE BEACH $$–$$$
20 Fordham Way
Newbury, MA 01951
(978) 465-7171
blueinn.com
The blue glass pebble walkway is the first sign that this is not your typical "olde New England" inn. Located on Plum Island—and close to the Parker River National Wildlife Refuge—this romantic beachfront property exudes an air of relaxed luxury. There are

only 14 rooms to go around, but they are all spacious and feature a white-on-white color scheme, flat-screen TVs, a separate seating area with either a gas or wood-burning fireplace, and a shared or private outdoor deck. Continental breakfast is included in all rates and arrives at your door in a picnic basket. Outside, enjoy the hotel's private beach and 2 hot tubs.

✳CONCORD'S COLONIAL INN $$–$$$
48 Monument Sq.
Concord, MA 01742
(978) 369-9200
concordscolonialinn.com
At this two-plus-century hospitality spot overlooking Concord's Monument Square, you can stay in cozy colonial-era rooms in the main inn. With exposed beams, original wood flooring, and period furniture, these rooms are as comfortable as they are historic. The rooms in the inn's newer wing had a major makeover in 2012 and are wonderfully up-to-date with flat-screen TVs and a contemporary style that is anything but fusty. Either way, be sure to spend some time on the inn's famed front porch whiling away an hour reading or people-watching.

✳EMERSON INN BY THE SEA $$
1 Cathedral Ave.
Rockport, MA 01966
(978) 546-6321
emersoninnbythesea.com
Located in Rockport's residential Pigeon Cove neighborhood, this grand 19th-century inn is a town landmark. The sweeping views of the Atlantic Ocean from the expansive veranda are picture-postcard perfect. The hotel is named for Ralph Waldo Emerson, who was once a guest at the hotel; look for framed quotations by the poet/

philosopher in the parlor and dining room. Each of the inn's 36 modernized rooms has a private bath (some have spa tubs) and is handsomely decorated in blue or red toile fabrics and cherrywood furniture. All rates include breakfast (buffet in the summer and fall, continental in the winter and spring). Behind the hotel is a large heated outdoor pool. And although the hotel is away from Rockport's hubbub, it is still close enough for a pleasant walk to Bearskin Neck's shops and restaurants.

ℹ️ The small red fishing shack on Rockport Harbor is instantly recognizable. Known as Motif No. 1, it has been a favorite subject of countless sketches, paintings, and photographs since the 1920s.

THE INN AT CASTLE HILL $$–$$$
280 Argilla Rd.
Ipswich, MA 01938
(978) 412-2555
thetrustees.org/the-inn-at-castle-hill
This elegant oceanfront inn provides a comfortable retreat on the grounds of the Crane Estate and is a short walk to Crane Beach, one of the most picturesque swimming beaches in all of New England. The grandeur is in the details here. Each of the inn's 10 guest rooms has a private bath and has its own distinct style and character with its own color scheme and custom furnishings. The inn is a quiet refuge; there are no TVs, but Wi-Fi is available (if you insist). A full gourmet breakfast and tea on the veranda are included in all rates.

Hotels & Motels

HAWTHORNE HOTEL $$–$$$
18 Washington St.
Salem, MA 01970
(978) 744-4080
hawthornehotel.com
In the heart of Salem, overlooking the Common and across the street from the Peabody Essex Museum, this historic hotel dates from 1925 but is in tip-top shape thanks to a recent refurbishment of its 93 rooms and suites. The idiosyncratic rooms present a handsome decor with cherrywood furnishings, warm hues, and refreshed linens. Even the smallest rooms are thoughtfully appointed with modernized bathrooms, flat-screen TVs, and free Wi-Fi. The Hawthorne is also known for its fabulous weekly Sunday jazz brunch and seasonal afternoon tea events. If you dare, ask about room 612—it's said to be haunted.

SALEM WATERFRONT HOTEL & MARINA $$–$$$
225 Derby St.
Salem, MA 01970
(978) 740-8788
salemwaterfronthotel.com
The waterfront location and views only slightly outshine the pleasant accommodations of this 6-story hotel, which features sunny rooms and a smart decor with contemporary furnishings, flat-screen TVs, free Wi-Fi, and a soothing taupe and beige palette. The Regatta Pub is a cozy spot for a casual meal or late-night bite; then you can unwind in the indoor heated pool or hit the fitness room. You can't beat the location on Pickering Wharf—Salem's sites are just a short stroll away.

RESTAURANTS

American

CENTRO   **$$**
24 Market St.
Lowell, MA 01852
(978) 453-4630
centrolowell.com

With high-caliber ingredients and unfussy presentations, this eatery draws locals and visitors alike for American comfort classics like chicken, cheddar, and apple paninis at lunch, and peppercorn beef filet and pistachio-crusted wild salmon at dinner. Or swing by the bar for surprisingly creative drinks and snacks, such as duck confit spring rolls.

SCRATCH KITCHEN   **$-$$**
245 Derby St.
Salem, MA 01970
(978) 741-2442
scratchkitchensalem.com

This cheery 40-seat eatery is open for lunch and dinner, serving innovative sandwiches piled high on oven-fresh bread. It's hard not to love the North Carolina–style pulled pork sandwich, and the cider-brined turkey with cranberry shallot marmalade and Gouda is a favorite of tourists. Check out the chalkboard for the wine and beer (draft and bottled) offerings to have with the house-cut fries with blue cheese fondue while you wait. Closed Mon.

Breakfast & Lunch

KANE'S DOUGHNUTS   **$**
120 Lincoln St.
Saugus, MA 01906
(781) 233-8499
kanesdonuts.com

Locals have been coming to Kane's since 1955 for the huge, fluffy honey-dipped doughnuts.

Recently named one of the top doughnut shops in the country by *Bon Appétit,* the shop now sees out-of-town multitudes join the lines and cram the small traditional shop. The coffee rolls are another tasty treat and can easily be shared by 3 or 4 people.

✳SUGAR MAGNOLIA'S   **$-$$**
112 Main St.
Gloucester, MA 01930
(978) 281-5310
sugarmags.com

The service is always warm at this Gloucester favorite. At Sugar Magnolia's, on the Main Street drag, visitors and locals flock for the packed omelets and especially for the carrot-cake pancakes slathered with maple cream cheese butter. On the lighter side there are bowls of fresh fruit with yogurt and at lunch there's an extensive menu of sandwiches and inventive salads.

WENHAM TEA HOUSE   **$-$$**
4 Monument St.
Wenham, MA 01984
(978) 468-1398
wenhamteahouse.com

Established in 1912, this little teahouse is reminiscent of days gone by. Fluffy omelets at breakfast and a classic lunch with the girls' menu of salads, soups, and sandwiches make way in the afternoon for scones, pastries, and pots of tea. There's also a selection of wine and beer—and in good weather, patio garden seating awaits. Delightful! Closed Mon.

Cafes & Coffeehouses

GULU GULU CAFE   **$**
247 Essex St.
Salem, MA 01970
(978) 740-8892
gulugulucafe.com

A salon, cafe, bar (beer and wine), and performance space—Gulu Gulu Cafe is all of these things. A diverse crowd gathers here day and night to tap away on their laptops (there's free Wi-Fi) and in the evening listen to a wide range of live entertainment. Ideal for a quick and affordable bite, the small kitchen turns out superb crepes (both sweet and savory) throughout the day as well as excellent coffee and enticing baked goods, plus a nice range of soups, salads, cheese plates, and sandwiches. There's patio seating in fine weather.

JAHO COFFEE & TEA   **$**
197 Derby St.
(978) 744-4300
Salem, MA 01970
jaho.com
If you need a jolt of java, the 2 Jaho Salem shops offer steady, reliable espresso drinks made from their own perfectly roasted beans. If you're adventurous (and patient), Jaho offers pour-over, press, siphon, or Chemex-style by-the-cup preparation. Both branches are spacious with lots of cafe seating; a second location (60 Wharf St.; 978-745-8322) houses the roastery and has a more hipster aesthetic, while the Derby Street location has sidewalk seating, is open later (until 11 p.m.), and attracts a more varied cross section of customers. Both branches serve pastries, gelato, and sandwiches, too.

NASHOBA BROOK BAKERY   **$**
152 Commonwealth Ave.
West Concord, MA 01742
(978) 318-1999
slowrise.com
This is the production facility for favorite regional artisan bread maker Nashoba Brook. It's also West Concord's neighborhood go-to bakery/cafe and is worth seeking out after visiting Concord's historic sites for a superb lunch of sandwiches, soups, cookies, scones, and coffee. The traditional slow-rise breads that are baked here throughout the day are used in the cafe sandwiches. Cheddar cheese, apple, and arugula on walnut and cranberry–studded Harvest bread, a cup of minestrone soup, and a lemon shortbread cookie make for a very nice lunch.

Deli

NEILLIO'S GOURMET KITCHEN   **$**
53 Bedford St.
Lexington, MA 02420
(781) 861-8466
neillioscatering.com
Everything is handmade at Neillio's: beef brisket, chicken Parmesan, and jambalaya—this is home cooking at its best. The lunch hour star is the Turkey Terrific: hand-carved fresh roast turkey with cranberry and stuffing served between whole-grain bread. There are no seats, but your sandwich can be brown-bagged to be enjoyed on Lexington Green.

Eclectic

ALCHEMY BISTRO   **$$**
3 Duncan St.
Gloucester, MA 01930
(978) 281-3997
alchemybistro.com
This funky, welcoming (and boisterous) space presents a shareable menu (both small plates and platters) with heavy Mediterranean influences and an emphasis on organic. Nosh on dishes like the fennel sausage flatbreads, confit duck pierogies, and crispy fried local turnips with lemon and thyme aioli. As you would expect with a

name like Alchemy, there is a strong bar program—from a refreshing Yuzu Gimlet to a "Perfect Storm" Dark and Stormy. It's a great choice for Sunday brunch, too; live bluegrass jazz accompanied by indulgent lobster eggs Benedict or standout blueberry pancakes, either chased by a classic Bloody Mary, of course.

Ice Cream

WHITE FARMS ICE CREAM $
326 High St.
Ipswich, MA 01938
(978) 356-2633

This nostalgic roadside ice cream stand is just a couple miles down the road from Crane Beach and is the place to go after a day spent swimming. It is easy to find, too—just look for the cow on the roof. The ice cream is homemade, sourced from local farms and churned into the essence of summer. White Farms boasts more than 60 flavors, with 30 or so available on any given day. If it's on the menu, Caramel Cow is the one to have—vanilla ice cream with a caramel swirl and both white and chocolate chips.

Italian

✳L'ANDANA $$$
86 Cambridge St.
Burlington, MA 01803
(781) 270-0100
landanagrill.com

Boston chef Jamie Mammano (Teatro, Mistral, Sorrelina) brings big-city dining to the suburbs with a Tuscan farmhouse-like space that is always warm with laughter and flowing wine. Wood-grilled meat is the cornerstone of the menu with dishes like a succulent veal chop with Marsala and a grilled rib eye based on the classic *bistecca*

Fiorentina. The hearty, authentic regional pastas are superb and desserts are wonderful, too, especially the intoxicatingly rich chocolate *crema*.

Mediterranean

✳CEIA KITCHEN + BAR $$–$$$
38 State St.
Newburyport, MA 01950
(978) 358-8112
ceia-newburyport.com

Just two years old, Ceia has a serious following, so the news that the restaurant has moved across the street and has expanded from 60 to 150 seats has been met with delight. The new space retains Ceia's rustic-romantic feel with exposed brick and soft lighting. Chef Patrick Soucy's stylish and seafood-heavy menu draws on the flavors of Spain, Italy, Portugal, and France while using mostly New England ingredients. The scallops with French lentils and duck prosciutto is outstanding. So, too, are the house-made pastas. Closed Mon, open for lunch and dinner Tues through Sun, and a late-night menu (until midnight!) is available Thurs through Sat.

ITHAKI $$
25 Hammett St.
Ipswich, MA 01938
(978) 356-0099
ithakicuisine.com

This modern taverna is an unexpected find in Ipswich, where the extensive lunch and dinner menus feature a wonderful combination of Greek- and Mediterranean-inspired dishes, some classic, some with a modern twist. Enjoy dishes like a grilled octopus salad with aioli, individually baked moussaka, stuffed grape leaves in lemon sauce, and braised lamb shanks. The appetizer platter with 4 types of spreads is delicious, as is the homemade pasta with Ipswich clams. The wine list is hefty and includes Greek vintages. Closed Mon.

Pizza

THE RIVERVIEW $
20 Estes St.
Ipswich, MA 01938
(978) 356-0500
Pizza aficionados brave the somewhat sketchy next-to-the-train-station setting of this Ipswich landmark for fantastic classic thin-crust pizza slathered with sweet-sauced cheese and generously loaded with toppings. There is good beer on tap (Bass, Magic Hat #9) and the wine is served in tumblers. Know that the Riverview is a place with an abundance of character—they serve only pizza, it comes in only one size, there are no plates, and it's cash only. Obviously, though, none of it matters, as the place is always packed. Closed Mon.

Pubs & Taverns

THE OLD SPOT $
121 Essex St.
Salem, MA 01970
(978) 745-5656
theoldspot.com
Drink well and dine heartily. Indeed. A stone's throw from the Salem waterfront, this snug English-style pub is properly dark and moody with an impressive array of taps (as many as 16 including Bass, Abbot Ale, Guinness, Stella Artois, and Sam Adams). The food, including shepherd's pie, fish and chips, steak tips, and cheddar chips with a curry cream sauce, is served in generous portions and is a cut above typical pub fare.

Seafood

✳CLAMBOX OF IPSWICH $$
246 High St.
Ipswich, MA 01938
(978) 356-9707
ipswichma.com/clambox
What is there left to say about the Clambox? For more than 75 years, this Ipswich landmark has served its multi-award-winning fried local Ipswich whole-belly clams to a devoted fan base from throughout New England. The building itself is a roadside attraction; it's shaped like a fried clam take-out container. Open mid-February through December; check website for hours.

RUDDER RESTAURANT $$-$$$
73 Rocky Neck Ave.
Gloucester, MA 01930
(978) 283-7967
rudderrestaurant.com
If you're looking for a casual seafood restaurant with outdoor seating and magical water views, you'll find it at the Rudder. It's located in picturesque Rocky Neck, a little off the beaten path from Gloucester Harbor, but well worth seeking out for its menu of baked day boat cod, seafood risotto, classic fried seafood, and boiled lobsters. Make your reservation for 8 p.m. so you can sit on the outside deck and watch the sun set over the harbor. Open Apr through Oct.

✳WOODMAN'S $$
121 Main St.
Essex, MA 01929
(978) 768-6057
woodmans.com
This is the "other" North Shore fried-clam shack. Don't let the crowds deter you from stopping by Woodman's, a local institution that claims to have invented fried clams in

1916. Woodman's buzzed-about fried clams are locally sourced: sweet, briny morsels of crispy fried goodness. Accompany them with an Ipswich Ale and you will be happy—as a clam. Open year-round.

DAY TRIP IN MERRIMACK VALLEY & NORTH SHORE

This day trip combines some of the Gloucester sights you couldn't get to in one day with a visit to the pretty seaside village of Rockport. Fuel up at **Two Sisters Coffee Shop** (275 Washington St., Gloucester; 978-281-3378), a local favorite breakfast spot for traditional egg and pancake dishes along with coffee served by lively, salt-of-the-earth waitresses. Cash only.

Head out of town following Main Street to Eastern Point Boulevard to visit **Beauport, the Sleeper-McCann House** (75 Eastern Point Blvd., Gloucester; 978-283-0800; historicnewengland.org/historic-properties/homes/beauport/beauport), a jaw-dropping, vaguely English-style seaside mansion. The summer home was built in 1907 and is noted for its 40 thematic rooms and the ideas of its owner, Henry Davis Sleeper, one of America's first professional interior designers. One-hour guided tours begin on the hour and take you through 30 of the wildly eclectic rooms (it's a bit of a sprint). Open May through Oct, Tues through Sat.

Take the scenic route, past the mansions on Eastern Point via Route 127A (8 miles), to reach Rockport in time for lunch. But first walk along **Bearskin Neck** at the very tip of **Cape Ann** to poke in the many fine shops and galleries. There's plenty of metered parking in the center of town or you can park in the free municipal Blue Gate Parking lot on Route 127 and walk the ¾ mile into Rockport. Some shops to consider include **Lula's Pantry** (5 Dock Sq.; 978-546-0010) for kitchen goods and gourmet foods and **Out of the Blue** (56 Bearskin Neck; 978-546-1622) for sea-glass jewelry. Dog lovers won't want to miss the **Good Dog! Gallery** (49 Bearskin Neck; 978-546-1364; gooddog gallery.com) for dog-themed art, gifts, and treats. And back toward the center of Rockport, **Toad Hall Bookstore** (47 Main St.; 979-564-7323; toadhallbooks.org) is a very classic, independent bookstore that feels almost like a personal library. Before you leave Bearskin Neck be sure to take your own photo of the iconic red fishing shack, **Motif No. 1,** said to be the most-painted building in America.

For lunch seek out **Roy Moore Lobster** (39 Bearskin Neck, Rockport; 978-546-6696) in Bearskin Neck. This weathered gray fish shanty features fresh-off-the-boat lobster. Order inside, then enjoy your whole boiled lobster or lobster roll on the back deck looking over the water. It doesn't get any better. Just 2 miles along Route 127 out of Rockport, the **Paper House** (52 Pigeon Hill St., Rockport; paperhouserockport.com) is a roadside attraction worth stopping for—a 2-room cottage made entirely of newspaper. Another mile along Route 127 and you'll realize that the lobster for lunch was a perfect segue to the next destination, **Halibut Point State Park** (Gott Avenue, Rockport; 978-546-2997; mass.gov/dcr/parks/northeast/halb.htm), where the rocky shoreline and granite tide pools are reminiscent of midcoast Maine. Before your amble, check in at the visitor center for trail maps and to have a look at the panoramic view from the visitor center fire tower. This area was formerly a quarry; on Saturday volunteers conduct granite-cutting demonstrations.

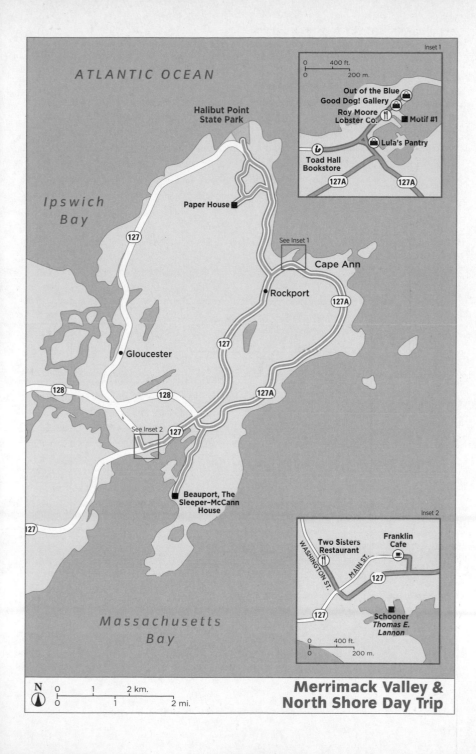

ATLANTIC OCEAN

Halibut Point
State Park

Ipswich
Bay

Paper House

See Inset 1

Cape Ann

• Rockport

127

127

127A

127A

• Gloucester

128

128

127A

See Inset 2

127

Beauport, The
Sleeper-McCann
House

127

Massachusetts
Bay

127

Inset 1

0   400 ft.
0   200 m.

Out of the Blue
Good Dog! Gallery
Roy Moore
Lobster Co.

■ Motif #1

Lula's Pantry

Toad Hall
Bookstore

127A

127A

Inset 2

Two Sisters
Restaurant

Franklin
Cafe

WASHINGTON ST.

MAIN ST.

127

127

Schooner
*Thomas E.
Lannon*

0   400 ft.
0   200 m.

N

0   1   2 km.
0   1   2 mi.

Merrimack Valley &
North Shore Day Trip

It's time to get out on the water. Head back to Gloucester Harbor along Route 127 for 7 miles. Hop on board the *Thomas E. Lannon* (45 Rogers St., Gloucester; 978-281-6623; schooner.org), a 65-foot 3-mast wood schooner that offers 2-hour public sails several times daily in the summer. After your sail, have dinner in Gloucester. From the harbor you're within walking distance of **Franklin Cafe** (118 Main St., Gloucester; 978-283-7888; franklincafe.com). Gloucester's stylish neighborhood eatery features a casual menu of seasonal fare, such as house-made linguini with clams and braised lamb shank with orange gremolata. There are house cocktails, an interesting wine selection, and local microbrews, too. Live jazz on weekend nights further adds to the Franklin's appeal.

SOUTHEAST MASSACHUSETTS & SOUTH SHORE

The South Shore is a geographic region that extends south of Boston from Quincy to Plymouth along the shores of Massachusetts Bay and Cape Cod Bay. Often ignored by tourists in a hurry to get down to the Cape, both Quincy and Plymouth offer histori- cally significant sites. Just 10 miles south of the city, Quincy (pronounced Kwin-zee) is known as the "City of Presidents," where at the Adams National Historic Park you can visit the birthplace and homes of John Adams and his son John Quincy Adams. In Plym- outh see the sites familiar to every American schoolchild as the birthplace of the first Thanksgiving: Plimoth Plantation, the *Mayflower II*, and Plymouth Rock.

Between Quincy and Plymouth, the string of pretty coastal towns—Hull, Hingham, Cohasset, Scituate, and Marshfield—are affectionately known by locals as the "Irish Riviera." In the early part of the 20th century prominent Irish-Americans like Mayor James Michael Curley and John F. Fitzgerald (President Kennedy's grandfather) built seaside summer homes here; true-blue union members soon followed. The area makes an outstanding summer side trip with excellent beaches and terrific seafood. On a hot summer Sunday, Hull's Nantasket Beach and its carousel still draw Bostonians just as they have since the middle of the 19th century. Hingham is a mecca for high-end shopping and chichi dining. Cohasset is a find with its cute seaport village—if it looks familiar it may be because many scenes from *The Witches of Eastwick* were filmed here. While in Scituate you can stroll the cove-like harbor and watch the lobster boats come in with the day's catch. And Marshfield's landscape of pristine salt marshes, dunes, and miles of gorgeous ocean beach puts the focus on the water with swimming, boating, and fishing.

Not to be confused with the South Shore, south coastal Massachusetts encom- passes the extreme southwest corner of the state, bordered by Buzzards Bay and Rhode Island. Venture to New Bedford, where whaling flourished in New England in the mid-1800s. Large numbers of immigrants came from the Azores and settled in New Bedford after being recruited as whalemen along the way. Today New Bedford is home to the largest commercial shipping fleet on the East Coast, the country's largest Portuguese-American community, and a restored historic wharf district. To the south, in Westport, the waves at Horseneck Beach make it a favorite among visitors and surf- ers alike. Another 8 miles takes you to Fall River, which capitalizes on its industrial past and is home to Battleship Cove, the world's largest collection of naval ships from World War II.

ATTRACTIONS

Historic Sites & Landmarks

✳ADAMS NATIONAL HISTORIC PARK

1250 Hancock St.

Quincy, MA 02169

(617) 770-1175

nps.gov/adam

The Adams National Historic Park has always had a lot of appeal for history geeks. It is, after all, the site of the country's oldest surviving presidential birthplaces: that of John Adams, the second US president, and his son John Quincy Adams, the sixth US president. It is also the site of the Stone Library, the nation's first presidential library. But since the acclaimed HBO miniseries *John Adams*, based on the Pulitzer Prize–winning book by David McCullough, the almost-forgotten historic site has experienced a surge in popularity. Two-hour ranger-guided tours begin at the visitor center in the Presidents Park Galleria (yes, it is a mall), where there's a snazzy 25-minute orientation film, *Enduring Legacy*, that features the voice talents of Tom Hanks, Laura Linney, and Paul Giamatti and chronicles four generations of the Adams family. A trolley bus then takes you for a short drive to the birth homes of John Adams and John Quincy Adams (they are next to each other) for a walk-through and a sense of how people lived in the early 1700s. The trolley then goes to the family estate, Peacefield, for a tour of the "old house" and the Stone Library. Throughout, you'll find that the National Park rangers really know their stuff, whether it's the details of the original family furnishings at Peacefield or recounting anecdotes from the "Dearest Friend" correspondence between John and Abigail Adams. Allow time for a stroll through the pretty English-style gardens. The tour season runs daily from mid-April through mid-November; the visitor center is open year-round (although Tues through Fri only from mid-November until mid-April).

i Built in 1896, atop Penn's Hill (at Viden Road), a fieldstone cairn (tower) marks the spot where in 1775 Abigail Adams and the then-7-year-old John Quincy Adams watched Charlestown burn during the Battle of Bunker Hill.

✳BATTLESHIP COVE

5 Water St.

Fall River, MA 02721

(508) 678-1100

battleshipcove.org

Battleship Cove is a "floating" maritime museum and war memorial that is the site for a collection of World War II naval vessels. The main attraction is the battleship *Massachusetts*. Climb aboard and enjoy almost total access to "Big Mamie" and imagine what a sailor's life was like—there are steep stairs, low doorways, and terribly uncomfortable-looking sailors' racks (bunks) for sleeping. Kids especially love the opportunity to crank the hand wheels of the ship's huge gun turrets. The destroyer *Joseph P. Kennedy* and the East German submarine the *Lionfish* are also open to explore. Also check out the two restored World War II–era PT boats displayed here. There are themed exhibits on several of the ships including one on "Women Protecting US," and the multimedia presentation *The Pearl Harbor Experience*, which re-creates the sights and sounds of the attack on December 7, 1941.

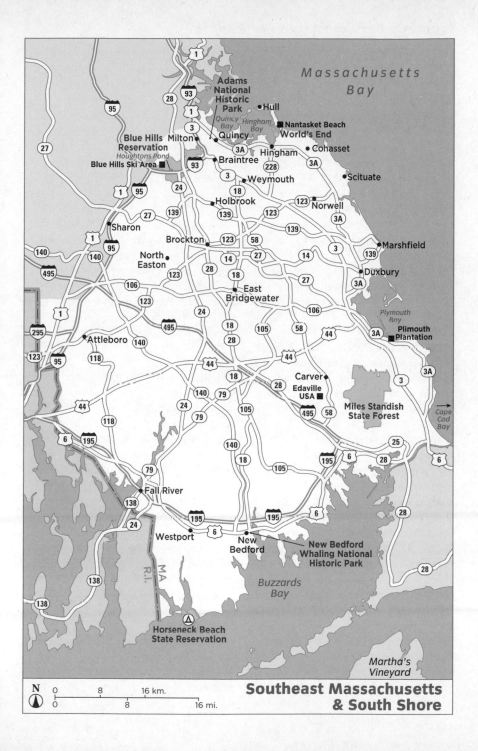

Southeast Massachusetts & South Shore

MAYFLOWER II
State Pier
Plymouth, MA 02360
(508) 746-1622
plimoth.org/what-see-do/mayflower-ii
The *Mayflower II* is a full-scale replica of the 1620 ship that set sail from Plymouth, England, bringing 102 colonists or "Pilgrims" to the New World. Built in England in the 1950s, the *Mayflower II*, like its namesake, sailed across the Atlantic. The ship is moored in Plymouth Harbor, where you can climb aboard and learn about the hardships endured on the 66-day journey—close quarters, disease, storms—from the point of view of both the Pilgrims and sailors. Open mid-March through Thanksgiving weekend.

i If you are visiting both Plimoth Plantation and *Mayflower II,* it's best to visit *Mayflower II* first because in the late afternoon parking near Plymouth Harbor is difficult.

✳PLIMOTH PLANTATION
137 Warren Ave.
Plymouth, MA 02362
(508) 746-1622
plimoth.org
Travel back in time at Plimoth Plantation, a living-history museum that showcases daily life for the Pilgrim colony and a typical Wampanoag Indian village during the 17th century. Throughout the site, interpreters describe the sometimes uneasy relationship between the two cultures and give a more honest account of the first Thanksgiving. You'll first encounter the Wampanoag Homesite, located along the Eel River. Visit a mat-covered wetu where local Wampanoag (and other native people) wearing traditional dress demonstrate age-old Native American skills and talk about their culture and history from a modern point of view. You'll then pass inside the wood stockade of the English Village, where several framed thatched-roof 1-room cottages, a meetinghouse, and a barn represent the colony's earliest buildings. Costumed guides are engaged in activities typical of early 17th-century life, such as gardening, military drills (including firing muskets), carpentry, and meal preparation. Visitors—especially children—are encouraged to ask questions and there is a hands-on element throughout; kids may be asked to stack firewood or help weed in the garden. In the crafts center, modern-day artisans practice making native hand-coiled ceramic pots, hand-woven blankets, and simple joined furniture.

PLYMOUTH ROCK
Pilgrim Memorial State Park
Water Street
Plymouth, MA 02360
(508) 747-5369
mass.gov/dcr/parks/southeast/plgm.htm
Located next to the *Mayflower II* under a granite portico on Plymouth Harbor, Plymouth Rock symbolically marks the spot where the Pilgrims first landed in the New World. And although more recent scholarship confirms that the Pilgrims first came ashore at the tip of Cape Cod near present-day Provincetown five weeks before they settled in Plymouth, the not-very-big boulder inscribed "1620" is nevertheless unexpectedly moving.

SCITUATE LIGHT
100 Lighthouse Rd.
Scituate, MA 02066
Activated in 1811, Scituate's granite and brick lighthouse stands at the northern edge of the

harbor. It is still used as a private aid to navigation. For an up-close approach, the lighthouse grounds are open from dawn to dusk (a caretaker lives in the adjacent keeper's house). Scheduled open houses during the summer allow visitors to climb up to the lantern room.

i Massachusetts children grow up hearing the story of how during the War of 1812 Abigail and Rebecca Bates, the Scituate lighthouse keeper's young daughters, saw British soldiers approaching the town in boats from a warship off the coast. "The American Army of Two" prevented a raid on Scituate by playing the fife and drum loudly and causing the British to retreat.

Museums

ART COMPLEX MUSEUM
189 Alden St.
Duxbury, MA 02332
(781) 934-6634
artcomplex.org
This small regional museum was established in 1971 to house the personal art collection of lumber heir Carl A. Weyerhaeuser. American paintings (mostly landscapes) by such artists as Charles Burchfield and George Bellows, print etchings and engravings (especially American, Dutch, and Japanese), and Shaker furniture are at the core of this collection. In the summer the museum's authentic Japanese tea hut is the setting for traditional tea ceremony presentations and classical music concerts.

✴THE FULLER CRAFT MUSEUM
455 Oak St.
Brockton, MA 02301
(508) 588-6000
fullercraft.org

Founded in 1946, the Fuller Craft Museum is New England's home for contemporary crafts. The museum's motto, "Let the art touch you," is evident everywhere. It's a dramatic campus both outdoors and in, with 22 acres of woodlands and modern, light-filled galleries. Throughout the year, works from the permanent collection share space with changing exhibits that are often built around an individual artist or a single theme. You might catch a show on cutting-edge ceramics or an exhibition of contemporary blacksmithing. The museum also offers a number of workshops throughout the year for adults and kids. And the museum gift shop is extraordinary, filled with museum-quality craft art pieces and whimsical jewelry. Closed Mon.

HULL LIFESAVING MUSEUM
1117 Nantasket Ave.
Hull, MA 02045
(781) 925-5433
lifesavingmuseum.org
Because of its treacherous rocky shoals and its peninsula location at the entrance to busy Boston Harbor, Hull has historically witnessed a high number of shipwrecks. Built in 1889, the Port Allerton Life Saving Station served in several capacities as part of the US Coast Guard. Now a museum, the site showcases Hull's maritime history and has loads of interesting exhibits including ship logs and other wreck artifacts, historic photographs, and newspaper clipping accounts of daring rescues. Open Nov through June, Mon, Wed, and Fri 10 a.m. to 1 p.m.; July through Oct, Mon, Wed, and Fri 10 a.m. to 1 p.m., Sat and Sun 10 a.m. to 2 p.m.

NEW BEDFORD WHALING MUSEUM

18 Johnny Cake Hill
New Bedford, MA 02740
(508) 997-0046
whalingmuseum.org

Anyone—young or old—fascinated by Herman Melville's *Moby-Dick* will find plenty to enjoy at this whaling museum. Kids will love the museum's 4 awesome whale skeletons (each of the specimens came to the museum as a stranding or as a death by unknown circumstances), and adults will be fascinated by the collection of finely detailed scrimshaw art and an impressive array of maritime artifacts including harpoons and tryworks kettles to melt whale blubber. In a dedicated gallery, climb aboard the *Lagoda*, a detail-perfect half-scale, fully rigged model of the whaling ship of the same name.

*NEW BEDFORD WHALING NATIONAL PARK

33 William St.
New Bedford, MA 02740
(508) 996-4095
nps.gov/nebe/index.htm

In its heyday during the mid-19th century, New Bedford's whaling captains brought enormous wealth back home. Uncover their stories by tracing their steps along the cobblestones of the New Bedford historic district and visit the sites, including the Seamen's Bethel Chapel, made famous in Herman Melville's masterwork, *Moby-Dick*. The National Park Visitor Center should be your first stop; its 22-minute orientation film, *The City that Lit the World,* is a must-see. One-hour ranger-led tours are offered daily at 10:30 a.m. and 2:30 p.m. in July and Aug, and by appointment the rest of the year.

USS *SALEM*/US NAVAL SHIPBUILDING MUSEUM

739 Washington St.
Quincy, MA 02169
(617) 479-7900
uss-salem.org/index.htm

Built here at the Fore River Shipyard in the mid-1940s and commissioned in 1949, the USS *Salem* was the flagship of the US Navy's Sixth Fleet in the Mediterranean and the Second Fleet in the Atlantic. In its 10 years of service, this US naval cruiser never saw action in war and is remembered mostly for serving as a hospital ship during the Ionian earthquake of 1953. Named after Salem, Massachusetts, home of the 1692 witchcraft trials, the ship was nicknamed the "Sea Witch" by sailors and is thought to be haunted. The ship is open for guided and self-guided tours June through Oct.

Kilroy Started Here

The Quincy Fore River Shipyard is widely regarded as the birthplace of the hand-drawn, bald-headed, long-nosed graffiti character of "Kilroy was here" fame. During World War II, shipyard-welding inspector James Kilroy would scrawl the character and text on the navy ships he inspected, and the catchphrase was adopted by American servicemen; Kilroy would turn up everywhere that American soldiers went and was a powerful morale booster for Allied troops.

Parks & Beaches

✳BLUE HILLS RESERVATION
695 Hillside St.
Milton, MA 02186
(617) 698-1802
mass.gov/dcr/parks/metroboston/blue
.htm

Ask most Bostonians to recommend a park and it's unlikely you'll hear Blue Hills mentioned very often. It's actually a huge park, a parcel that covers 7,000 acres in Dedham, Milton, Braintree, Quincy, Canton, and Randolph and offers a remarkable variety of activities just 15 miles from downtown. Among the attractions are Houghton's Pond, which has all the facilities for a full-day outing with a lifeguarded beach, grills, and picnic tables. Over 125 miles of woodland trails beckon weekend hikers and would-be adventurers. If time allows only one stop, make it Great Blue Hill. It's the site of the Blue Hill Observatory, the country's oldest continuously operating weather observatory (tours are held on weekends). Here at one of the highest points in eastern Massachusetts, the bird's-eye view of Boston is worth the hike. The **Blue Hills Ski Area** (see p. 129) is part of the reservation, as is Massachusetts Audubon's **Blue Hills Trailside Museum** (see p. 124), a family favorite for its conservation and environment programs.

FORT REVERE PARK
60 Farina Rd.
Hull, MA 02045
(781) 925-1777
mass.gov/dcr/parks/metroboston/
ftrevere.htm

A ½-mile uphill walk from the center of Hull to the top of Telegraph Hill garners fantastic views of Boston Harbor. The Massachusetts Bay colony set up a coastal defense here starting with a beacon tower in 1673. You can still see the abandoned remains of the ramparts of an American Revolution–era pentagonal fortification and a later 1890s fort here. The observation tower and small military museum on the site are currently closed to the public, but the 8-acre park has picnic benches and grills and is used for free summer outdoor concerts and movies.

HORSENECK BEACH STATE
  RESERVATION
5 John Reed Rd.
Westport, MA 02791
(508) 636-8816
mass.gov/dcr/parks/southeast/hbch.htm

Although this is one of the more remote Massachusetts beaches, Horseneck is hugely popular with local day-trippers. Horseneck has a sweep of nearly 2 miles of southwest-facing beach, so the water is generally warm. It's also popular with sailboarders, so you know this is also a great spot to fly a kite. And with 600 acres of salt dunes and marshlands, this is also a prime site for birding. The sunsets are gorgeous, too.

MOOSE HILL SANCTUARY
  (MASSACHUSETTS AUDUBON)
293 Moose Hill St.
Sharon, MA 02067
(781) 784-5691
massaudubon.org

One of the largest Massachusetts Audubon sanctuaries, Moose Hill has 25 miles of trails of extraordinary diversity. Visitors can walk through the vernal woods, look for frogs and spotted salamanders in the red maple swamp, enjoy the woodland wildflowers, and hear the chorus of migratory birds. In conjunction with **Ward's Berry Farm** (see p. 130), Moose Hill also runs a CSA (community-supported agriculture) program that provides a wide variety of sustainably grown vegetables to its members. If you have kids, be sure to check out the schedule of educational opportunities including weekend programs, seasonal special events, and children's vacation and summer camps.

NANTASKET BEACH
Route 3A
Hull, MA 02045
(781) 925-1777
mass.gov/dcr/parks/metroboston/
nantask.htm
Out-of-towners have been flocking to Nantasket Beach since the mid-1800s. Just 20 miles south of Boston, it's located on the ocean side of the peninsula that juts out into Boston Harbor. The nearly 3-mile stretch of beach features fine gray, pebbly sand. Check a tide chart before you come; high tide takes away almost the entire beach, bringing the ocean right up to the retaining wall.

i Taking the ferry is a terrific way to get to Boston from the South Shore. On weekdays you can take the MBTA commuter boat (mbta .com) to Boston from Quincy, Hull, and Hingham. You'll share the boat with workers reading newspapers, checking their smart phones, and drinking coffee while enjoying awesome skyline views of the city.

Wildlife & Zoos

BLUE HILLS TRAILSIDE MUSEUM
1904 Canton Ave.
Milton, MA 02186
(617) 333-0690
massaudubon.org

Families visiting Blue Hills Reservation will want to check out Massachusetts Audubon's Blue Hills Trailside Museum. The nature center highlights the wildlife common to the Blue Hills; the snakes and turtles are inside, and the outside exhibits feature the center's resident turkeys, hawks, otters, and snowy owls. On weekends naturalist-led programming often includes a live animal presentation. Guided nature walks and self-guided trails geared toward families begin and end here. Open Tues through Sun and holiday Mondays.

Wineries

WESTPORT RIVERS WINERY
417 Hixbridge Rd.
Westport, MA 02790
(508) 636-3423
westportrivers.com
Started in the early 1980s, family-owned Westport Rivers is a 200-acre vineyard winery that has been a pioneer in growing classic European grapes in Massachusetts. Its RJR Brut has been served several times at the White House and is considered one of the best sparkling wines made in the US. Wine tastings are held in the vineyard's historic 19th-century Long Acre farmhouse/wine shop. Public tours of the cellars take place Sat at 1 and 3 p.m. Closed Sun.

ACTIVITIES & EVENTS

Amusement Parks

EDAVILLE
7 Eda Ave.
Carver, MA 02330
(508) 866-8190
edaville.com
All aboard! Edaville provides amusement park fun on a small scale with just the right

amount of thrills for very young children ages 2 to 10. The centerpiece attraction at Edaville is the 20-minute narrow-gauge train ride through the cranberry bogs. Admission also includes unlimited access to the park's amusement rides—there's a Ferris wheel, spinning caterpillars, and flying elephants as well as an indoor play area and outdoor playground. The "Day Out with Thomas" events, which include Thomas the Tank Engine–themed activities, are very popular with young train fans. Annual events like the National Cranberry Festival during Columbus Day weekend and the Christmas Festival of Lights during December keep families coming back. Check website for park days/hours.

Arts Venues

SOUTH SHORE MUSIC CIRCUS
130 Sohier St.
Cohasset, MA 02025
(781) 383-9850
themusiccircus.org
Built as a summer theater in the seaside town of Cohasset in 1951, this open-air big-top pavilion hosts a variety of world-class performers during its June through August season. Such headliners as Willie Nelson, Chris Botti, the Beach Boys, the Golden Dragon Chinese Acrobats, and the Wiggles have recently played here. It's a circular stage and only 20 rows deep—so there isn't a bad seat in the house.

Cruises

CAPTAIN JOHN BOATS
10 Town Wharf
Plymouth, MA 02360
(508) 746-2643
captjohn.com

Experiencing a humpback whale surfacing is an unforgettable vacation memory. Captain John has a fleet of boats and their onboard naturalists are educational and entertaining. Each excursion makes a 4 hour round-trip excursion to the waters of the Stellwagen Bank Marine Sanctuary, a known feeding ground where humpback, minke, and finback whales feast on krill and plankton. Tours operate Apr through Oct.

Festivals & Annual Events

AMERICA'S HOMETOWN THANKSGIVING CELEBRATION
Along Water Street
Plymouth, MA 02360
(508) 746-1818
usathanksgiving.com
What better place to kick off Thanksgiving than in Plymouth? Taking place the weekend before Thanksgiving, the festivities include concerts, a New England–themed food festival, a re-created English settlement, and a Wampanoag pavilion. The highlight of the weekend is the Saturday parade, which chronicles the country's history from the 1600s to the present.

✴FEAST OF THE BLESSED SACRAMENT
Madeira Field
New Bedford, MA 02746
(508) 992-6911
portuguesefeast.com
This celebration of Portuguese culture and heritage is the largest ethnic festival in New England. Started by a group of New Bedford residents in 1915, today the festival welcomes nearly 100,000 visitors during its annual 4-day run the first weekend of August. Food is the centerpiece of this *festa* with linguica sausage sandwiches, a 40-foot grill to cook your own skewers of

beef, and casks of Madeira wine. All-day (and all-night) entertainment includes *fado* music and traditional folk dancing. There's a midway with rides and games and a Sunday Grand Parade with floats and dozens of marching bands.

KING RICHARD'S FAIRE
235 Main St.
Carver, MA 02330
(508) 866-5391
kingrichardsfaire.net
This annual fall festival celebrates all things medieval with a re-creation of a 16th-century English marketplace village. On the 80-acre wooded site, visitors can cheer on jousting knights, watch glass blowers, sample medieval food, test their knife-throwing skills, and visit the tigers and lions in the Royal Zoo. Adding to the merriment are the hundreds of performers who roam the grounds as minstrels, magicians, and "comely" wenches. If you really want to immerse yourself in the Renaissance experience, you can even rent a costume for the day. The festival takes place during the 8 weekends from late Aug through Columbus Day.

Fishing

HOUGHTON'S POND
Hillside Street
Milton, MA 02186
(617) 698-1802
mass.gov/dcr/parks/metroboston/houghtonsPond.htm
Located within the Blue Hills Reservation Area, this 24-acre spring-fed pond is stocked with 1,000 brown and brook trout each year. Anglers can also vie for bass and pickerel. This is bank-only fishing and although there are no docks, it's easy enough to walk the

trail that circles the pond and find a spot to drop a line.

Golf

GRANITE LINKS
100 Quarry Hills Dr.
Quincy, MA 02169
(617) 689-1900
granitelinksgolfclub.com
For top-notch golf with spectacular scenery close to Boston, this semiprivate club is a terrific option. It's a classic treeless link-style course set high on top of one of Quincy's old granite quarries. The 27-hole course is suitable for players of all levels and PGA pros are on hand to give lessons or quick swing tips.

Health & Wellness

WEYMOUTH CLUB
75 Finnell Dr.
Weymouth, MA 02188
(781) 337-4600
weymouthclub.com
The Weymouth Club is state-of-the-art, but not posh. It's a family-oriented health club that works hard to provide something for everyone, from toddlers in the child-care center to seniors in the "Young at Heart" class. The sprawling club has 13 indoor/outdoor tennis courts, 2 floors of fitness equipment with free weights and 60 pieces of cardio, 2 indoor pools, an outdoor pool, an indoor basketball court, as well as Jacuzzi, steam, and sauna. Opt into the club's countless group exercise classes. The Zumba classes are popular, as are classes in the spin studio.

Hiking & Walking

SKYLINE TRAIL AT BLUE HILLS RESERVATION

695 Hillside St.
Milton, MA 02186
(617) 698-1802
mass.gov/dcr/parks/metroboston/blue.htm

One of the most popular Boston-area day hikes, this 3-mile looping trail has a good deal of challenge that includes a 635-foot-high rocky climb with an equal payoff—stellar views of the Boston skyline. Pick up a map from the trailhead, which is the Blue Hills DCR (Department of Conservation and Recreation) headquarters.

i The original radio and television transmitters for Boston public radio and television were located on Great Blue Hill, hence the call letters WGBH Boston.

Kidstuff

BUTTONWOOD PARK ZOO

425 Hawthorn St.
New Bedford, MA 02740
(508) 991-6178
bpzoo.org

Creatures great and small abound at Buttonwood Zoo. This is a compact park, yet perfectly sized for small children, with a surprising collection of big zoo animals including black bears, cougars, and bison. The star attraction for many kids are Emily and Ruth, a pair of sweet-tempered Asian elephants. There are train rides and a carousel (both seasonal and weather permitting) along with a traditional New England farm animal exhibit that features rare-breed animals like the very cute Tamworth hogs and pretty Leicester Longwool sheep.

CAPRON PARK ZOO

201 County St.
Attleboro, MA 02703
(774) 203-1840
capronparkzoo.com

Capron is a darling little zoo (just 8 acres) that is a surefire hit for families with younger kids. Admission fees are low, too, making this a family entertainment bargain. Although small, Capron has all the regular zoo residents including monkeys, kangaroos, and leopards. Hands-down the highlight here is the lion exhibit, which features Ramses, a rare white African lion. In recent years the zoo has worked to upgrade its facilities; its water playground Splashpad Playspace is a popular draw in the summer—don't forget the kids' bathing suits and a towel.

CHILDREN'S MUSEUM IN EASTON

9 Sullivan Ave.
North Easton, MA 02356
(508) 230-3789
childrensmuseumineaston.org

The Children's Museum in Easton may be small in size, but its 3 floors of interactive exhibits in a charmingly renovated 100-year-old firehouse have plenty of activities to keep kids ages 1 to 8 occupied for hours. Highlights include the Wild Place Outdoor Area, with a two-story tree house; a Kids Clinic where aspiring MDs can X-ray a broken bone; and the Old Fishing Boat indoor play structure. Drop-in crafts, stories, and games geared toward the toddler set are offered Wednesday through Friday mornings and are free with admission. The museum also offers a wide variety of workshops, classes, themed events, and summer camps. Closed Mon.

*FALL RIVER CAROUSEL
One Central St.
Fall River, MA 02721
(508) 678-1100
battleshipcove.org
A fine example of American folk art, this restored carousel was designed by the Philadelphia Toboggan Company and dates from 1920. It sports 48 hand-carved galloping horses, 2 chariots, and a Wurlitzer band organ. Located in the grand Victorian pavilion next to the Battle Cove parking lot, it is open 7 days a week, Memorial Day through Columbus Day, weather permitting. Rides are just $1.

*PARAGON CAROUSEL
205 Nantasket Ave.
Hull, MA 02045
(781) 925-0472
paragoncarousel.com
For many, a day at Nantasket Beach is not complete without a ride on the Paragon Carousel. A Hull treasure, this 1928 carousel is the last vestige of the much-loved seaside Paragon Amusement Park. Manufactured by the Philadelphia Toboggan Company, it has 66 magnificent carved horses, 2 Roman chariots, and an antique Wurlitzer band organ. Housed under a restored pavilion, it operates Mar through Oct, weather permitting.

SOUTH SHORE NATURAL SCIENCE CENTER
48 Jacob's Ln.
Norwell, MA 02061
(781) 659-2559
ssnsc.org
Little naturalists and their parents will love exploring science together at the South Shore Natural Science Center. The indoor exhibits highlight the area's pond and woodland systems. Among the resident animals are an owl, a rabbit, and other small critters. Outdoors, there are 6 marked trails that skirt marshland and pass through piney woods and are easy walking for families. There are drop-in weekly programs where kids can watch a naturalist feed the animals or listen to "tales from the wild."

Nightlife

*TINKER'S SON
707 Main St.
Norwell, MA 02061
(781) 561-7361
thetinkersson.com
This is a dyed-in-the-wool Irish establishment, from the staff (and owner Brian Houlihan) to the decor that features stained-glass windows salvaged from a bar in Limerick and pews from a church in Belfast. There's Guinness on tap and a comfort-food menu with fish and chips made from cod fresh off the Scituate day boats and a first-rate shepherd's pie made with a mix of lamb, short rib, and ground beef topped with whipped potatoes and Irish cheddar. Late night, there's live Irish music several times a week. On Sunday tap your feet during a traditional Irish session while enjoying either the Tinker's Irish buffet or a la carte brunch.

Rock Climbing

QUINCY QUARRIES
Ricciuti Drive West
Quincy, MA 02169
(617) 698-1802
mass.gov/dcr/parks/metroboston/
quincyquarries.htm

Quincy was once the center of the American granite industry. Quincy granite was used in the construction of Boston's King's Chapel as early as the mid-1750s as well as the Bunker Hill Monument in the 1820s. Closed in 1963, the quarries have vast rock faces that are reminders of this period and are extremely popular for sport climbing. There are 20 short, easy to moderate routes and a decent bouldering area.

Skiing

BLUE HILLS SKI AREA
4001 Washington St.
Canton, MA 02021
(781) 828-5070
ski-bluehills.com
Want to jump in your car and be skiing in less than an hour? Blue Hills is the place. Just 17 miles from downtown, Blue Hills offers the closest skiing in the area, with 9 trails and 2 terrain parks that are serviced by 4 lifts. There is 80 percent snowmaking coverage and although it is a small slope (the vertical drop is only 309 feet), it is a great place if you are just learning or want to take up night skiing and grab a few turns after work. There's a rental shop and a ski school that offers private and group lessons for kids and adults. It does get crowded on weekends, but it is not nearly as crazy as the major ski resorts in Vermont and New Hampshire.

Theater

COMPANY THEATRE
30 Accord Park Dr.
Norwell, MA 02081
(781) 871-2787
companytheatre.com
Norwell's Company Theatre may challenge your idea of community theater. Their recent

original musical production, *Paragon Park* (based on the Nantasket Beach amusement park), was performed to critical acclaim. Five main-stage productions (lots of musicals, some comedy and drama) are staged annually using a diverse base of local talent. The theater also sponsors a concert series as well as a theater education program for children.

Watersports

NANTASKET KAYAK
48 George Washington Blvd.
Hull, MA 02045
(781) 962-4899
nantasketkayaks.com
Paddle along the sheltered Weir River Estuary, an area frequented by ospreys, egrets, and herons. Nantasket Kayak will supply kayaks and life jackets plus extras like whistles, maps, and dry bags. The kayaks are short, wide, and very stable—perfect for beginners. Open Memorial Day through Columbus Day.

SHOPPING

Farmers' Markets & Orchards

C. N. SMITH FARM
325 South St.
East Bridgewater, MA 02333
(508) 378-2270
cnsmithfarminc.com
This third-generation family farm has a loyal local following. The growing season begins in April when the greenhouses are stocked with potted flowers and vegetable plants for the home gardener. The farm's pick-your-own crop season begins in earnest with strawberries in June, followed by blueberries, raspberries, and peaches. In the fall, C. N. Smith offers a total New England

apple-picking experience with more than a dozen varieties of u-pick apples, an animal barnyard, tractor-driven weekend hayrides through the pumpkin fields, and an on-site cider mill. The farm stand is open Mar through Dec and carries farm-grown produce, jams, honey, and garden supplies.

WARD'S BERRY FARM
614 S. Main St.
Sharon, MA 02067
(781) 784-3600
wardsberryfarm.com

This quintessential family farm is open year-round, but June is when the pick-your-own season begins, with strawberries followed by blueberries in July and pumpkins in October. In late fall, fresh local turkeys, Christmas trees, and holiday decorations are the main attractions. Along with the locally grown seasonal produce, there's a deli for made-to-order sandwiches and a counter that sells soft-serve ice cream and smoothies. The bakery churns out everything from irresistible blueberry muffins to homey apple pies to downright addictive peanut butter chocolate chip cookies. For kids there's a picnic area, a playground, and cute farm animals to visit in the barns. They also offer several CSA (community-supported agriculture) share options.

Fashion & Shoes

CROSSING MAIN
5 Main St.
Hingham, MA 02043
crossingmain.com

Well-dressed women of distinction have been buying their serious statement pieces and fun and playful accessories here for years. Find iconic Diane von Furstenberg knit dresses, fur-trimmed sweaters by Class

Roberto Cavalli, and shoes and boots by Stuart Weitzman and Michael Kors to complete your look.

Gifts

MARSHFIELD HILLS GENERAL STORE
165 Prospect St.
Marshfield, MA 02050
(781) 834-8443
marshfieldhillsgeneralstore.com

This 150-year-old country store could have come right out of a Norman Rockwell painting and is a great little stop to or from nearby Humarock Beach. The store sells nostalgic favorites like penny candy, toys, fresh-popped popcorn, coffee, and the morning *Globe* and *Herald*. If you are not a local, though, the real draw is the Hollywood connection. Part-time Marshfield summer resident, actor Steve Carell, now owns the store and has been known to come in often when he's in town.

Mall

DERBY STREET SHOPPES
94 Derby St.
Hingham, MA 02043
(781) 749-7800
thederbystreetshoppes.com

Anchored by a Whole Foods, this open-air mall, with nearly 60 stores and a dozen or so restaurants, mimics a village center with landscaped sidewalks and storefront parking. You'll find national upscalers such as Williams-Sonoma, J. Crew, the Apple Store, and Hingham's own Talbots along with local chains like the London Harness Company (leather goods), Magic Beans (toys), and White's Pastry Shop. Nice shopping amenities here include a Serenity Garden behind the Barnes & Noble, a bocce court, and ice-skating on Hidden Pond (it's "hidden" behind Whole Foods). Healthy fast-food chain b.good is a family favorite for burgers, shakes, and fries, while several places including Bertucci's (pizza), Summer Shack (seafood), and Rustic Kitchen (Mediterranean) serve moderately priced fare.

Specialty Food

BIN ENDS
236 Wood Rd.
Braintree, MA 02185
(781) 817-1212
binendswine.com
The warehouse-like setting is an oenophile's haven and is the ideal place to stock up on odd lots of fine wine at serious savings. Soft-spoken, knowledgeable staff and generous spacing encourage quiet browsing among the well-curated selection. On the last Sunday of each month the fine wine flea market offers sometimes incredible savings (20–50 percent) on notable wines from independent vintners and family-run estates.

✳THE GOURMET OUTLET AT SID WAINER & SON
2301 Purchase St.
New Bedford, MA 02746
(508) 999-6408
sidwainer.com
This third-generation specialty/gourmet foods purveyor is a favorite resource of some of the top chefs in the Northeast. Headquartered in New Bedford, the company's gourmet outlet is a must-visit for foodies and serious home cooks. Open to the public, the store stocks its shelves with smoked fish and meats, wheels of aged and ripened cheeses, and hard-to-find comestibles from truffle butter to du Puy lentils to

almond flour. This is truly the good stuff. The best time of all to come is Saturday, when the demonstration kitchen hums with chefs cooking and offering advice (along with samples). Closed Sun.

ACCOMMODATIONS

Inns & Bed-and-Breakfasts

✳INN AT SCITUATE HARBOR   **$$**
7 Beaver Dam Rd.
Scituate, MA 02066
(781) 545-5550
innatscituate.com
Built overlooking Scituate Harbor, this inn has the most dramatic of natural amenities: a 180-degree view encompassing the Scituate Lighthouse and glorious ocean sunrises. Each of the inn's 29 nautically inspired rooms (white-on-white with touches of blue) has a fair share of the vistas. Rates include a continental breakfast and free Wi-Fi. The indoor pool is a nice plus, while Scituate's shops, pubs, and restaurants are just outside the inn's door.

WHITE SWAN BED & BREAKFAST   **$$**
146 Manomet Rd.
Plymouth, MA 02360
(508) 224-3759
whiteswan.com
Between the cheery innkeeper, full gourmet breakfasts, and garden grounds, you won't want to venture too far from this 1820 farmhouse inn. Each of the 3 large guest rooms is done up in New England country style (think floral wallpaper, oak furniture, and claw-foot tubs) with Wi-Fi throughout. The inn is located just a 5-minute walk from White Horse Beach.

Motels, Hotels & Resorts

∗COHASSET HARBOR RESORT $$
124 Elm St.
Cohasset, MA 02025
(781) 383-6650
cohassetharborresort.com

Fresh off a recent renovation and upgrade, the 50 guest rooms have soft-edged modern comfort with new pillow-top mattresses, luxurious bedding, and flat-screen TVs. Most of the rooms overlook the harbor and a simple continental breakfast is included in all rates. An indoor pool is an unexpected bonus. For dining under the sun or stars, Brisa Tapas and Wine Bar is open seasonally.

NANTASKET BEACH RESORT $$
45 Hull Shore Dr.
Hull, MA 02045
(781) 925-4500
nantasketbeachhotel.com

There are many reasons to stay here, but the universal favorite is the oceanfront location. There's also an indoor pool with retractable roof and a large fitness center. Lots of extras make this a solid choice in the good-value category. Each of the resort's 105 tidy marine-minimalist rooms comes with a gas fireplace, balcony, and jetted tub; many rooms have an ocean view. And all rates include a continental breakfast and free Wi-Fi.

PILGRIM SANDS ON LONG BEACH $$
150 Warren Ave.
Plymouth, MA 02360
(508) 747-0900
pilgrimsands.com

At this prime beachfront location—just across the street from Plimoth Plantation—Pilgrim Sands is a find. The well-maintained but utilitarian accommodations are pleasant—ask for a room facing the water. This is an especially good choice for families; besides swimming at Long Beach kids will enjoy the indoor and outdoor pools. All rates include a basic continental breakfast and free Wi-Fi.

Camping

MILES STANDISH STATE FOREST $
Cranberry Road
South Carver, MA 02366
(508) 866-2526
mass.gov/dcr/parks/southeast/mssf.htm

Straddling more than 14,000 acres across both Carver and Plymouth, Miles Standish is the state's largest recreational area. It's heavily treed with scrub oaks and pitch pines and crystal-clear kettle ponds in a quiet setting. The amenities are very basic—just campground restrooms with hot showers and picnic tables—but lots of recreational opportunities are available, including swimming, fishing, and canoeing. In the summer there are excellent ranger-led interpretive programs such as bird walks and stargazing that offer kids (and parents) a pleasant diversion.

RESTAURANTS

American

∗FAT CAT $$
24 Chestnut St.
Quincy, MA 02169
(617) 471-4363
fatcatrestaurant.com

Devotees of this hip neighborhood restaurant swear by the comfort food options, such as the truly addictive macaroni and cheese, pulled pork nachos, and deconstructed clam chowder. The vibe is as much relaxed bar as restaurant; there's a good selection of beers on draft and wine priced just above retail. It's open for lunch and dinner and is a great option if you are visiting the Adams National Historical Park. It's almost always crowded and they don't take reservations, so expect to wait.

ORO $$
162 Front St.
Scituate, MA 02066
(781) 378-2465
restaurantoro.com

Located on Scituate's scenic harbor, this casually upscale restaurant is awash in shades of white and beige and is a great little find for modern New England cuisine. Husband-and-wife Chef-Owners Robin and Jill King have created a menu that emphasizes seafood and local vegetables with dishes like cedar-roasted salmon with parsnip puree, and a lobster cake with spinach and a tomato *crema*. Be sure to save room for the warm chocolate pudding cake with salted caramel custard and coffee ice cream.

Breakfast & Lunch

DONUT KING $
151 Copeland St.
Quincy, MA 02169
(617) 786-9881

Totally old-school, Donut King is a tiny neighborhood shop that sells massive light and fluffy doughnuts that are among the best in the area. Purists will want to start with the classic glazed, then move on to the butternut. If you want a Boston cream (a cream-filled doughnut with chocolate glaze), come early—it's a daily sell-out. Cash only.

TOAST $
121 Nantasket Ave.
Hull, MA 02045
(781) 925-5221
toasthull.com

Locals start the day right with down-home breakfasts of blueberry pancakes (with real maple syrup), hefty 3-egg omelets, and bottomless cups of coffee. At lunch diners go for the clam chowder and sandwiches, such as the corned beef Reuben. It's a laid-back ambience and prices are reasonable, so expect to wait on a summer weekend. Closed Mon.

Burgers

✳WAHLBURGERS $–$$
The Launch at the Hingham Shipyard
19 Shipyard Dr.
Hingham, MA 02043
(781) 749-2110
wahlburgers.com

Hollywood celebrity draws the crowds to this South Shore retro-burger joint owned by local chef Paul Wahlberg and his brothers, actors Mark and Donnie Wahlberg. For a bite of classic Americana, order Our Burger: a house-ground natural beef 5-ounce patty with dill pickles, cheese, onions, lettuce, tomato, and special sauce. Specialty burgers, hot dogs, fries, and frappes round out the super-casual menu. And since the Wahlberg boys happen to be huge Boston sports fans, there are lots of flat screens in the full-service bar area, so you won't miss a minute of the action.

Cafes & Coffeehouses

＊FRENCH MEMORIES $
459 Washington St.
Duxbury, MA 02331
(781) 934-9020
frenchmemories.com
For buttery croissants, crusty baguettes, and artful tarts along with a perfect espresso, this is the best place on the South Shore to refuel with the ambience of St. Tropez—even if you are just heading over to Duxbury Beach.

＊RED EYE ROASTERS $
3 Otis St.
Hingham, MA 02043
(781) 740-2545
redeyeroasters.com
This small-batch locally owned roaster is dedicated to coffee's complex flavors, its origin, and its preparation. Overlooking picturesque Hingham Harbor, the shop caters to a vibrant, mixed clientele and has a cozy ambience with good music and friendly—not haughty—staff. Be sure to pick up a bag of whole beans for home.

Ice Cream

**CRESCENT RIDGE DAIRY BAR
HOLBROOK** $
176 S. Franklin St.
Holbrook, MA 02343
(781) 963-1016

**CRESCENT RIDGE DAIRY BAR
SHARON** $
355 Bay Rd.
Sharon, MA 02067
(781) 784-5892
crescentridge.com
Direct from the cow to you—Crescent Ridge is a local working dairy farm that still makes home milk deliveries in glass bottles. They

also still make their own premium ice cream. Crescent Ridge features more than 40 timeless New England flavors. Lots of sundaes and frappes are ordered, so the top sellers here are vanilla and strawberry. Kids go for the Black Bear, made with raspberry ice cream and chocolate chips, because of its cool purple color. Crescent Ridge portions are generous—the kiddie size is humongous! The Holbrook location is newer and has minigolf; the Sharon location is next to company headquarters and has the cows.

Italian

ITALY'S LITTLE KITCHEN $
1239 Hancock St.
Quincy, MA 02169
(617) 479-0984
This is Italian-American soul food—hefty meatball sandwiches, tasty chicken Parm subs—made even better than you remember. It really is a little kitchen; there are only 4 tables and the restaurant does a brisk take-out business. Sandwiches take up most of the menu, but there are plenty of other dishes worth trying, especially the antipasto salad and red-sauce pasta dishes. It is hard to find: Walk around the Hancock Street side of the building; the restaurant entrance is directly across the street from the Quincy T station. Open only until 6 p.m. Closed Sun.

＊TOSCA'S $$–$$$
14 North St.
Hingham, MA 02043
(781) 740-0080
toscahingham.com
Hingham is justifiably proud to have this gem in town. When it opened in 1993, Tosca was the first restaurant to bring big-city dining to the South Shore. Tosca's creative twists on regional rustic Italian cuisine are served in

a renovated 1910 market building overlooking the harbor. The dining room's exposed brick and an open wood-fire oven and kitchen both add to the perfect date-night ambience. Order a bowl of superbly made wild boar Bolognese or the chicken under a brick with Marsala glaze and polenta. They serve dinner only and are closed Mon.

Pizza

RIVA PIZZERIA $
24 Country Way
Scituate, MA 02066
(781) 545-5861
rivapizzeria.com
This invitingly modern pizza parlor offers its own twist on thin-crust Neapolitan pies. There's an enticing baked eggplant pizza lightly topped with ricotta, goat cheese, pecorino, and fresh herbs, and a simple Margherita pizza with crushed tomatoes, mozzarella, Parmesan, and basil. They also offer gourmet sandwiches, salads and cannoli. An additional location is at 307 Nantasket Ave., Hull, MA 02045 (781-925-1400).

Portuguese

✳ANTONIO'S $$
267 Coggeshall St.
New Bedford, MA 02746
(508) 990-3636
antoniosnewbedford.com
Entire extended local families as well as New Bedford tourists stop at this well regarded restaurant for down-home Portuguese cooking. Specialties include fried salted cod cakes and a fine seafood casserole in a tomato broth. For the meat fancier, a succulent sirloin steak topped with ham and a fried egg is one of several winning choices. The decor is basic, the portions are ample, the dishes are bargain-priced, and it's cash only.

Pubs & Taverns

✳SCARLET OAK TAVERN $$
1217 Main St.
Hingham, MA 02043
(781) 749-8200
scarletoaktavern.com
Seasonality and sustainability are the guiding principles at this New American gastropub, which incorporates produce from its own Gibbet Hill Farm in much of the menu. There are barbecue brisket sliders in the fireplaced bar, a pretty patio in warm weather, and a welcoming upscale New England tavern dining room. Enjoy dishes like baked goat cheese with grilled tomato salsa, potato-encrusted haddock, and a decadent lobster and scallop risotto. They are also known for their steaks.

Seafood

✳BLUE EYED CRAB & GRILLE $$
170 Water St.
Plymouth, MA 02360
(508) 747-6776
blue-eyedcrab.com
Salute the end of the day with a refreshing Cranberry Bog—bourbon, cranberry juice, honey, lime, and mint—on the lively patio. Great seafood is the focus, though; the comfortable menu has dishes that out-of-towners like to order, such as clam chowder and a lobster roll. But there are creative dishes (many with a tropical bent), such as lunch-perfect seared scallop salad with mango and jicama and grilled pineapple rum marinated steak tips.

✳HADDAD'S OCEAN CAFE $$
291 Ocean St.
Marshfield, MA 02050
(781) 536-5121
haddads-ocean-cafe.com

In the Brant Rock neighborhood for three generations, the Haddad family has replaced the 75-year-old family eatery with this brand-new, modern restaurant just yards away (and on higher ground) that is sure to be a crowd-pleaser. The dining room is much larger, there's a gorgeous 30-seat bar, and a wraparound deck with views of Green Harbor. The menu features all the old favorites, such as the deluxe seafood plate with fried haddock, clams, scallops, shrimp and lobster, and haddock fish and chips.

HINGHAM LOBSTER POUND $–$$
4 Broad Cove Rd.
Hingham, MA 02043
(781) 749-1984
hinghamlobster.com

No ocean views here—just an unassuming roadside take-out shack (formerly a bait shop) that sells some of the best lobster rolls, fried fish, and chowder around. Call ahead (2 hours) and they will have a steamed lobster ready for you. Open Mar through Dec, Wed through Sun; call for hours.

MARVELS' LUNCH BOX $
163 Nantasket Ave.
Hull, MA 02045
(781) 925-4614
marvelslunchbox.com

Directly facing Nantasket Beach, this strictly take-out joint is all about the lobster roll. Here, 5 ounces of fresh, sweet tail and claw meat are tossed in just enough mayo and celery and then heaped into a toasted roll. The addition of corn and carrots makes for

an untraditional—but still very good—clam chowder. Take your order to the beach or enjoy on the many benches out front. Open daily Memorial Day through Labor Day.

DAY TRIP IN THE SOUTH SHORE

Other than Plymouth, the South Shore often gets ignored. This day trip offers time to soak up some history and includes excursions for outdoor adventure and culture, too. Start the day with a doughnut and a coffee at the original **Dunkin Donuts** (543 Southern Artery, Quincy; 617-472-9502; dunkin donuts.com). Established in 1950, "Dunkin" is beloved by New Englanders and this shop, which has recently been "retro-renovated," is the one that started it all.

Around the corner is the National Park Visitor Center for the **Adams National Historic Park** (1250 Hancock St., Quincy; 617-770-1175; nps.gov/adam). If you have ever wondered how our founding fathers really lived, this is how. Park your car in the Galleria at Presidents Place public garage. From here you'll board a trolley bus to visit the birth homes of President John Adams and his son President John Quincy Adams. At the family estate, the "Old House" at Peacefield, the engaging ranger-led guided tour is sure to pique your interest in the Adams's presidencies and have you looking for the HBO miniseries *John Adams* on demand. Afterward it's a short walk and a quick stop to the **United First Parish Church** (1306 Hancock St., Quincy; 617-773-1290; ufpc.org) to visit the tombs of the two former presidents.

For lunch, follow Route 3A for 7 miles as it hugs the coast to the Hingham Shipyard complex. **Caffe Tosca** (15 North St., Hingham; 781-740-9400; caffetoscahingham .com) is the more casual, fun little sister to

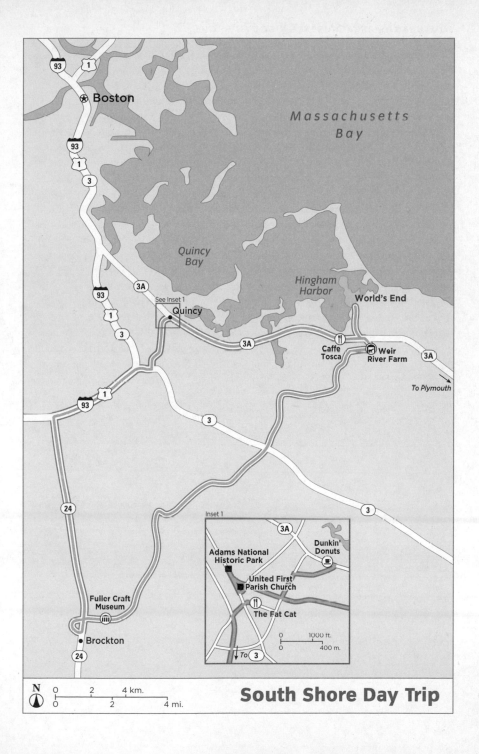

93 1

⊛ Boston

Massachusetts Bay

93
1
3

Quincy Bay

93
1
3

3A

See Inset 1
• Quincy

Hingham Harbor

World's End

3A

🍴 Caffe Tosca

🏛 Weir River Farm

3A

To Plymouth

3

24

Fuller Craft Museum
🏛

• Brockton

24

Inset 1

3A

Adams National Historic Park
🏛

Dunkin' Donuts
🍩

United First Parish Church
🏛

🍴 The Fat Cat

0   1000 ft.
0   400 m.

↓ To 3

N
0   2   4 km.
0   2   4 mi.

South Shore Day Trip

the upscale Italian restaurant Tosca. Caffe Tosca offers wood-fired pizzas, salads, and Italian-inspired sandwiches to eat inside, or outside on its umbrella-covered brick patio to enjoy if not a water view, an ocean breeze.

After lunch it's time to explore. It's just a 2-mile drive from the Hingham Shipyard to **World's End** (Martin's Lane, Hingham; 781-740-7233; thetrustees.org), a protected conservation area and park. This uniquely beautiful place offers a wooded trail that ends on a rocky promontory with a stunning view of the ocean and Boston in the near distance. If you have kids in tow, it's super easy to visit **Weir River Farm** (Turkey Hill Lane, Hingham; 781-740-7233; thetrustees .org), just another 2-mile drive away. This is another Trustees of Reservations property, a 10-acre working farm of gardens and orchards. Visit the chickens, pigs, sheep, and horses in the barns. At the farm stand you can purchase the farm's homegrown fruit, vegetables, meat, and eggs.

It's a 17-mile back-road drive to the **Fuller Craft Museum** (455 Oak St., Brockton; 508-588-6000; fullercraft.org), one of the country's finest museums of contemporary craft and decorative arts. The gallery's rich and diverse displays range from furniture to print to textiles and more. Exhibits include changing crafts exhibits and pieces from the museum's permanent collection. Crafts demonstrations, lectures, and musical performances are also part of the mix.

End your day the way you began. A quick 15-mile drive via Route 24 and I-93 north brings you back to Quincy Center. Plan for an early dinner to avoid the wait at neighborhood favorite **Fat Cat** (24 Chestnut St., Quincy; 617-471-4363; fatcatrestaurant .com) and order the famous lobster mac and cheese and a cold drink to wash it all down.

CAPE COD & THE ISLANDS

The salty-fresh waters of the Atlantic, warm sand between your toes, an abundance of homemade ice cream stands, and wind-weathered fried clam shacks. Cape Cod and the "Islands"—Martha's Vineyard and Nantucket—offer visitors a summer vacation that is as laid-back as it gets.

The Cape itself is a 62-mile-long arm-shaped peninsula that juts out into the Atlantic. Technically the Cape is an island, separated from the Massachusetts mainland by the man-made Cape Cod Canal and connected by the heavily trafficked Sagamore Bridge to the north and the only slightly less congested Bourne Bridge to the south. But endure the bridge traffic and you'll realize that the drive is worth it.

Each of the Cape's 15 charmingly distinct towns offers vacation opportunities for both explorers and strollers. At 400 square miles, the Cape is much bigger than most outsiders realize. So it is helpful to know the lay of the land. The Upper Cape refers to the towns closest to the bridges, including Falmouth and Sandwich. To the east, in the mid-Cape region, is Hyannis, famed as the summer home of the Kennedy clan. In practical terms, Hyannis is the transportation hub of the Cape. The Cape's major airport is here; so, too, the bus and railroad stations, while both Martha's Vineyard and Nantucket ferries as well as a veritable flotilla of whale-watch boats and fishing charters leave from Hyannis Harbor. The mid-Cape town of Yarmouth draws young families for its warm Nantucket Sound beaches, minigolf, and fast-food eateries. Lower Cape towns include affluent Chatham, with its picturesque lighthouse and postcard-perfect Main Street, and to the north, Brewster on Cape Cod Bay, historically known as the "Sea Captain's Town." Eastham doesn't have a defined center, but it is the gateway for the Cape Cod National Seashore, which for many defines the essence of the Cape—a 40-mile swath of sun-drenched, pristine Atlantic beach backed by marsh and dunes. The outer Cape towns of Wellfleet and Truro are known for their art galleries, while funky, bohemian Provincetown is a leading gay resort and has all the local color that you would ever want to see.

Across Nantucket Sound, Martha's Vineyard and Nantucket are both very special ports of call. Both islands are far less developed than the Cape: places of unrelenting beauty with fine, unspoiled beaches. The Vineyard is the bigger of the islands—it's nearly 100 square miles—and at 7 miles and a quick 35-minute ferry ride—it's a lot closer. Nantucket is a true island getaway destination. The name itself is a Native word that means "the land far away." Once the foremost whaling port in the world, today Nantucket sees yachts fill its harbor. Before or after dinner, stroll along the waterfront and select your dream boat.

ATTRACTIONS

Historic Sites & Landmarks

AQUINNAH CLIFFS
State Road
Aquinnah, MA 02535
On the extreme western end of the island, on tribal lands belonging to the Aquinnah Wampanoag, these sacred towering clay cliffs afford fantastic ocean views of Vineyard Sound and the Elizabeth Islands in the distance. Seek even higher ground and climb redbrick Gay Head Light (open daily mid-June through Columbus Day, 10 a.m. to 5 p.m.). Below the cliffs lies Moshup Beach, a small swath of Vineyard sand with far fewer people (and in some sections far fewer clothes than you would expect).

COTTAGE MUSEUM SHOP
Trinity Park
Oak Bluffs, MA 02557
(508) 693-7784
mvcma.org
Just behind Oak Bluffs's main street, the "Campgrounds" is a neighborhood of some 300 gaily painted Victorian summer cottages with ornate gingerbread trim. The cottages date from the 1860s and 1870s and were built by members of Oak Bluffs's summer Methodist retreat colony. The houses are all privately owned, but you can peek inside the Cottage Museum Shop, which has been set up with period furniture and artifacts.

i One of Martha's Vineyard's summer highlights is Grand Illumination Night, when the Campground community gathers for a sing-along at the open-air Tabernacle followed by the lighting of paper lanterns hung on the cottage porches.

DEXTER GRIST MILL
Water Street (behind Town Hall)
Sandwich, MA 02563
(508) 888-4910
Located on picturesque Shawme Pond, this weathered wood gristmill dates from the 1640s and still grinds corn into meal the old-fashioned way, with giant granite millstones. Guides on site demonstrate the milling process. Water-powered and stone-ground, the operation makes a lot of noise! Bags of fresh ground cornmeal are available for purchase and make a great souvenir. Be sure to take a picture, too; the Dexter Grist Mill pond scene is one of the Cape's most photographed. Open June through mid-October; call for hours.

i If you're looking to beat the summer Cape traffic, the new Cape FLYER train might be just the ticket. From Memorial Day weekend through Labor Day, departures from Boston's South Station on Friday evening and Saturday and Sunday mornings make the 2-hour trip to Hyannis. Return trips back to Boston take place on Saturday and Sunday evenings. The highlight of the trip is crossing the Cape Cod Canal via the Buzzards Bay Railroad Bridge, a vertical-lift bridge that is lowered for each railroad crossing.

HOXIE HOUSE
18 Water St.
Sandwich, MA 02563
(508) 888-1173
Just off Main Street, this early saltbox-style house dates from the mid-1600s and is one of the oldest on the Cape. Built for the Reverend John Smith, his wife, Susana, and their 13 children, the home is dark; the tiny casement

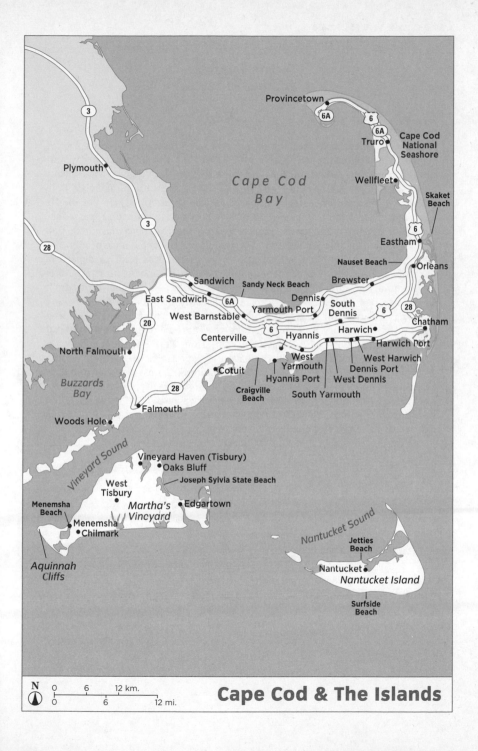

Provincetown

6A

6

6A

Truro

Cape Cod
National
Seashore

Cape Cod
Bay

Wellfleet

Skaket
Beach

3

Plymouth

3

28

6

Eastham

Nauset Beach

Orleans

Sandwich

Sandy Neck Beach

Brewster

East Sandwich

6A

Dennis

South
Dennis

6

28

West Barnstable

Yarmouth Port

Chatham

20

Centerville

6

Hyannis

Harwich

Harwich Port

North Falmouth

West
Yarmouth

West Harwich

Cotuit

Hyannis Port

Dennis Port

Buzzards
Bay

28

Craigville
Beach

West Dennis

South Yarmouth

Falmouth

Woods Hole

Vineyard Sound

Vineyard Haven (Tisbury)

Oaks Bluff

Joseph Sylvia State Beach

West
Tisbury

Martha's
Vineyard

Edgartown

Nantucket Sound

Menemsha
Beach

Menemsha

Chilmark

Jetties
Beach

Aquinnah
Cliffs

Nantucket

Nantucket Island

Surfside
Beach

N

0   6   12 km.

0   6   12 mi.

Cape Cod & The Islands

To the Islands:
Martha's Vineyard

Getting There
The vast majority of visitors take a ferry to the Vineyard. There are lots of choices. The **Steamship Authority** (508-477-8600; steamshipauthority.com) has the monopoly on auto and passenger ferries to the Vineyard and is your only choice if you are bringing over your car. Departures are from Woods Hole and arrive 45 minutes later in Vineyard Haven (year round) or Oak Bluffs (summer). The *Island Queen* (508-548-4800; islandqueen.com) passenger ferry is inexpensive and even quicker, making the Falmouth Harbor to Oak Bluffs crossing in just 35 minutes. For the *Island Queen,* it's cash only and reservations are not taken, so plan to arrive 45 minutes prior to departure to secure a space. **Hy-Line Cruises** (800-492-8082; hy-linecruises.com) offers both regular (95-minute) and fast-ferry (55-minute) passenger ferries from Hyannis to Oak Bluffs. Hy-Line also runs the only inter-island ferry making a daily round-trip run in summer between Straight Wharf in Nantucket and Oak Bluffs in Martha's Vineyard. Or take the seasonal 1-hour **New England Fast Ferry** (866-683-3779; nefastferry.com) from New Bedford to Vineyard Haven and Oak Bluffs and avoid the hassle of Cape traffic altogether. Finally, seasonal high-speed (90-minute) ferry service from Quonset, Rhode Island, is available on the **Vineyard Fast Ferry** (401-295-4040; vineyardfastferry.com).

Airlines providing service to the Vineyard include Cape Air year-round from Boston, Hyannis, Nantucket, and New Bedford. JetBlue and Delta provide daily seasonal service to the island from New York's JFK.

---

leaded glass windows let in the only light. In the house, suitably furnished with period artifacts, kindly docents give hourlong informative talks that describe what life was like for the 17th-century inhabitants. Open June through mid-October; call for hours.

PILGRIM MONUMENT AND
PROVINCETOWN MUSEUM
1 High Pole Hill Rd.
Provincetown, MA 02657
(508) 487-1310
pilgrim-monument.org
Provincetown, not Plymouth—and certainly not "the Rock"—was the first landing site of the *Mayflower* Pilgrims. After 35 days of exploring the Cape Cod peninsula, the Pilgrims continued on their way 50 miles across Cape Cod Bay to permanently settle in Plymouth. The exhibits at the Provincetown Museum tell the story of the Pilgrims' arrival and the drafting of the Mayflower Compact, an agreement for self-government. Next to the museum, Pilgrim Monument is the tallest all-granite structure in the US. Climb to the top of the 252-foot tower for incomparable vistas and see if you can spy Boston in the distance.

The Martha's Vineyard Chamber of Commerce information booth is located in Vineyard Haven across from the ferry terminal.

Martha's Vineyard Visitor Information: 24 Beach Rd., Vineyard Haven; (508) 693-0085; mvy.com.

Getting Around

A car isn't necessary but can be helpful if you're visiting for more than a few days. You can rent one on the island (check with A-A Island Rentals, 508-696-5300; mvautorental.com) or make arrangements to bring your car over on the Steamship Authority ferry (see above). Make car reservations well in advance, especially for August; spring is not too early.

Biking is one of the best ways to experience the Vineyard's charm. If you are coming for the day, you will want to rent your bike at one of the shops as you step off the ferry. If you are staying at a hotel or at a rental property and need a bike for just a day or two, all the island bike shops can deliver. Rental rates typically include helmets, locks, and a map of the island's bike trails. Both **Martha's Bike Rentals** (4 Lagoon Pond Rd., Vineyard Haven; 508-693-6593; marthasvineyardbikes.com) and **Anderson's Bike Rental** (Circuit Avenue Extension, Oak Bluffs; 508-693-9346; andersonsbikerentals.com) are great options.

The Martha's Vineyard Transit Authority (508-693-9940; vineyardtransit .com) runs a network of bus routes throughout the island (including the airport and out to Aquinnah) and is also used to picking up weary bikers who are too tired to pedal anymore (all the buses have bike racks). Rates are $1 per town (use exact change in cash or buy a pass).

PROVINCETOWN DUNE SHACKS
Snail Road and Route 6A
Provincetown, MA

Along an isolated 2-mile stretch of seashore from Race Point down to High Head in Truro lie a string of 19 weather-beaten cabins. In the first decades of the 20th century, these dune shacks were at the center of Provincetown's artist and writer colony. Among the shack's notable residents were Norman Mailer and Jack Kerouac. Now on the National Register of Historic Places, most of the shacks are still privately owned, but 3 are in frequent use for short-term artist-in-residency programs.

Museums

*EDWARD GOREY HOUSE
4 Strawberry Ln.
Yarmouthport, MA 02675
(508) 362-3909
edwardgoreyhouse.org

This rather ordinary Cape Cod home was the residence of eccentric artist and illustrator Edward Gorey, who lived here from 1986 until his death in 2000. Gorey was best known for his macabre yet charming book *The Ghastlycrumb Tinies*, the opening titles of PBS's Mystery series, and his Tony award–winning costume design for the Broadway production of *Dracula*. The home is a treasure trove of quirky Gorey artifacts, letters, and a collection of his drawings. In the compact but fascinating house museum, a tour guide will walk you through Gorey's unique world. Open Apr through Dec; check website for days and times.

i An unforgettable Cape Cod experience, Art's Dunes Tours (4 Standish St., Provincetown; 508-487-1950; artsdunetours.com) offer scheduled 4-wheel-drive guided tours of the Provincetown dunes. The 1-hour off-road adventure takes you to the Cape Cod National Seashore and the Provincetown Dune Shacks. In season (mid-April through mid-November), tours take place several times daily. Art's also offers 2-hour dune sunset tours and clambake tours.

✳HERITAGE MUSEUMS AND GARDENS
67 Grove St.
Sandwich, MA 02563
(508) 888-3300
heritagemuseumsandgardens.org
Experience memories of old-time fun at one of the nation's best collections of American folk art. The museum has 3 exhibit buildings and 100 acres of landscaped and naturalistic gardens and grounds. A reproduction of a Shaker round stone barn houses a collection of 30 antique automobiles, including a 1913 Model T Ford. The art gallery features a collection of scrimshaw, cigar store statues, and a 1908 carousel (with unlimited rides!). Traveling special exhibits take place in a replica Revolutionary War–era fort building and often highlight specific aspects of Americana, such as American kitchens through the years or the art of Norman Rockwell. Heritage also

has one of the state's most celebrated horticultural displays. Highlights include a magnificent collection of rhododendrons and azaleas in the spring; daylilies and hydrangeas in summer; chrysanthemums and blazing foliage in the autumn. The new Hidden Hollow nature area delights kids and their parents with story-time and musical programming. Open mid-April through October.

JOHN F. KENNEDY MUSEUM
397 Main St.
Hyannis, MA 02601
(508) 790-3077
jfkhyannismuseum.org
The Kennedy family and Hyannis are inextricably linked. The Kennedys have been summer residents of this seaside town since the early 1920s. Located in the center of Hyannis, this small museum captures with photos, memorabilia, and video memories of President Kennedy's time on the Cape from boyhood days through the years when the Kennedy compound served as the "Summer White House." Baseball fans will not want to miss the Cape Cod Baseball League Hall of Fame on the museum's lower level. The museum is open daily Memorial Day through Oct, closed in Dec and Jan; check website for days and times the rest of the year.

NANTUCKET LIGHTSHIP BASKET MUSEUM
49 Union St.
Nantucket, MA 02554
(508) 228-1177
nantucketlightshipbasketmuseum.org
This darling little museum is worth a spin for those interested in the fine art and craft of Nantucket lightship baskets. These rattan or cane woven baskets were first created in the early whaling days by the crewmen of

To the Islands:
Nantucket

Getting There

Most visitors arrive in Nantucket by ferry. The **Steamship Authority** (508-477-8600; steamshipauthority.com) is the most affordable option, offering both regular (2-hour) car and passenger ferries and in season, high-speed (1-hour) passenger-only ferry options from Hyannis. **Hy-Line Cruises** (800-492-8082; hy-linecruises.com) offers both regular (2-hour) and fast-ferry (1-hour) passenger ferries year-round from Hyannis. Hy-Line also runs a summer inter-island ferry between Nantucket and Martha's Vineyard. Or skip the busy Hyannis dock scene altogether and consider **Freedom Cruise Line's** (508-432-8999; nantucketislandferry.com) high-speed, 75-minute passenger ferry from Harwich. Freedom Cruise Line rates include free (and convenient) parking for day-trippers.

As for air, Nantucket Airlines, Cape Air, and Island Airlines operate scheduled flights to Nantucket. There is year-round service to Nantucket from Boston, Hyannis, and Martha's Vineyard. In the summer, there are nonstop flights from New York (JFK). Bear in mind that Nantucket is the "gray lady" for a reason and that planes won't fly to the island in dense fog.

The Nantucket Visitor Information Center (25 Federal St.; 508-228-0925, nantucket-ma.gov/Pages/NantucketMA_Visitor/index) is located a couple blocks from the ferry terminal. They can help you find a hotel if you want to stay last-minute overnight.

Getting Around

You really don't need a car in Nantucket. The island is small, just 48 square miles (about the size of Boston), and has excellent bike paths and public transportation options. Bring your bike on the ferry or rent a bike when you arrive on the island.

Public bus: **NRTA, the Nantucket Regional Transit Authority** (508-228-7025; nrtawave.com), seasonal Wave bus service covers nearly the entire island, including the beaches and airport. Fares range from $1 to $2, depending on the distance.

Bike rentals: **Young's Bicycle Shop** (Steamship Wharf, 6 Broad St., Nantucket; 508-228-1151; youngsbicycleshop.com).

---

the lightships (stationary vessels moored to warn sailors of the dangerous shoals) as a way to pass the time. The museum's Nantucket basket collection includes several prized examples from the 19th century as well as works by contemporary basket makers carrying on the tradition. Ongoing basket-weaving demonstrations take place throughout the day. Open late May through early Oct, Tues through Sat.

NANTUCKET WHALING MUSEUM
15 Broad St.
Nantucket, MA 02554
(508) 228-1894
nha.org

Housed in an 1847 spermaceti candle-making building (that still smells faintly of whale), the Nantucket Whaling Museum has some amazing tales to tell. Highlights in the small but nicely laid-out facility include a 46-foot skeleton of a mighty sperm whale that washed ashore in 1998, whale-hunting harpoons, and artifacts from the Essex ship-wreck that inspired the novel *Moby-Dick*. The museum's rooftop widow's walk offers a panoramic view of the island and Nantucket Harbor. The museum is open daily Apr through Oct and closed during Jan; check website for days and times the rest of the year.

PROVINCETOWN ART ASSOCIATION AND MUSEUM
460 Commercial St.
Provincetown, MA 02657
(508) 487-1750
paam.org

Central to Provincetown's artistic identity is this small museum, founded in 1914 by a group of artists led by artist/teacher Charles Hawthorne. Today this dynamic institution stages superb shows that attract national attention, and its large permanent collection holds works by Provincetown Art Colony luminaries Robert Motherwell, Hans Hoffman, Edwin Dickinson, and Blanche Lazzell. The museum is an active art association and stages monthly members' exhibits and sells their work in the gift shop. Open daily Memorial Day through Sept; Thurs through Sun, Oct through May.

SANDWICH GLASS MUSEUM
129 Main St.
Sandwich, MA 02563
(508) 888-0251
sandwichglassmuseum.org

This engaging museum pays tribute to the country's first glass factory, the Boston and Sandwich Glass Works, which was founded here in 1825 and flourished as a manufacturer of pressed glass until 1888. On view are 6,000 vintage pieces that represent Sandwich glass craftsmanship through the years, from utilitarian candlesticks to elaborate cut-crystal glass bowls. Take in one of the live glassmaking demonstrations that are given throughout the day. Be sure to browse one of the Cape's best gift shops, where you can pick up glass keepsakes including Sandwich Glass replica pieces as well as one-of-a-kind works from contemporary artists. Open daily Apr through Dec; Wed through Sun during Feb and Mar (check in advance); closed in Jan.

Parks & Beaches

CRAIGVILLE BEACH
Craigville Beach Road
Centerville, MA 02632
(508) 790-6345

Craigville Beach is located mid-Cape on Nantucket Sound and features warm water and few waves. The beach attracts a mix of residents and vacationing families but is especially popular with sunbathing teens and the college crowd. There's a large bath-house with changing rooms and showers and the Barnacle Snack Bar is conveniently located across the street.

JETTIES BEACH
4 Bathing Beach Rd.
Nantucket, MA 02554
nantucket.net/beaches/jetties.php

If you are coming off the ferry as a day-tripper, Jetties Beach is a terrific choice. It's an easy 1-mile bike ride or the Wave bus will whisk you over from Nantucket town. Jetties is a gorgeous Sound beach with fine powdery sand, warm ocean water, and an impressive array of amenities including a bathhouse and a beachside pavilion that sells sunscreen and rents chairs, umbrellas, and Boogie Boards. Also located directly on the beach, The Jetties (thejetties.com) serves a menu of lobster rolls, burgers, and salads and has a decent raw bar. Have a Whale's Tale Pale Ale and an oyster shooter as you enjoy the sunset and live music before you head back to the mainland.

JOSEPH SYLVIA STATE BEACH
180 Beach Rd.
Oak Bluffs, MA 02557

Located between Oak Bluffs and Edgartown, along Vineyard Sound, this 2-mile beach has pearly white sand along with calm, temperate waters. It's a favorite spot for families with young children. The parking tends to fill early, but the beach is easy to reach by the VTA shuttle or by the bike path, which runs its length.

i Recognize the bridge? Of course you do. The bridge along Beach State Road on the town line between Oak Bluffs and Edgartown is the "Jaws Bridge." Film buffs will remember that Martha's Vineyard portrayed Amity Island in the film *Jaws*. In the summer, jumping off this bridge into Sengekontacket Pond is hugely popular with teens.

MENEMSHA BEACH
Basin Road
Menemsha, MA 02552

On the western end of the Vineyard, the village of Menemsha boasts a small cove-like crescent of a beach that is a favorite with families because of its calm, warm waters. Menemsha clears out in the afternoon until early evening, when a new crowd gathers, bringing beach chairs and a picnic dinner to watch as the sun disappears into the Atlantic. Afterward everyone applauds. Really.

i Two local spots that do a healthy business catering to the sunset crowd include Larsen's Fish Market (508-645-2680; larsensfishmarket.com) for steamed lobsters (in advance) and The Bite (508-645-2680; thebitemenemsha.com) for fried clams and clam chowder.

✳NAUSET BEACH
299 Beach Rd.
Orleans, MA 02653
(508) 240-3780

Not to be confused with Nauset Light Beach, which is part of the Cape Cod National Seashore, Nauset is a public beach in the town of Orleans. A long boardwalk leads from the parking lot across the dunes to this 10-mile stretch of sand, giving beachgoers plenty of room to spread out. Nauset is an Atlantic Ocean–facing beach, with great waves for Boogie Boarding, and is refreshingly brisk even on the hottest day. Liam's is directly on the beach near the entrance and is famous for its fried clams and onion rings.

(Q) Close-up

Cape Cod National Seashore

Called the "Great Beach" by Henry David Thoreau in his 1865 book *Cape Cod,* this fragile peninsula of sand-swept hills and pristine beach still is. Established in 1961 by President Kennedy as the Cape Cod National Seashore, the 40-mile stretch of sea and sand from Chatham to Provincetown remains untainted by commercial development. Within its borders are 6 lifeguarded beaches, 11 marked walking trails, 3 paved biking trails, and numerous freshwater ponds. This shoreline has also seen a whole lot of history, including the "first encounter" between the *Mayflower* Pilgrims and Natives and the first wireless transatlantic communication between the US and England.

Be sure to stop by the **Salt Pond Visitor Center** (Nauset Road and Route 6, Eastham; 508-255-3421; daily 9 a.m. to 4:30 p.m. with increased hours during the summer), where you can pick up maps to the beaches, check the schedules for guided biking, hiking, and canoe trips, and buy park passes. Patch-crazy kids will want to check out the junior-ranger offerings. There is a rotating schedule of orientation films, a bookstore, and small nature center to check out, too. Recommended: Start off with an easy walking adventure like the 1.5-mile **Nauset Marsh Trail Loop,** which begins just outside the visitor center. The Cape Cod National Seashore's secondary visitor center in Provincetown is worth a visit, too. One of the Cape's best scenic overlooks is the rooftop observation deck at the **Province Lands Visitor Center** (Race Point Road, Provincetown; 508-487-1256; open daily from May 1 through Oct 31, 9 a.m. to 5 p.m.), which offers 360-degree views of the Province Lands sand dunes and the Atlantic Ocean.

Daily vehicle beach parking fees (currently $15) are collected at the Cape Cod National Seashore from Memorial Day through the end of September. If you plan on visiting the beaches for more than 3 days, consider purchasing the Cape Cod National Seashore Annual Pass (currently $45). All forms of the "America the Beautiful" pass cover Cape Cod National Seashore parking fees. All passes can be purchased at the visitor centers; the "America the Beautiful" pass can also be purchased online at nps.gov/findapark/passes.htm.

Coast Guard Beach. *Doane Road, Eastham.* This is the closest beach to the Salt Pond Visitor Center. In the summer, plan on bringing everything you need with you because although parking is plentiful, you will need to take the shuttle bus

PILGRIM BARK PARK
Route 6 and Shank Painter Road
Provincetown, MA 02657
(508) 487-5166
provincetowndogpark.org
Provincetown loves dogs. A lot. This community park was created with dogs and their owners in mind. This landscaped, gated off-leash park has plenty of space for pups to run around and mingle. There's even a separate area just for small dogs. Other dog perks include multilevel dog water fountains and the large-scale art pieces that double as places for dogs to climb and/or rest.

(free) to the beach itself. It's worth it, though, for a beach that has room for everyone, including the seals passing through.

Nauset Light Beach. *Ocean View Drive, Eastham.* A mile north of Coast Guard Beach, red and white Nauset Light keeps watch over this part of the coast, as it has since 1923. Backed by high dunes and a long set of stairs, the beach itself features fine, tawny sand. Only strong swimmers can ride these ocean waves; the surf is often heavy.

Marconi Beach. *Marconi Beach Road, Wellfleet.* Gaze out at the ocean and Cape Cod Bay from the viewing platform atop this massive sand cliff. A plaque tells the story of how the beach was named for Italian inventor Guglielmo Marconi, who sent the first US-to-England transatlantic telegraph message from this bluff in 1903. Make your way down the steep stairs to the long and generous beach below. An exposed beach break attracts lots of surfers. In the afternoon, the cliffs provide natural shade from the sun.

Head of the Meadow Beach. *Head of the Meadow, Truro.* Perhaps the most underused of the Cape Cod National Seashore beaches, this stretch of sand is adjacent to miles of salt marshes. The habitat supports a diversity of bird species, so bring binoculars. This is an ideal place to savor some quiet.

Herring Cove Beach. *Province Lands Road, Provincetown.* Herring is warmer than nearby Race Point Beach and has few waves. Facing southwest over the ocean, Herring Cove has some of New England's most spectacular sunsets. Know that walking down the trail to the left will land you in an area that has tacitly been given over to the gay and lesbian crowd.

Race Point Beach. *Race Point Road, Provincetown.* The final stretch of beach at the tip of the Cape features fine white sand, cold, bracing water, and just-right waves. Be on the lookout for whales, which come closer to the coast here than anywhere else on the eastern seaboard. Check out, too, the 1897 Old Harbor Life Saving Station, which once housed a unit of the US Lifesaving Service, the precursor of today's Coast Guard. Open during the summer, the station features original lifesaving equipment and new exhibits that tell the tales of Cape Cod shipwrecks and rescues at sea. Ranger staff perform rescue reenactments on Thurs evenings from June through Aug.

SANDY NECK BEACH
425 Sandy Neck Rd.
West Barnstable, MA 02668
(508) 362-8300
town.barnstable.ma.us/sandyneckpark/
default.aspx

This bayside beauty has pebbly brown sand, low waves, and a very gradual drop-off. The kids will dig the critter-filled tide pools and you'll dig the expansive vistas of Province-town in the far-off distance. This is also a great walking beach, providing nearly a 6-mile run of endless beach for your daily constitutional.

✳SKAKET BEACH
Rocky Harbor Road
Orleans, MA 02653

Skaket is small compared to other Cape beaches, with just ½-mile or so of sandy shoreline, but it's a favorite of area families. It's a Cape Cod Bay beach, so the waves are minimal and there is a slight drop-off, so kids can play without getting in over their heads. Splashers enjoy the tidal pools and looking for hermit crabs, the hard-packed sand is great for building castles, and the grassy sand dunes are perfect for kite-flying (they even sell kites at the beach concession stand). Other nice amenities include picnic tables and a bathhouse with changing rooms. There's plenty of parking adjacent to the beach, which is especially convenient for parents hauling sand toys and tots.

SURFSIDE BEACH
Surfside Road
Nantucket, MA 02554
nantucket.net/beaches/surfside.php

Located on the southern coast of the island, 3 miles from the ferry docks and easily reached by bike or the Wave bus, this long beach stretches to both the left and right, creating a feeling of remoteness and total beach escape. This is an Atlantic-side beach with surf that is particularly well suited to water sports and fishing.

Wildlife & Zoos

MONOMOY NATIONAL WILDLIFE REFUGE
30 Wikis Way, Morris Island
Chatham, MA 02633
(508) 945-0594
fws.gov/northeast/monomoy

This 7,000-acre wildlife preserve includes Morris Island (which is linked to Chatham by a causeway and can be reached by car) and the uninhabited barrier islands of North and South Monomoy. Morris Island is a great spot for birders; it is home to several bird species including nesting piping plovers, great cormorants, egrets, herons, and common terns. Check in at the refuge headquarters for a trail map or (in summer) sign up for a naturalist-led bird walk. The Monomoy Islands are accessible only by boat and are a haven for a thriving colony of harbor seals—thousands upon thousands of them. Keep your distance.

THORNTON BURGESS MUSEUM
4 Water St.
East Sandwich, MA 02563
(508) 888-4668
thorntonburgess.org

In the picture-perfect village of Sandwich, this charming museum dedicated to children's author and Sandwich native Thornton Burgess evokes the idyllic woodland setting of the author's beloved storybooks. The museum features memorabilia relating to both Thornton Burgess's role as an early conservationist and his famous animal characters, including Peter Rabbit, Reddy Fox, and Jimmy Skunk. Open Mon through Sat, early June through mid-October. Note: 2 miles down the road, the Thornton Burgess Society also maintains the Green Briar Nature Center and Jam Kitchen (6 Discovery Hill Rd., East Sandwich; 508-888-6870), where visitors can walk the trails and/or sign up for jam-making workshops.

WELLFLEET BAY WILDLIFE SANCTUARY (MASSACHUSETTS AUDUBON)
291 Route 6
South Wellfleet, MA 02667
(508) 349-2615
wellfleetbay.org

One of Mass Audubon's more far-flung reaches, Wellfleet Bay has 5 miles of interconnecting trails that wind through woodlands, salt marsh, and barrier beach dunes. Guided walks and a full slate of programs for kids are offered year-round. The spiffy Platinum LEED-certified nature center is a model of green architecture, utilizing solar panels, composting toilets, and gray-water gardening methods.

i Wellfleet Bay has a small (20-site) family campground that is highly sought after and available exclusively to Massachusetts Audubon members.

Wineries & Breweries

✳CISCO BREWERS
5 Bartlett Farm Rd.
Nantucket, MA 02554
(508) 325-5929
ciscobrewers.com

A rare three-in-one drinking opportunity, Cisco Brewers is also home to Triple Eight Distillery and Nantucket Vineyards and is purportedly one of only 8 producers in the world that make beer, spirits, and wine. Visit the tasting-room bars where the atmosphere is laid-back and welcoming. There's often live music in the courtyard in the late afternoon to enjoy the sunset along with your glass of the brand's flagship, Whale's Tale Pale Ale. Cisco doesn't sell any food, but

there are lots of picnic tables on the property (regulars know to stop by Bartlett Farm on the way and pick up gourmet sandwiches). Brewery tours are also offered (by appointment). Open daily year-round; check website for hours.

TRURO VINEYARD
11 Shore Rd., Route 6A
Truro, MA 02652
(508) 487-6200
trurovineyardsofcapecod.com

On the way to Provincetown stop for a sip at this pretty seaside winery. The Cape's microclimate of sandy soil and warm ocean breezes has proved perfect for the growing of Chardonnay, Merlot, and Cabernet Franc grapes. Pinot Grigio is Truro Vineyards' specialty, but they also produce a highly regarded estate Chardonnay. Tastings are offered year-round ($10 for 5 pours) and in summer there are daily free tours at 1 and 3 p.m.

ACTIVITIES & EVENTS

Arts Venues

CAPE COD MELODY TENT
21 W. Main St.
Hyannis, MA 02601
(508) 775-5630
melodytent.org

The Cape Cod Melody Tent opened in the summer of 1950 and continues the tradition of summer music circus tents with a 2,500-seat theater in the round. Today the Melody Tent is an even better summer music venue with a state-of-the-art sound and a computerized lighting system. National pop, folk, and country acts are scheduled every summer. Watch for performances by the likes of the Beach Boys, a cappella group Straight No Chaser, and comedian Bill Maher.

CAPE PLAYHOUSE
820 Route 6A
Dennis, MA 02638
(877) 385-3911
capeplayhouse.com
This venerable playhouse has entertained the Cape since 1927. The most polished and consistent of Cape summer stock theater companies, the Cape Playhouse offers crisply produced shows starring freshly minted musical theater grads working alongside equity actors. Six shows are produced throughout the summer. Recent productions have included *The Graduate, Legally Blonde,* and *Footloose.* The Kids Bits series of family performances packs them in with a varied selection of plays, storytelling, puppetry, music, and magic on Thurs and Fri at 11 a.m. all summer.

COTUIT CENTER FOR THE ARTS
4404 Falmouth Rd., Route 28
Cotuit, MA 02635
(508) 428-0669
artsonthecape.org
The Cotuit Center is a handsome, modern building that serves as a year-round performance space and fine arts center for the Cape's growing corps of talented visual and performing artists and residents. Ongoing classes are given in pottery, painting, photography, and drawing, and there are numerous workshops for both adults and children. Visitors are welcome to attend the gallery shows, join the weekly Cape Cod drum circle, and take in the concerts and theater productions.

Cruises

✳SCHOONER *LIBERTÉ*
227 Clinton Ave.
Falmouth, MA 02540
(508) 548-26262
theliberte.com
To fully appreciate the Cape, get out on the water in a boat using nothing but the wind for power. The *Liberté,* a 74-foot, 3-mast schooner, is docked in Falmouth Harbor every summer from late June through the end of August. It takes passengers out on the harbor several times a day, but the sunset cruise is the one to choose. You can also charter the boat and its crew for a private sail.

WHALE WATCH DOLPHIN FLEET
305 Commercial St.
Provincetown, MA 02657
(508) 240-3636
whalewatch.com
Provincetown is the closest port to the nutrient-rich waters of the Stellwagen Bank Marine Sanctuary, the summer feeding ground of minke, humpback, and finback whales. Leaving from Macmillan Wharf, Dolphin's naturalist-led whale excursions get you to and from the sanctuary quickly, which allows you more time to spend viewing the whales.

Festivals & Annual Events

DAFFODIL FESTIVAL
Throughout the island
Nantucket, MA 02554
daffodilfestival.com
In spring 3 million daffodils create a sea of yellow (and white and pink) blossoms throughout the island of Nantucket. During the last weekend of April, Nantucket honors

its favorite flower with an antique car parade, a daffodil hat pageant, and parades where both kids and canines don daffodil-themed finery (and look awfully cute).

PROVINCETOWN ARTS FESTIVAL
Venues throughout Provincetown
Provincetown, MA 02657
provincetowngalleryguild.org
One of the country's oldest working art colonies, Provincetown opens its doors for 10 days in mid-September. Temporary public art installations pop up all over town and there are dozens of events, most of them free, including open galleries, play readings, and musical performances.

WELLFLEET OYSTER FEST
Center of Wellfleet
Wellfleet, MA 02667
wellfleetoysterfest.org
Organizers expect 100,000 local Wellfleet oysters to be consumed during the festival's 3-day run, and you can do your part by sampling from among the many types of succulent bivalves available from the dozen different raw bar tents. The festival's signature event is the shuck-off, where you can expect to see high drama as both amateurs and professionals (fishermen, fishmongers, chefs) compete for cash—and local bragging rights. Held the 3rd weekend in Oct.

Fishing

BILL FISHER TACKLE
127 Orange St.
Nantucket, MA 02554
(508) 228-2261
billfishertackle.com
Both Jetties and Surfside draw anglers from dusk into the night surfcasting for blues and stripers. Bill Fisher is the place to go on the island to get the tackle, bait, and veteran advice you need.

SANDWICH FISH HATCHERY
164 Route 6A
Sandwich, MA 02563
(508) 888-0008
This state-run fish hatchery is the oldest in the country and is a great quick stop to pass some time with the kids after a morning at the beach. Nearly 200,000 trout (rainbow, brown, brook, and tiger) are raised here annually to stock the state's lakes and ponds. Visitors can see how the hatchery operates, walk along the fish raceways, and give the fish meal pellets provided from the coin-operated machines. Have the kids make the fish jump by feeding them one pellet at a time, or toss in a handful of pellets and watch the feeding frenzy. Open daily 9 a.m. to 3 p.m.

Golf

DENNIS GOLF
825 Old Bass River Rd.
Dennis, MA 02638
(508) 385-8347
dennisgolf.com
Few Cape public golf courses offer as much as Dennis Golf. Take your pick from one of two 18-hole courses, Dennis Highlands and Dennis Pines. The Highlands is pleasing to the eye and the easier of the two, while tree-lined Pines is ranked as one of the best public courses in the state. It's also a good value thanks to its reasonable green fees.

CAPE COD & THE ISLANDS

Health & Wellness

MID-CAPE RACQUET & HEALTH CLUB
193 Whites Path
South Yarmouth, MA 02664
(508) 394-3511
midcaperacquet.com
Grab your racket and fine-tune your skills at Mid-Cape Racquet & Health, which has 9 indoor tennis courts. They offer a full range of lessons, round robins, and clinics as well as competitive tennis leagues for adults and kids. Mid-Cape Racquet is also a full fitness club. Enjoy everything from cardio machines to spin classes to top-notch Pilates fitness instruction. Other amenities include child care, Jacuzzi, sauna, and steam. Drop-ins are welcome—and common. The club offers visitors a day pass, weekly pass, or 10-visit punch card.

SOLSTICE SPA
408 Main St.
Hyannis, MA 02601
(508) 775-7400
solsticedayspa.com
Solstice Spa is the Cape's day spa of choice to escape the stress of everyday life and enjoy a few hours of pampering. Delicious body wraps and scrubs, relaxing massages, and expert facials await you in a soothing atmosphere. Vacation beauty emergency? Solstice excels at blowouts and last-minute mani-pedis, too.

Hiking, Biking & Walking

ART'S BIKE SHOP
91 County Rd.
North Falmouth, MA 02556
(508) 563-7379
artsbikeshop.com
Just a few minutes from the beginning of the Shining Sea Bikeway, this full-service bike shop features a well-rounded selection of bikes to rent. And if the terrain takes a toll on your bike, your repairs will be mended with efficiency.

BARBARA'S BIKE SHOP
430 Route 134
South Dennis, MA
(508) 760.4723
barbsbikeshop.com
Rent and ride! Located at the very beginning of the Cape Cod Rail Trail in Dennis, this bike shop rents all manner of bikes (including children's and adult tandems). And if you don't feel like riding back, you can drop off your rental at their Nickerson State Park location in Brewster, 11 miles away.

CAPE COD CANAL BIKE PATH
60 Ed Moffitt Dr.
Sandwich, MA 02563
(508) 833-9678
This arrow-straight 7-mile bike/walking path follows both banks of the Cape Cod Canal between the Bourne Bridge and the Sagamore Bridge. The paved paths are the access roads for the US Army Corps of Engineers and you will find that the Cape side trail is used much more than the mainland side. Along the way, you'll also often see quite a lot of boat traffic moving through the canal. The path passes under 3 bridges (the Cape Cod Rail, Bourne, and Sagamore) on the way to the path's end point at quiet Scusset Beach on Buzzards Bay.

*CAPE COD RAIL TRAIL
Route 134
Dennis, MA 02660
Enjoy some of the best nature that the Cape has to offer on the Cape Cod Rail Trail, one of the most popular bike paths in the entire

state. The trail starts from Dennis, crossing much of mid-Cape before ending at the Cape Cod National Seashore in Wellfleet. The flat, paved 22-mile path follows the Old Colony railroad track bed past Harwich's cranberry bogs, dipping into oak and pine woods at Nickerson Park before ending with cool ocean headwinds at Le Count Hollow Beach. Along the way there are plenty of places to stop for a bite to eat or to take a dip.

GREAT ISLAND TRAIL
Parking lot off of Chequessett Neck Road
Wellfleet, MA 02667
This Wellfleet hike is a favorite for beach lovers who enjoy solitude. It's a moderately strenuous 6-mile round-trip hike on a mostly sandy trail taking you through an extraordinary diversity of Cape Cod National Seashore scenery, including pitch pine–covered hills and tidal flats along the way to Jeremy Point at the ocean's edge.

NATURE WATCH
455 State Rd., Suite 178
Vineyard Haven, MA 02568
(508) 693-4908
The Vineyard offers a superb opportunity to see a great variety of birds, including as many as 30 species of ducks. Robert Culbert of Nature Watch is among the most experienced birders in the region. He offers a weekly (May through Oct) Saturday morning bird-watching tour suitable for both first-time birders who need instruction on how to use binoculars and seasoned birders who are looking to add new species to their life list. Birding trips typically depart by caravan from Martha's Vineyard Regional High School at 9 a.m. and last 2½ hours in the field. Call in advance to confirm tour time or to arrange a private tour.

SHINING SEA BIKEWAY
Routes 151 and 28A
North Falmouth, MA 02556
This bike trail is named the Shining Sea to honor Falmouth native Katharine Lee Bates, who wrote the words to the song "America the Beautiful." This easy 10-mile route begins in North Falmouth, passing farmland and cranberry bogs. The route hugs Vineyard Sound for a mile or so before swinging you into the fishing village of Woods Hole. This route is also a favorite for runners and walkers.

Horseback Riding

EMERALD HOLLOW FARM
235 Run Hill Rd.
Brewster, MA 02631
(508) 685-6811
emeraldhollowfarm.com
Travel along the shaded trails and enjoy the flora and fauna of the 835-acre Punkhorn Parklands conservation area on an hourlong guided trail ride. Emerald Hollow caters primarily to first-time riders: The pace is leisurely and the staff are friendly and safety minded.

Kidstuff

CAPE COD MUSEUM OF NATURAL HISTORY
869 Main St., Route 6A
Brewster, MA 02631
(508) 896-3867
ccmnh.org
This engaging nature center is packed with hands-on exhibits and a small collection of wildlife residents helping to introduce kids to the unique ecosystem of the Cape. Special hikes and activities geared toward young trailblazers take place every week. There are 2 marked 1-mile trails for families to explore

that are short enough for even the youngest scout in the family to complete.

CAPE COD POTATO CHIP FACTORY
100 Breed's Hill Rd.
Hyannis, MA 02601
(888) 881-2447
capecodchips.com
The Cape Cod Potato Chip factory tour is one of the Cape's top attractions: a fun, quick stop—and super crowded on a rainy summer day. Tours are a self-guided walk down a glass-enclosed corridor where you can watch (and smell!) the manufacturing process from spud to chip. At the end, you are given 2 sample bags of Cape Cod hand-stirred kettle-cooked potato chips (and the opportunity to buy more in the gift shop). Open Mon through Fri 9 a.m. to 5 p.m., closed Sat and Sun.

FLYING HORSES CAROUSEL
15 Lake Ave.
Oak Bluffs, MA 02557
(508) 693-9481
mvpreservation.org
There's plenty of old-time fun to be had on this vintage carousel located inside a quaint red barn. The carousel itself dates from 1876 but was almost scrapped in the 1980s. The Martha's Vineyard Preservation Trust rallied to save the carousel and have it designated a National Historic Landmark. Now the 1923 Wurlitzer band organ plays and the 20 hand-carved horses have been beautifully restored, each featuring real glass eyes and a horsehair mane and tail. Open Easter Saturday through Columbus Day; check for times.

PIRATE'S COVE MINI GOLF
782 Main St.
South Yarmouth, MA 02664
(508) 394-6200
piratescove.net
With an over-the-top pirate theme, this is the most elaborate of the Cape's many minigolf courses. And because one is never enough, there are two 18-hole courses here, both with lots of water features and trick shots that make minigolfing such a blast.

i Woods Hole is a world center for marine, biomedical, and environmental studies. Those with a scientific bent may want to check out the Woods Hole Oceanographic Institute (15 School St.; 508-289-2663) and the Marine Biological Lab (100 Water St.; 508-289-2252; mbl.edu). Both institutions have exhibit centers open to the public and offer behind-the-scenes summer walking tours of their facilities. The guides are often retired scientists or teachers who really love their work.

WOODS HOLE SCIENCE AQUARIUM
166 Water St.
Woods Hole, MA 02543
(508) 495-2001
aquarium.nefsc.noaa.gov
The operative word in this aquarium's name is "science." This is not a world-ranging mega-aquarium, but a friendly, small facility that concentrates on marine animals from the Northeast and Mid-Atlantic waters. Among the creatures that live here are turtles, lobsters, jellyfish, fresh- and saltwater fish, and 2 harbor seals, Bumper and Luseal. Dating from 1875, this is the nation's first public aquarium. Although the exhibits are somewhat dated, the easy-to-view tanks,

accessible touching pool, free admission (!), and absence of crowds make this a great outing with small children. Open daily from Memorial Day weekend through Labor Day; open Tues through Sat the rest of the year.

Nightlife

BRICK CELLAR BAR
137 Main St.
Edgartown, MA 02539
(508) 627-5850
atriamv.com/bar.html
Downstairs from the restaurant Atria, Brick boasts a dark, sultry ambience and is a Vineyarder go-to spot for a late-night cocktail and jazz. Comfortable, with leather armchairs, a burnished brass bar, and lots of nooks and crannies, it is the perfect hideaway—and now you're in on the secret.

CHICKEN BOX
14 Dave St.
Nantucket, MA 02584
(508) 228-9717
thechickenbox.com
The atmosphere is lively, even raucous, over at the Box, a live music venue of long standing that features reggae, rock, and rhythm and blues bands nightly in the summer and on the weekends in the off-season. The Box is a Nantucket institution attracting a crowd of mostly young locals and visitors with cheap beer, a low cover charge, and a large dance floor.

EMBARGO
453 Main St.
Hyannis Port, MA 02601
(508) 771-9700
No website
Bringing urban flair to the Cape, Embargo has a global tapas-style menu that features dishes like ahi tuna sliders and grilled lamb

lollipops with pomegranate sauce. A huge (96-foot-long) central bar and potent cocktails complete the picture. After 10 p.m. the space becomes a full-on nightclub with live bands and DJ music.

Cod Ball: The Cape Cod Baseball League

A well-loved Cape summer tradition since 1885, the Cape Cod Baseball League (capecodbaseball .org) is one of the premier amateur leagues in the country. The 10-team league attracts some of the country's best college baseball players. While the players are hoping to catch the attention of visiting scouts, you just might catch the next Jason Varitek (Hyannis '91 and '93) or Tim Lincecum (Harwich '05) before he lands in the major leagues. The 44-game season runs from mid-June to mid-August and games are played almost nightly (under the lights) at town or high school fields across the Cape. Admission is free, but you may want to toss in a few dollars when they pass around the baseball hat.

Theater

WELLFLEET DRIVE-IN THEATRE
51 State Hwy., Route 6
Wellfleet, MA 02667
(508) 349-7176
wellfleetcinemas.com/drive-in-theatre
One of the last of its kind, the 1950s-era Wellfleet Drive-In schedules first-run double-feature movies all summer long. You can

CAPE COD & THE ISLANDS

take in a movie under the stars and fill up on popcorn and ice cream from the concession stand. The gates open at 7 p.m. and the films start at sundown. Cash only. Open Memorial Day weekend through Labor Day weekend.

Water Sports

＊FLYER'S BOAT RENTAL
131 Commercial St.
Provincetown, MA 02657
(508) 497-0898
flyersrentals.com
Flyer's is a full-service boatyard. Rent a kayak to explore sheltered Provincetown Harbor and paddle to the lighthouse at Long Point. Learn to sail, or if you are an "old salt," take a refresher course—you can rent sailboats here by the hour. Flyer's also rents power-boats, from easy-to-handle 2-passenger personal watercraft to 6-person, 19-foot cruisers.

i Experience a nearly secluded Cape Cod beach. In the summer season, Flyer's runs a pontoon shuttle boat to Long Point, at the very tip of Cape Cod. You can spend some time on the beach and visit the abandoned lighthouse. Take one of the later shuttles back or better yet, trek the 1 mile across the breakwater jetty to Provincetown.

RIDEAWAY KAYAK
449 Route 6A
Sandwich, MA 02537
(508) 247-0827
rideawaykayak.com
Putter along Scorton Creek in Sandwich to explore a marsh island frequented by ospreys or choose to rent from RideAway's New Sea-bury location and venture to Popponesset Island, where the beach makes a perfect

break point. They also operate guided excursions, including a popular sunset tour, as well as give lessons and rentals for the current "it" sport, stand-up paddleboarding.

SHOPPING

Antiques

ANTIQUES CENTER OF YARMOUTH
325 Route 28
West Yarmouth, MA 02673
(508) 771-3327
antiquescenterofyarmouth.com
The Cape is well-known as a prime destination for antiques hounds. One of the easiest ways for visitors to go antiques shopping is to try this collection of 150 independent dealers where you can lose yourself among the china, clocks, silver, lighting fixtures, and furniture.

MARINE SPECIALTIES
235 Commercial St.
Provincetown, MA 02657
(508) 487-1730
ptownarmynavy.com
In keeping with P-town's quirky individuality, nothing is off limits at Marine Specialties. The warehouse-size space is filled to the rafters with nautical surplus, gas masks, lobster pots, combat boots, and feather boas. In the summer the store stays open until 1 a.m.—it's a scene.

Art Galleries

JULIE HELLER GALLERY
2 Gosnold St.
Provincetown, MA 02657
(508) 487-2169
juliehellergallery.com

This is one of Provincetown's most established galleries—and friendly, too. The specialty here is 20th-century modernist American art, including some early Provincetown figures. There is also a secondary space, Julie Heller East at 465 Commercial St., that shows works mostly by established, contemporary artists.

i Join the party that is Provincetown during the weekly summer Friday night gallery stroll. Galleries up and down Commercial Street stay open late and host openings (often with wine and snacks) that give art-lovers an opportunity to meet and chat with the artists.

✳SCARGO POTTERY & ART GALLERY
30 Dr. Lord's Rd. South
Dennis, MA 02638
(508) 385-3894
scargopottery.com
Nestled in the woods near Scargo Lake, this unique working indoor/outdoor pottery studio is worth a stop to watch potters at the wheel and browse items in the showroom gallery that features the work of the four Holl sisters and resident artist Meden Parker. Signature pieces include glazed earthenware mugs, plates, birdbaths, tiles, and large-scale sculptural pieces.

Auctions

SANDWICH AUCTION HOUSE
15 Tupper Rd.
Sandwich, MA 02563
(508) 888-1926
sandwichauction.com
A diverse audience of art and antiques dealers, collectors, and vacationers keep prices reasonable at these weekly sales that specialize in unloading whole house contents. You never know what you'll find, but sample wares include Persian rugs, rare books, antique furniture, and choice knickknacks. Auctions are held every Wed during the summer and on Sat the rest of the year with previews beginning at 2 p.m.

Books

BREWSTER BOOKSHOP
2648 Main St.
Brewster, MA 02631
(508) 896-6543
brewsterbookstore.com
This cozy, neat-as-a-pin year-round neighborhood bookstore stocks classics and the *New York Times* best sellers along with the best of the best in children's books. They also stock a delightful selection of educational toys and games that after a string of rainy days may save your family vacation.

BUNCH OF GRAPES BOOKSTORE
35 Main St.
Vineyard Haven, MA 02568
(508) 693-2291
bunchofgrapes.com
This 40-year-old Vineyard landmark has recently moved into new digs across the street from its original location. The modern, bright 3,000-square-foot space is now all on one floor with stock ranging from best-selling fiction and nonfiction to local-interest and children's books. Count on lots of author book signings during the summer—sometimes as many as 4 a week—after all, everyone wants to be on the Vineyard. Open year-round.

i On summer Friday nights, Grace Church (Woodlawn Avenue and William Street, Vineyard Haven; 508-693-0332, gracechurchmv.com) famously hosts a lobster roll church dinner that is so popular, it's a tourist attraction in its own right. The lobster roll—a hot dog bun filled with lobster meat mixed with a touch of mayonnaise, is generous and the price—$15—includes a beverage and a bag of chips. Enjoy at the picnic tables on the church lawn or have it packed to go.

Farmers' Markets & Pick Your Own

BARTLETT FARM
33 Bartlett Farm Rd.
Nantucket, MA 02554
(508) 228-9408
bartlettsfarm.com

The shelves at Bartlett's are stocked with produce, fresh-baked breads and pastries, local cheeses, and handmade pastas and sauces. The addition of a sandwich counter makes this a must-stop on the way to **Cisco Brewers** (see p. 151). Both the garden center and the farm stand are open daily year-round, and in-season Bartlett's homegrown corn and tomatoes are the best on the island.

MORNING GLORY FARM
120 Meshacket Rd.
Edgartown, MA 02539
(508) 627-9674
morninggloryfarm.com

What makes it so convenient for food-loving Vineyarders who come to Morning Glory Farm for the selection of homegrown seasonal produce, farm-raised grass-fed beef, fresh eggs, and fresh-baked cranberry-blueberry pie is that they can also check off an entire grocery list in the process. In the back there are made-to-order sandwiches, homemade soups, and a wonderful salad bar. Closed in the winter.

Fashion & Shoes

MURRAY'S TOGGERY
62 Main St.
Nantucket, MA 02554
(508) 228-0437
nantucketreds.com

Nantucket Reds—that iconic symbol of carefree summer days spent on the Faraway Island—were invented at Murray's in the 1950s. The light red chinos get better with age as they fade to a light salmon pink. The clothing line has expanded to include pants, shorts, and shirts for men, women, and children along with all types of accessories including baseball hats, socks, and shoes. The store also stocks other brands of resort wear. Closed Sun.

✳PURITAN CAPE COD
408 Main St.
Hyannis, MA 02601
(508) 775-2400
puritancapecod.com

On Main Street in the heart of Hyannis, generations of Cape Codders have shopped at Puritan since the department store's founding in 1919. Don't let the name "Puritan" mislead you; the store carries only the finest fashions for the entire family: steadfast but thoroughly modern brands like Vineyard Vines, Barbour, Burberry, and Eileen Fisher. They also have a house brand, the Chatham Chino Company, which is solidly made and isn't off-the-chart expensive. Closed Sun. Additional location information is available on the company's website.

VINEYARD VINES

56 Narragansett Ave.
Oak Bluffs, MA 02557
(508) 687-9841
vineyardvines.com

Sporty, summery, preppy. Clothing retailer Vineyard Vines was founded in Edgartown in 1998 by brothers Shep and Ian Murray and is the embodiment of all that is the Vineyard. The brand is best known for its whimsical ties, including ones with whales, lighthouses, and Red Sox logos. Real New England weddings always have the groom and groomsmen wearing Vineyard Vines ties! The company has since expanded to well beyond ties with a full line of men's, women's, and children's clothing that brings fun updates to traditional New England staples. The Edgartown store is the brand's original location, but the Oak Bluffs store is open year-round. Additional location information is available on the Vineyard Vines website.

Flea Markets

WELLFLEET FLEA MARKET

51 State Hwy., Route 6
Wellfleet, MA 02667
(508) 349-0541
wellfleetcinemas.com/flea-market

An anything-goes spirit prevails at the huge Wellfleet Flea Market, which takes place in the parking lot of the Wellfleet Drive-In Theatre. As many as 200 vendors set up hawking antiques, used books, record albums, nostalgic knickknacks, handmade jewelry, and vintage clothing. On summer gray-weather days, it's packed. Bring cash. Summer markets: Wed, Thurs, Sat, and Sun from 8 a.m. to 3 p.m.; check website for spring/fall dates.

General Store

ALLEY'S GENERAL STORE

1041 State Rd. (Martha's Vineyard)
West Tisbury, MA
(508) 693-0088
mvpreservation.org

Alley's is a Vineyard landmark, an old-time general store dating from 1858. Now operated under the auspices of the Martha's Vineyard Preservation Society, the store stocks its shelves with pantry necessities including milk, bread, home-style jams and jellies, and cereal. Because of the hot coffee, the *Boston Globe* (and *New York Times*), and a community bulletin board, Alley's is still the place to go for island news and gossip. Open daily year-round.

Gifts

BIRD WATCHER'S GENERAL STORE

36 Route 6A
Orleans, MA 02653
(508) 255-6974
birdwatchersgeneralstore.com

The Outer Cape is a birding hot spot. Conveniently located on the way to the Cape Cod National Seashore, Wellfleet Bay Wildlife Sanctuary, and Monomoy National Wildlife Refuge, this store is a great stop for both serious and aspiring birders. Find a terrific selection of field guides, binoculars, and spotting scopes. They also carry bird seed and bird feeders for your backyard birding needs, along with quality bird-themed gifts.

✳NANTUCKET LOOMS

51 Main St.
Nantucket, MA 02554
(508) 228-1908
nantucketlooms.com

Nantucket Looms produces a style of muted, hand-woven textiles to create rugs, throws, and upholstery fabrics that put a fresh spin on New England decor. The weaving studio is located on the second floor; the first-floor gallery carries the company's full line of products including its signature brushed mohair throw. This is also an artist collective and the shop showcases local artisan work, including handmade jewelry, ship models, and Nantucket lightship baskets.

SHELL SHOP
276 Commercial St.
Provincetown, MA 02657
(508) 487-1763
theshellshop.com
Sought out by both local interior designers and lovers of kitsch, this shop is a treasure trove of seashell art and loose shells from tasteful to delightfully tacky. It's also a great choice for inexpensive souvenir sea trinkets for the kids.

Jewelry

✳CB STARK JEWELERS
53 Main St.
Vineyard Haven, MA 02568
(508) 693-2284
cbstark.com
Since 1966 CB Stark has been the place on the Vineyard to go for a pear-shaped engagement ring or a strand of pearls. But don't think you can't afford anything here. Some of the best-selling items include Vineyard charms and charm beads (to fit Pandora bracelets) and a just-for-fun sand dollar pendant. If you find a special piece of frosted sea glass on the beach, bring it here and Stark can turn it into a custom pendant. A second location is at 27 N. Water St., Edgartown, MA 02359.

Specialty Food

✳ATLANTIC SPICE COMPANY
2 Shore Rd.
Truro, MA 02652
(800) 316-7965
atlanticspice.com
Vacationing professional chefs and serious home cooks know to make the trek to this Truro warehouse store to stock up on exotic and traditional spices, herbs, and more than 250 other provisions. The great prices on gourmet pantry basics such as vanilla beans, saffron threads, and arborio rice are reason enough to go, as are the friendly staff, who are happy to provide tips on how to use everything.

CAPE COD SALT WATER TAFFY
984 Route 28
South Yarmouth, MA 02664
(508) 394-7557
capecodsaltwatertaffy.com
A trip to the beach isn't complete without buying a box of saltwater taffy. Shaded by a red-and-white-striped awning, this quaint roadside stand displays a colorful selection of 30 varieties of saltwater taffy that's been cooked, stretched, and wrapped right on site. Bring the kids and watch the candy-makers at work. Open seasonally Apr through Oct.

✳CHATHAM JAM & JELLY SHOP
10 Vineyard Ave.
Chatham, MA 02669
chathamjamandjellyshop.com
Husband and wife Robin and Carol Cummings launched their jam business from their home kitchen in 1983. Today all the jams and jellies sold at this adorable Cape Cod cottage are still kettle-cooked in small batches from the tiny kitchen in the back. At any one time, the shop's shelves are filled

with more than 100 varieties of preserves from Cape Cod Rose Hip Jelly to Strawberry Rhubarb Jam to Cranberry Apple Butter.

i For more than 80 years in Chatham, Friday evenings have been filled with the sound of town-band concerts. The free concerts are held in the gazebo (where else!) on the grounds of Kate Gould Park on Main Street and begin at 8 p.m. There's something for everyone; these days you'll hear "The Bunny Hop" and "Sweet Caroline" along with rousing patriotic tunes. Bring your beach chairs, blankets, and a picnic.

✳CHILMARK CHOCOLATES
19 State Rd.
Chilmark, MA 02535
(508) 645-3013
It's a bit of a drive to Chilmark, but that doesn't stop legions of fans from making the pilgrimage to this small, homey shop for its hand-dipped chocolates. Favorites include the almond chocolate toffee, dark chocolate peanut butter bars, and truffles. It's not just that the chocolates are delectable; both the candy-making and retail operation employ workers with disabilities. Closed Mon through Wed and late Dec through Jan.

PROVINCETOWN FUDGE FACTORY
210 Commercial St.
Provincetown, MA 02657
(508) 487-2850
ptownfudge.com
It's hard not to be drawn in by the smell of freshly made fudge wafting from this confectionary/ice cream shop. Indeed, on a summer day you'll see just about every kind of person imaginable (this is P-town!) pause by the door, sigh, and give in to temptation.

The shop makes more than a dozen flavors of smooth and creamy fudge including wonderfully old-fashioned penuche fudge made with vanilla and brown sugar. The shop's other signature treat is the homemade peanut butter cups, which have a soft, creamy inside and are made in milk, dark chocolate, and white chocolate varieties.

Sporting Goods

✳GOOSE HUMMOCK
15 Route 6A
Orleans, MA 02653
(508) 255-0455
goose.com
Need gear? Goose Hummock is a one-stop shop to rent or buy everything you need for outings on the water. They rent canoes, kayaks, and stand-up paddleboards (like walking on water) as well as sell saltwater, freshwater, and fly fishing tackle. Goose Hummock also offers a variety of classes and expeditions including a popular guided wade-fishing trip. You can launch kayaks right from their dock. And if you need a fishing charter, they can set you up.

ACCOMMODATIONS

Inns & Bed-and-Breakfasts

DAN'L WEBSTER INN $$–$$$
149 Main St.
Sandwich, MA 02563
(508) 888-3622
danlwebsterinn.com
This fine inn offers traditional "olde New England" elegance—with the price you might expect from an average motel. The inn's 48 rooms come in all shapes and sizes and are individually appointed with dark woods and rich fabrics. There are 3 restaurants on the

property and room rates typically include a breakfast voucher. Inn amenities include an outdoor pool, pretty landscaped gardens, and on-site Beach Plum Spa. The inn always has lots of great weekend packages that make it a great pick for spontaneous getaways.

DOCKSIDE INN $$$
9 Circuit Ave.
Oak Bluffs, MA 02557
(508) 693-2966
vineyardinns.com
Overlooking the busy harbor and located in the heart of Oak Bluffs, this Victorian inn has recently been totally revamped in the clean, modern style that is practically de rigueur for new lodgings. Each of the 21 rooms is done up in an ocean-inspired palette of soft blue and plum and features high-end linens and toiletries, a flat-screen TV, and free Wi-Fi. All rates include a continental breakfast. This inn is more child-friendly than many Vineyard inns and some suites have kitchenettes. Other extras include ice cream and snacks in the afternoon and complimentary beach gear to borrow. You'll love sitting out on the front veranda in a rocking chair as the world passes by.

PLATINUM PEBBLE INN $$$
186 Belmont Rd.
West Harwich, MA 02671
(508) 432-7766
platinumpebble.com
Luxury without pretense makes this 8-room retreat both a style-conscious and budget-conscious choice. The beds are piled high with pillows, down duvets, and Italian linens. All the rooms have marble baths with glass walk-in rain showers; some have soaking tubs. Breakfast is included and brought to your room or, if you prefer, poolside.

UNION STREET INN $$$–$$$$
7 Union St.
Nantucket, MA 02544
(508) 228-9222
unioninn.com
This 12-room luxury boutique property is tucked away from the center of town, yet within walking distance of the harbor. The gracious 1770s whale captain's home has been totally renovated and features gorgeous sun-flooded rooms appointed with designer fabrics, exceptional linens, antiques and custom-designed pieces, flat-screen TVs, and free Wi-Fi. Several rooms feature wood-burning fireplaces. Breakfasts are sumptuous and included in all rates.

WOODS HOLE INN $$$
28 Water St.
Woods Hole, MA 02453
(508) 495-0248
woodsholeinn.com
Experience total relaxation at this gray-shingled 1870 inn overlooking the harbor and located a stone's throw from the bustle of the picturesque fishing village of Woods Hole. The 14 rooms feature luxury linens and duvets and lavishly restored bathrooms that include pedestal sinks, claw-foot tubs, and rain-head showers. Wake up each morning to a gourmet continental breakfast served in the breakfast room or on the patio.

Hotels & Motels

CROWNE POINTE HISTORIC INN
& SPA $$
82 Bradford St.
Provincetown, MA 02657
(508) 487-6767
crownepointe.com
The Crowne Point is a good choice if you appreciate the intimacy of a B&B with the

style and sophistication of an upscale hotel. Each of the 40 rooms and suites is spacious and decorated with soothing neutral colors. Rates include a gourmet cooked-to-order breakfast conveniently served until 11 a.m. for late risers. The best rooms are located in the mansion and have balconies overlooking the landscaped courtyard. Other nice touches? Free parking (not so easy in P-town!), a late-afternoon wine and cheese social, and use of the spa's sauna and steam room.

PEQUOT HOTEL $$–$$$
19 Pequot Ave.
Oak Bluffs, MA 02557
(508) 693-5087
pequothotel.com
Blessed with a prime location close to Oak Bluff's Camp Meeting Grounds (the "gingerbread cottages") and just 1 block from State Beach, this Victorian inn offers 32 charmingly quirky rooms (all with private bath) spread across 3 buildings. Room rates are affordable and include an expanded continental breakfast and afternoon cookies. Free Wi-Fi is available in the hotel's common areas. Children are welcome.

SEA CREST BEACH HOTEL $$
350 Quaker Rd.
Falmouth, MA 02556
(508) 540-9400
seacrestbeachhotel.com
You'll love this hotel, a perfect base for a family vacation, for its private powdery soft white sand beach, freshly renovated rooms in fun, vibrant colors, 2 pools (indoor and outdoor and both are saline), and water sports. Each of the 260 rooms has a flat-screen TV and free Wi-Fi; some rooms have beach views and/or a cozy fireplace.

VINEYARD SQUARE HOTEL $$$
38 North Water St.
Edgartown, MA 02539
(508) 627-4711
vineyardsquarehotel.com
Located in the heart of Edgartown, this beautifully run 34-room hotel dates from 1911. In honor of the hotel's 100th anniversary, the hotel's spacious rooms and suites were totally renovated in a modern beach style, and they feature exceptionally comfortable beds. Lots of little extras including free Wi-Fi, free parking (reserve in advance), complimentary bike rentals, a generous continental breakfast, and afternoon sweet treats make this a great value.

Resorts

BAYSIDE RESORT $$
225 Route 28
West Yarmouth, MA 02673
(508) 775-5669
baysideresort.com
For a sandy family Cape escape that won't break the bank, you won't go wrong here. The hotel's spacious rooms are a little dated, but it offers several pleasant extras including free continental breakfast and free Wi-Fi, an indoor and outdoor pool, a game room, and a fitness room. It's not that much more to upgrade to a room with a view of Lewis Bay, perfect for greeting the morning sun.

NANTUCKET HOTEL & RESORT $$$$
77 Easton St.
Nantucket, MA 02554
(508) 228-4747
thenantuckethotel.com
Reopened in 2012 after a total rebuild, this impressive island resort getaway proves that "family vacation" isn't an oxymoron. The 1891 shingled facade is a Victorian

beauty, now wonderfully up-to-date with luxe amenities and family-friendly New England beach-cottage styling. The property offers lots of room options to suit all sizes of families—hotel rooms as well as 1- to 4-bedroom suites and cottages—and there is a casual bar and eatery called The Breeze so you can avoid public meal meltdowns. Its location ensures easy access to Nantucket and the beaches (take advantage of the free shuttle service to the beach and the ferry dock). And the complimentary day camp is a godsend for parents who appreciate some "me time" in the fitness room and some much needed R&R poolside.

Vacation Rentals

KINLIN GROVER
1990 Main St.
Brewster, MA 02631
(508) 896-7004
kinlingrover.com
Kinlin Grover has been in business on the Cape since 1992, listing and selling vacation homes, investment properties, and residential housing and retirement properties. The firm has 16 offices that span the Cape but it's the Brewster office that specializes in vacation property rentals with listings for more than 600 private homes covering everything from 1-bedroom condo golf villas to impressive beachside 8-bedroom compounds ideal for multigeneration family reunions.

Hostels

HOSTELLING INTERNATIONAL CAPE COD $
111 Ocean St.
Hyannis, MA 02601
(508) 775-7990
capecod.hiusa.org/index.php

This 37-bed newly renovated award-winning hostel is the largest of the Cape hostels and has a prime location just steps from the ferries and downtown Hyannis. Rooms are spacious, clean, and basic. Rates include linens, continental breakfast, and free Wi-Fi. Open late May through mid-October. For additional area location information, check out the Hostelling International website.

Camping

✳NICKERSON STATE PARK $
Route 6A
Brewster, MA 02631
(508) 896-3491
mass.gov/dcr/parks/southeast/nick.htm
If you can snag a space, this is an excellent, inexpensive lodging option in high summer. The more than 400 sites are fairly well spread out across 1,900 acres of pitch pine and scrub oak forest. Go swimming in one of the clear freshwater kettle ponds, fish for bass, or rent a canoe or pedalboat from on-site Jack's Boat Rental (508-349-9808; jacksboatrental.com). Also on site: Barb's Bike Rentals (508-896-7231; barbsbikeshop.com), with bikes at the ready to explore the park's 8 miles of paved bike paths (some of the Cape Cod Rail Trail passes through Nickerson).

RESTAURANTS

American (New)

CAPE SEA GRILLE $$$$
31 Sea St.
Harwich Port, MA 02646
(508) 432-4745
capeseagrille.com
This bistro originated as a sea captain's house and serves beautiful coastal New England food, from crispy duck confit with a stuffed

swiss chard to a pan-seared whole lobster with pancetta and a calvados saffron reduction. The service is professional and the atmosphere is upscale but not stuffy. Reservations are a must. Open Apr through Dec; check hours in the off-season.

GRILL ON MAIN $$-$$$
227 Upper Main St.
Edgartown, MA 02539
(508) 627-8344
thegrillonmain.com
A little off the beaten path, Grill on Main doesn't get caught up in the island's dining scene but focuses on consistently excellent and creative American bistro fare. Make a reservation and you will still have to wait, but enjoy a cocktail at the bar. Once seated you'll relish offerings like baked codfish with a citrus beurre blanc and grilled lamb chops with a minted raspberry glaze—all aided by delightful service (with no attitude). Above all, Grill on Main is a good value compared to other Vineyard restaurants.

✳STATE ROAD $$-$$$
688 State Rd.
West Tisbury, MA 02575
(508) 693-8582
stateroadrestaurant.com
There's a lot to love about this casual, local-leaning eatery that boasts the sort of food that people want to eat with regularity. Breakfast features dishes like ricotta pancakes with blueberries and at lunch there's a very nice lamb burger and a green fried tomato BLT. But there are also upscale dishes you won't find everywhere, including braised pork ragout with mustard spaetzle at dinner.

TEN TABLES PROVINCETOWN $$$
133 Bradford St.
Provincetown, MA 02657
(508) 487-0106
tentables.net/provincetown.html
Like its much-buzzed-about sibling restaurants in Jamaica Plain and Cambridge, Ten Tables Provincetown offers an intimate dining experience (there really are just 10 tables) and a dinner menu featuring creative bistro fare and local, seasonal ingredients like Nauset striped bass with gigante bean and corn succotash and Cape Cod scallops with snap peas from the restaurant's garden. Reservations are a must for the dining room, but the upstairs bar works well for drinks and oysters with friends or a casual weeknight dinner of buttermilk fried chicken or the famed TT burger. Open seasonally for dinner only Apr through Oct.

WATER STREET $$$
131 North Water St.
Edgartown, MA 02539
(508) 627-3761
harbor-view.com/dining/water-street
Lovely Water Street is the main dining room of the Harbor View Hotel. It boasts lots of windows with views of Edgartown Harbor and the lighthouse, which provide the backdrop for a leisurely meal of New American fare. The menu selections showcase fresh local seafood (although, the Good Farm chicken, a half bird with pan jus, is the dish to get), and are complemented by extraordinary wines. Open year-round for breakfast, lunch, or dinner.

American (Traditional)

MARSHLAND $-$$
109 Route 6A
Sandwich, MA 02563
(508) 888-9824
marshlandrestaurant.com

This casual all-day restaurant delivers unpretentious and good American dishes of the type loved by all. Locally, it's best known for its wonderful traditional breakfasts, but it is also a comfortable choice for lunch and dinner. Lately Marshland has gained some notoriety for its stuffed quahogs (clams), featured on Food Network's *The Best Thing I Ever Ate*.

Breakfast & Lunch

AMONG THE FLOWERS $$
17 Mayhew Ln.
Edgartown, MA 02539
(508) 627-3233
mvol.com/menu/amongtheflowers

Exit the summer chaos of the Vineyard on the patio of this cute cafe just steps away from the docks at Edgartown Harbor. Breakfast features from-scratch muffins and omelets made with Vineyard farm-fresh eggs. Lunch is all about the lobster-salad roll and fancy salads like the seared tuna with mixed greens and pineapple salsa. At dinner the entrees are upscale but not pretentious. Find pan-roasted chicken with roasted tomato ragout and jumbo lump crab cakes with roasted corn and pepper relish, while the prices are downright reasonable for the island. Open May through Oct.

CENTERVILLE PIE $
1671 Falmouth Rd.
Centerville, MA 02632
(774) 470-1406
centervillepies.com

Centerville Pie's chicken potpie is an Oprah "favorite thing" and it can be yours, too. This quaint little bakery/cafe sells scrumptious pies in all guises from savory to sweet and to eat in or take out. The clam pie is especially popular on Friday as a take-home dinner choice for locals. You can savor a slice of hot pie—from apple to apple cranberry to pecan—straight out of the oven or get a pie to go (and get an extra chicken potpie for the freezer). If you cannot live by pie alone, they serve breakfast all day and sandwiches and soups at lunch.

✳CORNER STORE $
1403 Old Queen Anne Rd.
Chatham, MA 02633
(508) 432-1077
freshfastfun.com

From burritos to paninis, the standout sandwiches at the Corner Store will leave you satisfied. Good burritos are hard to come by on the Cape but here you can build your perfect burrito because there are tons of choices (including 3 kinds of beans!) and just about everything—the grilled-corn salsa, the slow-roasted pork, and the pico de gallo—is handmade. Leave room for a carrot cake whoopee pie or giant Rice Krispy treat. There are a few seats, but basically this is a take-out place, ideal for the beach.

✳KELTIC KITCHEN $-$$
415 Route 28
West Yarmouth, MA 02673
(508) 771-4835
thekeltickitchen.com

Irish expats have long settled on Cape Cod. Get a proper Irish breakfast (likely served by a lad with a brogue) at this delightful breakfast/lunch spot. The Irish farmhouse breakfast is tremendous and includes black and white pudding, Irish bacon and sausage, baked beans, home fries, brown bread toast, perfectly cooked eggs, and an ocean of coffee. You won't need to eat again until dinner! Afterward the attached Keltic Kottage is a cute shop to browse for Aran sweaters or to pick up iconic Irish grocery brands like Hob-Nobs cookies and Tayto Crisps.

*PROVINCETOWN PORTUGUESE
   BAKERY $
299 Commercial St.
Provincetown, MA 02657
(508) 487-1803

In a city where Portuguese heritage runs deep, this bakery/cafe is a local favorite. Take a seat at one of the few tables, then order up breakfast with a Portuguese twist. Try the Portuguese egg and linguica sausage breakfast sandwich made on a soft Portuguese roll. Order it to go and it will be wrapped in wax paper for the beach. At lunch count on kale and potato soup to make an appearance. And day and night, *malasadas*—sugary Portuguese doughnuts without holes—fly out of the bakery. They sure are hard to resist—the fryer is located in the bakery window. Closed Nov through Feb.

*SOMETHING NATURAL $
50 Cliff Rd.
Nantucket, MA 02554
(508) 228-0504
somethingnatural.com

A sandwich is only as good as the bread used to make it. To that end, Something Natural bakes 10 to 12 types of bread daily as the foundation for its outstanding sandwiches. The bakery is located just outside of town and is a convenient spot on the way to Jetties Beach. Stop for a smoked turkey and Swiss on rye or sprouts, vegetables, and avocado on 6-grain. There's a wonderful picnic spot here, with tables set on the lawn beneath shady trees (which kids love to climb).

Cafes & Coffeehouses

HOT CHOCOLATE SPARROW $
5 Old Colony Way
Orleans, MA 02653
(508) 240-2230
hotchocolatesparrow.com

This Cape chocolatier doubles as a cafe and gourmet shop selling hand-dipped chocolates and coffee beans. The Mocha Sparrow—a shot (or two) of espresso with house-made melted chocolate fudge sauce and steamed milk—is a must-have and is available hot, iced, or frozen. With its excellent pastries, perfect paninis, spacious seating, and strong Wi-Fi, there's really no better place to take a coffee break on the Cape.

MARTHA'S VINEYARD GOURMET
    CAFE & BAKERY (AND HOME OF
    BACK DOOR DONUTS) $
5 Post Office Sq.
Oak Bluffs, MA 02557
(508) 693-3688
mvbakery.com

One of the Vineyard's best spots for coffee, breakfast treats, and cupcakes, this bakery is best known for its "after-hours" activity. For the best doughnut-eating experience you'll ever have, join the late-night line (beginning at 7 p.m.) behind the shop for doughnuts that are served warm out of the fryer until the wee morning hours. The apple fritters reign supreme here; enormous, deep-fried to a crisp, dark brown with bits of apple and a heavy sugar glaze, they are indeed the finest fritter anywhere. The bakery is open year-round; Back Door doughnuts are available Apr through Oct (cash only).

PIE IN THE SKY $
10 Water St.
Woods Hole, MA 02453
(508) 540-5475
woodshole.com/pie

When the scientists from Woods Hole need coffee, a sandwich, or a scone—or just a place to chat or surf the Internet—they come here. Order house-blend roast coffee and a fresh-from-the-oven popover. They also do more meal-sized fare; a breakfast sandwich of egg and linguica and the turkey, bacon, and avocado wrap is a great lunch, especially in combination with a soup, coffee, and cookie of your choice.

French

✳PAIN D'AVIGNON $–$$$
15 Hinkley Rd.
Hyannis, MA 02601
(508) 778-8588
paindavignon.com

There's a reason many of the Cape's best restaurants serve this artisan bakery's crusty French breads that are brimming with ingredients like olives, walnuts, and seeds. Locals adore the bakery/cafe for its croissants, muffins, and perfect coffee at breakfast and sandwiches and soups at lunch. At dinner the space becomes an authentic sit-down bistro complete with white table linens and candles, serving continental comfort food such as beef stroganoff with homemade noodles and coq au vin at an equally good value.

Ice Cream

FOUR SEAS $
360 S. Main St.
Centerville, MA 02632
(508) 775-1394
fourseasicecream.com

All Cape Codders have some childhood memory of standing in line at Four Seas. Since 1934 this no-frills ice cream parlor in a former blacksmith shop has been serving up massive cones of their homemade super-rich ice cream. They make 30 flavors or so; among the most popular are vanilla (they make a lot of sundaes) and chip chocolate. In August it's all about fresh peach. Now open year-round.

JUICE BAR $
12 Broad St.
Nantucket, MA 02554
(508) 228-5799

On a typical summer afternoon at around 3 p.m., a line forms outside the Juice Bar—just a hop, skip, and jump from Steamship Authority Wharf—as the beach crowd heads home from another day of sun and sand. The ice cream flavors aren't overly gourmet—toffee crunch, blackberry, and triple chocolate are as fancy as it gets here—but the ultra-rich ice cream is made on the premises and the super-friendly college kids behind the counter offer generous samples if you can't decide. Open seasonally.

MAD MARTHA'S ICE CREAM $
8 Union St.
Vineyard Haven, MA 02568
(508) 693-5883

Locals and visitors alike are positively mad for this local ice cream chain. The homemade super-premium ice cream is second to none and comes in two dozen flavors—the Oreo cream is their signature flavor. Make this your last stop before you board the ferry—with a view of Vineyard Haven Harbor this becomes an unparalleled vacation cone. Open seasonally.

SUNDAE SCHOOL $
381 Lower County Rd.
Dennisport, MA 02639
(508) 394-9122
sundaeschool.com
Sundae School, with 3 locations on the Cape, has been dishing out its ice cream to summer vacationers since 1976. The store has an old-fashioned marble soda fountain and a dedicated following for its sundaes, frappes, and ice cream cones. They typically offer 30 flavors, including an espresso crunch, rum raisin, and fresh blueberry. Or order the 4-flavor sampler if you can't decide. Open seasonally, mid-April through October. For information on additional area locations, check out the website.

Italian

BUCA'S TUSCAN ROADHOUSE $$–$$$
4 Depot Rd.
Harwich, MA 02645
(508) 432-6900
bucasroadhouse.com
If you seek Italian food on the Cape, journey to Harwich to this small treasure where a polished northern Italian menu is known among dining cognoscenti for its intriguing and even exquisite flavors. The menu starts with grilled goat cheese polenta with orange fig compote—and only gets better from there with house specialties like boar-meat Bolognese over tagliatelle and veal scaloppine with red wine, sun-dried cherries, and roasted tomatoes.

Japanese

INAHO $$$
157 Route 6A
Yarmouth Port, MA 02675
(508) 363-5522
inahocapecod.com
The Cape does fried fish very, very well but good sushi is surprisingly difficult to find. The sushi offerings here are highly respected (even by Boston urbanites) and you'll likely find your go-to *nigiri* and *maki* favorites on the extensive menu. In addition to sushi, there are familiar preparations of teriyakis, tempuras, and dinner bento boxes.

Mediterranean

PAZZO $$$
130 Pleasant St.
Nantucket, MA 02554
(508) 325-4500
pazzonantucket.com
When you are tired of seafood, head to this new Nantucket gem, which features a casual but stylish setting and an eclectic menu. Small plates of chicken-liver mousse with pickled red onion and whipped feta with plums and shallot go along with shareable dishes like the tagines with tender couscous, chicken, and preserved lemons. Add in a lively bar scene and Pazzo works as both an island and visitor hangout.

Mexican

✳AÑEJO $$
188 Main St.
Falmouth, MA 02540
(508) 388-7631
anejomexicanbistro.com
Añejo is sparkling new and already a hot spot, serving up beautifully presented Mexican food and tremendous cocktails in an

exuberant atmosphere. The menu is heavy on *antojitos* like mole poblano chicken wings and coconut shrimp with mango habanero jam. Overall the menu is seafood-centric and features items you won't find at other Cape Mexican cantinas, such as corn flake–encrusted cod with fire-roasted corn and a verde sauce and a deeply flavored tomatillo-braised pork shank.

Pizza

✳PALIO PIZZA $-$$
435 Main St.
Hyannis, MA 02601
(508) 771-7004
paliopizzeria.com
This crowd-pleasing pizza parlor is a solid choice when you arrive just off the ferry from Nantucket or the Vineyard. The thin-crust pizzas come from a wood-burning oven and are made with high-quality ingredients, there are pitchers of Sam Adams, unfussy salads, and booth seating, and it all comes at reasonable prices. What more could you want?

✳SWEET TOMATOES PIZZA $
155 Crowell Rd.
Chatham, MA 02633
(508) 348-0200
sweettomatoescapecod.com
Cape Codders have their local Sweet Tomatoes on speed-dial. The Neapolitan-style thin crust is addictive and features fresh chopped, uncooked tomatoes and enticing combinations (the Pizza Sarah with bacon, goat cheese, and caramelized onions is a standout) along with specialty sandwiches and salads. There is limited cafe seating inside and out, but most customers take their pies to go. For additional area location information, check out the website.

Pubs & Taverns

✳BROTHERHOOD OF THIEVES $$
22 Broad St.
Nantucket, MA 02554
(508) 228-2551
brotherhoodofthieves.com
At the end of the day, the libations at the downstairs 1840s Whaling Bar are a good capper. Along with 12 beers on tap, the atmospheric bar nods to its historic roots with a focus on upscale rums and bourbons. Or join the party at the outdoor *biergarten* for a Cisco brew, a New England cod po' boy, or a seasonal flatbread pizza.

WHARF PUB & RESTAURANT $$
5 Lower Main Rd.
Edgartown, MA 02539
(508) 627-9966
wharfpub.com
Offering refuge from the Vineyard crowds, this is a great place to pop in for a pint and hearty eats. The traditional American menu travels from classic bar snacks like house-made onion rings and steamed mussels to burgers and pastas and fried seafood. If in doubt, the clam chowder and fish and chips are reliably excellent.

Seafood

✳CHATHAM PIER FISH MARKET $-$$
43 Barcliff Ave.
Chatham, MA 02633
(508) 945-3473
chathampierfishmarket.com
A favorite Cape retail fish market, this is also a great spot for take-out lobster rolls, fried fish plates, clam chowder, lobster bisque, and steamed lobsters. Take your meal to the picnic tables where you can watch seals swim among the fishing boats as they

unload the day's catch on the docks. Open May through Oct.

*COOKE'S SEAFOOD $$
1120 Iyannough Rd.
Hyannis, MA 02601
(508) 775-0450
cookesseafood.com

This busy restaurant is popular with both visitors and locals. This isn't an elegant place; you order your seafood at the counter and then find a booth and wait for someone to call your number. But the food is ultra-fresh and expertly prepared. The many fried seafood options include clams, scallops, shrimp, and haddock. You can also opt for broiled fish and shellfish. Be forewarned: All the portions are humongous. A second location is in Mashpee at 7 Ryan's Way (508-477-9595).

KREAM 'N' KONE $$
961 Main St.
West Dennis, MA 02670
(508) 394-0808
kreamnkone.com

Watch the occasional lone kayaker slice through the Swan River's placid waters from an expansive patio while feasting on fried fisherman's plates—plus stellar chowder and memorable onion rings. For dessert, Kream 'n' Kone has every soft-serve flavor imaginable, including cheesecake and tutti frutti, but the chocolate/vanilla twist is as perfect as it gets.

MARTHA'S VINEYARD CHOWDER
COMPANY $$
9 Oak Bluffs Ave.
Oak Bluffs, MA 02557
(508) 696-3000
mvchowder.com

As you would expect from the name, the chowder is the thing to order here. Their clam chowder is made without butter or flour—just clams and fresh, creamy broth. Fast, friendly servers bring terrific sandwiches and salads, including the standout lobster tail salad. In the evening the menu includes various seafood specials. It's located across the street from the Flying Horses Carousel, so don't be afraid to bring your kids—everyone else does!

NAKED OYSTER $$-$$$
410 Main St.
Hyannis, MA 02601
(508) 778-6500
nakedoyster.com

Depending on the day's haul, this restaurant's extensive raw bar features several varieties of oysters, along with clams, lobster, and shrimp. There are also steamed local mussels with Chablis and salmon with a pistachio crust that share space on the menu with pasta, steak, and chicken dishes.

*QUICK'S HOLE $$
6 Luscombe Ave.
Woods Hole, MA 02543
(508) 495-0792
quicksholewickedfresh.com

This spiffed-up fish shack is casual but with more interesting than usual offerings, such as a yellowfin tuna BLT and a blackened fish sandwich. For Mexican food fans there is instant gratification with better than average Mexican street food specialties, such as fish tacos and slow-roasted-pork quesadillas. The fresh lobster tacos are a perfect blend of Baja and Cape Cod, and when you wash them down with a glass of house-made sangria, you're well on your way (happily) to the ferry. Open seasonally, May through Oct.

(Q) Close-up

See the Light(s)

A guiding light perched high on a rocky cliff, on a sandy shore at a harbor's entrance, or sometimes on a remote island—more than 20 lighthouses stand watch along the coastline of Cape Cod, Martha's Vineyard, and Nantucket. Lighthouses are some of Cape Cod's most iconic and alluring images and are among the region's most visited attractions. Most of these lighthouses were built in the 19th century to mark the shore for ships to avoid running aground on rocky shoals at night or when the coast was shrouded in fog.

Sadly, there are no more lighthouse keepers; the lighthouse beam and the wail of the foghorn have long been automated. But even today, with radar and GPS, seven Cape lighthouses remain active aids in navigation and are still owned by the Coast Guard. The National Park Service and town historical associations own the remaining decommissioned lights. They each have a story to tell. Here is a list of the best Cape lighthouses to visit.

Nobska Light. *Church Street, Falmouth; lighthouse.cc/nobska.* With its charming Victorian keeper's house, this is arguably the Cape's most photographed lighthouse. Overlooking Vineyard Sound, it marks the entrance to Woods Hole Harbor and is seen by ferrygoers traveling to and from Martha's Vineyard. This 1876 lighthouse is owned by the US Coast Guard and is still an active aid in navigation. The keeper's house serves as the living quarters for the Woods Hole Coast Guard commander but the grounds are open to the public. There are occasional open-house days to climb the lighthouse; check the website for schedule.

Chatham Light. *Shore Road, Chatham; lighthouse.cc/chatham.* Located on the "elbow" of the Cape overlooking Chatham's Lighthouse Beach, this 1877 cast-iron lighthouse is an active US Coast Guard station. Ascend the 44 spiraling steps for great views of the crashing surf below, seals basking on the sandbars, and deserted South Monomoy Island and its lighthouse in the distance. Open for visits Wed from May through Oct; check schedule for times.

Nauset Light and the Three Sisters Lighthouses. *Ocean View Drive, Eastham; nps.gov/caco.* Combine some time at the beach with a visit to 4 lighthouses all in one afternoon. Nauset Light looks out over the cliffs of the Cape Cod National Seashore's Nauset Light Beach. You may recognize its distinctive red and white painted tower as the logo from the Cape Cod Potato Chips bag. This cast-iron lighthouse, built in 1877 and the "twin" of the Chatham tower to the south, was moved here in 1923 to replace the 3 white wooden lighthouse towers that were nicknamed the "Three Sisters." Tours of Nauset Light are offered from May through Oct on Sun, with additional tours on Wed during July and Aug. Follow the signed path from the parking lot to visit the Three Sisters in the clearing.

Highland Light. *Highland Light Road, Truro; capecodlight.org.* Located high on a bluff above the Atlantic, the Cape's first lighthouse station was built here in 1797. Although it's in the middle of the Highland Links Golf Course, this is actually the Cape's most accessible lighthouse. Tours of the current vintage 1857 lighthouse include the opportunity to climb its 69 winding steps to the lantern room. Not for the claustrophobic, but great fun for kids! Open daily from mid-May through mid-October.

Race Point Light. *Race Point Beach, Provincetown; racepointlighthouse.org.* This 1876 cast-iron lighthouse is on the northernmost tip of the Cape. From the beach parking lot, it's a 2-mile hike over sand to the lighthouse. Public tours are offered on the 1st and 3rd Saturdays of the month from June through Oct. If you want to get the full lighthouse experience, you can even stay overnight in shared accommodations in the keeper's house or book use of a private 2-bedroom cottage. Rest assured, you will overnight in conditions far more comfortable than the keepers ever experienced.

Edgartown Light. *121 N. Water St., Edgartown; mvmuseum.org/edgartown.php.* It's a 10-minute walk from Edgartown to the small cast-iron lighthouse that sits on a rock breakwater in Edgartown Harbor. In the summer season, this lighthouse is open on Friday until 8 p.m., which means you can watch the sunset from the catwalk balcony that circles the lighthouse top before you head back to town for a late dinner. Open Memorial Day weekend through Labor Day; check hours.

Great Point Light. *Coskata-Coatue Wildlife Refuge, Nantucket; thetrustees.org.* At the extreme northeast corner of Nantucket, Great Point is one of the most desolate lighthouses in all of New England. It's accessible only by 4-wheel drive vehicle (your own or rent one from town), unless you are up for walking 7 miles in deep sand. Alternatively, you can sign up for one of the excellent 2½-hour guided 4x4 SUV natural history tours offered by the Trustees of Reservations. The climb to the top of the lighthouse, a towering white concrete structure that is a replica of an 1818 structure that was claimed by the sea in 1984, is the trip highlight. If you are using your own car, purchase an overland permit at the gatehouse. Tours offered daily May through Oct; sign up in advance.

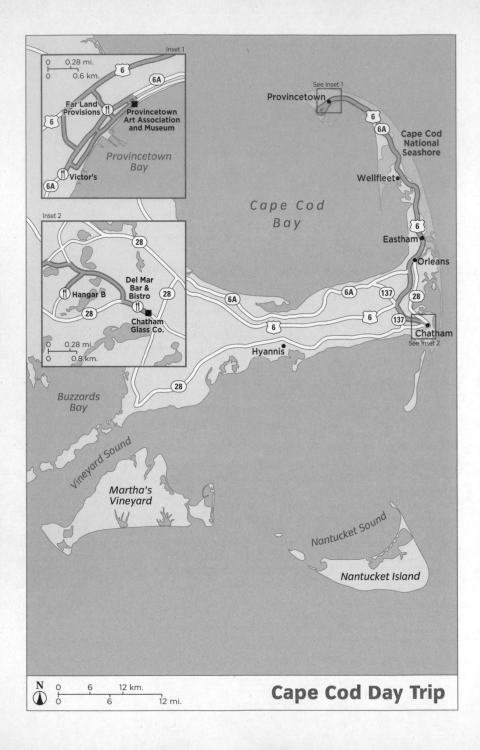

Inset 1

0 — 0.28 mi.
0 — 0.6 km.

6 6A

Far Land Provisions

Provincetown Art Association and Museum

6

Provincetown Bay

6A Victor's

Inset 2

28

Del Mar Bar & Bistro

Hangar B 28

28

Chatham Glass Co.

0 — 0.28 mi.
0 — 0.8 km.

Provincetown

See Inset 1

6

6A

Cape Cod National Seashore

Wellfleet

Cape Cod Bay

6

Eastham

Orleans

6A 137

28

6

137

Chatham
See Inset 2

Hyannis

28

Buzzards Bay

Vineyard Sound

Martha's Vineyard

Nantucket Sound

Nantucket Island

N

0 — 6 — 12 km.
0 — 6 — 12 mi.

Cape Cod Day Trip

DAY TRIP IN CAPE COD

Head out to the Chatham Airport. Not because you're leaving town, but because overlooking the landing strip is **Hangar B** (240 George Ryder Rd.; 508-593-3655; hangar bcapecod.com), a retro modern eatery that is one of the Cape's best breakfast/lunch spots. It's a small restaurant and you may have to wait, but it's worth it for the reasonably priced lemon ricotta pancakes and the house-made red flannel hash (it has beets) with 2 eggs and toast, served with fresh-squeezed juice and local Chatham coffee.

Now that you are fueled, it's time to explore. A trip to the Cape wouldn't be complete without a visit to lively **Provincetown.** Buzz up to Provincetown before the traffic on Route 6 slows to a trickle. From Chatham pick up Route 6 E and drive 32 miles to Provincetown. Park at the main municipal parking lot at Commercial Street and McMillan Wharf and you can be car-free for the rest of your visit.

For lunch pick up some gourmet sandwiches and drinks from **Far Land Provisions** (150 Bradford St.; 508-487-0045; farlandprovisions.com) before you head over to the McMillan Wharf and pick up the Flyer's shuttle to Long Point at the very tip of the Cape for a picnic lunch on the nearly secluded 1-mile beach. You can swim, stroll over to the abandoned lighthouse, or just laze in the sand. Walk back along the stone jetty (1 mile) or take the shuttle back.

Art is all around in Provincetown. At **Fisherman's Wharf** you can't help but notice the 5 oversize black and white portraits of Portuguese women mounted on the sides of the defunct fishing cannery building that make up *They Also Faced the Sea* by Norma Holt. Spend some time peeking into the wonderful galleries and funky shops along Commercial Street. Finish your stroll and shop at the **Provincetown Art Association and Museum** (460 Commercial St.; 508-487-1750; paam.org). Seek out the paintings by Charles Hawthorne and Robert Motherwell and step back into Provincetown's early days as an arts colony. Compare and contrast with the modern and contemporary works of the current juried show.

At sunset one of the liveliest happy hours in Provincetown takes place at **Victor's** (175 Bradford St.; 508-487-1777; victors ptown.com). Enjoy potent cocktails such as a white Cosmo with cranberries along with 99-cent raw-bar selections amid a friendly mix of locals and visitors.

Or skip the evening Provincetown party in favor of a quiet late dinner back in **Chatham.** It's an easy 38-mile drive back down Route 6 W. Pre-dinner, take in a glass-blowing demonstration at **Chatham Glass Company** (758 Main St.; chathamglass.com), which specializes in contemporary sculptural pieces that you would be proud to display in your home. Dinner at **Del Mar Bar & Bistro** (907 Main St.; delmarbistro.com) means upscale Cape fare—the wood oven turns out excellent prosciutto and fig pizza, roasted Chatham cod, and a bananas Foster with vanilla ice cream that will have you licking your bowl clean.

WORCESTER COUNTY

Known as "the heart of Massachusetts," Worcester County is the geographic center and the largest county in the state, encompassing a swath of mostly agricultural farmland and hilly forest. Worcester County effectively separates the state between Boston—and, as Bostonians will tell you, "western" Massachusetts—the Berkshires and everything else in between.

Worcester is the region's largest city and its county seat. The Nipmuc tribe, or "people of the freshwater pond," were the first known inhabitants of this area. The name perhaps refers to Lake Quinsigamond, the narrow four-mile-long lake that is one of Worcester's most prominent geographical features (the other being its seven hills). The first English settlement was established here in 1673 and was called Quinsigamond Plantation. Driven out by the Nipmucs during King Philip's War in 1698, the English didn't resettle the area until 1713. The settlement was then incorporated as a town and named in honor of Worcester, England. The British way has survived to this day; here Worcester is properly pronounced "Wuss-ter."

By 1828 the opening of the Blackstone Canal and the building of the Boston & Worcester Railroad brought manufacturing—first textiles, then steel wire—to the city. The city's many cultural and educational institutions, including the Worcester Art Museum, Mechanics Hall, and Worcester Polytechnic Institute, were established as a result of the prosperity that followed. Today, Worcester's principal industry is education. The city is home to 10 college and universities, among them Holy Cross, Worcester Polytechnic Institute, Clark University, and UMass Medical School. Undeniably, the college students give Worcester a youthful vibe (and better bars and restaurants).

Beyond Worcester the landscape offers wooded countryside punctuated by towns large and small. To the south, experience early-19th-century New England life at Old Sturbridge Village, a re-created historic settlement. Head north from Worcester and there are under-the-radar sites that charm: Rural Boylston is home to the Tower Hill Botanic Garden, and the mill town of Clinton draws visitors from around the world to its Museum of Russian Icons.

In Leominster, in the far northern reaches of Worcester County, folk hero and roaming pioneer apple orchard farmer John Chapman, popularly known as Johnny Appleseed, was born in 1775. Follow the Johnny Appleseed Trail along Route 2 from Harvard to Orange. It's an area for leaf peeping, country drives, and as you would expect, lots of apple orchards.

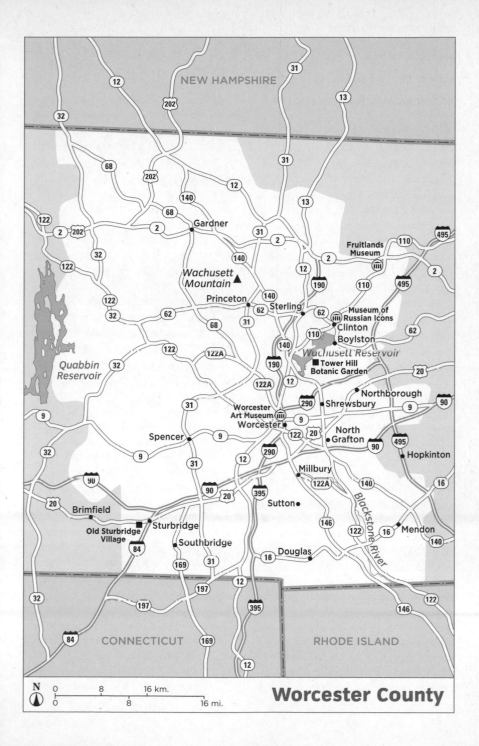

NEW HAMPSHIRE

12

202

31

13

32

68

202

31

122

2 202

68

140

2

Gardner

12

31

2

13

Fruitlands
Museum

110

495

32

122

32

140

Wachusett
Mountain ▲

140

12

190

110

2

495

122

122

62

Princeton

140

62

Sterling

62

Museum of
Russian Icons

110

62

68

31

Clinton

32

122A

140

Boylston

Quabbin
Reservoir

122

32

122A

190

Wachusett Reservoir

Tower Hill
Botanic Garden

20

9

31

12

Worcester
Art Museum

290

Shrewsbury

Northborough

9

90

32

Spencer

9

Worcester

9

122

20

North
Grafton

90

495

Hopkinton

9

31

12

290

Millbury

122A

140

16

90

20

395

Sutton

146

20

Brimfield

Old Sturbridge
Village

Sturbridge

84

Southbridge

169

31

16

Douglas

122

16

Mendon

140

146

32

197

197

12

395

122

84

CONNECTICUT

169

RHODE ISLAND

12

N

0   8   16 km.

0   8   16 mi.

Worcester County

ATTRACTIONS

Historic Sites & Landmarks

AMERICAN ANTIQUARIAN SOCIETY

185 Salisbury St.

Worcester, MA 01609

(508) 754-6116

americanantiquarian.org

This cathedral of American historical scholarship was established in 1812 from a founding gift by colonial printer Isaiah Thomas. It is a treasure trove of Americana including not only books but prints, newspapers, magazines, maps, sheet music, and even advertisements and board games—nearly 4 million volumes in all—from the colonial period through 1876. Among the society's holdings is the first book printed in America, *The Bay Psalms Book,* published in 1640, as well as the first American cookbook. The library is open Mon through Fri, and while this is a closed-stack library (the books are available for use by qualified scholars only), the library is very much open to the public. Public tours describing the work and scholarship of the Society and its members take place at 3 p.m. every Wednesday. There are also regularly scheduled lectures (nearly weekly) by well-known historians, authors, and American Antiquarian curators that are open to the public.

✳OLD STURBRIDGE VILLAGE

1 Old Sturbridge Village Rd.

Sturbridge, MA 01566

(508) 347-3363

osv.org

With 40 original buildings on 200 acres, this living history museum provides a glimpse into 18th- and 19th-century rural life in America. Old Sturbridge Village has been carefully re-created, from the period furnishings in the homes to the tools that were used in the blacksmith's and potter's shops. The "villagers," costumed historical interpreters and tradespeople, can be seen baking bread in a wood-fired oven, cutting lumber at the working sawmill, or tending to longhorn livestock in the fields, completing the film-set effect. For families, there are loads of daily activities geared just to kids: They can try on 19th-century clothing, dip candles, and meet the animals in the barn. Your kids will learn a lot and have more fun than they expect. There is a lot to see here, so plan on spending at least half a day. The food choices feature strictly modern-day fare. At the Village Cafe sandwiches, salads, soups, fresh baked goods, and coffee are offered. The Bullard Tavern Cafe is larger; it's a cafeteria setup that offers some hot lunch choices along with sandwiches and salads. The museum is open year-round and closed Mon. And as this is an outdoor museum, wear comfortable shoes and dress for the weather. In winter the buildings are heated—but only by "cozy" fires (it's cold!).

✳TOWER HILL BOTANIC GARDEN

11 French Dr.

Boylston, MA 01505

(508) 869-6111

towerhillbg.org

All of New England's seasons are on full display at this living plant museum located just 10 miles north of Worcester. This 132-acre property is a mix of towering trees and open green space that contains 8 distinct gardens of exotic and native plantings—there's a wildlife garden, a cottage and vegetable garden, and a grand lawn garden that leads to a secret garden. In the winter, the 18th-century-style Orangerie and Limonaia (very fancy greenhouses these) feature flowering forced bulbs, camellias, ferns, citrus, and several water features. With 3 miles of paved, intricate pathways, it's easy to enjoy the scenic beauty. No visitor should leave without taking the 1-mile loop trail to the Tower Hill Summit for a sweeping view of the Wachusett Lake Reservoir with Wachusett Mountain in the near distance. Tower Hill is open year-round Tues through Sun and on holiday Mondays.

UNION STATION
34 Washington Sq.
Worcester, MA 01614
No website
The marble vastness of Union Station is where 2 regal lions preside over traffic and an ever-shifting sea of people still does much to heighten the excitement of arriving in Worcester. Behind the station's 1911 marble facade are the platforms that service Amtrak and the MBTA (Massachusetts Bay Transportation Authority) commuter rail line. Next door is the terminal for the Greyhound and Peter Pan bus lines and the Worcester Regional Transit Authority local city bus service.

i Put your ear to the marble floor of the Grand Hall—that's not the rumble of an arriving train, it's the sound of water from the Blackstone Canal underneath.

Museums

*FREDERICK HISTORIC PIANO COLLECTION
30 Main St.
Ashburnham, MA 01430
(978) 827-6232
frederickcollection.org

Why would some of the world's best classical musicians trek to the tiny hamlet of Ashburnham in northern Worcester County? To have the opportunity to try out their repertoire on a European grand piano similar to what the composers would have used. Housed in the former Ashburnham town library, this collection of historic pianos is the passion of local residents (and accomplished musicians) Michael and Patricia Frederick. Currently numbering 23 instruments (with several more in the process of restoration), they range from a 1795 Viennese piano to a 1907 Blüthner from Leipzig. The Fredericks host public tours on Thurs from 10 a.m. to 4 p.m. and Sat from 1 to 4 p.m. or by appointment. Tours last 3 hours and include lecture and demonstration. You'll learn that Schumann's Papillons sounds very different—much more clear—on an 1840 Erard than on the family upright. And as these pianos are meant to be played, bring your music. The center also sponsors a fall and spring concert series by renowned musicians at nearby Ashburnham Community Church.

FRUITLANDS MUSEUM
102 Prospect Hill Rd.
Harvard, MA 01451
(978) 456-3924
fruitlands.org
Located on the former site of Fruitlands, the short-lived utopian community experiment that took place here in 1843, this scenic small museum focuses on the history of the Nashua River valley. The Fruitlands Farmhouse is the main museum, focusing on transcendentalism and Fruitlands' Alcott connection (Bronson Alcott, the father of Louisa May Alcott, was one of Fruitlands' leaders). The museum also has on site a 1796 Shaker house that was moved here from nearby, with exhibits on Shaker life.

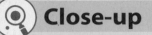

Close-up

Worcester's Farmer Patriots

One of the first acts of colonial civil disobedience against the British took place in Worcester, months before the first shots rang out in Lexington and Concord. In the aftermath of the 1773 Boston Tea Party, Worcester blacksmith Timothy Bigelow, along with local farmers, formed the American Political Society to challenge local British rule.

By the summer of 1774, Worcester was a town divided. At the Worcester town meeting of June 3, Clark Chandler, the Worcester town clerk and a British Loyalist, entered into the town record what has since become known as the "Tory Protest." The statement expressed the sentiment of 52 Worcester Loyalists that those who had participated in the Boston Tea Party "we esteem enemies to our King and Country, violators of all law and civil liberty."

The American Political Party drafted its own resolution to force the Loyalist supporters to recant their statement and by August they called for a town meeting. The Patriots ordered Chandler to draw his pen through each line of the protest in public view. Next, Chandler was told to make scroll marks through each line to obliterate the wording. After that, each Loyalist protester was forced to cross out his own name. But that wasn't enough. It appears that a mob mentality took over. Chandler was then forced to put his fingers in the inkwell and his hand was dragged across the page, smudging ink along the way. The Tory Protest is among the city's most treasured documents and is held in a vault in Worcester City Hall. In Worcester Common (next to City Hall) there is a monument to Timothy Bigelow.

Other buildings in the complex include a Native American Gallery, which showcases artifacts from local Native people including a longhouse and a dugout canoe. The Art Gallery has several fine Hudson River valley paintings (including one from Albert Bierstadt) and a large collection of New England primitive portraiture. The museum grounds are criss-crossed with 3 miles of marked trails with views of fields, meadows, and rolling hills not unlike when the Alcotts lived here.

✳**MUSEUM OF RUSSIAN ICONS**
203 Union St.
Clinton, MA 01510
(978) 598-5000
museumofrussianicons.org

Here, on display in the small industrial town of Clinton, just north of Worcester, is the largest collection of Russian icons in North America. It's an art museum that you might more likely find in a major metropolitan area, not in a town of just 13,000 people.

Located in a renovated 150-year-old carpet mill building, the museum was founded in 2006 by local plastics tycoon Gordon Lankton to house his collection of Russian Orthodox art. Rich in symbolism, icons typically depict saints or holy events painted with egg tempera on wood panels and decorated with gold leaf. The museum's collection includes more than 500 icons and artifacts dating back 6 centuries. The high-end museum gift shop stocks lots of one-of-a-kind items, including exquisite Russian lacquer boxes. Closed Sun and Mon.

WILLARD HOUSE AND CLOCK MUSEUM
11 Willard St.
North Grafton, MA 01536
(508) 839-3500
willardhouse.org

The 4 Willard brothers of Grafton were early American clockmakers renowned for their particularly fine mechanical work and for designs that were innovative for their time. Tours of the 1718 homestead include a visit to the original 1766 clock workshop with its collection of 18th-century tools and a guided walk through the main gallery rooms, which are filled with more than 80 examples of Willard clocks, including both shelf and tall (grandfather) clocks. Some are still running after more than 200 years! The museum is always closed on Mon and Tues, and Wed, too, during the winter; double-check museum days and hours before you visit.

*WORCESTER ART MUSEUM
55 Salisbury St.
Worcester, MA 01609
(508) 799-4406
worcesterart.org

First opened to the public in 1898, the Worcester Art Museum's collection (more than 35,000 works) has a depth and breadth that is unrivaled among small American art museums. In particular, the museum is strong in American, European, and Asian art. Come here to see masterpieces by some of the world's most famous painters: El Greco, Gainsborough, Gaugin, and Monet, to name only a few. The treasure of the museum is the Renaissance Court with its 500-square-foot mosaic dating from the 6th century. Named

the Worcester Hunt Mosaic, the highly patterned scene was discovered in the 1930s at a villa in Antioch in present-day Turkey. The Worcester Art Museum Cafe is well regarded for its soups (the pear and wild mushroom soup is fantastic), salads, and sandwiches. It can get busy, as it is as popular with the downtown workforce as it is for museum visitors. Open Wed through Sat.

Parks & Beaches

BROAD BROOK MEADOW CONSERVATION AND WILDLIFE SANCTUARY (MASSACHUSETTS AUDUBON)
414 Massasoit Rd.
Worcester, MA 01604
(508) 753-6087
massaudubon.org

Located within Worcester city limits, this is an ideal place to visit if you have a couple hours on your hands for a good walk. The series of small interconnected looping trails totals 4 miles, taking you through woodlands and meadows, then across a narrow boardwalk through marsh and by Green Heron Pond. The small nature center features a covered area to comfortably (and stealthily) watch the activity around the bird feeders. Day and weekend programs for both adults and kids are scheduled throughout the year, as well as a very popular children's summer day camp.

i Hollywood would have you believe that Forrest Gump invented the smiley face, but it was Harvey Ball, a Worcester graphic artist, who designed the original in 1963 as part of an employee morale campaign for a local insurance company. The Harvey Ball Conservation Area and the Smiley Trail adjoin Broad Brook Wildlife Sanctuary.

BREEZY PICNIC GROUNDS
WATERSLIDES
520 NW Main St.
Douglas, MA 01516
(508) 476-2664
breezysummer.com

Pack a lunch and spend the day lake swimming at this wholesome, family-oriented amusement park. There is swimming at Whitins Reservoir and lots of picnic tables and barbecue grills (don't forget the charcoal!) under the shady trees. Best of all, admission includes unlimited rides on Breezy's 3 giant waterslides. Afterward enjoy late-afternoon ice cream from the snack bar. Open daily, early June through Labor Day.

ELM PARK
Highland and Park Avenues
Worcester, MA 01609
(508) 929-1300
worcesterma.gov

It is easy to imagine earlier days when parents strolled baby carriages and couples promenaded along the winding footpaths and over the bridges that cross the 3 pretty ponds of this park, designed by the firm of Frederick Law Olmsted in the mid-1800s. These days Elm Park is still a favorite destination for Worcesterites because of the excellent variety of activities it offers, including playgrounds, tennis courts, winter ice-skating, and a concert series in the summer.

HOPKINTON STATE PARK
Route 85
Hopkinton, MA 01748
(508) 435-4303
mass.gov/dcr/parks/northeast/hpsp.htm

Hopkinton State Park is a tremendous outdoor recreational resource for those living in the Metro West area. Hopkinton is big—there are actually 2 swimming beaches here and extensive recreational facilities including more than 300 tables and 165 or so grills—so the park is extremely popular (particularly on Sunday) for large family and group events. In season, boating enthusiasts can rent a kayak, sailboat, canoe, or even a pedal boat for a little spin around the pretty reservoir. There are also 10 miles of marked, multi-use trails through the woods that are open to hikers, bikers, equestrians, cross-country skiers, and snowmobilers. Open daily year-round.

Wildlife & Zoos

SOUTHWICK'S ZOO
2 Southwick St.
Mendon, MA 01756
(800) 258-9182
southwickszoo.com

Occupying 175 acres, Southwick's is New England's largest zoo, with more than 500 animals, many of which are rare or endangered species. The natural habitat settings enable animal lovers to come practically face-to-face with their favorite creatures. At Deer Forest, you can buy feed (bring quarters) and the deer will come to you. Southwick's boasts lots of kid-favorite large land animals, including giraffes, lions, tigers, and elephants. Enjoy a breathtaking bird's-eye view of the animals and the park and cap your visit with a ride on the SkyFari aerial ride (additional charge). Open daily mid-April through October.

Wineries & Breweries

*NASHOBA VALLEY WINERY
92 Wattaquadock Hill Rd.
Bolton, MA 01740
(978) 779-5521
nashobawinery.com

With mature trees and rolling hills, this is a picture-perfect orchard for pick-your-own apples in the fall. But the real attraction here is the wine. Nashoba produces more than 20 unique fruit wines including a popular cranberry apple wine and a well-regarded blueberry Merlot. There is also a microbrewery on site that offers fresh beer you can purchase to go in a half-gallon growler—perfect for your orchard picnic or for future imbibing. Nashoba offers tastings every day in the wine shop (something of a shopper's paradise) and tours of its winemaking facilities during the weekends. J's Restaurant at Nashoba Valley Winery (see below) offers fine dining in a rustic farmhouse setting. Or have lunch al fresco. There's a nice covered porch area with lots of tables for enjoying your own picnic lunch, or order boxed gourmet picnic lunches in advance to pick up at the wine shop. And this is a dog-friendly orchard, too—pets on a leash are welcome.

ACTIVITIES & EVENTS

Arts Venues

HANOVER THEATRE FOR THE PERFORMING ARTS
2 Southbridge St.
Worcester, MA 01608
(508) 831-0800
thehanovertheatre.org
The Hanover Theatre opened in 1904 as a small-time vaudeville hall. With the advent of movies, the theater foundered and in 1925 underwent a full-scale renovation that transformed the space into a movie theater with ornate plasterwork, grand chandeliers, and stately marble columns that captured the gilded glamour of the time. By the late 1990s the theater was shuttered. Newly refurbished and now state-of-the-art, the Hanover is hailed as a gem—and ranks among the city's most beautiful buildings. Touring productions from New York perform here, such as *Mary Poppins* and *American Idiot*, as well as shows by performers such as Whoopi Goldberg and the group Celtic Woman. Historian and Pulitzer Prize–winning author Doris Kearns Goodwin packed the house recently (and everyone is still talking about it).

MECHANICS HALL
321 Main St.
Worcester, MA 01608
(508) 752-0888
mechanicshall.org
Mechanics Hall is considered by many to be one of the finest concert halls in the country. Built in 1857 by the Worcester County Mechanics Association, the concert hall represented the cultural aspirations of the skilled workers who made up its membership—which would have been practically every family in town. Inside, the visual centerpiece of the hall is a 3,504-pipe Hook organ dating from 1864. Today, in addition to concerts and lectures, the hall is often used for recordings because of its excellent acoustics.

Festivals & Events

BRIMFIELD ANTIQUE SHOW
Route 20
Brimfield, MA 01010
brimfield.com
What started in 1959 as a one-off antiques market with a handful of dealers has expanded into a mega-show with as many as 5,000 vendors along a 1-mile stretch of both sides of Route 20. Now taking place 3 times a year (in mid-May, mid-July, and early September for 6 consecutive days),

the show features items that run the gamut from American and continental furniture and paintings, to garden statuary, to 1920s watches, to books, along with other unusual finds.

FIRST NIGHT WORCESTER
Various venues throughout downtown
Worcester, MA 01609
(508) 799-4909
firstnightworcester.org
First Night Worcester is the second-longest running First Night (after Boston's) and is easily the largest New Year's celebration in central Massachusetts. It's a community- and family-oriented (alcohol-free), multicultural festival of the arts featuring music, dance, comedy, puppetry, theater, and magic—more than 100 events in all! Activities generally run from late afternoon on Dec 31 and culminate with midnight fireworks. Events take place at locations throughout the city including the Worcester Common, Mechanics Hall, the DCU Arena, National Guard Armory, Hanover Theater, and everywhere in between. It's a free event but buttons are needed to enjoy most of the events at the indoor venues.

PAN MASS CHALLENGE
Sturbridge, MA 01566
panmasschallenge.org
Attracting more than 5,000 cyclists, this bike-athon raises money for Boston's Dana-Farber Cancer Institute and is the country's largest mass-participation charity event. There are now 11 routes for the riders to choose from, but the original route starts in Sturbridge and is the most grueling. The first Saturday of August, the streets of Sturbridge are lined with residents and thousands of supporters cheering on the cyclists as they begin a trek that ends 192 miles and 2 days later in Provincetown on Cape Cod.

Hiking, Biking & Walking

PURGATORY CHASM STATE
   RESERVATION
190 Purgatory Rd.
Sutton, MA 01590
(508) 234-3733
mass.gov/dcr/parks/central/purg.htm
Although Worcester County is more hilly than mountainous, Purgatory Chasm State Park offers hikers a small dose of adventure with piles of boulders to climb and hidden caverns to explore. The main trail, the Chasm Looping Trail, is just 1 mile but it features challenging sections with names like Lover's Leap and the Devil's Coffin. Conquer this and you'll feel on top of the world.

Kidstuff

DAVIS FARMLAND
145 Redstone Hill Rd.
Sterling, MA 01564
(978) 422-6666
davisfarmland.com
Your kids can practically talk to the animals at Davis Farmland. In the farm showcase area there is always a friendly farmer on hand to introduce the kids to the animals in the barn and show them how to milk a cow, collect eggs, or help with bottle-feeding a new baby animal. If you want to stay longer or if you need to entertain a child who is timid with animals, there is a large playground area. In the summer Davis has a "sprayground" for the kids to cool off. Open mid-April through late October, weather permitting.

DAVIS MEGA MAZE
145 Redstone Hill
Sterling, MA 01564
(978) 422-8888
davisfarmland.com
Getting lost means having fun finding your way through an 8-acre field planted with an estimated 3 miles of trails lined with 10- to 12-foot towering walls of corn. Each year features a different elaborately designed maze theme; past seasons have featured an Indiana Jones–like adventure, "The Lost Tomb," and a "Clue"-like murder/mystery to solve. The maze attractions vary each year, too, but there are always several bridges and an observation tower to watch others wander into dead ends. The maze is always challenging and takes 1 to 2 hours to complete—and often takes parents longer than their children! Davis Mega Maze is a seasonal attraction, open daily from early Aug through early Oct and weekends through Halloween.

ECOTARIUM
222 Harrington Way
Worcester, MA 01604
(508) 929-2700
ecotarium.org
The Ecotarium in Worcester is a wonderful science and environmental museum that stresses conservation and appreciation of the natural world. The weekly Wednesday drop-in program is ideal for ages 3 to 5, where kids can listen to a story, make a craft, and discover the unique features of one of the Ecotarium's small mammals, birds, or reptiles. The Budding Scientist program on the first Thursday of the month introduces fun, hands-on science activities for kids ages 4 through 6. Both programs are designed for kids and parents to enjoy together. The Ecotarium is also home to an impressive number

of animals, including fun-loving otters and a pair of beautiful red foxes.

Nightlife

NICKS' BAR & RESTAURANT
124 Millbury St.
Worcester, MA 01610
(508) 753-40030
nicksworcester.com
Live jazz and cabaret music along with perfect cocktails distinguish this home-away-from-home for a friendly mixed urban/artist crowd. The food is German, no-frills and hearty with items like warm soft pretzels with herbed cheese and liverwurst sandwiches served with sauerkraut.

RALPH'S ROCK DINER
148 Grove St.
Worcester, MA 01605
(508) 753-9543
ralphsrockdiner.com
The heart of Worcester's indie rocker scene, there are three separate rooms within this old diner car/factory space—a burger joint, a bar, and an upstairs live music venue that lines up an eclectic calendar of local bands Thursday through Saturday nights (usually with a cover). Sunday night is movie night. Open nightly.

Skiing

SKI WARD
1000 Main St.
Shrewsbury, MA 01545
(508) 842-6346
skiward.com
Dating back to 1939, this family-owned ski area offers affordable skiing. Ward Hill has 220 vertical feet, and 1 triple chairlift, a T-bar, and a carpet lift that service the 9 beginner

trails. Nonexistent lines and uncrowded trails are the rule here. Ward has all the amenities of mountain skiing—snowmaking, lights for night skiing, a rental shop, ski school, a terrain park, a lodge with a snack bar/grill, and the very popular "Tubaslide" tubing hill—and is an excellent choice for first-time skiers and young families.

i Take the rails to the trails. Every winter Wachusett Mountain, in conjunction with the Massachusetts Bay commuter rail (mbta.com), runs a ski train (with a car that has been modified to accommodate ski gear) from Boston's North Station. A free Wachusett shuttle bus then takes skiers directly to the mountain, 20 minutes away.

WACHUSETT MOUNTAIN
499 Mountain Rd.
Princeton, MA 01541
wachusett.com
You can hit the slopes less than an hour's drive from downtown Boston at Wachusett Mountain. Wachusett has a long history of strong children's programs and is renowned as a family resort. With a 1,000-foot vertical drop, 22 trails, and 8 lifts, Wachusett is near big-time status. Beginners have their own learning area while intermediate and expert skiers have access to the upper mountain by 3 quad chairlifts. The post-and-beam base lodge is expansive with a rental shop, a large stone fireplace, and plenty of seating options, including a large outdoor deck. The lodge feeds many a hungry skier; the cafeteria serves standard après fare (chili and sandwiches), and the upstairs Black Diamond is the place for less hectic pub-style dining (nacho platters, salads, fish and chips) with a view of the mountain, while

the Copper Top Lounge is a friendly bar with the sports channel always on. Lift tickets are available for day, twilight, and night skiing and are priced even better when you buy in advance online.

Spectator Sports

DCU CENTER
50 Foster St.
Worcester, MA 01608
(508) 755-6800
dcucenter.com
Frank Sinatra performed the inaugural concert when it opened as the Centrum in 1982. Now known as the DCU Center (Digital Federal Credit Union), the 15,000-seat arena has since hosted countless artists including Madonna, Andrea Bocelli, and Bruce Springsteen. The DCU Center is home ice to the Worcester Sharks of the American Hockey League (the NHL's top minor league division) and there's plenty of sports action from area college teams as well. Among the annual events taking place here are the Harlem Globetrotters, Stars on Ice, truck and tractor pulls, and sometimes even the rodeo.

SHOPPING
Art

✳MOLE HOLLOW CANDLES
208 Charlton Rd.
Sturbridge, MA 01566
(800) 445-6653
molehollowcandles.com
This family-owned artisan candle company has been making gorgeous handmade tapers, pillars, and votives since 1969. These are slow-burning candles that soothe. Their tiny tapers (3 inches) look lovely on a birthday cake. Each season brings a new color palette and the tapers and votives come in

both unscented and scented varieties (but not the kind that make you woozy).

*VAILLANCOURT FOLK ART STUDIOS
9 Main St.
Sutton, MA 01590
(508) 476-3601
valfa.com
Founded in 1984 by husband and wife Gary and Judy Vaillancourt, the main attraction in the village of Sutton is the Vaillancourt chalkware factory. Visitors can watch the artists hand-paint the exquisitely detailed, collectible holiday-themed figurines for which Vaillancourt is famous. Afterward visit the Christmas Museum and the company store to purchase unique gifts and souvenirs.

Farmers' Markets & Pick Your Own

STOWE FARM ORCHARD
15 Stowe Rd.
Millbury, MA 01527
(508) 865-9860
stowefarm.com
Plan on spending an afternoon at this orchard—there is so much to do! Pick apples, visit the country store, go on a hayride, let the kids see the animals in the petting zoo and play in the playground. Other unique features? A 25-foot climbing wall, a gem-mining area, and an aerial adventure course.

*TOUGAS FAMILY FARM
234 Ball St.
Northboro, MA 01532
(508) 393-6406
tougasfarm.com
Tougas is one of the area's finest pick-your-own farms, offering a variety of fruit from spring through fall. Strawberry season begins in late May and continues through Father's Day weekend; blueberry picking season begins soon after in July. During the height of the summer, the blueberry, peach, and raspberry crops typically overlap, so in one visit, you can pick all 3 fruits. In the fall, enjoy the changing of the seasons and the pleasure of eating a crisp, red apple picked fresh from the tree. The Tougas farm stand sells ice cream and cold drinks as well as a wide variety of freshly baked fruit pies, crisps, and doughnuts. You can bring your own lunch or buy sandwiches to eat at the picnic tables. Afterward the kids can visit the barn area and feed the animals (bring quarters) or play in the playground.

Furniture

LACHANCE FURNITURE SHOWROOMS
25 Kraft St.
Gardner, MA 01440
(978) 630-3299
lachancefurniture.com
Once the furniture capital of New England, Gardner is a great place to go if you're interested in new home furnishings. Low prices and selection are the draw at LaChance. Expect more than 150 well-known brands and some pieces at below manufacturer direct prices. Among the well-known brands are Lexington, Harden, and Sarreid. LaChance also has a furniture outlet around the corner (501 W. Broadway; 978-630-3299) that has deep discounts on overstock and slightly imperfect items.

Specialty Food

HEBERT'S CANDY MANSION
575 Hartford Turnpike
Shrewsbury, MA 01545
(508) 845-8051
hebertcandies.com

Generations of local families have come to Hebert's to indulge in the legendary "make your own" sundae bar with 17 toppings and 15 flavors of ice cream. The Tudor stone mansion is an amazing backdrop as the main retail outlet for Hebert's Candy—definitely pick up some of their small-batch handmade fudge.

Toys & Comic Books

THAT'S ENTERTAINMENT
244 Park Ave.
Worcester, MA 01609
(508) 755-4207
thatse.com
Why are comic book stores so hard to find? That's Entertainment is an enormous store that has a full selection of popular comics and graphic novels. They also stock every kind of music imaginable, including progressive rock, country, world, jazz, and soul. You can also fill your need for books, videos, sports memorabilia, video games, action figure novelties, CD tracks, and even used vinyl—some records are just $1!

ACCOMMODATIONS

Inns & Bed-and-Breakfasts

MAGUIRE HOUSE B & B   **$$**
30 Cobb Rd.
Ashburnham, MA 01430
(978) 827-5053
maguirehouse.com
A beautiful setting on more than 40 private acres overlooking Upper Naukeag Lake with views of Mount Monadnock makes this 1764 property a country idyll. This 3-room inn's airy, antiques-laden, and TV-free guest rooms harken back to simpler times. You can doze by the welcoming fire in the lounge or take a

walk on the grounds. It's blessedly quiet, but don't oversleep—among the hearty New England–style breakfast choices are pumpkin waffles that are not to be missed.

RED MAPLE INN   **$$**
217 Main St.
Spencer, MA 01512
(508) 885-9205
theredmapleinn.com
For a romantic retreat with a gourmet twist, look no further than the Red Maple Inn. This award-winning colonial-era estate has gourmet dine-and-stay packages with multicourse themed menus and wine pairings and also offers a monthly in-house cooking class. Each of the 6 rooms is Victorian pretty with period antique furniture, luxurious bedding, and modern conveniences like free Wi-Fi. Breakfasts are sophisticated, featuring blueberry cream cheese–stuffed french toast or spinach frittata—perfect fuel for a day of antiquing at nearby Brimfield.

YANKEE CRICKET B & B   **$$**
106 Five Bridge Rd.
Brimfield, MA 01010
(413) 245-0030
yankeecricket.com
Perched on a wooded ridge, this small inn looks like a well-restored 18th-century home but the rustic barn–red clapboard exterior belies its 2002 origins. The brand-new interior was custom crafted for the inn's owners and features a keeping room with an open hearth and a dining room painted with wall murals depicting early New England life. The inn's 5 rooms are comfy with unique touches—pleasingly painted woodwork, rooms filled with antiques, and good-sized private bathrooms.

Hotels & Motels

✳BEECHWOOD HOTEL $$–$$$
363 Plantation St.
Worcester, MA 01605
(508) 754-5789
beechwoodhotel.com
Conveniently located across the street from UMass Medical Center, this hotel has also been discovered by families of students from WPI, Holy Cross, and Clark. Guest rooms are big, many have sofa beds, and connecting rooms are available if you really want to spread out. Rooms are decorated in soothing taupes, beds are dressed with white *matelassé* bedspreads while bathrooms have granite counters and nickel fixtures. The hotel offers lots of value; all room rates come with free Wi-Fi, free continental breakfast, and free parking. The hotel's Ceres restaurant has a popular weekly Sunday buffet brunch.

SOUTHBRIDGE HOTEL & CONFERENCE CENTER $$
14 Mechanic St.
Southbridge, MA 01550
(508) 765-8000
southbridgehotel.com
This property opened in 2002 after extensive renovations to the turn-of-the-20th-century former American Optical Factory mill building. This well-equipped business hotel has more than 200 rooms that are generic, but generously sized and well maintained. You'll be pleasantly surprised by the hotel's amenities, which include a huge fitness center with an indoor pool, sauna, and Jacuzzi. The hotel is in a less than scenic neighborhood, but Old Sturbridge Village and the Brimfield Antiques Show are both just a short drive away.

RESTAURANTS

American

GEORGE'S CONEY ISLAND LUNCH $
158 Southbridge St.
Worcester, MA 01608
(508) 753-4362
coneyislandlunch.com
Not much changes at this 1918 Worcester landmark; the wood benches date from 1938 and are carved with the initials of decades of patrons, the 60-foot neon sign is from the 1940s, and it's still cash only. The menu is old school: egg salad sandwiches, grilled cheese, and hamburgers. But hot dogs are the main draw; get yours "up" and it will come with yellow mustard, finely chopped onions, and a special chili sauce (more sauce than chili). Beer is on the menu, but the drink of choice is chocolate milk. Not sure why. Closed Tues.

KENMORE DINER $
250 Franklin St.
Worcester, MA 01609
(508) 792-5125
Home of the now-defunct Worcester Lunch Car Company, which manufactured more than 600 diners during the first half of the last century, Worcester is still a city of diners, with several classic boxcar diners in the area. The Kenmore is a new reconstruction diner; it literally rose from the ashes in the wake of the next-door 1999 Worcester Cold Storage Warehouse fire, which took the lives of 6 firemen. Open all day and night, this is the place in the city for late-night eats. You'll still find retro portion sizes and prices—the raved-about spinach, sausage, and cheese omelet with home fries is just $5. Cash only.

✳LUCKY'S CAFE $$
102½ Grove St.
Worcester, MA 01605
(508) 756-5014
luckyscafeworcester.com

The 40-seat place in a subterranean space at Northworks in the old wire mill complex may not look sophisticated, but the food is exceptional: thick-cut pork chops with apple rum sauce, Portuguese fish stew with fennel in an orange broth, rosemary polenta with fresh mozzarella. Regulars come for breakfasts that feature omelets and there are sandwiches and salad for the lunch crowd. Friday and Saturday nights feature live music; take advantage of the BYOB policy and bring a special vintage to enjoy with your meal.

Barbecue

B.T.'S SMOKEHOUSE $$
392 Main St.
Sturbridge, MA 01566
(508) 347-3188
btsmokehouse.com

Who needs fancy digs when you can chow down on slow-smoked ribs or tangy pulled pork? They are serious about their sides, too; spicy and perfectly cooked collard greens, black-eyed peas, and authentic skillet corn bread. And be sure to order an appetizer of "Pig Newtons"; bite-size morsels of flaky crust filled with pulled pork and fig chutney. No longer a trailer and finally a restaurant (albeit a small one), the place limits seating to just 3 booths and a few counter stools—but take-out is always an option. Closed Mon.

Eclectic

EVO $–$$
234 Chandler St.
Worcester, MA 01609
(508) 459-4240
evodining.com

The decor is trendy urban with an eclectic mix of global (pesto arancini, lobster rangoon) and American comfort food (the Phat Albert, an 8-ounce Angus burger stuffed with cheese, then baked in a screaming-hot oven for a perfect sear, is a star). Look over the menu carefully and you'll find some unexpected gems, too, like Port Said chicken with mushrooms, allspice, and white wine over authentic Lebanese rice pilaf made with broken vermicelli. The menu is designed to please diners on either end of the meat spectrum with lots of vegetarian and vegan choices and also offers gluten-free options—and it's all clearly (and refreshingly) marked as such.

Italian

DINO'S RISTORANTE ITALIANO $$
13 Lord St.
Worcester, MA 01604
(508) 799-6068
dineatdinos.com

This is your father's Italian joint, and it's still great with a dining room filled with old-time charm and families enjoying good-value meals. The menu is heavily southern Italian cuisine, with hearty and earthy dishes such as homemade manicotti and sausage cacciatore as well as elegant dishes such as veal piccata and seafood in a white wine sauce over pasta. Be sure to loosen your belt, though—most dishes are big enough for two.

Pizza

CORNER GRILLE $
806 Pleasant St.
Worcester, MA 01602
(508) 754-8884
cornergrille.com
You'll need to go off the beaten path to
the west side of Worcester for this one. The
Corner Grille offers wondrous cracker-thin-
crust pizza in a funky storefront that keeps
the crowds lined up. The sweet tomato and
basil pies emerge from the wood-fired oven
with an immaculate char, plenty of mozzarella, and slivers of basil. Among the set
combos, the Caveman pizza with pepperoni,
sausage, bacon, and hamburger has lots of
fans among the college guys. If you can stop
yourself from ordering a second pie (they are
small), reward yourself with any of the excellent homemade baked goods, such as the
chocolate chip cookies and whoopee pies.
The lemonade and ice tea "for two" comes
in a quart Mason jar with 2 paper straws
(very cute).

Polish

STANLEY'S LUNCH $
231 Pleasant St.
Gardner, MA 01440
(978) 632-9891
This homey little Polish lunch spot was
launched in Gardner during the Great
Depression and is well worth your time for
its authentic menu of filling fare: homemade
kielbasa, cabbage rolls, and stuffed peppers.
Make sure you try the imported beers, too.
Tip: If you are furniture shopping at the
Gardner outlets, this would be a great lunch
choice (compensation) for a "tag-along" husband. Open Mon through Sat 11:30 a.m. to 2
p.m.; cash only.

Pubs & Taverns

✳ARMSBY ABBEY $–$$
144 Main St.
Worcester, MA 01608
(508) 795-1012
armsbyabbey.com
Worcester's first real gastropub regularly
makes the local "best of" lists in several categories for its well-executed fare—the mac
and cheese is made even better with beer
as its secret ingredient, generous plates of
home-cured charcuterie and "stinky" artisan cheeses are served with house-baked
breads and gourmet sandwiches. Cutting-
edge cocktails—the Abbey Manhattan
features a torched orange peel—and a
rotating beer selection of 20 local and international taps along with 200 bottles draw
a grab bag of beer fanatics and casual
drinkers alike. The long wood bar, exposed
brick walls, and chalkboard signs create an
upscale feel, while the prices reflect that
this is Worcester.

Seafood

✳SOLE PROPRIETOR $$
118 Highland St.
Worcester, MA 01609
(508) 798-3474
thesole.com
Freshness is a given at the Sole Proprietor,
where more than 20 varieties of seafood
are on the menu daily, from an excellent
clam chowder to basic broiled, grilled, or
fried seafood to New American dishes like
pecan-crusted mahimahi. Or have it all with
a classic surf-and-turf pairing of a 6-ounce
steak tenderloin with baked shrimp. For
dessert try the irresistible chocolate terrine
with 2 (dark and white chocolate) sauces.
The elegant and subtly nautical dining

room and an upbeat atmosphere make this the go-to special occasion dining choice in Worcester.

> **i** Nestled in the shadows of Mount Wachusett, the rural town of Sterling is known as the real-life setting for the poem "Mary Had a Little Lamb." In 1815 a young Mary Sawyer was followed to school by her pet lamb. A small statue of Mary's lamb stands on the town common—its ears worn shiny from love by generations of schoolchildren.

DAY TRIP IN WORCESTER

For breakfast, hit **Shaker's Cafe & Restaurant** (296 Hamilton St.; 508-797-5550), a neighborhood spot where you'll discover an impressive array of omelets and egg dishes. The regulars can't seem to get enough of the Lebanese breakfast; 3 eggs any way you like, Syrian toast with feta, and house-made hash with kibbe. And like most really great breakfast joints, it's cash only.

Locals are proud to say that Worcester, like Rome, is a city of 7 hills. **Bancroft Tower** provides an excellent overview of the city and is a fun roadside attraction to boot. From Shaker's pick up I-290 and travel east for a mile. Make a left on Route 9 and follow for 2 miles. Take a right on Westland Road, a quick left on Institute Road, and another quick right turn onto Farnum Street as it becomes Bancroft Tower Road. Bancroft Tower (Bancroft Tower Road, Worcester) is a strangely small facade of a castle. It was built in 1900 by Stephen Salisbury III (founder of the Worcester Art Museum) as a tribute to Worcester native George Bancroft, secretary of the navy under James Polk and founder of the US Naval Academy. The stairs inside the

tower are closed, but there are good views of Worcester and a locater map stone on the ground that identifies each of Worcester's 7 hills.

From Bancroft Tower, follow Massachusetts Avenue down the hill and make a right on Salisbury Road. The affluent homes here are among the nicest in Worcester. You'll pass the campus of WPI and after a mile reach Worcester's not-so-hidden gem, the **Worcester Art Museum** (55 Salisbury St.; 508-799-4406; worcesterart.org), for a brush with culture. Among the significant works in the collection are the second largest collection in the world of Paul Revere silver, and works by Whistler and Monet. Linger for lunch at the excellent Museum Cafe or consider the Skyline Bistro at **Worcester Technical High School** (One Skyline Dr.; 508-799-1964; portal.techhigh.us) and help students with their on-the-job training. From the museum, follow Belmont Street for 1 mile. Along the way you'll pass the sprawling UMass Medical Center. With 13,000 employees, it is practically a city unto itself and is a key player in every aspect of Worcester city life. Make a left onto Skyline Drive and follow for ⅓ mile to Worcester Technical High. **Skyline Bistro** is a cute 80-seat cafe that is open to the public and serves as a classroom and ongoing exam for students enrolled in Worcester Tech's culinary arts program. The New England–centric menu might include a grilled chicken Caesar salad, an open steak sirloin sandwich, or baked scrod. It's always a grade-A lunch. Open Tues through Fri 10:30 a.m. to 12:30 p.m.

After lunch continue along Skyline Drive to the **Massachusetts Vietnam Veterans Memorial** (Green Hill Park; massvvm.org), which sits on a 4-acre landscaped site within Green Hill Park. The memorial's tranquil

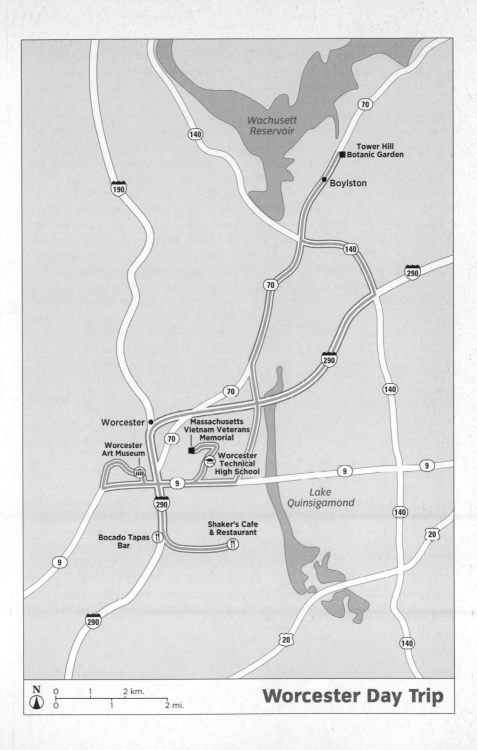

Wachusett Reservoir

■ Tower Hill
Botanic Garden

● Boylston

Worcester ●

Massachusetts
Vietnam Veterans
Memorial

Worcester
Art Museum

Worcester
Technical
High School

Lake
Quinsigamond

Bocado Tapas
Bar

Shaker's Cafe
& Restaurant

N

0   1   2 km.
0   1   2 mi.

Worcester Day Trip

beauty makes it a special place for reflection. Near the entrance is perhaps the most poignant section. At the **Place of Words,** 4 granite pillars are inscribed with portions of text from letters to home from 13 Vietnam servicemen, all of whom died very young. Follow the winding walking path beside the duck pond to the **Place of Names,** where 6 granite pillars are inscribed with the names of the 1,546 men and 1 woman from Massachusetts who gave their lives to (or remain missing as a result of) the Vietnam War. As you exit, there's a moving memorial to the 4,000 war dogs that served in Vietnam.

Head out of town for some outdoor recreation. No matter the season, **Tower Hill Botanic Garden** (11 French Dr., Boylston; 508-869-6111; towerhillbg.org) always has something to see. To get there, work your way back down Skyline Drive. Make a right onto Route 9 and follow for 1 mile. Make a left on Plantation Street and drive for 2 miles.

Turn right onto Route 70 and follow 4 miles to the Tower Hill Botanic Garden.

If the weather's chilly, you can keep warm in the conservatory. When the sun is out and the weather is fine, explore the gardens and walk the trails with views of Mount Wachusett.

The better route back to Worcester and a leisurely dinner is via I-290 for 7 miles to exit 14. It's always fun to mix and match tapas at casually upscale **Bocado Tapas Bar** (82 Winter St.; 508-797-1011; bocadotapasbar.com), where the sangria, cava, and Rioja flow. Stay all evening, sampling all manner of delectables: *pan con tomate,* pheasant sausage, sautéed littleneck clams with chorizo. Don't miss the fried goat cheese with almonds and honey. Few would consider Worcester a hot spot for nightlife, but Bocado comes close with its Thursday salsa nights and an ongoing fixed-price menu and flamenco show on the 3rd Friday of the month.

PIONEER VALLEY

Sandwiched between the Berkshire Mountains to the west and the Quabbin Reservoir to the east, the rural Pioneer Valley is a vast three-county swath of fertile farmland and country villages, vibrant college towns, and the industrial city of Springfield.

The Connecticut River bisects the region from the Vermont border in the north to the Connecticut River in the south. It was the river that first brought English colonists to the Pioneer Valley around present-day Springfield in 1635. These settlers really were pioneers, as this frontier formed the westernmost border of the state until the 1720s.

Less well-known than the Berkshires and far less populated than adjacent Worcester County, the Pioneer Valley offers family-friendly attractions, a cluster of lesser-known specialty museums, and ample natural scenery.

Springfield is best known as the home of the Basketball Hall of Fame and it is the prime reason for families to visit the region. But there is such an abundance of kid-centric sights—including Six Flags New England, the Forest Park Zoo, and the Dr. Seuss National Memorial—that you could spend a couple days in Springfield and leave begging for more.

The Pioneer Valley has an unparalleled concentration of higher education institutions, known as the Five College Consortium. It includes the flagship campus of the University of Massachusetts and four colleges: Amherst, Mount Holyoke, Smith, and Hampshire. The five campuses are located in neighboring towns that are all within 10 miles of each other and together they offer visitors access to museums, public lectures, and sporting events in inviting college environs. Amherst is the liveliest of the towns; it is home to UMass, Amherst, and Hampshire. The campus of Smith College is located in Northampton. Dubbed Noho, it has an interesting mix of academics and artists, and a large gay and lesbian community, along with eclectic restaurants and quirky shops that align perfectly with the town's free-spirited culture. South Hadley (home to Mount Holyoke) is the most isolated (and quietest) of the college towns, but orchards and farmland have their charms.

To the far north, follow the Mohawk Trail, America's First Auto Road, as it parallels the Deerfield River. Just off the highway, a sense of nostalgia permeates the small town of Deerfield with its tree-lined Main Street and perfectly preserved historic district. Spend a morning or afternoon here, and you'll get the feeling that you may have just stepped back in time.

ATTRACTIONS

Historic Sites & Landmarks

BRIDGE OF FLOWERS
Bridge Street off Route 2
Shelburne Falls, MA 01370
bridgeofflowersmass.org

The Bridge of Flowers that crosses the Deerfield River in Shelburne Falls is simply terrific repurposing. In 1908 the arched trolley bridge was built in the center of Shelburne Falls. It was closed in 1928 and soon after the Shelburne Falls Women's Club spearheaded an effort to develop a community garden across its 400-foot span. Today dense plantings of trees, bulbs, annuals, and perennials create a floral blanket of color throughout the spring, summer, and fall growing season that is enjoyed by visitors from far and wide. And to this day, the Shelburne Falls Women's Club, along with a dedicated group of volunteers (and with support of public donations), lovingly plants and maintains the garden.

*HISTORIC DEERFIELD
80 Old Main St.
Deerfield, MA 01342
(413) 775-7214
historic-deerfield.org

Farsighted preservation by local citizens has saved more than 50 historic buildings dating back to the 18th century along a mile-long section of Deerfield's Main Street. The result is a unique outdoor living-history museum that examines early rural New England life. The district's 11 museum houses make up the core of Historic Deerfield and are available for either guided or self-guided tours. They date from 1720 to 1850; some are restored to a particular period, some are used for exhibits, and some are viewed from the outside only. Perhaps the most

opulent home is the Stebbins House, a 1799 brick federal-style mansion decorated in the neoclassical style of the period. The Dwight House is a working studio that demonstrates weaving, ceramics-making, and woodworking skills. The Flynt Center for Early New England Life is a modern, state-of-the-art museum with notable exhibits of powder horns, textiles, and early American furniture. Upstairs, "The Attic" is a visible storage facility for works not currently on view in the museum. The museum store is exceptional, with high-quality reproduction 18th-century wares, such as hand-wrought silver jewelry, needlework kits, cornhusk dolls, and furniture including early American–style tavern and trestle tables.

Museums

BENESKI MUSEUM OF NATURAL HISTORY
11 Barrett Hill Rd.
Amherst, MA 01002
(413) 542-2165
amherst.edu/museums/naturalhistory

This museum on the campus of Amherst College delves deep back in time, displaying eons-old artifacts and specimens that fascinate both adults and kids. Highlights include Ice Age skeletons of a mammoth and a mastodon, taxidermied birds and mammals, and one of the world's largest collections of dinosaur footprints. Closed Mon.

*EMILY DICKINSON MUSEUM
280 Main St.
Amherst, MA 01002
(413) 542-8161
emilydickinsonmuseum.org

As is often the case with historic houses, the docent makes the tour—and these docents are very well versed (pun intended) on the

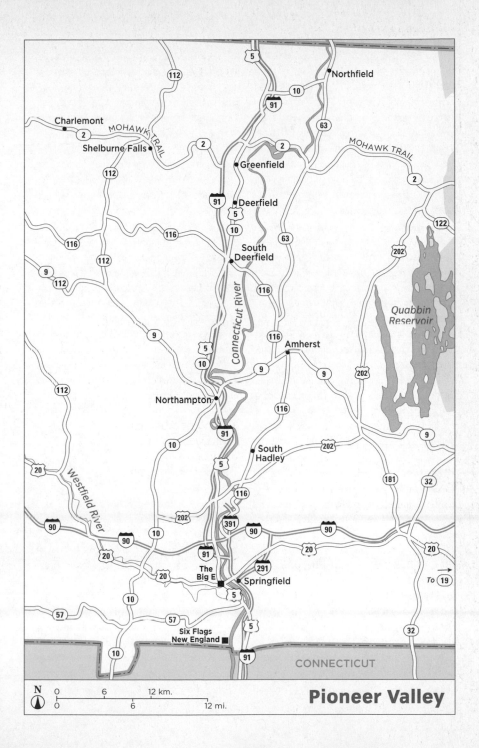

Pioneer Valley

life of Emily Dickinson and her poetry. The 90-minute guided tours include visiting the Dickinson Homestead, where Emily was born and spent most of her life. She wrote many of her poems in her sunny 2nd-floor bedroom. Emily was reclusive in her later years and was known in Amherst as the "woman in white." You'll see a replica "white dress" at the top of the 2nd-floor stairs. The simple cotton house dress with mother-of-pearl buttons is distinctive, too, for its special sewn-on pocket so that Emily would always have a scrap of paper and a pencil at hand. You'll also visit the Evergreens next door, the Italianate house owned by her brother Austin, with its collection of Dickinson family furniture and artifacts. Serious poetry buffs should check ahead for information on the extensive schedule of special events and programs that take place—often in conjunction with leading academics from Amherst College. If you are not familiar with Emily's poetry ("I'm nobody, who are you?"), the museum's bookstore carries many excellent compilations. The museum is closed during Jan and Feb.

i It's pronounced AM-erst. In a community where righteously liberal politics dominate, locals are proud of their town's unofficial motto, "Amherst, where only the 'h' is silent."

ERIC CARLE MUSEUM OF PICTURE BOOK ART
125 W. Bay Rd.
Amherst, MA 01002
(413) 658-1100
picturebookart.org
Ask any teenager or young adult and they will tell you that *The Very Hungry Caterpillar* by Eric Carle is one of the coolest picture

books ever. Eric Carle and his wife established this museum, devoted to national and international picture-book art, in 2002. The museum appeals to all ages but was designed with children in mind; the artwork is hung lower than normal. The 3 galleries display a rotating series of exhibits. Eric Carle has illustrated more than 70 picture books and the West Gallery always features some aspect of his work; past exhibits have included "Bears and Beyond," which examined Carle's collage technique, and "Beyond Books," a retrospective of his other artistic endeavors: photography, sketches, painting, and sculpture. The other galleries feature various other children's picture-book authors; past exhibitions have included Maurice Sendak, Arnold Lobel, Leo Lionni, Lucy Cousins, and Latino folk tales. The gift shop has a phenomenal selection of classic picture books and related gifts. Before you go, make a list of kids you need to buy a gift for this year and get it done in advance.

MEAD ART MUSEUM
Amherst College
41 Quadrangle Dr.
Amherst, MA 01002
(413) 542-2335
amherst.edu/museums/mead
Set in a classic redbrick building on the campus of Amherst College, the museum has 6 galleries that cover a diverse range of culture and time periods. While the Mead's holdings are expansive, with works as diverse as ancient Assyrian sculptures, European masters paintings, and Russian modern art, its American collection is its most renowned, with works by John Singleton Copley, Frederic Edwin Church, Winslow Homer, Childe Hassam, and Robert Henri. The museum is closed Mon but open until midnight Tues

through Thurs and Sun—a boon in early-closing Amherst.

NAISMITH MEMORIAL BASKETBALL HALL OF FAME
1000 Hall of Fame Ave.
Springfield, MA 01105
(877) 466-6752
hoophall.com
You can't miss the Basketball Hall of Fame—the hall's giant basketball-shaped dome positively looms over the city. Springfield is considered the birthplace of basketball. James Naismith was working as a coach at the local YMCA and invented the game here in 1891. Most decide to start their visit on the 3rd floor, where plaques bearing the pictures and biographies of the more than 300 inductees line the walls of the Honors Ring, the actual hall of fame. The 2nd floor is dedicated to the history of the game along with exhibits (videos and memorabilia) relating to the NBA, college basketball, and international play. On the regulation 1st-floor Center Court there are lots of ball carts filled with basketballs waiting for visitors to shoot a few.

SHELBURNE FALLS TROLLEY MUSEUM
15 Depot St.
Shelburne Falls, MA 01370
(413) 625-9443
sftm.org
Around the corner from the Bridge of Flowers, this small museum operates on tracks originally used by the Shelburne Falls and Colrain Street trolley. Admission includes a 15-minute narrated trolley ride on the restored 1896 No. 10 trolley car (for 65 years it served as a chicken coop!) and the opportunity to pump the handcar along a section of track in the rail yard. The former freight house serves as the museum's exhibit space

with an assortment of vintage equipment on display. The museum is open weekends from Memorial Day through Oct, and also Mon in July and Aug; check for hours.

SMITH COLLEGE MUSEUM OF ART
Elm Street at Bedford Terrace
Northampton, MA 01063
(413) 585-2760
smith.edu/artmuseum
Thanks in large part to generous alumnae donors, Smith has an art museum that rivals those in major metropolitan areas. Housed on campus in the Brown Fine Arts Center, the modern redbrick and steel building's 4 floors of sky-lit galleries bring together an impressive permanent collection with strong selections of 19th- and 20th-century European and American art. You can't miss one of the museum's most notable works; Mexican artist Rufino Tamayo's 43-foot mural *Nature and the Artist: The Work of Art and the Observer* was commissioned by the college in 1943 and is the centerpiece of the museum's atrium space. Closed Mon.

SPRINGFIELD MUSEUMS
21 Edwards St.
Springfield, MA 01103
(413) 263-6800
springfieldmuseums.org
Spend a couple hours exploring this complex of 5 small museums that house fascinating collections relating to art, science, and history. The Museum of Fine Arts houses an eclectic collection that includes paintings by American artists John Singleton Copley and Winslow Homer, a gallery devoted to Currier & Ives lithographs, and sculpture by contemporary artist Dale Chihuly. The George Walter Vincent Smith Museum focuses on 19th-century American paintings and a collection

of Japanese art. At the Science Museum, the life-size replica of *Tyrannosaurus rex* is the big crowd-pleaser, while the hall of stuffed African animals in a diorama-like setting engrosses young and old. A museum of Springfield history and a Connecticut Valley Museum are also on the campus. With one admission ticket you gain access to all 5 museums. The cluster of museum buildings surrounds a grassy quadrangle, the Dr. Seuss National Memorial Sculpture Garden, which features whimsical, larger-than-life bronze statues of the Cat in the Hat and other characters from the books of native son Theodor Geisel (aka Dr. Seuss). The museums are closed Mon; the sculpture garden is open to the public daily dawn to dusk.

Wildlife & Zoos

MAGIC WINGS BUTTERFLY
CONSERVATORY & GARDENS
281 Greenfield Rd.
South Deerfield, MA 01373
(413) 665-2805
magicwings.net
More than 4,000 native and tropical butterflies are allowed to flutter freely in this 8,000-square-foot, rain forest–like glass conservatory that features paved pathways, a small pond, birds, and lush, flowering vegetation. If you sit still on one of the benches for a few minutes, an electric-blue *Morpho peleides* butterfly might just land on you. Also on the premises is a large gift shop, an outdoor butterfly garden, and the restaurant Monarchs, serving breakfast, lunch, and light dinners.

THE ZOO AT FOREST PARK
302 Sumner Ave.
Springfield, MA 01138
(413) 733-2251
forestparkzoo.org

Dating from the early 20th century, this charming park-like zoo has more than 150 species of domestic and exotic animals. There's the Heritage Breeds barnyard, where kids can peek in the chicken coop and get a glimpse of eggs hatching, or they can buy special feed and offer the goats a snack. Kids are always entertained by the childlike playfulness of the capuchins and lemurs. Other family faves: the Outback exhibit with its kangaroos, emus, and wallabies, and the rubber-tire train ride around the park. The admission fees at this zoo are low too—priced just right for multiple visits. The zoo is closed Dec through Mar.

i From Thanksgiving weekend through New Year's Day, Springfield's Forest Park is transformed into a 2.5-mile glittering wonderland with a 600,000-light display. Tune your radio to the Bright Nights frequency to hear the musical simulcast as you drive through the more than 20 illuminated themes. Seussland is the perennial favorite.

ACTIVITIES & EVENTS

Amusement Parks

SIX FLAGS NEW ENGLAND
1623 Main St.
Agawam, MA 01002
(413) 786-9300
sixflags.com/newengland
Located just a few miles from Springfield, this is by far the region's largest amusement park. The 10 roller coasters, close to 60 other rides and attractions in 7 themed areas, water park, and numerous shows could keep any family busy for days. This Six Flags has a reputation for satisfying the needs of

thrill-seekers. So, if you like roller coasters, this is the park for you. Bizarro turns riders upside-down 6 times and makes a 15-story dive at almost 80 miles per hour into a fog-filled tunnel. For less daring parents and very young children, there are lots of tamer choices in Kidzopolis and the Looney Tunes Movie Town area including bumper cars, a teacup ride, and a carousel. Take a break from riding and cool off at Hurricane Harbor water park (bathing suits are required and lockers are available), which has a lazy-river tube ride, a wave pool, and more than a dozen waterslides. On summer weekends wait times for the big roller coasters are as long as 2 hours. You may want to consider purchasing a Flash Pass (the price is in addition to admission), which allows holders to jump to the front of the line. Open May through Oct; check website for days and times.

Arts Venues

IRON HORSE MUSIC HALL
20 Center St.
Northampton, MA 01060
(413) 586-8686
iheg.com
The Iron Horse is the area's most well-known venue for live music. Noisy and crowded, the hall provides table service for drinks and food. It is best known for its rock, folk, jazz, and blues acts, having played host to the likes of Peter Wolf, Joan Osborne, Winton Marsalis, and Bo Diddley. Most often, local or regional acts take the stage. Closed Mon.

NATIONAL YIDDISH BOOK CENTER
1021 West St.
Amherst, MA 01002
(413) 256-4900
yiddishbookcenter.org

From a distance the building looks like an isolated settlement on a hilltop overlooking an apple orchard. Built to resemble an Eastern European Jewish village, or shtetl, from the outside, the 37,000-square-foot Jewish cultural center has a bright, modern design inside and abundant natural light. In 1980 then–graduate student Aaron Lansky set out to save Yiddish books from Dumpsters and rescue unwanted texts from basements and attics in an effort to preserve Jewish language and culture. To date, more than 1.5 million volumes have been collected. Visit the library and art galleries or participate in the center's extensive cultural programming, including concerts, films, and author talks. The center is located adjacent to Hampshire College; closed Sat (Sun, too, during the winter) and all major Jewish and legal holidays.

Cruises

QUINNETUKUT II RIVERBOAT CRUISE
Northfield Visitor Center
99 Millers Falls Rd.
Northfield, MA 01360
(800) 859-2960
firstlightpower.com/northfield
For a different perspective of the Mohawk Trail, take a riverboat cruise. The Quinnetukut II or "QII" is a 44-seat riverboat that takes passengers on a narrated 1-hour cruise along the Connecticut River. Highlights include passing under the steel-arch French King Bridge and spotting eagles at Barton Cove. Bring binoculars. Season runs from late June through mid-October; cruises depart 3 times a day, Fri through Sun.

Festivals & Annual Events

*THE BIG E (EASTERN STATES EXPOSITION)
875 Memorial Ave.
West Springfield, MA 01089
(413) 737-2443
thebige.com
For 2 weeks beginning in mid-September, the Big E brings together the 6 New England states in a celebration of the region's agricultural heritage. There are livestock shows, prize-winning pumpkins, midway rides, country music concerts, and fried everything (Girl Scout cookies, lasagna, Twinkies, and more). Experience all of New England at the Avenue of States, where you can walk through a bigger-than-life replica of each New England state's capitol building with exhibits that showcase the state's products and attractions.

Hiking, Biking & Walking

NORWATTUCK RAIL TRAIL
446 Damon Rd.
Northampton, MA 01060
(413) 586-8706
mass.gov/dcr/parks/central/nwrt.htm
In the days before the car was king, the central Massachusetts branch of the Boston & Maine railroad passenger train worked this route between Boston and Northampton 3 times a day. This 11-mile scenic and well-maintained multi-use (bike, walk, cross-country ski) trail connects Northampton, Hadley, and Amherst. The meandering, flat route through woods and farmland is easy even for a novice. Favorite spot: the long iron trestle bridge that crosses the Connecticut River in Northampton.

Nightlife

NORTHAMPTON BREWERY
11 Brewster Ct.
Northampton, MA 01060
(413) 584-9903
northamptonbrewery.com
Venerable Northampton Brewery churns out nearly 950 barrels of beer a year from its on-site brew house. Fans always go straight for the Blue Boots IPA but the real reason to visit the source is the interesting seasonal and specialty beers. A good option for the indecisive is the 6-glass sampler that might include Black Cat Stout, with hints of coffee. In the winter, near the fireplace is the place to be and in the summer (day or night) the huge rooftop beer garden is a must. The all-day menu features better-than-average, beer-friendly fare like homemade soups, sandwiches on locally baked bread, an 8-ounce Black Angus burger, and other pub favorites like fish and chips and a ploughman's platter with braised bratwurst, local cheddar cheese, roasted beets, sweet cornichons, and homemade flatbread. Open daily until 1 a.m.

TUNNEL BAR
125 A Pleasant St.
Northampton, MA 01060
(413) 586-5366
This abandoned century-old underground train station has all the trappings of a speakeasy: an unmarked entrance, overstuffed leather chairs, and dim lighting. Martinis are the specialty and the menu has dozens of choices. The narrow room is often packed, so go early if you want to chat.

SHOPPING

Art

ARTISAN GALLERY
162 Main St.
Northampton, MA 01601
(413) 586-1942
theartisangallery.com
A haven for those who prize local and hand-made crafts, this shop showcases a broad selection of items from some of the best artists in the valley. Recent finds include an elegant silk and hand-felted Merino wool evening wrap and handmade jewelry in antique architectural patterns.

Books

✳AMHERST BOOKS
8 Main St.
Amherst, MA 01002
(413) 256-1547
amherstbooks.com
The Amherst community is well served here; this friendly independent bookstore hosts regular readings and book launches and is a fantastic place to peruse, shop, and get acquainted with local and national authors. The store is known for its comprehensive new-release section (some are from small-press publishers) and noteworthy sections in poetry, literature, and philosophy.

FOOD FOR THOUGHT BOOKS
106 N. Pleasant St.
Amherst, MA 01002
(413) 253-5432
foodforthoughtbooks.com
Since 1976 this book shop (it actually follows a workers-collective model) has been on the front lines of raising political and

social awareness in the Amherst community. Unapologetically far left of center, it stocks books from ecological/environmental issues to feminism to justice in the developing world. Feel free to join in and debate the issues of the day at the store's frequent book and community events.

✳ODYSSEY BOOK SHOP
9 College St.
South Hadley, MA 01075
(413) 534-7307
odysseybks.com
A fixture in South Hadley since 1963, Odyssey is the largest bookstore in the Pioneer Valley. Its inventory caters to the artsy and the intellectual (Mount Holyoke is its neighbor). The store is also known for its first-edition program that offers members signed, newly published books. There is a well-established sense of community here as well, with as many as 125 literary events yearly including readings, lectures, and children's story hours.

Farmers' Market & Grocery Stores

ATKINS FARMS COUNTRY MARKET
1150 West St.
Amherst, MA 01002
(413) 253-9528
atkinsfarms.com
This once-modest little farm stand has evolved over the years to become an upscale country market with loads of local produce and flowers and a unique selection of grocery items from the region. The farm stand bakery regularly incorporates seasonal produce in its lineup of sweets; in the fall there are sweet and subtle cider-y apple doughnuts; in the summer they make a mighty fine 3-berry pie.

GREEN FIELDS MARKET
144 Main St.
Greenfield, MA 01301
(413) 773-9567
greenfieldsmarket.coop

Selling wholesome foods in the Pioneer Valley since 1977, this locally supported grocery co-op has a deep-rooted commitment to the young famers and food entrepreneurs of the local food scene. The produce and grocery bulk departments are among the best in the area, and the cheese department features lots of cheese from Massachusetts and nearby Vermont. Pick up a made-to-order sandwich and made-from-scratch soup, then eat in the mezzanine sitting area. The grilled Cheesosaurus, with Swiss, cheddar, and vegetables on oatmeal bread, and a bowl of tomato bisque is the perfect soup-and-sandwich pairing.

Gifts

SCANDIHOOVIANS
150 Main St.
Northampton, MA 01060
(413) 586-0002
scandihoovians.com

This little boutique sells unique women's clothing, jewelry, and home goods inspired by Scandinavian design and its simple elegance of form and color. Among the finds: delicate sterling-silver jewelry with crystals and pearls, pretty embroidery-trimmed tunic tops, Ekelund tea towels, and table runners.

YANKEE CANDLE VILLAGE
25 Greenfield Rd.
South Deerfield, MA
(413) 665-8306
yankeecandle.com

This is the flagship store of the Yankee Candle Company and is a shopping and tourist destination in its own right. The huge 90,000-square-foot store is filled with every type of the company's signature style of scented glass-jar candles, soaps, and knickknacks. The store keeps the Christmas spirit alive all year with its Bavarian Christmas Village, where Santa is on hand every day and it "snows" even in summer. Afterward head to Mrs. Claus' Bakery Cafe for a snack or enjoy a more leisurely meal at Chandler's.

Malls

✳THORNE'S MARKETPLACE
150 Main St.
Northampton, MA 01060
(413) 584-5582
thornesmarketplace.com

The 30 independent galleries, shops, studios, and restaurants on 5 floors of an 1873 building (it was once a department store) perfectly capture the spirit of shopping in Northampton. Browse the latest best sellers at Booklink, and find casual-cool menswear at Jackson & Connor, handmade contemporary jewelry at Rebekah Brooks, baby and maternity wear at Impish, and LGBTQ gifts from Northampton's Pride and Joy.

Outdoors

✳ZOAR OUTDOOR
7 Main St.
Charlemont, MA 01339
(800) 532-7483
zoaroutdoor.com

Step out of your comfort zone. Learn to kayak or canoe, go on a guided whitewater rafting trip (floats to Class IV) along the Deerfield River, learn to rock climb, or fly through the air on a zip-line canopy tour with Zoar Outdoor, a full-service outfitter with an extensive base in Charlemont. The retail store sells top-brand gear, outerwear, and equipment for outdoor enthusiasts.

Specialty Foods

*HUNGRY GHOST BREAD
62 State St.
Northampton, MA 01060
(413) 582-9009
hungryghostbread.com

Fans from all over the Pioneer Valley flock to this tiny Northampton bakery that turns out natural sourdough breads (sourdough french, rosemary studded 8-grain, and more) from a wood-burning brick oven that baker/owners Jonathan Stevens and Cheryl Maffei helped build themselves. Though this is strictly a bakery (there isn't any seating), they do take orders for pizza after 5 p.m. And although you'll come for the loaves, you'll likely leave with chocolate chip cookies and fig bars to get you through the week. Cash only.

*RICHARDSON'S CANDY KITCHEN
500 Greenfield Rd.
Deerfield, MA 01342
(413) 772-0443
richardsonscandy.com

This local chocolate institution has been turning out small batches of handmade confections for more than 65 years. You'll find a large assortment of old-school favorites like peanut butter twirler cups and copper-kettle-made fudge. Be sure to take home a box of Dixies, handmade caramel and roasted nuts drenched in milk or dark chocolate.

ACCOMMODATIONS

Inns & Bed-and-Breakfasts

DEERFIELD INN $$
81 Main St.
Deerfield, MA
(413) 774-5587
deerfieldinn.com

A pleasing throwback to simpler times, this 1884 inn has recently undergone a rebuild as a result of damage suffered from Hurricane Irene. The property's 24 rooms are spread between the main inn and a carriage house. No two rooms are alike—each has its own personality and varies in size and color, but expect period antiques and updated chintz and gingham fabrics and braided rugs; each has a private bath. The handsome wood-worn Champney's Restaurant & Tavern has been transformed as well with an American menu that celebrates locally inspired ingredients. The real reason to book this inn is its on-site Historic Deerfield location, and all guests receive complimentary tickets to the museum.

*LORD JEFFERY INN $$–$$$
30 Boltwood Ave.
Amherst, MA 01002
(413) 256-8200
lordjefferyinn.com

Following a 2011 major renovation, the 1926 Lord Jeffery Inn now perfectly blends modern convenience with historical significance. Every inch of the inn exudes refined New England country elegance, from the lobby with its fireplace and many intimate seating areas to the flagstone terrace of 30 Boltwood, the inn's farm-to-table restaurant. The inn's 49 guest rooms have been updated as well in a variety of pleasing color palettes and feature plush linens, flat-screen LCD HD TVs, and bathrooms with walk-in frameless glass showers.

Hotels & Resorts

HOTEL NORTHAMPTON $$
36 King St.
Northampton, MA 01060
(413) 584-3100
hotelnorthampton.com
Built in 1927, this hotel is traditional in every detail. Rooms are decorated with floral spreads and dark cherrywood furnishings, and bathrooms are smallish. But you'll find that rates include a few extra amenities: free Wi-Fi, continental breakfast, and parking. And you can't beat the location in the heart of Northampton, within walking distance of Smith College.

SPRINGFIELD MARRIOTT $$
2 Boland Way
Springfield, MA 01115
(413) 781-7111
marriott.com
While there's plenty of lodging in and around Springfield, there isn't much variety. The Springfield Marriott offers reasonably priced accommodations that feature spacious rooms, an indoor pool, and a fitness center. Request a room on a higher floor and wake up with a view of the Connecticut River.

RESTAURANTS

Burgers & Sandwich Shops

✳LOCAL $
16 Main St.
Northampton, MA 01060
(413) 586-5857
localnorthampton.com

This Northampton eatery flips seriously delicious grass-fed burgers that are worth seeking out. The 6-ounce juicy patties are reasonably priced and garnished to order with premium components. Among the specialty burgers, the Westhampton, with applewood bacon, good cheddar, and slathered with both barbecue sauce and ranch dressing, is a messy favorite. And make any burger more awesome with a heap of sweet potato fries and an order of fried pickles. The Local is open late, until 3 a.m. Fri and Sat.

Cafes & Coffeehouses

RAO'S COFFEE $
17 Kellogg Ave.
Amherst, MA 01002
(413) 253-9441
This is exactly what a college campus coffeehouse should be, offering serious study space with more than 90 seats inside (and additional patio seating) and free (strong) Wi-Fi. Rao's coffee beans are roasted locally and the result is a noticeable freshness. Their espresso is better than most and their iced coffee is cold-brewed with care. And since Amherst is a college town, the bakery case is mega-stocked with trays of home-spun treats: pumpkin chocolate chip cookies and carrot cake muffins with cream cheese frosting (isn't that a cupcake?), which keep the kids coming back for more.

Chinese

AMHERST CHINESE FOOD $-$$
62 Main St.
Amherst, MA 01002
(413) 992-6181
amherstchinesefood.com
The nondescript name of this Amherst mainstay belies the much better than average

Chinese food. Amherst Chinese Food has been doing farm-to-table before practically anyone else; since 1995 the restaurant has been sourcing much of its vegetables from its own 40-acre organic family farm. Check the blackboard for the day's specials. To try: organic stir-fried vegetables with shiitake mushrooms and tofu or the bitter melon with black beans and pork.

Eclectic

✳JUDIE'S RESTAURANT $$
51 N. Pleasant St.
Amherst, MA 01002
(413) 253-3491
judiesrestaurant.com
An Amherst mainstay since 1977, Judie's has catered to generations of UMass students with its eclectic, art-filled space and something-for-everyone menu; pan-seared scallops with a tomato tarte tatin and lamb shanks with a shredded potato pancake have great appeal to visiting parents, while the burgers, meal-size Caesar salads, seafood bisque, and shareable potato skins are among the college kids' favorites. Whatever you do, order the to-die-for popover with apple butter (it's giant—one is big enough to share).

German

STUDENT PRINCE CAFE AND FORT DINING ROOM $$
8 Fort St.
Springfield, MA 01103
(413) 788-6628
studentprince.com
Before there was craft beer and charcuterie, there was German food. For more than 75 years this Springfield original has been

doling out German sausage and wiener schnitzel, and now offers new American fare as well. The dark-wood, tchotchke-packed bar (beer steins and cuckoo clocks) offers lots to look at and features a German-heavy beer selection.

Ice Cream

✳HERRELL'S ICE CREAM $
8 Old South St.
Northampton, MA 01060
(413) 586-9700
In 1973 Steve Herrell pioneered the idea of "smoosh-ins," offering customers the option to choose a customized mix of chopped candy, crushed cookies, or fresh fruit folded into any flavor of exceptionally rich hand-made ice cream. Herrell's makes their ice cream at the shop—an ever-changing roster of flavors, and 30 or so are offered daily. If you can't decide, try the malted vanilla or chocolate pudding.

Middle Eastern

MOTI $$
25 N. Pleasant St.
Amherst, MA 01002
(413) 259-2150
motiamherst.com
Located in the center of Amherst, this small restaurant is owned by a young UMass graduate who has named the restaurant after his mother. Moti serves Persian cuisine in a casually elegant space with stucco walls inset with decorative grottos and a kilim pillow–strewn lounge area. Among the exotically flavored dishes specialties are familiar kebabs, falafel, and homemade hummus as well as Persian home-style fare, such as rice with lima beans, dill, and lamb.

Pizza

MAGPIE WOODFIRED PIZZERIA $$
21 Bank Row
Greenfield, MA 01301
magpiepizza.com
Judging by the 1-hour wait for a table, the best pizza in the Pioneer Valley is in tiny Greenfield. This pizzeria speaks to the local/seasonal sensibility of the area, offering wood-fired pizza topped with artful ingredients like fennel, arugula, and goat cheese. Don't hesitate to order something other than pizza. They also make excellent plates of pasta, including a true lasagna Bolognese made with beef short rib. Open for dinner only; closed Tues.

Pubs & Taverns

THE PEOPLE'S PINT $$
24 Federal St.
Greenfield, MA 01301
(413) 773-0333
thepeoplespint.com
More often than not, you can expect to wait for a table at this local brewpub that has been making its own beer (nearby on Hope Street) since 1997. Sample their Imperial Stout as you look over a menu that surprises with creative entrees like duck breast with mashed turnips and kale, smoked chicken chili, and a goat cheese quiche. This is a family-friendly pub, too, with a "half-pint" menu that features a turkey burger just for the kids. There's also live entertainment, usually Irish or Quebecois music, on some weekend nights.

Southern

BIG MAMOU $$
63 Liberty St.
Springfield, MA 01103
(413) 732-1011
chefwaynes-bigmamou.com
From a small but cheery storefront in downtown Springfield, Chef Wayne serves up New Orleans–style eats to appreciative regulars. Enjoy shrimp and sausage jambalaya or chicken étoufée in a spicy gravy. The catfish specialties are tried and true—enormous plates of fried catfish with rice and beans or fat, perfect po' boys. Desserts like sweet potato pie and bread pudding with a whiskey sauce round out the down-home picture. Open for lunch and dinner, but closed Sun.

DAY TRIP IN THE PIONEER VALLEY: THE MOHAWK TRAIL

Considered one of America's great road trips, the **Mohawk Trail,** also known as Massachusetts Route 2, runs east to west from Orange to Williamstown. The road traces the vestiges of a Native footpath between the Connecticut River and Hudson River valleys. Pioneers and their wagons then followed the Mohawk Trail west. By 1914 the old thoroughfare was paved and designated as America's first scenic byway. The Mohawk Trail really comes into its own during autumn with the added attraction of a breathtaking display of fall foliage. The most scenic stretch of the trail is the 40-mile section between Greenfield and North Adams. You'll experience the thrill of motoring along twisting mountain roads, stopping at several vantage points, and visiting off-the-beaten-path sites along the way. It's a road to take slow and enjoy the view.

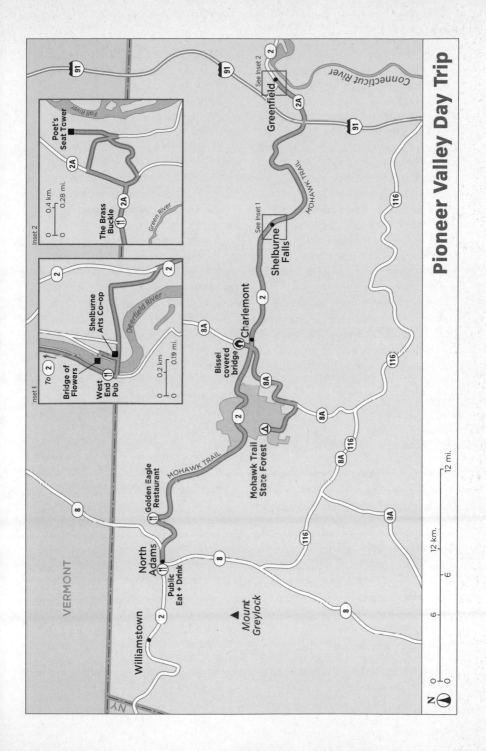

Pioneer Valley Day Trip

Located just off I-91 with Route 2A passing through its downtown, **Greenfield** makes an ideal starting point for the Mohawk Trail. Kick off your road trip with a hearty breakfast of huevos rancheros or grit cakes at the **Brass Buckle** (204 Main St., Greenfield; 413-475-3268; brassbucklegreenfield.com) served in a lively environment with local artwork adorning the walls. Drive east along Main Street to High Street and follow the signs to **Poet's Seat Tower.** It's a short (¼-mile) walk to the sandstone tower, which was built in 1912 as a tribute to local poet Frederick Goddard Tuckerman. You may be inspired, too, with the views of Greenfield and the Connecticut River valley.

Head 12 miles west along Route 2 for an extended stop in the town of **Shelburne Falls,** home of the **Bridge of Flowers,** an arched trolley bridge high above the Deerfield River that has been transformed by a garden of flowers into a pedestrian walkway. Also in Shelburne, Salmon Falls, and just below are glacial potholes left behind during the Ice Age. Worth a browse is the **Shelburne Arts Cooperative** (26 Bridge St.; 413-625-9324; shelburneartscoop.com), where nearly 50 local artists exhibit a mix of goods that includes jewelry, ceramics, clothing, and framed art and prints. For lunch overlooking the Bridge of Flowers, it has to be **West End Pub** (16 State St., Shelburne Falls; 413-625-6216; westendpubinfo.com). Local burgers and salads are popular and the food is made mostly from local sources. Closed Mon.

Just 2 miles out of Shelburne, you can't miss **Native Views** (2217 Mohawk Trail; 413-625-2331). For practically forever it has been known as the "Big Indian Shop." An 18-foot giant Indian statue stands outside—it is as kitsch as they come. Inside, the store sells Indian crafts and souvenirs and retro postcards with pictures from the Mohawk Trail's heyday.

Back on the road again, it's 8 more miles of winding road until you reach the pull-off for the *Hail to the Sunrise* statue. The 8-foot bronze statue of a Native American with his arms outstretched is the Mohawk Trail's most recognizable attraction. From here take a short detour along Route 8A to the **Bissell covered bridge,** spanning the Deerfield River.

You don't have to be a hiker to enjoy the mountains, but a leg-stretching walk is definitely in order. Turn into the **Mohawk Trail State Forest** (175 Mohawk Trail, Charlemont; 413-359-5504), where the Indian Lookout trail is an easy 1-mile walk through old-growth forest and ends in terrific vistas of the Berkshire Mountains.

Back to the car and continuing along Route 2, the road rises as you reach **Whitcomb Summit,** which at 2,173 feet is the top of the trail and offers a 4-state view. At this point, you have crossed into the Berkshires. From here, it's a 4-mile drive and a precipitous drop to the Mohawk Trail's infamous hairpin turn. Recover at the **Golden Eagle Restaurant** (1935 Mohawk Trail, Clarksburg; 413-663-9834; thegoldeneaglerestaurant.com), which is worth a stop for a pre-dinner drink to enjoy along with a stunning view. But best hold off dinner until North Adams, where an eclectic dining experience awaits at **Public Eat + Drink** (34 Holden St.; 413-664-4444). The menu ranges from flatbread pizza to burgers to a decidedly upscale butter-poached cod with mussels, pancetta, and arugula. And because road-tripping is hard work, be sure to save room for a slice of bourbon pecan pie with vanilla ice cream.

THE BERKSHIRES

The mountainous region of far western Massachusetts is hardly an undiscovered vacation spot. After all, since the mid-1800s the Berkshires has been a popular summer enclave that has attracted writers, artists, musicians, and the wealthy. They came to the Berkshires for inspiration, for the cool mountain breezes, for a reprieve from the city heat, and to enjoy the region's sylvan beauty.

Today the Berkshires are a vacation destination for everyone. The rolling hills and mountain ranges are still largely unspoiled, offering spectacular views and lots of outdoor recreational opportunities. In summer the arts scene abounds with world-class music, theater, and art. In the fall the forests blaze with color; in winter the mountain slopes lure skiers; and in spring there is maple sugaring and a burst of green nearly everywhere.

Lenox is the most resort-like town in the Berkshires. It is the home of Tanglewood, the famed summer music festival of the Boston Symphony. Lenox is hugely popular with the Tanglewood crowd for its stellar restaurants, lovely shops, and genteel country inns. Neighboring Stockbridge is also home to Tanglewood (the campus straddles both towns) but is decidedly quainter. As painted by Norman Rockwell—who lived here from 1953 until his death in 1978—Stockbridge is small-town America.

But the Berkshires also has a crunchy, outdoorsy vibe, nowhere more so than in Great Barrington. The Old Trinity Church, immortalized in the song *Alice's Restaurant,* is now the Guthrie Center, a community music hall. Great Barrington is also popular with vacation homeowners from New York, making this one of the few places in Massachusetts where a Yankees hat is tolerated. Nearby, the tiny village of Sheffield draws avid antiquers who hunt for undiscovered treasures in the shops along Route 7.

Located in the center of Berkshire County, bustling Pittsfield is the largest community in the Berkshires—really a bona fide city. Pittsfield has redefined itself as a cultural center with its restored Colonial Theater, lively art galleries, and new eateries. Continue north to Williamstown, home to prestigious Williams College and its Williamstown Theatre Festival. And funky North Adams has lately experienced an influx of young contemporary artists who have made the city their home.

ATTRACTIONS

Historic Sites & Landmarks

BASH BISH FALLS
Bash Bish Falls State Park
Falls Road
Mount Washington, MA 01258
(413) 528-0330
mass.gov/dcr/parks/western/bash.htm

Located on the Massachusetts/New York state border just outside of Great Barrington is Massachusetts's highest waterfall, which is as unexpected as it is inspiring. This natural wonder of multi-tiered cascades continues nearly 200 feet before splitting into 2 falls that tumble around a boulder before dropping 60 feet into a deep pool at the base. From the overlook next to the parking lot there is a view of Bash Bish Gorge below and the Catskill Mountains in the distance. From here there's a well-marked (and well-traveled) ½-mile hiking trail downhill to the falls. And although it's a mighty tempting swimming hole, it is a dangerous spot, and rangers do patrol the area. Feet wading, though, is fine.

BERKSHIRE BOTANICAL GARDENS
5 W. Stockbridge Rd.
Stockbridge, MA 01262
(413) 298-3926
berkshirebotanical.org

This little-known gem, not far from the Norman Rockwell Museum, is one of America's oldest botanical gardens. The many specialty gardens are the highlight of the 15-acre formally designed landscape, which is open daily from May through Oct. The Procter garden features a charming display of blue-purple perennial blooms amid benches sheltered by vine-covered bowers. The rose garden dazzles in late June with a touch of fragrance from thyme planted between the paving stones and a children's garden is tailor-made for budding horticulturalists. Everything is well labeled to help in identification (some 3,000 cultivars are represented) so that you can add your favorites to your home garden.

What's in a Name?: Bash Bish Falls

So why are the falls named Bash Bish? Bash Bish is said to be the name of a beautiful local Indian woman who was unjustly accused of being unfaithful to her husband. She was condemned to death and was to be tied to a canoe to be sent over the waterfall. At the time of her punishment, a fine mist appeared and Bash Bish escaped, flinging herself over the falls followed by a cloud of white butterflies. Bash Bish's body was never recovered and some say in certain light that they can see the image of a woman's face under the cascading water.

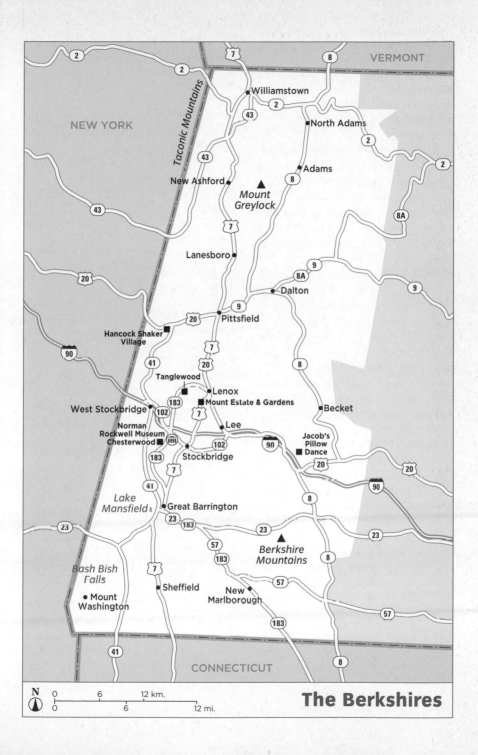

The Berkshires

MOUNT GREYLOCK

Mount Greylock State Reservation
30 Rockwell Rd.
Lanesboro, MA 01237
(413) 499-4262
mass.gov/dcr

For truly awe-inspiring views that stretch as far as 100 miles across 5 New England states, a visit to the summit of Mount Greylock is a must. At 3,491 feet, this is the highest peak in Massachusetts. You can opt to reach the summit via the 9-mile auto road (expect hordes of cars slowly winding their way up in the autumn). Or choose to hike from the base (and you will easily fulfill your day's exercise quota!). If you decide to drive to the top, consider a short, looping hike. The reservation has a total of 50 miles of marked walking trails—several start from the summit parking lot and are doable for casual day hikers. At the top, **Bascom Lodge** (see p. 236) offers dining and rustic overnight accommodations. Note, too that the auto road is open only from late May through Oct.

SHEFFIELD COVERED BRIDGE

Bridge Road (off of Route 7)
Sheffield, MA

Massachusetts's oldest, newest covered bridge is located just outside of the village of Sheffield. Spanning the Housatonic River, this is a 1999 wooden replacement of what was once the state's oldest covered bridge, which dated from 1832 and was destroyed by arson in 1994. Inside, be sure to admire the post-and-beam construction; the new bridge incorporates the historic bridge's lattice truss design.

Museums

ARROWHEAD

780 Holmes Rd.
Pittsfield, MA 01201
(413) 442-1793
mobydick.org

Between 1850 and 1863, Herman Melville and his family lived in this farmhouse just outside of Pittsfield. The view of nearby Mount Greylock from his study window inspired him to write *Moby-Dick*: "I look out my window in the morning when I rise as I would out of the porthole of a ship in the Atlantic." The house is open from May through Oct.

*CHESTERWOOD

4 Williamsville Rd.
Stockbridge, MA 01262
(413) 298-3579
chesterwood.org

Chesterwood was the summer home of Daniel Chester French, most famously known as the artist who created the monumental sculpture of the seated Lincoln in Washington, DC. French summered at Chesterwood from 1897 to 1931. The house and its next-door studio were designed for French by his friend Henry Bacon (Bacon was the architect of the Lincoln Memorial and the two men collaborated often on projects.). Guided tours allow access to the studio, which is artistically cluttered with clay models, drawings, and sculpting tools. The house is modest by the grand Berkshire summerhouse standard of the time, but it has lovely formal gardens. Afterward check out the annual exhibit, "Contemporary Sculpture at Chesterwood," which features a dozen or more large-scale pieces scattered on the manicured lawn and in the estate's small forest. The house is open for tours May through Oct; check website for days and times.

CLARK ART INSTITUTE
225 South St.
Williamstown, MA 01267
(413) 458-2303
clarkart.edu

These are exciting times at the Clark. Located next to Williams College, this excellent small art museum is currently undergoing a renovation and expansion, scheduled to be completed in June 2014. The museum is open during construction; Clark Remix exhibits highlights of the museum's collection, including its notable French Impressionist paintings by Renoir and Pissarro, and American paintings that include important works by John Singer Sargent and Winslow Homer. Galleries are open Sept through June, Tues through Sun; daily in July and Aug.

*CRANE MUSEUM OF PAPERMAKING
40 Pioneer St.
Dalton, MA 01226
(413) 684-7780
crane.com/about-us/
crane-museum-of-papermaking

If you have an interest in American history or the art of letter writing, stop here to follow the paper trail of one of the country's most distinguished firms. Well-known today for its elegant stationery, Crane is a 7th-generation family business that has been manufacturing 100 percent cotton paper since before the Revolutionary War. You likely have Crane paper in your wallet; since 1879 the company has made the paper used for US currency. Tucked behind the company's Dalton headquarters, its museum is housed in the company's Old Stone Mill. Here you can watch a video about the papermaking process and see antique molds and tools. Other displays chronicle some of the more than 200 years of events that have been announced on Crane stationery. You'll also see a copy of the museum's most prized possession, a 1775 ledger that details the purchase of currency paper by Paul Revere. At the end of your visit, you'll receive lovely free stationery samples for your own correspondence. The museum is open from June through mid-October, Mon through Fri from 1 to 5 p.m. Admission is free.

FRELINGHUYSEN MORRIS HOUSE & STUDIO
92 Hawthorne St.
Lenox, MA 01240
(413) 637-0166
frelinghuysen.org

Suzy and George were not your ordinary Lenox couple. Suzy Frelinghuysen and her husband, George L. K. Morris, were both talented abstract artists in their time. They also had a good eye and collected the work of their contemporaries, including Pablo Picasso, Georges Braque, and Fernand Leger. On a guided tour of their furnished, modernist home you'll see the couple's art and that of their very famous friends. It's a refreshing change from the area's other historic home tours. Guided tours are available June through Oct; call ahead to confirm.

HANCOCK SHAKER VILLAGE
1843 Housatonic St.
Pittsfield, MA 01201
(413) 443-0188
hancockshakervillage.org

The Shaker community thrived in Hancock Village from 1790 to 1960. Its inhabitants made their living through farming and creating simple but exquisitely well-made furniture. Today Hancock Village is not only a working farm (the public can buy CSA shares) but also a museum that chronicles the history of the Shakers. The Round Stone Barn is the centerpiece of the restored village. Kids especially enjoy visiting the calf nursery and watching milking demonstrations. The village offers engaging interactive/learning programs that include options like learning about turbines in the Laundry & Machine room and touring the village heirloom gardens.

✳MASSACHUSETTS MUSEUM OF CONTEMPORARY ART (MASS MOCA)
87 Marshall St.
North Adams, MA 01247
(413) 664-4111
massmoca.org

The 13-acre campus of mill factory buildings is the perfect industrial setting for Mass MoCA's permanent collection and frequent special exhibitions of art, music, dance, and film. One of the advantages of having warehouse-like gallery space is the ability to display large public art pieces like the very popular Sol LeWitt Retrospective, which features 105 of the artist's large-scale drawings. Art is extremely accessible at Mass MoCA; the public can even watch art being made in the fabrication studios or see a computer music ensemble rehearse.

i Art-minded? DownStreetArt (downstreetart.org) is a free night of gallery and cultural events that take place along Main Street in North Adams on the last Thursday of the month from June through October. Local artists keep things lively with a dizzying array of events that run the gamut from pop-up concerts and dance to museum nights and gallery shows.

✳THE MOUNT
2 Plunkett St.
Lenox, MA 01240
(413) 551-5104
edithwharton.org

A visit to the Mount, the stately summer home of novelist Edith Wharton, is a twofold treat, providing historical insight into the life and times of the Gilded Age, while exploring interior and garden design. Although best known for her novels *The House of Mirth, Ethan Frome,* and *The Age of Innocence* (which won the 1921 Pulitzer Prize), Wharton also wrote several interior- and garden-design books. Built in 1902, this stately 3½-story white stucco villa mansion and its landscaped gardens were designed by Wharton. She lived here for just 10 years, but it was from this home that she established herself as a writer. The house is open from May through Oct, and although you can tour the home on your own, go for the tour—the docents are both knowledgeable and passionate about Wharton's legacy. Wharton devoted as much attention to her gardens as she did her home. The elaborate Italianate walled garden, with its series of "garden rooms" and fountains, will blow you away. The Terrace Cafe overlooks the formal gardens and is the perfect choice for a light lunch of sandwiches and salads.

NAUMKEAG
5 Prospect Hill Rd.
Stockbridge, MA 01262
(413) 298-3239
thetrustees.org

A Gilded Age estate known for its gardens as much as for its home, this 1885 shingle-style estate was built for Joseph Hodges Choate, a New York lawyer who was ambassador to Great Britain from 1899 to 1905.

American Icons

Save money on admission fees to some of the Berkshires's most popular destinations with the American Icons Program. Participating attractions include the Norman Rockwell Museum, Edith Wharton's The Mount, Hancock Shaker Village, and Daniel Chester French's Chesterwood. From Memorial Day weekend through Columbus Day weekend, visitors can purchase passes at the ticket booths of any of the sites. Passes are flexible; you can choose a Pick Two, Pick Three, or American Icons Pass and enjoy savings on two, three, or four attractions. (You'll also save time not having to wait in lines.) Visit american-icons.org/about for current pricing.

He named his summer home Naumkeag, which is the Indian name for his birthplace of Salem, Massachusetts. The home is popular with historic-home enthusiasts because the 44-room estate was donated together with its original furniture. Gardeners enjoy the 8 terraced acres and the garden "rooms," including an Afternoon Garden, a Chinese Garden, and the Blue Step fountain garden. Open seasonally from the end of May to mid-October.

✳NORMAN ROCKWELL MUSEUM
9 Route 183
Stockbridge, MA 01262
(413) 298-4100
nrm.org
Beloved American artist Norman Rockwell lived in Stockbridge from 1953 until his death in 1978. This museum holds the largest collection of his works, including all 322 of his *Saturday Evening Post* covers. Highlights of the collection include "The Four Freedoms" paintings, which were inspired by Franklin Delano Roosevelt's 1941 State of the Union address. "Freedom from Want," or the "Thanksgiving Picture," is the most well-known. The dedicated gallery has an almost reverential feel and there are benches for

quiet contemplation. Check out, too, Rockwell's actual art studio, which was moved to the museum site from its original location on Main Street. Apparently Rockwell was a very neat artist.

VENTFORT HALL MANSION & GILDED AGE MUSEUM
104 Walker St.
Lenox, MA 01240
(413) 637-3206
gildedage.org
Built between1893 and 1895, this imposing redbrick Jacobean revival mansion is one of the most impressive of the Berkshires's many estates. It was the home of heiress Sarah Morgan, sister of financier J. P. Morgan, and among its marvels are an elaborate wood-paneled 3-story great hall and staircase and a music salon with extraordinary plasterwork ceilings and stained-glass windows. Shuttered for many years, the mansion is presented as a work in progress. Admission includes a guided tour of the 1st floor (self-guided on winter weekdays) and access to the "Les Petites Dames de Mode" (The Little Ladies of Fashion), sixty 29-inch gorgeously costumed dolls that portray fashion from 1855 to 1914.

WILLIAMS COLLEGE MUSEUM OF ART
15 Lawrence Hall Dr.
Williamstown, MA 01267
(413) 597-2429
wcma.williams.edu

The Williams College Museum of Art princi-pally collects American and 20th-century art pieces. It's open to the public Tues through Sun. Among the highlights are Edward Hopper's *Morning in the City* and a yellow and black Andy Warhol self-portrait. You can't miss Louise Bourgeoisie's *Eye*; the large-scale landscape pieces sit near the museum's entrance and just seem to draw you in.

Parks & Beaches

KENNEDY PARK
Routes 7 and 20
Lenox, MA 01240
townoflenox.com

A perennial favorite among locals and part-time summer residents, Kennedy Park offers 15 miles of shady woodland trails for walking and jogging. In winter the trails are used for cross-country skiing. The park is owned by the town of Lenox and is well maintained. The park is located in the center of Lenox and the best parking is anywhere along Main Street.

LAKE MANSFIELD
Lake Mansfield Road
Great Barrington, MA 01230
townofgb.org

Located just a short walk outside of Great Barrington, Lake Mansfield is a hugely popu-lar local spot for swimming, fishing, and rowing. At adjoining Lake Mansfield Park you'll find nearly 30 acres of wooded forest that are criss-crossed by several excellent walking footpaths. Lake Mansfield has lots of free parking; grills and shaded picnic tables

are available; and there's a terrific playground for kids.

NATURAL BRIDGE STATE PARK
McCauley Road
North Adams, MA 01247
(413) 663-6392
mass.gov/dcr/parks/western/nbdg.htm

For a maximum dose of nature for minimum effort, this 48-acre park is worth a detour. This park has one very special attraction: a 30-foot naturally formed marble bridge that crosses Hudson Brook. Walk along the path and you'll find the remnants of the marble quarry that operated here from the early 1800s to the mid-1900s.

Wineries

*LES TROIS EMME VINEYARD & WINERY
8 Knight Rd.
New Marlborough, MA 01230
(413) 528-2051
ltewinery.com

Located less than a mile from the entrance to the Butternut Ski area, this small winery is making some of the most drinkable wines in the state. Les Trois Emme is owned by Mary Jane and Wayne Eline, who make unique blends of traditional grape wines includ-ing an award-winning Cayuga white and a French oak-aged Cabernet Sauvignon. This is a small, intimate operation; the winery is located on the family's 3 acres of vine-yards. After you visit the winemaking facility, tastings are paired with homemade hors' d'ouevres. You'll find that Mary Jane and Wayne are kind and generous hosts who treat visitors to their winery like honored guests. Afterward buy a bottle (or two!) from the shop and while away the afternoon on the patio overlooking the grounds. The winery is generally open weekends mid-April through December with additional days during the high summer season. Call or check the website to confirm hours before visiting.

ACTIVITIES & EVENTS

Arts Venues

COLONIAL THEATER
111 South St.
Pittsfield, MA 01201
(413) 997-4444
berkshiretheatregroup.org
The intricate carved balconies, gold leaf, and plaster ornamentation evoke turn-of-the-20th-century glamour. Built in 1903 as a vaudeville theater, the recently renovated Colonial is a year-round performing arts venue that hosts **Berkshire Theatre Festival** performances (see below) and books artists with local and regional followings such as Ronan Tynan and James Taylor. The Colonial is also popular with touring Broadway productions.

MAHAIWE PERFORMING ARTS CENTER
14 Castle St.
Great Barrington, MA 01230
(413) 528-0100
mahaiwe.org
Extensive renovation has returned this Great Barrington landmark back to its original 1905 glory. When it isn't hosting acts like the Temptations and events like "An Evening with Patty LuPone and Mandy Patinkin," the Mahaiwe packs audiences in for screenings of *The Met: Live in HD* and for community theater productions.

Festivals & Annual Events

BANG ON A CAN SUMMER FESTIVAL
Massachusetts Museum of Contemporary Art (Mass MoCA)
87 Marshall St.
North Adams, MA 01247
(413) 662-2111
bangonacan.org
It's a 3-week blowout of contemporary music and contemporary art at this annual July festival on the campus of Mass MoCA. Each year since 2001, the Bang on a Can festival has brought together a new group of emerging young contemporary musicians with returning faculty to create and perform new music. Daily concerts in the museum's art galleries (free with museum admission) are an opportunity to look at art in a new way and interpret it within the context of the performance. The festival culminates with a Bang on a Can Marathon, an audience-friendly (you don't have to stay the entire time) 6-hour mega-concert.

BERKSHIRE THEATRE FESTIVAL
6 East St.
Stockbridge, MA 01262
(413) 298-5576
berkshiretheatregroup.org
Since 1929 this festival has presented a full summer season of classic and new, musical and nonmusical productions. The 2012 season included *A Chorus Line* and its lesser known companion piece, *A Class Act*, a smaller musical about the artists behind *A Chorus Line*.

✳JACOB'S PILLOW DANCE FESTIVAL
358 George Carter Rd.
Becket, MA 01223
(413) 243-9919
jacobspillow.org

This mountain retreat showcases the best in contemporary dance in all its genres: ballet, folk, modern, and ethnic. Dating back to 1933, Jacob's Pillow is the country's longest-running dance festival. Famous performers who have attended the festival in the past include Alvin Ailey and Marc Morris. Throughout the summer, the Pillow typically stages nearly 300 performances on its scenic 163-acre campus. Its signature event is the "Inside/Out" performance series, which takes place at dusk on an outdoor stage beneath the trees and against the backdrop of the Berkshire Hills.

Cheap Seats

Score a Berkshire bargain. On the day of a performance, half-price tickets for many Berkshire cultural events (including the biggies: Tanglewood, Jacob's Pillow, Shakespeare & Company, and the Williamstown Festival) may be purchased at one of the seasonal 1/2 TIX booths, sponsored by the Berkshire Visitors Bureau. Purchases must be made in person and are cash only. Check out berkshires.org for current ticket booth locations and daily performance availability.

✳SHAKESPEARE & COMPANY
70 Kemble St.
Lenox, MA 01240
(413) 637-1199
shakespeare.org
The Berkshire Hills are an appropriate setting for this year-round repertory company dedicated to all things Shakespeare. Established in 1978, and now under the leadership of director Tony Simotes, the troupe balances familiar Shakespeare repertoire with unorthodox Shakespeare stagings, such as *The Tempest* with Olympia Dukakis playing a female Prospero. The company also presents works "of social and political significance" by up-and-coming playwrights, along with spirited Shakespeare educational programming for children.

✳TANGLEWOOD
297 West St.
Lenox, MA 01240
(888) 266-1200
bso.org
Tanglewood, the summer home of the Boston Symphony Orchestra, beckons classical music lovers year after year to its summer outdoor concerts. From early July to late August, the BSO typically performs 3 concerts a week at its open-sided outdoor concert hall, the "Shed." The symphony's Tanglewood schedule features regular visits from internationally known guest artists including Joshua Bell, Itzhak Perlman, and Lang Lang. But the essential Tanglewood experience is to buy lawn tickets, arrive early with a blanket and a picnic, and listen to the concert under the stars. The Tanglewood Music Center is also an integral part of the BSO's Tanglewood season. Young professional musicians from around the world audition a year in advance to have the opportunity for intensive music study as a Tanglewood Fellow for the summer. The Fellows perform as part of the Tanglewood Music Center Orchestra and their performances are also ticketed events and open to the public.

i The Boston Symphony Orchestra's summer home in the Berkshires is named in homage to Nathaniel Hawthorne's *Tanglewood Tales for Girls and Boys*. Hawthorne lived in a small cottage in Lenox from 1850 to 1851 on what is now the BSO property and wrote the book during that time.

*WILLIAMSTOWN THEATER FESTIVAL
1000 Main St.
Williamstown, MA 01267
(413) 597-3400
wtfestival.org

Since it was founded in 1954 on the campus of Williams College, this pioneering summer theater festival has attracted top talent (in 2012 Blythe Danner, Tyne Daly, and David Hyde Pierce were the festival stars) who come to this corner of the Berkshires to hone their stagecraft. Each season artistic director Jenny Gersten offers a selection of 7 wonderfully diverse productions. Recent seasons have included *The Importance of Being Earnest*, *The Elephant Man*, and the musical, *Far from Heaven*. The Williamstown Festival intern program is a training ground for the next generation of stage talent. A few years from now you may be able to say, "I saw [so-and-so] at Williamstown before they made the big time."

Golf

WAUBEEKA GOLF LINKS
137 New Ashford Rd.
Williamstown, MA 01267
(413) 458-5869
waubeeka.com

Known for its Berkshire Hills views and challenging play, this par 72, 18-holer is an excellent public golf option. On this recently renovated course with new tees and bunkers, greens fees are still very reasonable and twilight rates (after 2 p.m.) are even better.

Health & Wellness

CANYON RANCH
165 Kemble St.
Lenox, MA 01240
(413) 637-4100
canyonranch.com/lenox

The forested mountain vistas from this spa's floor-to-ceiling windows will relax you even before your spa treatments begin. Canyon Ranch's 100,000-square-foot spa complex makes this the most luxurious spa resort retreat in New England, hands-down. Overnight resort guests enjoy accommodations at the Bellefontaine Mansion, all-inclusive gourmet meals, and a full roster of exercise classes, outdoor activities, and indulgent therapies. Or "ahhh" the day away with a day spa package that includes use of all resort facilities and an allowance toward spa services (a sea salt body scrub? a canyon stone massage?), followed by a wholesome spa lunch.

KRIPALU CENTER FOR YOGA & HEALTH
57 Interlaken Rd.
Stockbridge, MA 01262
(866) 200-5203
kripalu.org

Looking for a no-frills holistic hideaway experience? Housed in a former Jesuit seminary on 150 acres, Kripalu is the country's largest and most well-established year-round yoga retreat. Totally health focused, the center buzzes with activity; dozens of yoga classes and lifestyle workshops are offered each day, yet the place still manages to exude a general air of quietude. Overnight guests can choose from either shared or dormitory

🔍 Close-up

Tanglewood Picnic: Where to Get the Goods

Enjoying a stylish picnic on the perfectly manicured lawn while enjoying an open-air concert by the Boston Symphony Orchestra is the essential Tanglewood experience. But how to pull it all off?

Plan to arrive at least 90 minutes before the concert begins. Tanglewood traffic is famously "challenging"—it just isn't possible to buzz into Lenox only minutes before the concert. Know, too, that most of the Tanglewood parking lots are far from the main gate, so be prepared to haul your picnic equipment some distance to a spot on the lawn.

Besides your picnic basket, don't forget these other essentials: a large blanket and a waterproof tarp for underneath (the lawn is always perfectly lush because of its sprinkler system!), a bottle of wine (and a corkscrew), and a citronella jar candle (both romantic and practical). Low beach chairs are a good idea or consider lawn chair rentals that are available for $5 cash near the main entrance.

For a sumptuous, no-fuss spread for your Tanglewood picnic, here's a list of favorite Berkshire-area gourmet-food purveyors.

Nejaime's. *60 Main St., Lenox, MA 01240; (800) 946-3978; 3 Elm St., Stockbridge, MA 01262; (800) 946-3987; nejaimeswine.com.* Nejaime's is everyone's favorite local wine shop. Nejaime's is also well-known for its themed picnics to go that are available for 2 or 4 people. Their Mediterranean picnic tempts with a meze selection of stuffed grape leaves, tabouli, and lentil salad along with homemade baklava; the French basket includes a double-cream brie and pâté, smoked chicken, and a berry tart; the Berkshire classic features chevre, roast salmon filet, sesame lo mein, and cookies. Nejaime's 2 locations are equidistant to Tanglewood; either will work. Advance ordering is recommended.

accommodations in the main house or a private room in the Green Annex. Rates include 3 buffet-style (mostly vegetarian) meals and full participation in program activities. Spa treatments are offered (they call them "healing arts" here) but they are extra. You can also purchase a day pass, if you just need a kickstart to a new and improved you.

LENOX FITNESS CENTER
90 Pittsfield Rd.
Lenox, MA 01240
(413) 637-9893
lenoxfitnesscenter.com

Very used to out-of-towners and visitors, Lenox Fitness Center offers 1-day, 1-week, and 1-month pass plans, along with a 6-month punch-card option. Lenox Fitness Center has dozens of cardio and weight machines, 2 strength-training areas, and a full slate of fitness classes. The spa offers a roster of indulgences and whether you stop in for a deep hydration facial or a quickie weekend manicure, the staff will leave you looking and feeling your best.

Patisserie Lenox. *30A Church St., Lenox, MA 01240; (413) 551-9050; patisserielenox .com.* Patisserie Lenox is a cozy and elegant French pastry shop—the opera cake and macaroons are divine and are so worth the calorie splurge—that also offers light meal options that make excellent Tanglewood picnic fare: cucumber avocado gazpacho, beet and goat cheese salad, savory tarts, and quiches.

Rubiner's. *264 Main St., Great Barrington, MA 01230; (413) 528-00488; rubiners .com.* You'll find that the impressive international cheese and charcuterie selection (including excellent locally made foie gras) and artisan breads at this cheese shop/gourmet market are an excellent picnic launching pad.

Bizalion's. *684 Main St., Great Barrington, MA 01230; (413) 644-9988; bizalions .com.* This is not the kind of market where you pop in for a gallon of milk. Rather, this is where you will find groceries and gourmet foods of the highest quality. You'll find local and imported cheese and charcuterie plates, specialty sandwiches, composed salads, and a nice range of wines to pair with it all.

Guido's. *1020 South St., Pittsfield, MA 01201; (413) 442-9912; 760 S. Main St., Great Barrington, 01230; (413) 528-9255; guidosfreshmarketplace.com.* Guido's is the Berkshires's biggest independent grocery store (see p. 231). It also offers a good variety of picnic provisions, an expansive array of prepared food, beer, and wine. Be sure to grab some napkins, forks, and knives from the salad bar before you check out.

Finally, Tanglewood makes it easy with boxed dinners and picnic totes to go. Order in advance online or by phone and your picnic will be waiting for you (413-637-5152; bso.org).

Hiking, Biking & Walking

*ASHUWILLTICOOK RAIL TRAIL
3 Hoosac St.
Adams, MA 01220
(413) 442-8928
mass.gov/dcr/parks/western/asrt.htm

The tranquil Ashuwillticook Rail Trail is a dedicated, mostly flat, paved bike path that courses 11 miles from the center of Adams through the towns of Cheshire and Lanesborough. The trail, along the bed of the old Pittsburgh and North Adams Railroad, follows the Hoosac River and the banks of the Cheshire Reservoir, between Mount Greylock and the Hoosac Mountain range. In the autumn, the foliage is especially spectacular. Most bikers choose to start in Adams and take the north–south route, but the trail is also accessible at Farnham Street in Cheshire and at the southern trailhead at Berkshire Mall Road. "Ashuwillticook" is said to come from the Native American word for "a pleasant river in between the hills"—and that it is.

BARTHOLOMEW'S COBBLE
105 Weatogue Rd.
Sheffield, MA 01257
(413) 229-8600
thetrustees.org

This 330-acre nature reserve is a favorite spot that provides a near-perfect day hike for beginning trekkers. Orient yourself at the visitor and nature center, next to the entrance. Pick up a trail map and check out the schedule of special programs offered including canoeing, hiking, and bird watching. The reservation features 5 miles of well-marked trails; the Ledges Trail is the most popular. Here, the gentle ½-mile loop ascends through wooded forest to reach an ancient formation of exposed bedrock, or cobble (primarily quartzite and limestone), which offers panoramic vistas of the Housatonic River valley. This is an especially good walk for families with small children; there are 2 small caves along the way and the undergrowth of wildflowers and ferns in the woods has an almost prehistoric feel. Leave some time to visit the Ashley House, a 1735 colonial house named after its owner, Colonel John Ashley, one of Sheffield's founding citizens, who helped draft the Sheffield Resolves, a 1773 manifesto for individual rights. In 1781 Ashley's slave Mum Bett argued for her freedom against him in court—and won. The success of Mum Bett's suit was instrumental in ending slavery in Massachusetts in 1783.

MONUMENT MOUNTAIN
Route 7
Great Barrington, MA 01230
(413) 298-3239
thetrustees.org
The huge boulders at the 1,642-foot summit boast crowd-pleasing sights like Mount Greylock to the north, the Catskills to the west, and the Housatonic River valley below. The popular Indian Monument Trail is a moderate 3-mile climb and shouldn't take more than 2 hours. Monument Mountain has inspired thinkers for years. Locally the

mountain is also referred to as the Poet's Hike. In 1815 Great Barrington native William Cullen Bryant wrote "Monument Mountain," a poem that tells the legend of how a young local Indian girl took a lover's leap from this mountain. In 1850 Bryant arranged a hiking excursion whose participants included Herman Melville and Nathaniel Hawthorne. The story goes that a thunderstorm caused the group to take shelter under a ledge and it was here that the group passed time reciting Bryant's poem and drinking champagne.

Horseback Riding

BERKSHIRE HORSEBACK ADVENTURES
293 Main St.
Lenox, MA 01240
(413) 637-9090
berkshirehorseback.net
Saddle up for a relaxing guided horseback ride along gentle trails through shady Kennedy Park and into the wooded conservation land of Lenox Mountain. Berkshire Horseback Adventures mounts are sturdy and amble slowly along the well-worn paths, making this a good choice for novice riders. Hour, half-day, and overnight camping rides are available.

Kidstuff

BERKSHIRE MUSEUM
39 South St.
Pittsfield, MA 01201
(413) 443-7171
berkshiremuseum.org
Lots of museums promise something for everyone; with its mix of art, history, and science, the Berkshire Museum actually delivers. Zenas Crane, grandson of the founder of the Crane papermaking family, founded the museum in 1903. As you approach the

2-story Italian Renaissance revival building, you'll almost always find preschoolers gleefully scampering over and on Wally, the giant (26 feet long, 12 feet tall, and 7 feet wide) fiberglass stegosaurus replica that stands out front. School-age kids will be intrigued by the World of Miniatures diorama collection, which dates from the 1950s and gives a sense of ecology and geography from around the world at that time. Kids of all ages love mummies, and the Berkshire Museum has a good one, a 2,300-year-old Egyptian mummy known as Pahat. And of interest to adults, the museum has a nice collection of Hudson River School landscapes.

IOKA VALLEY FARM
3475 Route 43
Hancock, MA 01237
(413) 738-5915
iokavalleyfarm.com
For many kids an afternoon on a farm is pure bliss. This working family farm does raise beef cattle and sells vegetables, but its activities are designed mainly to entertain kids. In the spring, from mid-February through March, visit the maple sugar shack and enjoy a pancake breakfast at the farm's seasonal "Calf-A." June brings strawberry fields for pick-your-own berries and the opening of Uncle Don's Barnyard (admission charge), where kids can get friendly with the squeaky-clean pigs, rabbits, goats, sheep, and cows. Other activities here are a hay maze, pedal carts, a playground, and a 40-foot tunnel slide (fun for grown-ups, too!). In the fall, take a hayride out to the pumpkin patch and after Thanksgiving this is the place for cut-your-own Christmas trees.

Nightlife

DREAM AWAY LODGE
1342 County Rd.
Becket, MA 01223
(413) 243-6697
thedreamawaylodge.com
Prohibition-era speakeasies are all the rage, but this is the real deal. Located deep in the woods near October Mountain, this legendary restaurant/bar/live music venue has been in operation since the early 1920s and in its time has hosted big-name talent such as Pete Seeger, Arlo Guthrie, and Joan Baez. On Wednesday the music room hosts open-mic night; Thursday through Sunday local bands and other artistic events (poetry readings, etc.) are featured. The restaurant is a draw, too, with a reasonably priced eclectic menu that features dishes like Hungarian chicken paprika and South African curried meatloaf.

MOE'S TAVERN
10 Railroad St.
Lee, MA 01238
(413) 243-6697
nocoorslight.com
It's a little out of the way, located on a side street in Lee, but Moe's is quickly becoming a New England craft beer destination that's also a comfortable, reliable bet any day of the week for locals. Moe's serves a large selection of small-batch bottled American beers along with more than a dozen regionals on tap including selections from Mayflower, Jack's Abby, and Brooklyn Brewery. Know that there's no kitchen, but the bar does sells snacks (and several local eateries are used to delivering here).

Skiing

BOUSQUET MOUNTAIN
101 Dan Fox Dr.
Pittsfield, MA 01201
(413) 442-8316
bousquets.com
Bousquet is all about affordable family skiing. The mountain has 3 double chairlifts and 2 carpet lifts for its 23 trails. There's a ski school, 3 new terrain parks, and a small tubing center. In the summer, Bousquet runs an Adventure Park that has a zip line, waterslides and activity pool, bungee trampoline, minigolf, and more.

BUTTERNUT
38 State Rd., Route 23
Great Barrington, MA 01230
(413) 528-2000
skibutternut.com
With a 1,000-foot vertical drop and 100 percent snowmaking, Butternut is the ideal mountain for families that ski. There are 22 trails, and the varied terrain (mostly intermediate) is served by 11 lifts, plus 2 top-to-bottom snowboard parks. There's nighttime boarding and skiing and a 7-lane snow tubing center.

JIMINY PEAK
37 Corey Rd.
Hancock, MA 01237
jiminypeak.com
Jiminy Peak is easily Massachusetts's biggest ski/summer adventure recreation area. The ski area has 45 trails with 18 typically open for night skiing. Jiminy Peak has 3 terrain parks for snowboarders with enough space for both new boarders and those looking for a challenge. In summer, area families, summer campers, and clusters of newly independent teens flock to the Mountain Adventure Park with its alpine slide and mountain coaster. In 2012, Jiminy Peak added an Aerial Adventure Park that features a forest ropes course.

Theater

BARRINGTON STAGE
Boyd Quinson Mainstage
30 Union St.
Pittsfield, MA 01201
(413) 236-8888
barringtonstageco.org
One of the guiding forces in the resurgence of Pittsfield as a cultural arts center, the Barrington Stage Company produces some of the best theater in the country including premieres like 2004's *The 25th Annual Putnam County Spelling Bee*, which moved on to Broadway and beyond.

Watersports

BERKSHIRE SCENIC TREKS & CANOE TOURS
Decker's Landing
Lenox, MA 01240
(413) 442-2789
berkshirecanoetours.org
Take a flat-water guided canoe and kayak tour along the Housatonic River. These guided tours include all equipment rental and last 1½ to 2 hours and are suitable for paddlers of all ages and abilities.

SHOPPING

Antiques

ASIA BARONG
199 Stockbridge Rd.
Great Barrington, MA 01230
(413) 528-5091
asiabarong.com

One of the country's largest direct Asian furniture and antiques importers, this huge gallery is chock-full of fantastical pieces: colorful Indian fabric-covered benches, intricately carved Balinese temple doors, and Chinese apothecary cabinets, along with other one-of-a-kind curiosities. Or consider purchasing an Asian-inspired statue, fountain, or stone lantern to bring calm and serenity to your garden space.

GREAT BARRINGTON ANTIQUES CENTER
964 S. Main St.
Great Barrington, MA 01230
(413) 644-8848
greatbarringtonantiquescenter.com
More than 30 established galleries offer furniture, textiles, art, jewelry, and decorative accessories from New England, Europe, and Asia in this 50,000-square-foot multidealer store. Highlights among the encyclopedic selection are antique maps and prints, Persian rugs, French seating, American country tables and cupboards, and mid-20th-century modern furniture.

*PAINTED PORCH
102 S. Main St.
Sheffield, MA 01257
(413) 229-2700
paintedporch.com
Sheffield has been dubbed the antiques capital of Massachusetts, and while there are dozens of shops scattered along picturesque Route 7, this is one of the nicest. The handsome 1815 colonial farmhouse and the next-door barn make an attractive setting for the formal and country French, English, American, and Canadian antiques. These are coveted, one-of-a-kind pieces, such as a

painted, marble-topped French shop counter or an English pine settle bench.

Art Gallery

FERRIN GALLERY
437 North St.
Pittsfield, MA 01201
(413) 442-1622
ferringallery.com
This small but long-established gallery specializes primarily in contemporary sculpture and studio ceramics. The shows at this striking, modern space tend toward more experimental pieces. The popular Dish + Dines series pairs local art with food from local restaurants and offers a lively salon-like evening out. Ferrin is an extremely welcoming gallery, but hours vary by season, so be sure to check the website or call prior to visiting.

Books

BOOKLOFT
322 Stockbridge Rd.
Great Barrington, MA 01230
(413) 528-1521
thebookloft.com
Independent bookstores are alive and well in the Berkshires. The well-organized shelves here offer shoppers a wide selection of new and used books—from best sellers and literary classics to arcane academic titles. The Bookloft also has an exceptional section of regional titles including Appalachian Trail guides. The genial employees are happy to offer book suggestions, and the store's sponsored book groups and author appearances are community events. The Bookloft is pet-friendly, too; well-behaved dogs on leashes are welcome while their owners browse.

BerkShares

Spend any time in the Berkshires and you will likely notice the "BerkShares Accepted Here" signs in store windows nearly everywhere. BerkShares (berkshares .org) is the region's alternative currency, the largest alternative currency system in the US, and a source of great community pride. Residents and visitors can exchange US dollars at a discount—95 dollars will buy 100 BerkShares—and use them at over 400 local businesses. The colorful bills are issued in 1, 5, 10, 20, and 50 denominations and bear the images of local heroes: a Mohican Indian, writer and civil rights activist W. E. B. DuBois, organic farmer Robyn Van En, writer Herman Melville, and artist Norman Rockwell. Funny money it's not.

THE BOOKSTORE
11 Housatonic St.
Lenox, MA 01240
(413) 637-3390
bookstoreinlenox.com

For booklovers this eclectic, independent bookstore is a welcome haven from the Tanglewood crowds. The bookshelves are filled with a handpicked selection of works by Berkshire-area writers, the latest national best sellers, and classic children's literature. The shop also hosts author readings and other free events throughout the year. Feeling social? The Get Lit wine bar offers yet another reason to stop in.

Craft Stores

JWS ART SUPPLIES
38 Railroad St.
Great Barrington, MA 01230
(413) 644-9838
jwsartsupplies.com

For more than 150 years the Berkshire Hills have inspired artists to practice their passion. JWS Art Supplies draws Berkshire dabblers and professionals alike with its array of high-end pastels, acrylics, and oils, as well as sculpting and drafting supplies. The store is worth a look, too, for gifting needs—the front stocks gorgeous handmade wrapping papers and quirky greeting cards while the walls of the store serve as a de facto gallery space for pieces for sale by local artists. Plus, store employees are super nice and happy to lend their expertise and wisdom—just ask.

Farmers' Markets & Pick Your Own

LAKEVIEW ORCHARD
94 Old Cheshire Rd.
Lanesboro, MA 01237
(413) 448-6009
lakevieworchard.com

This idyllic hillside farm overlooking Hoosac Lake has everything you need for a fun day in the country. Lakeview offers season-long pick-your-own fruit opportunities, beginning with cherries and raspberries in late June, peaches in August, and ending with apples throughout the fall. The Lakeview Orchard bakery/farm stand sells homemade cider donuts and pies along with produce harvested from their own fields. Families with kids will want to stop by the mill and watch fresh-pressed cider being made. Plan your outing to stay for lunch. The farm stand also offers sandwiches and drinks to enjoy at the picnic tables under the shade trees. Cash only.

LENOX FARMERS' MARKET
70 Kemble St.
Lenox, MA 01240
(413) 528-8950
No website
Wander among bushel baskets filled to overflowing with peaches, wooden bins of apples, and piles of pumpkins. Taking place every Friday (1 to 5 p.m.) from mid-May through early October on the campus of Shakespeare & Company (abundant parking here), the Lenox Farmers' Market features not only local produce but also staples such as milk, eggs, bread, and meat plus specialty items that make great foodie souvenirs: honey, maple syrup, jams, and wines.

Gifts

MISTRAL
7 Railroad St.
Great Barrington, MA 01230
(413) 528-1618
mistralshome.com
Find a little bit of France in the heart of the Berkshires. Most of the items in this lovely gift shop are decorative. Find glassware, mustard yellow and olive green Provencal pottery, Laguiole knives, and assorted linen tablecloths. The shop also carries candles as well as body-care products and lingerie. Ooh la la!

Grocery

GUIDO'S FRESH MARKETPLACE
1020 South St.
Pittsfield, MA 01201
(413) 442-9912
guidosfreshmarketplace.com

Since 1979 this independent, family-owned grocery store has delivered the gourmet goods to both year-round Berkshire residents and visitors with an expansive cheese and deli counter, outstanding homemade prepared foods, fancy chocolates, and artisanal baked goods along with a whole lot of local and organic grocery, meat, and produce choices. This is a true one-stop shopping experience—Guido's even sells wine and beer! A second location is in Great Barrington at 760 S. Main St. (413-528-9255).

Home Goods

CHEF'S SHOP
31 Railroad St.
Great Barrington, MA 02130
(413) 528-0135
thechefsshop.com
Established in 1991, the Chef Shop supplies both restaurants and the kitchens of serious home chefs with top-notch cookware. The shelves overflow with kitchen stuff: copper pots, enameled cast-iron cookware, oodles of gadgets, tabletop accessories, and cookbooks to help you make it all happen. And although the shop has a professional feel, it is still beginner friendly with frequent in-store cooking classes and live demonstrations by local chefs and cookbook authors.

✳COUNTRY CURTAINS
371 Main St.
Sturbridge, MA 01566
(508) 347-2158
The flagship store of the national mail-order curtain company is located within the Red Lion Inn. Founded by the Fitzpatrick family in 1956, the company operated out of the family's home until 1969, when the Fitzpatricks purchased the Red Lion Inn and moved the business there. Enter the showroom from

Main Street or from within the hotel and you'll find rack after rack of ready-to-hang curtains, tablecloths, and bedcovers. Not just "country curtains," the store also stocks an impressive array of sophisticated striped, floral, and toile designs as well as fine, lined silk panels at affordable prices. Don't forget to bring your window measurements!

Kids' Fashions & Toys

PERSNICKETY TOYS
13 Eagle St.
North Adams, MA 01247
(413) 662-2990
No website
This delightfully old-fashioned toy store carries all the newest and latest toys for kids. And with a name like Persnickety, you know that this place will feature only top-quality playthings: clever games, beautifully illustrated books, award-winning science kits, and life-size stuffed animals. Among the shelves you'll also find a wealth of arts-and-craft supplies for a rainy-day escape. And everyone who works here obviously loves what they are doing.

Malls & Outlets

LEE PREMIUM OUTLETS
17 Prime Outlets Blvd.
Lee, MA 01238
(413) 243-8186
premiumoutlets.com/lee
Located just off the Mass Pike (at exit 2), this outlet center features 60 stores in an outdoor village setting. Although not everything is a bargain, and some of the merchandise is out of season or irregular, savvy bargain-hunters can find deep discounts (up to 65 percent) on everything from men's, women's, and children's apparel to cosmetics and household goods. Popular retailers include outlet stalwarts Brooks Brothers, Polo, J.Crew, and BCBG Max Azria. Easily the most popular store here is the Coach outlet.

Specialty Foods

BARRINGTON BITES
31 Railroad St.
Great Barrington, MA 02130
(413) 528-0660
barringtonbites.com
In the back of the Chef Shop you'll find Barrington Bites, a cupcake bakery that specializes in gourmet, made-from-scratch mini-cupcakes. The repertoire includes more than 30 flavors, from a gluten-free flourless chocolate soufflé to a salted caramel to strawberries and cream. A recommendation? The chocolate chai, a bite-size morsel of confectionary heaven.

BARRINGTON COFFEE ROASTING COMPANY
165 Quarry Hill Rd.
Lee, MA 01238
(413) 243-3008
barringtoncoffee.com
To bring home some of the world's best coffee beans, head to Barrington Coffee Roastery. Roasting in the Berkshires since 1993, Barrington Coffee Roasters is locally owned by Gregg Charbonneau and Barth Anderson. Well-known for both its signature blends and single-origin, certified organic coffees, Barrington Coffee sources its beans worldwide only from sustainable farms. Staff diligently coaxes great flavor and aroma from the beans to create outstanding coffee. The Colombian La Esperanza is a classic.

*CHARLES H. BALDWIN
1 Center St.
West Stockbridge, MA 01266
(413) 232-7785
baldwinextracts.com

For anyone who loves to bake, a stop at the Charles Baldwin shop, family-run since 1888, to stock up on pure vanilla extract is a must. This high-quality vanilla extract is made in small batches from imported Madagascar vanilla beans that are aged in 100-year-old oak barrels. Charmingly cluttered, this country store also sells other extracts, flavorings, and baking supplies. Near the vintage metal cash register, pick out something sweet from the old-fashioned candy counter stocked with retro favorites like Mary Janes, Vanilla Bullseyes, and Chocolate Turkish Taffy.

*CHOCOLATE SPRINGS CAFE
55 Pittsfield Lenox Rd.
Lenox, MA 01240
(413) 637-9820
chocolatesprings.com

Worth the short drive outside Lenox center, this European-style chocolate shop emits aromas that will seduce any chocolate lover. Cozy up on one of the couches with a decadent cup of hot sipping chocolate. Or stop for a pick-me-up coffee and a slice of passion fruit mousse cake. Prefer to nibble? Individual chocolates—particularly the champagne cognac truffle—are some of the best confections around. And for that ice cream fix, they make their own sorbets and gelato, too.

Sporting Goods

BERKSHIRE OUTFITTERS
169 Grove St.
Adams, MA 01220
(413) 743-5900
berkshireoutfitters.com

So you want to go canoeing? Or how about the latest adventure craze, stand-up paddleboarding? Berkshire Outfitters is staffed by a crew of outdoors enthusiasts who can gear you up for most any outdoors adventure. In addition to selling a full selection of top-of-the-line mountain bikes, skis, tents, backpacks, clothing, and hiking boots, Berkshire offers canoe, kayak, winter sports, and car-rack rentals.

Women's Clothing

KAREN ALLEN FIBER ARTS
8 Railroad St.
Great Barrington, MA 01230
(413) 528-8555
karenallen-fiberarts.com

Actress Karen Allen (*Animal House*, *Raiders of the Lost Ark*) makes her home in the Berkshires, where she pursues her second calling: designing eye-catching knitwear. The array of goods at her Great Barrington shop includes cozy cashmere sweaters, brilliantly colored scarves, and fun, reversible knit hats.

ACCOMMODATIONS

Inns & Bed-and-Breakfasts

BERKSHIRES SHIRAKABA $$$$
20 Mallery Rd.
New Ashford, MA 01237
(413) 458-1800
berkshires-shirakaba.com

Set on a ridge amid 21 wooded acres just outside of Williamstown, Berkshires Shirakaba is a traditional Japanese guest house that offers first-class pampering and hospitality by hosts Louise Palmer and Sadao Yagi from the moment you arrive until the time when you (regretfully) leave. There are just 2 guest suites here, ensuring almost total privacy. The property itself is tranquil, featuring lots of *shirakaba,* or white birch trees, along with a landscaped koi pond and fountain. Common areas include an indoor pool, hot tub, and tearoom. Both suites have Tempur-Pedic beds and spa-quality linens and feature some of the hallmarks of traditional Japanese style with low furniture, rice-paper lamps and tatami straw matting. Rates include a choice of either a traditional Japanese or Western-style breakfast. A traditional 6-course Japanese dinner is offered at an additional cost.

CHAMBERY INN   **$$**
199 Main St.
Lee, MA 01238
(413) 243-2221
chamberyinn.com
This delightful reincarnation of an 1885 parochial school surrounds guests with elegance and charm—all with the value you might expect from a roadside motel. Each of the 9 rooms is unique, but all have private bathrooms and are prettily appointed; most have poster or canopy beds and spa tubs and some have sitting rooms with fireplaces. A home-cooked breakfast basket is delivered to your room each morning—no dressing up early to dine with strangers!

✳GARDEN GABLES INN   **$$$$**
135 Main St.
Lenox, MA 01240
(413) 637-0193
gardengablesinn.com
Nestled on 5 acres of beautifully wooded grounds in the heart of Lenox, this elegant inn has everything a discerning traveler would expect—from plush rooms to gourmet meals to hospitality so attentive you don't need to do a single thing other than relax. Its accommodations include 13 guest rooms and 2 suites, all have private bathrooms, and some have a fireplace and/ or private deck. The rooms are classic New England luxe: comfy beds with great linens, a sprinkling of formal antiques and rustic painted pieces, designer fabrics, old-school plaids, regional art, leather wing chairs, LCD TVs, and free Wi-Fi. A highlight of a stay here is the included gourmet buffet breakfast, which features cooked-to-order entrees. The innkeeper's specialty, the apple strudel french toast, is a must-order. During the summer weekends, the inn offers a prix-fixe gourmet dinner, exclusive to guests. A gracious library (with a piano—this is Lenox after all) awaits guests in the main house. The property also boasts an outdoor heated Olympic-size swimming pool—it's an antique, one of the first to be built in the region—and it's a beauty.

INN AT SWEET WATER FARM $$$–$$$$
One Prospect Lake Rd.
Great Barrington, MA 01230
(413) 528-2882
innsweetwater.com
You may audibly sigh as you cross the threshold of this gorgeous 19th-century post-and-beam inn that feels more like a well-appointed home than a B&B. The 6 bedrooms (each has a private bath) have gleaming wide-plank wood floors and are decorated with clean-lined antiques and are also wonderfully upscale with line-dried high-count sheets and feather comforters. The farm-to-table breakfasts feature fruit, yogurt and granola, fresh-baked bread, homemade pastries, and eggs straight from the backyard henhouse.

Motels

BRIARCLIFF MOTEL $$
506 Stockbridge Rd.
Great Barrington, MA 01230
(413) 528-3000
thebriarcliffmotel.com

Located in the shadow of Monument Mountain, this reincarnation of a roadside 1950s motel has a hipster sensibility and a budget-friendly price tag. The 16 rooms have a mix of retro furnishings and modern amenities including flat-screen TVs, plush-top mattresses, and organic linens along with brand-new bathrooms. Other flourishes include free Wi-Fi and complimentary breakfast, which features homemade granola, local yogurt, made-from scratch muffins, and Barrington Roasters coffee. Good to know, too, there's no minimum stay required in the summer.

Hotels & Resorts

CRANWELL RESORT $$$-$$$$
55 Lee Rd.
Lenox, MA 01240
(413) 637-1364
cranwell.com

Once upon a time, grand summer cottages dotted the Berkshires. And few places capture the spirit of the Gilded Age better than the Cranwell Resort. Located on 380 acres of gorgeous grounds, the 1894 estate boasts 3 restaurants, an 18-hole championship golf course (open for public play), cross-country skiing, tennis courts, an outdoor heated pool, an indoor pool, and a spacious upscale spa. The 114 rooms and suites vary in size, but all are well appointed, and there is something to make everyone happy. Once you check in, you don't really need to leave

until departure day, making this an excellent lodging choice for families.

*PORCHES $$-$$$
231 River St.
North Adams, MA 01247
(413) 664-0400
porches.com

Once a cluster of dilapidated 19th-century mill-worker row homes, the Porches is a stunning example of an affordable retro-chic boutique hotel. Located across the street from Mass MoCA, this 47-room hotel offers lots of smart design elements like high-end bed linens, wood-painted floors topped with deep, patterned wool rugs (fun to dig your toes into!), and super-wired rooms with free Wi-Fi, iPod clock/radio docking stations, and TV/DVDs. The well-fitted bathrooms have slate floors and come with either a Jacuzzi or claw-foot tub and a separate shower. Kitsch touches abound throughout the property; walls are decorated with paint-by-numbers art and your complimentary continental breakfast arrives in a vintage metal lunch box. The fire pit area and the year-round heated outdoor pool and hot tub draw guests together to socialize.

*RED LION INN $$$
30 Main St.
Stockbridge, MA 01262
(413) 290-5545
redlioninn.com

If this historic inn conjures up images of a Norman Rockwell painting, there's a good reason. The Red Lion was prominently featured in Rockwell's *Stockbridge Main Street at Christmas* painting. A Stockbridge fixture since 1773, the Red Lion offers 108 rooms and suites that are spread across the Main Inn and 4 adjacent houses. The rooms are of different shapes and sizes, but all exude cozy New England country charm with lots of antiques and folk art along with modern touches (high-count thread sheets, pillow-top mattresses, totally wired rooms and public spaces) that present-day travelers expect. Other amenities include a year-round heated outdoor pool and several on-site restaurant options, including the Main Dining Room (see p. 237), the Widow Bingham's Tavern for pub fare, and courtyard dining from June through October. Sit a spell on the inn's wide front porch—it has rocking chairs and wicker seating aplenty—and enjoy the sights of Main Street USA.

Camping

**BASCOM LODGE ON MOUNT
  GREYLOCK** $-$$
Rockwell Road
Lanesboro, MA 01237
(413) 743-1591
bascomlodge.net
Talk about a room with a view. This mountain aerie crowns the summit of Mount Greylock, the state's highest peak. Popular with Appalachian Trail thru-hikers, the lodge is also accessible via an 8-mile auto road. A Depression-era work project, the Arts and Crafts–style stone and wood lodge was built in 1937 by the Civilian Conservation Corps. The lodge operates a full-service restaurant that is open to the public serving hearty meals like pecan buttermilk pancakes for breakfast and pulled pork sandwiches or hummus plates at lunch. Lodge dinners are a decidedly more fancy affair; a 3-course prix fixe, by reservation only, that features dishes like an arugula and beet salad, followed by chicken cacciatore and hazelnut gelato with butter cookies. Overnight guests can choose from either private or bunk room–style

accommodations, both of which include your bedding and a towel. There isn't any TV or phone service (but there is Wi-Fi) and the bathrooms are shared, but just look at those rates. Open June through Oct.

RESTAURANTS

American (New)

*MEZZE $$$
777 Cold Spring Rd.
Williamstown, MA 01267
(413) 458-0123
mezzerestaurant.com
Impress your out-of-town friends with your dining savvy. Located in a 19th-century farmhouse on 3 stunningly beautiful country acres (there's a kitchen-supplying garden on the property), Mezze is a perennial favorite dining spot with the Williamstown Festival crowd. Expect sublime, seasonal New American fare that is thoughtfully prepared with local ingredients and layers of complexity. To try: the house-made charcuterie plate; seared scallops with vegetable ragout; s'mores tart.

*OLD INN ON THE GREEN $$-$$$
134 Huntsville New Marlborough Rd.
New Marlborough, MA 01230
(413) 229-7924
dining.oldinn.com
Epicures appreciate Chef Peter Platt's fresh, sophisticated New American cuisine served in the intimate, antique-filled dining rooms at the Old Inn on the Green, considered by many to be one of the best restaurants in the Berkshires. Recent stars of the seasonally changing menu have included braised lamb shank with autumn vegetables and a lobster, saffron, and sweet pea risotto. For dessert, consider any one of the breathtaking

homemade gelati or sorbets. Reasonable tabs (including several prix-fixe options) are an unexpected bonus, leaving enough in your wallet to afford that nice bottle of wine.

American (Traditional)

✳RED LION INN $$–$$$
30 Main St.
Stockbridge, MA 01262
(413) 298-5545
redlioninn.com

At the Red Lion Inn sustainable, organic, and local food meets historic fine dining. Surrounded by antiques, floral wallpaper, and soft candlelight, the dining room harks back to the country elegance of a bygone era. And while the menu offers visitors century-old standbys like roast native turkey and Indian pudding made with cornmeal and molasses, you'll find lots of dishes that have been rejiggered for modern palates, too. You can sample cinnamon-cured pork tenderloin with mashed sweet potatoes or lamb and kale meatballs with Parmesan risotto. For dessert there's a warm brown sugar baby bundt cake with coffee ice cream and caramel sauce or Callebaut chocolate pudding.

Breakfast & Lunch

GREAT BARRINGTON BAGEL COMPANY $
777 Main St.
Great Barrington, MA 01230
(413) 528-9055

Authentic New York–style bagels in the Berkshires? Who knew? Since 1995 the Great Barrington Bagel Company has served freshly baked bagels, more than a dozen homemade cream cheese spreads, and classic Jewish soul food. The standards—chicken matzo ball soup, pastrami sandwiches, and

smoked fish—are as good as it gets while their (not-at-all-kosher) lobster rolls are among the deli's most popular summer menu items.

SPOON $
26 Housatonic St.
Lenox, MA 01240
(413) 881-4040
spoonlenox.com

The most important meal of the day is served all day long at this adorable breakfast/lunch spot where the menu features Barrington Roaster's fair-traded coffee, local free-range eggs, and artisan-made breads. Locals and visitors flock here for the house-cured corned beef hash and eggs and the home-style fried chicken and waffles. Lunch offerings skew eclectic; find a hummus plate, a leafy bean and grain salad, and sandwiches like a portobello melt and a turkey and bacon club that feature a side of homemade potato chips. Spoon doesn't serve dinner, but they do scoop ice cream (New York's Golden Organics) in the afternoon and into the evening.

Cafes & Coffeehouses

BREWHAHA $
20 Marshall St.
North Adams, MA 01247
(413) 664-2020
cafebrewhaha.com

Ease into the day with coffee and a warm, home-baked pumpkin muffin at this favorite northern Berkshires gathering spot across the street from Mass MoCA. The coffee menu is long and the espressos and lattes are well crafted. Breakfast is served all day and the lunch menu of healthy and inexpensive sandwiches, salads, and soups features lots of vegan and vegetarian-friendly options.

Completing the indie coffeehouse vibe is the world and jazz music soundtrack and artwork by local artist friends and customers on the walls.

＊HAVEN CAFE AND BAKERY $
8 Franklin St.
Lenox, MA 01240
(413) 637-8948
havencafebakery.com

The service may be rushed and it may be elbow-to-elbow crowded, but it's worth the wait at this buzzing Berkshire breakfast and lunch bakery/cafe for heaven-sent pastries (blueberry muffins, homemade doughnuts, brownies) and perfect cups of coffee all day. Light and casual meals feature sophisticated takes on home cooking like croissant french toast and signature rolled omelets at breakfast to dishes like grilled polenta topped with pesto and goat cheese to an 8-ounce grass-fed burger with hand-cut fries at lunch.

Eclectic

ALTA WINE BAR $$
34 Church St.
Lenox, MA 01240
(413) 637-0003
altawinebar.com

This casual spot is modeled after quaint European wine bars. You'll find the list of bottles and glasses is both impressive and accessible and the knowledgeable servers will guide you to the perfect selection. For those with commitment issues, perhaps the best way to experience several is to order one of the reasonably priced ($10 for 3 pours) wine flights. The menu isn't too serious either, a combination of Mediterranean-influenced and New American fare. Appetizers such as a foie gras terrine with peach and apricot chutney or an entree such as a pan-seared

duck breast with a salty caramel sauce and local vegetables deliver lots of flavor. The restaurant has a prime Church Street location, and reservations are always a good idea in season. The tables on the covered front porch provide a good vantage point for people-watching or escape the Lenox crowd and dine in the charming back room.

ELIZABETH'S $$
1264 East St.
Pittsfield, MA 01201
(413) 443-8244

Located a little off the beaten path in Pittsfield, this no-frills spot stays just under the radar but is without a doubt one of the Berkshires's best restaurants. Watch the action in the open kitchen and order from a menu that is deliciously laden with buttery pasta dishes like baked shells with Gorgonzola and baby sweet peas and a 4-cheese lasagna with caramelized onions and spinach. There's also a market-driven fish and a meat entree per night and everything is very gently priced. Note: It's cash or check only and reservations are essential. Open for dinner only Memorial Day to Labor Day, Wed through Sun, and Wed through Sat the rest of the year.

NUDEL RESTAURANT $$–$$$
37 Church St.
Lenox, MA 01240
(413) 551-7183
nudelrestaurant.com

Equally popular with Tanglewood habitués and Birkenstock-clad hippies, Nudel offers a long list of reasonably priced small plates, pastas, entrees, and wine. The menu changes weekly and is filled with serious yet crowd-pleasing possibilities such as linguine with a roasted marrow tomato sauce or fried

Vermont quail with peach and fennel salad. Expect inventive dessert choices, too, like the very popular (and shareable) dark chocolate ganache with peanut butter–bacon brownies. The vibe is casual yet upscale, but it's a no-reservation and dinner-only spot, so come early (before 6 p.m.) or plan to wait for a table.

French

✳ROUGE RESTAURANT & BISTRO $$$
3 Center St.
West Stockbridge, MA 01266
(413) 232-4111
rougerestaurant.com
With the lovingly prepared authentic French bistro food and its quirky setting (a warren of dining rooms flamboyantly painted in red and yellow, festooned with strands of outdoor lights and an abundance of playful local art), dining at Rouge is a feast for the senses. French-born Chef-Owner William Merelle presides over the kitchen; his charming wife, Maggie, takes care of the front of the house. Merelle even expertly butchers his own meat. His signature dish is duck with seasonal vegetables in a balsamic vanilla sauce, or order the steak au poivre with cognac sauce. In the front of the restaurant, the hopping bar is where Berkshire neighbors all seem to hang out on Friday night, ordering burgers and tapas plates along with draft beer and wine by the glass.

Ice Cream

SOCO $
5 Railroad St.
Great Barrington, MA 02130
(413) 528-9420
sococreamery.com

A lot of care goes into the making of the small-batch ice cream at this Berkshire scoop shop. SoCo's super-rich 16 percent butterfat content and its wide range of seasonal and exotic flavors make this the region's most beloved ice cream maker. A summer standout is Berkshire Berry, which is made with whatever local berries are in season. Year-round, though, SoCo's top-selling flavor is Dirty Chocolate, an obscenely rich chocolate ice cream that uses 3 different chocolates and is said to be the messiest ice cream to make at the creamery. Especially lively on a summer evening at 9 p.m., the shop has both inside seating and outdoor benches for hanging out.

Italian

BABA LOUIE'S $
286 Main St.
Great Barrington, MA 01230
(413) 528-8100
babalouiespizza.com
For pizza aficionados nothing can top the remarkable thin-crust pies from Baba Louie's—except of course the interesting toppings themselves (the Isabella Pizzarella features roasted sweet potatoes and shaved fennel, the Dolce Vita figs, prosciutto, and Gorgonzola). Pizza is the star of the menu, but don't write off the special salads (especially the antipasto salad, a meal by itself) and daily pasta special that always features lots of local vegetables. Baba Louie's is so popular, there's often a wait. A second location is in Pittsfield at 34 Depot St. (413-499-2400).

CAFE LUCIA $$
80 Church St.
Lenox, MA 01240
(413) 637-2640
cafelucialenox.com

Set in an 1840s farmhouse on Lenox's main restaurant drag, Cafe Lucia is Italian to the core, serving approachable northern Italian cuisine. Start with the wild mushroom medley with soft polenta. Then order the osso bucco if only because the dish elicits a dreamy depth of flavor that can be achieved only by an all-day braise. The place is consistently mobbed during the summer season, so make reservations in advance.

TRATTORIA RUSTICA $$
27 McKay St.
Pittsfield, MA 01201
(413) 499-1192
trattoria-rustica.com

Almost a throwback to another era, with its candle-lit grotto-like subterranean space, Trattoria Rustica offers traditional Italian meals with a focus on classic preparations and ingredients. While a few up-to-date twists dot the menu, for the most part it's a reassuring roster of antipasti (Caprese salad), *primi piatti* (linguine with clams), and *secondi* (brick-oven roasted chicken with potatoes). Portions are generous, so dessert may seem impossible, but the homemade tiramisu is too good to refuse. A well-chosen wine list and service that is friendly and informed help make Trattoria Rustica a fine Berkshire choice for date night or a low-key dinner with friends.

Japanese

BIZEN $$
17 Railroad St.
Great Barrington, MA 01230
(413) 528-4343

Bizen has an ardent following of vacationing urbanites who come for the well-presented food and a comfortable interior with tatami mats, rice-paper partitions, and centerpiece sushi bar. The menu is a mix of sushi and sashimi standards along with excellent specialty rolls. Landlubbers will find plenty to like, too, with offerings such as teriyaki, tempura, and *nabemono* (one-pot soup meals) and it's all supplemented by a large sake menu.

Pubs

BARRINGTON BREWERY & RESTAURANT $-$$
420 Stockbridge Rd.
Great Barrington, MA 01230
(413) 528-8282
barringtonbrewery.net

Located in a barn, this brewpub is a magnet for those seeking good food and company—not to mention fine small-batch beer. Barrington Brewery prides itself on brewing "solar beer," with the help of 30 solar panels. They pour expertly crafted beers for every palate including seasonal fruit varieties; their malty Black Bear Stout is a favorite year-round. There's a locavore's dream pub-grub menu that features items like a grass-fed burger, a local sausage sampler, a free-range chicken half, and chocolate stout cake.

PUBLIC EAT + DRINK $$
34 Holden St.
North Adams, MA 01247
(413) 664-4444
publiceatanddrink.com

This local smart-casual joint provides a laid-back ambience to enjoy refined American classics such as gourmet burgers, flatbreads, and entrees like a flatiron steak with herbed butter and balsamic glazed grilled salmon.

On weekends walk-ins hang at the bar for up to an hour, but the warm welcome, a selection of a dozen craft beers on tap, and live music make the wait easier.

DAY TRIP IN THE BERKSHIRES

If you base yourself in and around Lenox and Stockbridge for the summer festival season, this itinerary introduces the best of northern Berkshire County, combining outdoor recreation with not one but two world-class art museums that are still largely undiscovered by the crowds.

If breakfast is not included as part of your accommodations, then start your day at always-bustling **Haven Cafe and Bakery** (8 Franklin St., Lenox; 413-637-8948; havencafe bakery.com). The baked blueberry french toast is hard to resist and should fortify you for the day ahead. After breakfast, you are headed toward Pittsfield (ironically landlocked), where Herman Melville wrote *Moby-Dick,* one of the greatest sea tales ever told. Follow Main Street north out of Lenox for 1 mile and make the first right onto Route 20, which merges with Route 7, and follow for 2 miles. Turn right onto Holmes Road at the traffic light and **Arrowhead** (780 Holmes Rd., Pittsfield; 413-442-1793; mobydick.org) will be 1.5 miles on the left. Arrowhead is open for guided tours from May through October beginning on the hour and also by appointment in the off-season (the offices of the Berkshire Historical Society are located here, so ask the docents nicely).

The whale-like shape of **Mount Greylock**'s forested slopes in the distance inspired Melville to write *Moby-Dick*—now you must venture forth to the summit of Massachusetts's tallest peak yourself. Follow Holmes Road north for 1 mile, make a left

on Pomeroy Avenue, and continue for 1.6 miles. Make a left on East Street and the next right onto Route 7 heading north (toward the mountain; you can't miss it) for 5.5 miles, as it becomes North Main Street. From here, follow the auto road signs up Rockwell Road to Mount Greylock and **Bascom Lodge** (30 Rockwell Rd., Lanesboro; 413-499-4262; bas comlodge.net). It's a nearly 9-mile climb to the summit where memorable views stretch across 5 New England states. To get your heart rate up after all the driving you can climb the 5-story **War Memorial Tower** for a bird's-eye view of the region or hike one (or just part) of the 4 well-marked summit trails that cross this part of the Appalachian Trail. Rest up at the restaurant inside Bascom Lodge. A bowl of chili or a grilled cheese on sourdough bread make for a simple meal with a view before you continue your descent down the mountain.

You are headed to the Berkshires's (and Massachusetts's) most far-flung reaches at the very northwest corner of the state. Both **Williamstown** and **North Adams** are college towns (Williams College and the Massachusetts College of Liberal Arts, respectively) and both host big-deal art museums. To reach them, backtrack to Rockwell Road and then Greylock Road. Make a right onto Scott Road and a left onto Old Williamstown Road and follow it for 12 miles to South Street. **The Clark** (225 South St., Williamstown; 413-458-2303; clarkart.edu) has important holdings of European and American masterpieces. The museum's benefactors, Sterling and Francine Clark, established their museum in rural Williamstown in 1955 far away from their native New York City, in part because of Cold War fears.

Around the corner on Main Street, the **Williams College Museum of Art** (15

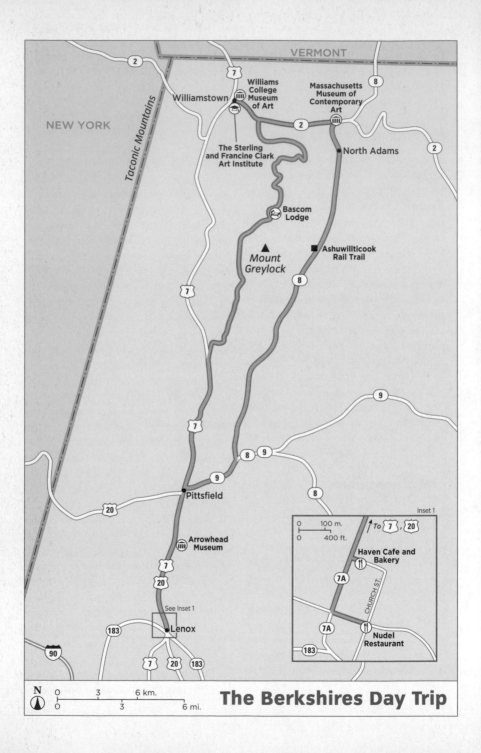

VERMONT

2

7

Williams College Museum of Art

Williamstown

Massachusetts Museum of Contemporary Art

8

NEW YORK

Taconic Mountains

2

The Sterling and Francine Clark Art Institute

2

North Adams

2

Bascom Lodge

Mount Greylock

Ashuwillticook Rail Trail

7

8

8

9

7

8   9

9

Pittsfield

8

20

9

Arrowhead Museum

Inset 1

0   100 m.

To 7 , 20

0   400 ft.

7

20

Haven Cafe and Bakery

7A

See Inset 1

183

Lenox

CHURCH ST.

90

7A

Nudel Restaurant

7   20   183

183

N

0   3   6 km.

0   3   6 mi.

The Berkshires Day Trip

Lawrence Hall Dr., Williamstown; 413-597-2429; wcma.williams.edu) is worth a spin (and it's free, so if you spend just a short time here you won't feel guilty) for its collection of modern art. Be sure to factor in some time for **Mass MoCA** (87 Marshall St., North Adams; 413-664-4111; massmoca.org) and its collection of über-modern, cutting-edge art. It's located just a short 5-mile drive along Main Street in downtown North Adams. Rest your weary feet and have an espresso or ice cream at Lickety Split, located in the lobby of Mass MoCA. As you head south along Route 8 back toward Lenox, wrap up the day with a relaxing walk along the **Ashuwillticook Rail Trail** (3 Hoosac St., Adams; 413-442-8928; mass.gov/dcr/parks/western/asrt.htm). The trailhead in the middle of downtown Adams on Hoosac Street offers free parking. The first mile or so is urban with brick former mill buildings and funky stores and eateries. Following the Hoosac River to the Cheshire Reservoir makes a logical turn-around point back to Adams and your car. Return to Lenox via Route 8 south for 12 miles and Route 7 south for 6 miles. The drive is a total of just over 60 miles and takes from 6 to 8 hours depending on stops. Low-key **Nudel Restaurant** (37 Church St., Lenox; 413-551-7183; nudelrestaurant.com), a cozy bistro that serves up an oft-changing menu of farm-to-table artisanal pasta dishes, is a worthy finish to a very full day.

LIVING HERE

The metropolitan Boston area is the third–most expensive housing market in the country. In 2012 the median price of a single-family home in the state was $300,000. The high price of real estate is reflected as well in an overall high cost of living, as much as 38 percent higher than the rest of the country, but higher average salaries somewhat compensate for it. The housing sector in Massachusetts is generally stable and avoids the problems that affect other regions because of an economy that is based on health care, higher education, and the banking and insurance industries. In 2012 the unemployment rate in the state averaged 7 percent, lower than the US average of 8.6 percent.

RELOCATION

There are many things to consider when purchasing a home. This section reviews the Massachusetts real estate market, highlighting several cities, towns, and neighborhoods that you may just want to call home. Many of the large national real estate companies, including Century 21, Coldwell Banker, Keller Williams, and RE/MAX along with regional company William Raveis, have local offices throughout the state. Contact information for some of the area's best independent real estate companies is listed for each region. The main office number is listed, but in many cases the company has offices in several area towns.

Boston & Greater Boston

Attracting Boston commuters and workers who work in the tech corridor of Route 128, towns such as Newton and Wellesley draw families for their stellar schools. Houses in both of these towns command top dollar and go quickly when they come on the market. In Newton the median house value is $685,000, which will buy a three-bedroom on a small lot on the south side of town. In Wellesley homes are generally bigger and start at just under $1 million and go as high as $3 million. Boston itself offers a tremendous variety of housing options from a one-bedroom $400,000 downtown loft to a gut-renovated $900,000 triple-decker in artsy Jamaica Plain to high-end multimillion-dollar "finds" in the Back Bay. Residential tax rates are generally high in these communities and hardly any of these towns ever experience a decline in prices, but prestigious zip codes, amenities, and proximity to the city don't come cheap.

BOSTON REALTY ADVISORS
745 Boylston St.
Boston, MA 02116
(617) 375-7900
bradvisors.com

PRESERVATION PROPERTIES
439 Newtonville Ave.
Newton, MA 02460
(617) 527-3700
preservationproperties.com

North of Boston

Concord and Lexington both have top-drawer schools and attractive historic town centers, and are close enough to get to work easily almost anywhere in the city. Lexington has a reputation for a global vibe and diversity as a result of a large Chinese and Indian population. The median home price in Lexington is $723,000; a small starter home will get you in the market for $600,000.

On the North Shore, towns such as Manchester-by-the-Sea and Essex offer pristine beaches and rich housing stock, but because of the sometimes-challenging commute to Boston, there are bargains to be found. The median home price in Essex is $439,000, which will buy you a four-bedroom antique with loads of charm. Consider telecommuting.

THE HIGGINS GROUP
1688 Massachusetts Ave.
Lexington, MA 02420
(781) 862-1700
higginsgrouprealtors.com

LILLIAN MONTALTO SIGNATURE
** PROPERTIES**
34 Park St., Ste. 1
Andover, MA 01810
(978) 475-5222
andoverhomes.com

South of Boston

The communities south of Boston represent two distinct locales. The inland Neponset Valley towns, such as Westwood and Sharon, offer great proximity (via the MBTA commuter rail line) to both Boston and Providence. Then there is the better-known South Shore, with its mix of affordable, community-minded towns, such as Quincy, and posh "Gold Coast" towns, such as Cohasset.

As a whole, the suburban towns of Westwood and Sharon both offer tremendous value for families—home prices are affordable and the high schools here are among the most highly ranked in the state. Both towns have a rural feel and significant

conservation land set aside for recreational use by residents. Westwood is the more expensive address; the median home price is $467,000, which will get you a small three-bedroom colonial or Cape. In Sharon there's plenty for even less, with lots of starter homes in the mid-$300,000s.

Quincy is located just five miles outside of Boston and has always enjoyed an affordability factor that has traditionally made it a first stop for immigrants (originally the Irish, now Chinese immigrants) on the way to home ownership. Other pluses? Wollaston Beach is nearby and Quincy is directly on the Red Line. The median home price in Quincy is a shade under $300,000, a 10 percent rise since last year—no doubt in anticipation of the city's plan to revitalize 20 blocks of the downtown area with new shops and condos. Tiny Cohasset was once a seaside retreat for Boston's elite. Today the seaside mansions along Jerusalem Street occupy the top of the market and range from $1.5 million to $12 million. Older clapboard homes clustered closer to town are much more reasonable and list in the $800,000s.

JACK CONWAY REALTY
137 Washington St.
Norwell, MA 02061
(781) 871-0080
jackconway.com

HAMMOND REAL ESTATE
15 Leavitt St.
Hingham, MA 02043
(781) 749-3650
hammondre.com/hingham

Cape Cod & the Islands

The region's scenic beauty and an abundance of cultural attractions convince summer visitors to buy on the Cape. The median price for a single-family home in Barnstable County has fallen 18 percent since 2005 and is now down to $320,000. On the Upper Cape, with its proximity to the Sagamore and Bourne Bridges, there are as many year-round residents as seasonal homeowners. Sandwich is a popular commuter town and prices are generally stable, with lots of homes on the market in the $300,000s. The mid-Cape encompasses the "village" of Hyannis, the Cape's transportation hub and urban center, and has a low tax rate because of its tourist-supported commercial base. Homes clustered outside downtown also list in the $300,000s. Even at the highest end of the spectrum, opportunity knocks at places that once seemed immune. In Nantucket the entry-level price for a home is down to around $1 million, representing a one-year decline of 10 percent in value.

ROBERT PAUL PROPERTIES
867 Main St.
Osterville, MA 02655
(508) 420-1414
robertpaul.com

SANDPIPER REALTY
60 Winter St.
Edgartown, MA 02539
(508) 627-3737
sandpiperrealty.com

Greater Worcester

Homebuyers looking for affordability would do well to look at Worcester County and enduring a longer commute. Worcester has great accessibility to Boston, it's located on both the Mass Pike and Route 495, and it's the last stop on the commuter rail. Most of Worcester's schools have made tremendous

progress in their MCAS test scores over the past five years with 41 percent of 3rd graders proficient in English language arts, up from 30 percent in 2008. The median sales price of a home in 2012 was $155,000 and has increased 12 percent over the past year. The housing stock offers a wide range of affordable options from condos in the $200,000s, 2-family homes in the $300,000s and large single-families in the $400,000s. The major employers in Worcester are UMass Medical and the universities WPI, Clark, and Holy Cross.

CENTRAL MASS REAL ESTATE INC.
3 Park St., Ste. 203
Leominster, MA 01453
(877) 537-9997
centralmass.com

Pioneer Valley

The three counties that make up the Pioneer Valley—Franklin, Hampshire, and Hampden—represent a great diversity in lifestyle choices including rural, college town, and urban. Recently the number of home sales has risen 9 percent as the overall economy in the region has improved. In 2012 the median home sales price was $210,000 for the region. Tourism (Deerfield Village) and farming are the biggest industries in rural Franklin County. Hampshire County is the home of five colleges: Amherst, UMass Amherst, Mount Holyoke, Hampshire, and Smith. The college community provides the most employment in the county. The Northampton area is an especially appealing city with a lively commercial district. A new home in an outlying suburb like Leeds or Florence can be built for $350,000 or a charming in-town Victorian can be had for $400,000. Springfield is the largest city and is the economic and transportation hub for western Massachusetts. Its job base is diverse and includes several corporate headquarters, such as Massachusetts Mutual Life Insurance Company and Bay State Health. Springfield's median home price in 2012 is low at $114,000. Springfield is sometimes called the "City of Homes" because of its Victorian residential architecture. The area offers a variety of affordable housing options to include single-family houses and a substantial stock of two- and three-family homes.

JONES GROUP REALTORS
200 Triangle St.
Amherst, MA 01002
(413) 549-3700
jonesgrouponline.com

LANDMARK REALTORS
2133 Boston Rd.
Wilbraham, MA 01095
(413) 596-4500
landmarkre.com

The Berkshires

The Berkshire real estate market is a Boston/New York City vacation home market, which puts a lot of upward pressure on the housing stock, locking out younger buyers and year-round residents.

Located in southern Berkshire County, picture-perfect Great Barrington is a favorite second-home choice for urban escapees. *Smithsonian Magazine* recently named Great Barrington one of the "best small towns in America." The median price for a three-bedroom house in 2012 was $345,000, up 52 percent from the previous year. But the data tells only half the story. Home prices vary greatly from $345,000 for a four-bedroom/two-bath in downtown Barrington, to $2

million for a large spread on a private tract outside the city.

Pittsfield is located in the heart of the Berkshires and is the largest city in the county, with a year-round population of 45,000 and a revitalized downtown. Home prices are stagnant (they used to be falling) and offer lots of affordable choices. The average listing price of a home in 2012 was $226,000, which will buy a 3-bedroom, 2½-bath colonial on a cul-de-sac.

HARSCH ASSOCIATES BERKSHIRE
   REAL ESTATE
311 Main St.
Williamstown, MA 01267
(413) 458-5000
harschrealestate.com

LANCE VERMEULEN REAL ESTATE
283 Main St.
Great Barrington, MA 01230
(413) 528-6011
lancerealestate.com

THE BUSINESS OF MOVING TO MASSACHUSETTS

Vehicle Registration & Driver's Licenses

MASSACHUSETTS REGISTRY OF MOTOR VEHICLES
25 Newport Ave.
Quincy, MA 02205
(617) 351-4500
massrmv.com

Once you have established residency in Massachusetts, you have 30 days to get your Massachusetts driver's license. You will have to make an in-person RMV visit and provide proof of identity and proof of residency, Social Security number, birthdate, signature, and transfer fee ($125). You will also have to take a simple vision-screening test. If you have a valid license from another state, you will not need to take either the written test or road test.

After moving permanently to Massachusetts, you also have 30 days to properly register your vehicle and get a vehicle inspection. This also must be done in person at the RMV. You will simultaneously transfer the title and register the vehicle at the same time. Prior to visiting the branch, you will· need to get insurance certification issued by a Massachusetts-licensed insurance company. You will also need to bring proof of title. After paying the registration fee (currently $50 for two years), you will receive your registration, plates, and decal. You're not done yet, though. Within seven days you must also get a vehicle safety and emissions inspection (currently $29). Getting your license, insurance, registration, and inspection does takes time. Allow half a day.

Voter Registration

ELECTIONS DIVISION OFFICES OF THE SECRETARY OF THE COMMONWEALTH
One Ashburton Place, Room 1705
Boston, MA 02108
(617) 727-2828
sec.state.ma.us/ele
Registering to vote in Massachusetts is easy and empowers you to have as much say as anyone else about statewide and federal laws. You can register to vote at the Registry of Motor Vehicles when you apply for your driver's license or ID card. You can register in person at your local election office (it's usually in your city or town hall) or through the mail, by contacting your city or town clerk's office and asking for an application to be sent. Before state and federal elections, college-student political groups actively register students who may have forgotten to register or those who have just turned 18.

EDUCATION

In the late 1830s educator Horace Mann advocated for a free, compulsory public school system in Massachusetts that later became the model for the nation. Massachusetts still excels in providing a quality public education for its students and is accustomed to accolades for its high overall test scores and its high learning standards.

Child Care

DEPARTMENT OF EARLY EDUCATION & CARE (EEC)
51 Sleeper St., 4th Floor
Boston, MA 02210
(617) 988-6600
mass.gov/edu/birth-grade-12/
early-education-and-care
Finding high-quality child care is a real concern for parents of young children. In Massachusetts the Department of Early Education and Care (EEC) licenses family child care homes and early childhood programs. Unlicensed care may be provided in the child's home by a babysitter or by relatives. Family child-care homes with 6 or 10 children (with an additional assistant) must be licensed by the state. Early childhood programs, both full- or part-time care in a nonresidential setting or in a home, must also be licensed. In Massachusetts this includes child-care centers, nursery schools, preschools, prekindergarten, Head Start, and before- and after-school programs.

Daycare costs in Massachusetts are among the highest in the country. The average day-care cost for full-time infant care in the state in 2011 was nearly $15,000 per year. For a 4-year-old preschooler, the full-time day-care cost was $11,669. The EEC makes funds available to families to assist them with child care payments. The amount of the payments depends on family size and income.

i Dial 2-1-1 is a toll-free number that connects callers in the state to health and human services resources available in the community, such as disaster relief, disability services, counseling, senior services, health care, child care, educational and volunteer opportunities, and much more.

Primary & Secondary Education

Public Schools
MASSACHUSETTS DEPARTMENT OF ELEMENTARY & SECONDARY EDUCATION
75 Pleasant St.
Malden, MA 02148
(781) 338-3000
doe.mass.edu

Measuring K–12 achievement through national test scores, Massachusetts has consistently ranked at or near the top over the past four years (2008–2012). High school graduation rates are high as well, at 83 percent. In per pupil spending in 2011, Massachusetts ranked 13th in the country; given Massachusetts's students' high testing outcomes, it seems the state is getting some bang for its buck.

Although test results are only one measure of student achievement, they have become increasingly important in assessing student learning in Massachusetts. The state uses the Massachusetts Comprehensive Assessment System (MCAS) to test students in grades 3 through 8 and 10 in language arts and math, and students in grades 5, 8, and 9/10 in science and engineering technology. Children must meet a minimum level of "proficient" on the grade 10 test to graduate from high school. Kids do, however, have several opportunities to pass MCAS— and tutoring help is available if they need it.

Charter & Magnet Schools
Most cities and towns in Massachusetts operate their own school districts. The state also offers public charter and magnet school choices in some locales. Some school districts have magnet schools, which are public schools that focus on a theme such as the arts, language, or science and math. Magnet schools accept children from the neighborhood and then children from the city or town by lottery for the remaining slots. Charter schools are also public schools, but they are independently run from the local school committee. Massachusetts currently has 64 charter schools. Many are located in urban districts and serve underserved children, and often feature a more flexible curriculum and school environment. Charter schools are popular—most have long waiting lists.

Private Schools & Homeschooling
There are more than 500 private and non-public schools in Massachusetts that provide parents of school-age children diverse alternatives to the public schools. Private schools are available at all grade levels including kindergarten, elementary, and secondary schools of virtually every educational philosophy and religious denomination. There are also schools for special education as well as private academies and boarding schools. Parents and guardians may also choose to

LIVING HERE

homeschool their children in accordance with their local school district policies.

Higher Education

In Massachusetts more than 69 percent of 18- to 24-year-olds are enrolled in higher education or have a degree—the highest of all the states. Massachusetts is also the only state where more than half of those ages 25 to 64 have a postsecondary degree. Seems Massachusetts residents are "smaaht"!

Public Universities & Colleges
UNIVERSITY OF MASSACHUSETTS
Amherst, MA 01003
(413) 545-0111
umass.edu
Located 90 miles from Boston, in the western part of the state, the University of Massachusetts was originally known as the Massachusetts Agricultural College or "Mass Aggie." The campus is surrounded by farmland and the school still offers programs in agriculture, but over the years the scope of the curriculum has changed dramatically to include 85 majors across a range of educational opportunities. UMass is an exceptional educational value; in-state tuition and fees are $13,000 or $26,000 annually for out-of-state students. Amherst is also a great college town (it's also home to Amherst College and Hampshire College) but it is isolated and sports are a major focus for students. The UMass Minutemen compete in NCAA Division I sports. Ice hockey and basketball are the most popular sports; football less so now that home games are played at Gillette Stadium in Foxboro, 2 hours away. Besides Amherst, the UMass system includes campuses in Boston, Dartmouth, Lowell, and the UMass Medical School in Worcester.

Private Universities & Colleges
BABSON COLLEGE
231 Babson Park
Wellesley, MA 02457
(781) 239-5522
babson.edu
Babson is a small private college that specializes in business education. Located outside of Boston in the town of Wellesley, it has a total undergraduate enrollment of 2,000 students. The school offers undergraduate concentrations in traditional business fields like marketing, finance, and accounting, but is particularly well-known for its program in entrepreneurship, for which it is consistently ranked number one in the country by *US News & World Report*. The graduate school enrolls 1,400 students and offers both full-time and part-time programs that lead to an MBA or a master of science in accounting degree. Babson's part-time evening graduate track is a popular choice for working professionals who have corporate tuition remission benefits. As for community programs, the Babson Skating Center is an indoor ice rink that offers public open skate and ice lessons year-round.

BERKLEE COLLEGE OF MUSIC
1140 Boylston St.
Boston, MA 02215
(617) 266-1400
berklee.edu
Straddling the Back Bay and Fenway neighborhoods, Berklee is a relatively new college, founded in 1945 by Lawrence Berk, an MIT engineer and musician who saw a need to provide practical training for working musicians in the then-new fields of radio and television. Today Berklee is one of the most renowned contemporary music schools in the country, with strengths in

jazz, rock, and popular music performance—both instrumental and vocal. Berklee's music production, songwriting, and film scoring departments are also well regarded. Its undergraduate enrollment is 4,300 and the school can count among its famous students Quincy Jones, John Mayer, Bruce Hornsby, Melissa Etheridge, and Esperanza Spalding. The Berklee Performance Center (136 Massachusetts Ave.; 617-266-7455; berklee.edu/bpc) is the college's principal stage. Or you can see up-and-coming Berklee musicians at the school's on-campus coffeehouse, Cafe 939 (939 Boylston St.; 617-747-6038; cafe939.com).

BOSTON COLLEGE
140 Commonwealth Ave.
Chestnut Hill, MA 02467
(617) 552-8000
bc.edu

Boston College opened as a Jesuit school with just 22 students in 1864. The college was established to serve the immigrant Irish community of the city; today its 9 schools enroll more than 9,000 undergraduates and 5,000 graduate students. The main campus is situated on 175 acres of lush greenery in Chestnut Hill overlooking Boston and features outstanding examples of gothic revival architecture. BC's signature building is stone Gasson Hall, which has a terra-cotta tile roof, stained-glass windows, and a majestic 200-foot bell tower. BC has a second residential campus 1 mile away in Newton, which is home to the BC Law School. Fall is a big season for the BC Eagles (NCAA Division I), whose football program has historically been a big local draw—even before Doug Flutie's Hail Mary pass over Miami in 1984.

BOSTON UNIVERSITY
One Silber Way
Boston, MA 02215
(617) 353-2000
bu.edu

Founded in 1839 as a small Methodist theological school, Boston University has grown from its humble beginnings as the Newbury Biblical Institute to become a powerhouse of academics, research, and ice hockey. Seemingly continuously expanding, BU is the fourth largest private university in the country, with 18 schools and colleges and a student population of over 30,000 (undergraduate and graduate). BU's academic offerings are highly regarded, especially business, engineering, and education, as well as the graduate medical and law programs. With classrooms and dorms of its main Charles River campus scattered along Commonwealth Avenue and throughout the Fenway/Kenmore Square neighborhood and its medical school across town in the South End, the university doesn't have a traditional campus feel, but with 5 national championships, the BU Terriers NCAA Division I men's hockey team generates plenty of school spirit. Metropolitan College offers professional degrees and certificate programs in a wide variety of disciplines including criminal justice, tourism management, and health informatics as well as one-time courses open to the general public, including very popular evening seminars in food, wine, and the arts.

CLARK UNIVERSITY
950 Main St.
Worcester, MA 01610
(508) 793-7431
clarku.edu

Clark was founded in 1887 as the country's first university dedicated to graduate studies.

Clark's programs leading to master's and doctoral degrees in psychology, physics, and geography are nationally recognized. More recently Clark was one of the 40 colleges featured in Loren Pope's landmark college guidebook *Colleges That Change Lives*. Clark is particularly credited with promoting the development of psychology as a discipline. In 1909 Sigmund Freud delivered a lecture series on psychoanalysis at Clark—it was the only time he spoke at an American university. The Robert H. Goddard Library is named after Robert Goddard, the "father of the American rocket program", who received both his master's degree and PhD in physics from Clark. (A true Worcesterite, Goddard received his undergraduate degree from WPI.) Today Clark is a liberal arts, research-based university, but considered small in size with undergraduate enrollment of 2,300 students and graduate enrollment of 1,150 students. Its undergraduate program offers 32 majors as well as a very attractive accelerated BA/master's program with the fifth year of study tuition-free. Located in Worcester's Main South neighborhood, Clark has been nationally recognized for its exceptional effort at urban revitalization of its community. Since 1985 Clark's University Park Partnership has worked to renovate local housing, offer adult education classes, and provide free-tuition scholarships to neighborhood residents.

COLLEGE OF THE HOLY CROSS
1 College St.
Worcester, MA 01610
(508) 793-2443
holycross.edu

Holy Cross is a small, exclusively undergraduate liberal arts Catholic college. Founded in 1843 by the Jesuits, the school has a reputation for academic excellence and ranks as one of the country's top Catholic colleges. The leafy 175-acre campus is set high on a hill overlooking Worcester and features an abundance of buildings with gothic flair—it's all very Hogwarts-esque. Holy Cross enrolls about 3,000 students and offers more than 27 majors with the social sciences, English, psychology, foreign languages, and history among the more popular majors. The Holy Cross Crusaders are members of the NCAA Division I Patriot League, and in the tradition of former Crusaders and Celtics Basketball Hall of Famers Bob Cousy and Tommy Heinsohn, Holy Cross is especially competitive in basketball. There is huge school spirit at Holy Cross. These students bleed purple—the basketball games especially bring out huge crowds.

HARVARD UNIVERSITY
1350 Massachusetts Ave.
Cambridge, MA 02138
(617) 495-1000
harvard.edu

The best-known university in the world is Harvard; the list of notable people associated with the university is legion and includes 8 US presidents, John F. Kennedy, George W. Bush, and Barack Obama among them. Other distinguished Harvard alumni include Helen Keller, Yo Yo Ma, and Tommy Lee Jones. Founded in 1636, Harvard is the oldest college in the US. Undergraduate enrollment is 7,000 students; graduate school enrollment is 14,000 students. Harvard comprises the College, the Graduate School of Arts and Sciences, and 12 professional schools. Included in the professional schools are the top-ranked Law School, MBA program, and School of Medicine. The Harvard Kennedy School of Government, the Engineering and

Applied Sciences School, and Divinity School are also well-regarded graduate programs. The Harvard Museum of Natural History is the public face of Harvard. The university has several other museums, too, including the Harvard Art Museums, the Peabody Museum of Archaeology and Ethnology, and the Semitic Museum. Adult learners can experience these hallowed halls by pursuing a part-time Harvard degree (associate's, bachelor's, or master's). Harvard also offers 5-course professional certificates in topics as varied as religious studies, software engineering, and sustainability.

LESLEY UNIVERSITY
29 Everett St.
Cambridge, MA 02138
(617) 868-9600
lesley.edu

The institution known as Lesley University was founded as a "teachers college" in 1909. Today degrees and programs for education professionals are still the school's focus. Lesley offers undergraduate, graduate (masters and PhD), and certificate programs in education, as well as the fields of human services including psychology and expressive therapies. The school's enrollment numbers tell the story; Lesley has 1,857 undergraduate students and 7,768 postgraduate students. Lesley is known for its flexible learning opportunities; courses are offered on evenings and weekends to accommodate the working professionals who take them. Among Lesley's most popular offerings are its "fast-track" programs that provide focused education training and teach the skills required to obtain licensure in the education field.

MASSACHUSETTS COLLEGE OF PHARMACY AND HEALTH SCIENCES
179 Longwood Ave.
Boston, MA 02115
(617) 732-2800
mcphs.edu

Located in the heart of the Longwood Medical area, the Massachusetts College of Pharmacy and Health Sciences is well-known for its undergraduate and graduate pharmacy programs. More than a pharmacy school, MCPHS offers 30 undergraduate degrees in a wide range of health-related fields including chemistry, public health, pre-med, nursing, dental hygiene, and medical imaging. MCPHS also offers 21 master's and PhD programs including an accelerated 6-year doctor of pharmacy (PharmD) program. It's a small college with undergraduate enrollment at 1,890 students and graduate enrollment at 3,437 students. As medical/health science majors, MCPHS students look forward to plenty of employment opportunities when they graduate.

MASSACHUSETTS INSTITUTE OF TECHNOLOGY
77 Massachusetts Ave.
Cambridge, MA 02139
(617) 253-3400
mit.edu

Sometimes referred to as "the other" Cambridge university, MIT is one of the world's leading science and technology research institutions. MIT can lay claim to 78 Nobel laureates and an equally impressive number of National Medal of Science recipients and Rhodes Scholars. The undergraduate enrollment is 4,384 students while the graduate school program has an enrollment of 6,510. Besides engineering and science disciplines (of which electrical engineering and computer science are the most popular), MIT has strong departments in economics, linguistics, political science, and management. The campus itself is located on the Charles River and is spread across 168 acres in East Cambridge. The "innovation economy" isn't the latest business policy trend at MIT. Over the years, MIT alumni have gone on to found several prominent companies including Intel, Texas Instruments, Raytheon, and Bose. Today dozens of smaller MIT-spawned labs and technology companies dot the university's Kendall Square neighborhood and new eateries and hip loft living have followed.

NEW ENGLAND CONSERVATORY
290 Huntington Ave.
Boston, MA 02115
(617) 585-1101
necmusic.edu

New England Conservatory was established in 1867 and is one of the oldest and most prestigious conservatories in the country. Located on Huntington Avenue across from Symphony Hall, NEC is a neighbor to the Boston Symphony Orchestra and the ties between the two organizations are strong. Several BSO orchestra members teach at NEC and many current members of the orchestra are NEC alumni. The school is home to 750 undergraduate and graduate (master's and doctor of musical arts) students. Among the majors offered are piano, all the orchestral instruments, jazz, composition, conducting, and voice. Dating from 1903, Jordan Hall (617-585-1260) is NEC's signature performance space, a glorious acoustical and architectural gem. The 1,000-seat concert hall is used for student concerts and also regularly features prominent musicians from around the world. Of the nearly 600 student and faculty concerts that take place during the school year, the vast majority are free and open to the public. Not as well known is that through its community-based preparatory school for children and its continuing education division for adults, NEC also trains musicians of every age and every level—even awkward beginning adults!

NORTHEASTERN UNIVERSITY
360 Huntington Ave.
Boston, MA 02115
(617) 373-2000
northeastern.edu

Northeastern is on the rise. Ranked 56th overall in the 2013 *US News & World Report* ranking, Northeastern has transformed itself over the past 15 years from being a largely local commuter school to a national research university. Northeastern began in 1898 as an evening institute at the Huntington Avenue YMCA. Today Northeastern has bought some of that YMCA building for dorm space and has taken over much of the rest of the neighborhood to include parts of Roxbury, Fenway, and the Back Bay. The university undergraduate enrollment is 15,339 students and its graduate programs enroll an additional 5,410 students. In its undergraduate school, Northeastern offers majors in 65 departments. Its business, engineering, health sciences, computer, and information science colleges are its most popular. Since 1909 a cooperative education program that sends students to work for an employer to get on-the-job experience has been an integral part of a Northeastern education. When students aren't working or in class, there is plenty to do. The neighborhood is extremely student-centric with Wentworth Institute of Technology next door and Boston University across the Fens.

The Northeastern Huskies compete in NCAA Division I athletics. Home to Huskies ice hockey and basketball, Matthews Arena, which opened in 1910, is the nation's oldest indoor hockey arena still in use.

WENTWORTH INSTITUTE OF TECHNOLOGY
550 Huntington Ave.
Boston, MA 02115
(617) 989-4000
wit.edu

Located on Huntington Avenue in Boston's Fenway neighborhood, Wentworth is a small engineering college that offers undergraduate degrees in 14 majors including architecture, computer science, and electro-mechanical engineering. Wentworth also offers master's degree programs in architecture and construction management. The undergraduate enrollment numbers 3,855 students and like that of a lot of technology-based universities, the student population is heavily male, with only 19 percent of the students women. There is an emphasis on hands-on learning and most majors require students to complete a cooperative work experience designed to give them an opportunity to make connections in their field. The most compelling reason to come to Wentworth is that graduates find their way into the workforce with better than decent entry-level engineering jobs. Wentworth has extensive continuing education offerings including journeyman electrician programs and AutoCAD workforce training.

WORCESTER POLYTECHNIC INSTITUTE
100 Institute Rd.
Worcester, MA 01609
(508) 831-5286
wpi.edu

Founded in 1865, Worcester Polytechnic Institute, better known as WPI, has an attractive New England–style campus on a hill on the outskirts of Worcester. The university offers 50 undergraduate and graduate degrees and is focused on cutting-edge science and engineering. It's a small university with 3,849 undergraduates and 1,929 graduate students. Among its most popular majors are mechanical engineering, biology and biotechnology, and robotics engineering. The translation of WPI's German motto, *Lehr und Kunst,* is "Theory and Practice," which reflects the school's learn-by-doing approach of project- and presentation-based course work. WPI graduates typically land jobs right out of school, recently ranking No. 6 among all national universities for average starting salary by Payscale.com. WPI's selective and small (200-student) part-time MBA program is technology focused and is consistently ranked highly by *Businessweek.*

HEALTH CARE

Massachusetts has medical care options that are among the very best in the country. From cutting-edge cancer treatment to emergency psychiatric care to educating families about pediatric asthma, Massachusetts hospitals take comprehensive health care to the next level. Included on this list are large teaching institutions—sprawling multicampus behemoths like Brigham and Women's and UMass Worcester Medical Center that treat hundreds of thousands of patients a year, as well as specialty hospitals, such as orthopedic care center New England Baptist Hospital, and community hospitals like Newton Wellesley that deliver top-notch emergency room care.

Health Departments

MASSACHUSETTS DEPARTMENT OF PUBLIC HEALTH
250 Washington St.
Boston, MA 02108
(617) 624-6000
mass.gov/dph

There's no shortage of doctors, hospitals, and pharmacies in Massachusetts, but sometimes you need help finding what is best for your health-care needs. The Massachusetts Department of Public Health is a one-stop source that provides links to emergency medical service providers, hospitals, doctors, and wellness programs, such as flu clinics. The Health Connector link also provides access to affordable health insurance options until all the provisions of the national health care reform law take effect in 2014.

BOSTON PUBLIC HEALTH COMMISSION
1010 Massachusetts Ave.
Boston, MA 02118
(617) 534-5395
bphc.org

Boston's Public Health Commission has an illustrious past. The commission dates back to 1799 and claims Paul Revere as its first health officer (silversmith, dentist, and message deliverer; Revere was a busy guy). The city's public health commission is totally connected to Boston's medical community. Among its useful services are free flu clinics, emergency weather shelters for heat and cold, addiction and recovery support, as well as child, adolescent, and family health services.

Hospitals

BETH ISRAEL DEACONESS MEDICAL CENTER
330 Brookline Ave.
Boston, MA 02115
(617) 667-7000
bidmc.org

Beth Israel Deaconess is a 631-bed, full-service tertiary teaching hospital associated with Harvard Medical and is affiliated with both the Joslin Diabetes Center and the Dana-Farber/Harvard Cancer Center. Beth Israel conducts top-flight research, both basic and clinical, and virtually every patient just diagnosed with cancer is offered the chance to participate in a study. Beth Israel helped to develop the first implantable cardiac pacemaker in 1952 and is known for its care for the full range of heart conditions. Beth Israel is a popular hospital choice for mothers-to-be. In 2012 the Beth Israel obstetrics team delivered approximately 5,000 babies. Located in the Longwood Medical area around the corner from Fenway Park, Beth Israel Deaconess is also the official hospital of the Red Sox.

BOSTON MEDICAL CENTER
One Boston Medical Center Place
Boston, MA 02118
(617) 638-8000
bmc.org

Boston Medical Center is a 626-bed community teaching hospital that was created through the merger of the old (since 1864) Boston City Hospital with Boston University Medical Center. The hospital offers health care to meet the specific needs of its community (Dorchester, Mattapan, the South End), with an emphasis on outreach and ambulatory services. Boston Medical is also a leader in disaster management and has New

England's largest Level I Trauma emergency room center.

BRIGHAM AND WOMEN'S HOSPITAL
75 Francis St.
Boston, MA 02115
(617) 732-5500
brighamandwomens.org

Brigham and Women's is consistently ranked among the top 10 hospitals in the country by US News & World Report. Located in the Longwood Medical area, the hospital is a Harvard Medical School–affiliated institution and is internationally acclaimed for excellence in clinical care, education, and scientific research in medicine with unparalleled programs in cancer, heart surgery, neurology, orthopedics, and obstetrics. The Brigham has one of the most active and successful heart transplant programs in the world, established in 1984. Its surgeons have already performed more than 600 heart transplants—more than any hospital in New England. Its neurosciences institute has been an internationally recognized center for the treatment of brain disorders. The Brigham also has one of the largest obstetrics and gynecology programs in the country, providing everything from routine screening tests to the most advanced diagnosis and management of high-risk births.

CAPE COD HOSPITAL
27 Park St.
Hyannis, MA 02601
(508) 771-1800
capecodhealth.org

What started out as a small cottage hospital in 1920 has since grown to a 259-bed facility that is the largest hospital on the Cape. This is one of the busiest emergency centers in the state year-round, seeing more than 90,000 people come through its ER doors annually. The hospital offers impressive cardiovascular services with a dedicated 4-bed cardio triage unit for coronary intervention and 2 cardiac surgery rooms.

CHILDREN'S HOSPITAL BOSTON
300 Longwood Ave.
Boston, MA 02115
(617) 355-6000
childrenshospital.org

When it comes to serious illness in the lives of children, only the best will do. Children's Hospital Boston is a 395-bed comprehensive center that is nationally ranked as one of the best pediatric hospitals in the country with strengths in cardiac surgery, neurology, cancer, orthopedics, urology, and kidney disorders. Children's is a teaching hospital for Harvard Medical School and is located in the Longwood Medical area. Children's is also the world's largest research pediatric medical center and is a leader in the treatment of autism. Children's is particularly known for going the extra mile to ensure the comfort of kids and their families with toy-filled play rooms on every floor and beds built into window alcoves for parents to sleep overnight in their child's hospital room.

MASSACHUSETTS GENERAL HOSPITAL
55 Fruit St.
Boston, MA 02114
(617) 726-2000
massgeneral.org

Arguably the best hospital in the country, Mass General is also one of the most historic. Located in Boston's Beacon Hill neighborhood, Mass General is the state's largest hospital with 1,051 beds. It was founded in 1811 and is the third oldest hospital in the country. Its original building was designed by colonial architect Charles Bulfinch and is still in use. Mass General is Harvard's oldest and biggest affiliated teaching hospital and is nationally ranked in 16 adult specialties and 4 pediatric specialties. Whatever ails you, getting it treated at Mass General is a safe bet: The hospital's patient-safety record is exemplary.

MCLEAN HOSPITAL
115 Mill St.
Belmont, MA 02478
(617) 855-2000
mcleanhospital.org

Founded in 1811 and located in residential surroundings on the Belmont/Cambridge line, McLean Hospital is a Harvard-affiliated psychiatric institution offering comprehensive treatment in both inpatient and outpatient settings for adults, adolescents, and children. Ranked among the top psychiatric hospitals in the country by *US News & World Report* for the past 20 years, McLean's is especially known for its on-site Pathways Academy, a fully accredited independent private school that caters to children and teens.

NEW ENGLAND BAPTIST HOSPITAL
125 Parker Hill Ave.
Boston, MA 02120
(617) 754-5800
nebh.org

New England Baptist is one of the city's smaller hospitals that has an established niche—in this case for orthopedic care—that compares favorably to the city's "Big Three": Mass General, Beth Israel, and the Brigham. Affiliated with Tufts Medical School and UMass Medical School, the 141-bed facility is located in Boston's Mission Hill neighborhood. New England Baptist offers a team of experts in orthopedic surgery,

plastic surgery, radiology, and physical and occupational therapy and a comprehensive approach to orthopedic patient care. New England Baptist is the official hospital of the Boston Celtics, so it's a good bet they can take care of your knee surgery, too.

NEWTON WELLESLEY HOSPITAL
2014 Washington St.
Newton, MA 02462
(617) 243-6000
nwh.org

Boston isn't the only place in the state to get top-notch medical care. Newton Wellesley is a 313-bed community teaching hospital offering many of the inpatient, outpatient, emergency, and diagnostic services of the city teaching hospitals—with fewer hassles and valet parking. The hospital is located at mile 17 of the Boston Marathon and its emergency room is extremely experienced in every sort of running injury. The wellness and education center is comprehensive, offering everything from nutrition counseling to baby massage, support groups for caregivers, and babysitter certification for teens.

SOUTH SHORE HOSPITAL
55 Fogg Rd.
South Weymouth, MA 02190
(781) 624-8000
southshorehospital.org

South Shore Hospital is a regional health resource for nearly 725,000 residents of Boston's South Shore. The facility has 321 beds and is staffed by more than 300 physicians in 30 specialties. The hospital is best known for its knee and hip replacement surgeries, but it has also received recognition in many other specialties, such as diabetes and endocrinology, urology, and ear/nose/throat. Its South

Shore Visiting Nurse Association is one of the state's largest home-health service providers.

UMASS MEMORIAL MEDICAL CENTER
55 Lake Ave. North
Worcester, MA 01655
(508) 334-1000
umassmemorial.org
It's tough to compete with the big Boston hospitals, but in many ways UMass Medical holds its own. Affiliated with UMass Medical School, this is the largest health-care system in central and western Massachusetts, with 3 campuses in downtown Worcester, 4 community partner hospitals, and a network of community health centers. Virtually every department provides high-quality care, among its strengths cardiology, diabetes, orthopedics, cancer, emergency medicine, surgery, women's health, and children's medical services.

MEDIA

Print Media

Magazines
BOSTON MAGAZINE
300 Massachusetts Ave.
Boston, MA 02115
(617) 262-9700
bostonmagazine.com
For 40 years this monthly Boston glossy lifestyle magazine has featured articles on the city's best dining, entertainment, and shopping trends. The magazine also runs thought-provoking pieces on politics and culture such as "M.I.T. Rising: How Harvard Became the Second-Best University in Cambridge" and "Put a Casino in the Seaport Now. Seriously." But it is its annual guides *Best of Boston* and *Boston's Best Schools* that fly off the shelf.

BOSTON PARENTS PAPER
639 Granite St.
Braintree, MA 02184
(617) 522-1515
boston.parenthood.com
The *Boston Parents Paper* is a free monthly newspaper that is the area's go-to resource for parents and families with children from newborn through the early teens. Each issue features a good mix of substantive local stories, humorous parenting essays, and sound advice, along with a calendar of family-oriented events so you are never at a loss for things to do with your kids on weekends or during school and summer vacations.

Daily Newspapers

BOSTON GLOBE
135 Morrissey Blvd.
Boston, MA 02125
(617) 929-2000
bostonglobe.com
Founded in 1872, the *Globe* is the region's largest general daily newspaper (circulation 225,000). Over the years the *Globe* has won 21 Pulitzer Prizes in journalism and is considered the region's most influential newspaper. To find out what's going on in the area day by day, check out the *Globe*'s G section; the Thursday Weekend section is particularly helpful for visitors. Access to online newspaper content is by paid subscription (print subscribers have free access). Some of the *Globe*'s online edition can also be found for free at the *Globe*'s community portal, boston .com. Changes are on the horizon; the *Globe* has been owned by the *New York Times* since 1993 and is currently on the selling block.

BOSTON HERALD
70 Fargo St.
Boston, MA 02210
(617) 426-3000
bostonherald.com
Started in 1864, the *Boston Herald* is the city's other broadsheet. The *Herald's* circulation is just under 100,000. The *Herald* is columnist driven and is generally viewed as the less liberal of the Boston papers.

WORCESTER TELEGRAM & GAZETTE
100 Front St.
Worcester, MA 01608
(508) 793-9100
telegram.com
Worcester's only daily newspaper, *T&G* covers Worcester politics (its editorial offices are located in the shadow of Worcester City Hall) and happenings on Beacon Hill—especially those that affect residents of Worcester and central Massachusetts communities. *T&G* coverage also includes business news, sports, and lifestyle features. Its Sunday edition features the Entertainment and Travel sections that come from the *Boston Globe*. Established in 1866, *T&G* has been owned by the *New York Times* since 1999 and like the *Boston Globe*, it is currently up for sale.

Other Regional Newspapers
BAY WINDOWS
28 Damrell St.
Boston, MA 02127
(617) 464-7280
baywindows.com
Boston's largest-circulation lesbian and gay newspaper, *Bay Windows* comes out every Thursday and focuses on LGBT local and national news and politics along with reviews of the club, restaurant, and theater scene around town. It's a free publication and distributed at Shaw's and Stop & Shop grocery stores and gay-friendly establishments throughout the city.

JEWISH ADVOCATE
15 School St.
Boston, MA 02108
(617) 367-9100
thejewishadvocate.com
The *Jewish Advocate* is the oldest continuously circulating Jewish publication in the US, a weekly newspaper that can trace its history back to 1902. The *Jewish Advocate* provides news articles, reviews, and features on a wide-ranging mix of local, national, and international events and issues of concern to the Jewish community in Boston and New England.

THE PILOT
66 Brooks Dr.
Braintree, MA 02189
(617) 779-3780
thebostonpilot.com
The official newspaper of the Archdiocese of Boston, *The Pilot* was first published in 1829 and is the oldest Catholic newspaper in the country. *The Pilot* is a weekly with print circulation of 26,000. The paper has a decided Irish-American slant and measures events (local, national, international) against Catholic morals and ethics.

Television Stations

Each of the three major commercial networks (ABC, CBS, NBC) and PBS have affiliate stations in Massachusetts. The state is also home to several large regional cable networks including New England Cable News and NESN.

COMCAST SPORTSNET NEW ENGLAND

42 3rd Ave.
Burlington, MA 01803
(781) 270-2610
csnne.com

Comcast SportsNet is the sister cable station to NECN, covering all of the New England professional sports teams including the Red Sox, Patriots, Celtics, and Bruins, as well as the region's many college teams. You can get Boston sports breaking news, scores, updates, and interviews 24 hours a day.

NECN

160 Wells Ave.
Newton, MA 02459
(617) 630-5000
necn.com

The nation's largest 24-hour regional cable news network reaches close to 4 million households in the six-state New England region. On-air and online, NECN is a full-service news channel that delivers world and national stories, but the predominating content is decidedly local. Although owned by Comcast, the station is carried on most cable systems in New England.

NESN

480 Arsenal St.
Watertown, MA 02472
(617) 536-9233
nesn.com

NESN, pronounced "Ness-en", is a regional cable network that covers a variety of sports events but is mostly known as the principal broadcaster of Red Sox and Bruins games (NESN is owned by both teams). Available locally in all six New England States, it is included as part of all basic cable and satellite packages. How could it not?

WBZ CHANNEL 4

1170 Soldiers Field Rd.
Boston, MA 02134
(617) 787-7145
boston.cbslocal.com

The studios of the local CBS affiliate are located in the Allston-Brighton section of Boston. WBZ broadcasts local news, weather, traffic, and sports from 4:30 a.m. to 7 a.m., noon, 5 p.m., 5:30 p.m., 6 p.m., and 11 p.m. The station is also known for its live local event coverage, including First Night, the Boston Marathon, and the Fourth of July Boston Pops Fireworks Spectacular.

WCVB CHANNEL 5

5 TV Place
Needham, MA 02494
(781) 449-0400
wcvb.com

WCVB is the Boston ABC affiliate and is the market's top-rated and most-watched news station. WCVB broadcasts local news, weather, traffic, and sports beginning with its *EyeOpener* broadcast from 4:30 a.m. to 7 a.m., and news also at noon, 5 p.m., 5:30 p.m., 6 p.m., and 11 p.m. WCVB also produces original programming, including the long-running (since 1982) local nightly news magazine *Chronicle*. *Chronicle* showcases stories with a local flavor, such as "best of" Boston restaurants and growing up biracial in Boston.

WGBH BOSTON

1 Guest St.
Boston, MA 02135
(617) 300-2000
wgbh.org

WGBH is a PBS powerhouse station— besides delivering the best of PBS educational programming and acclaimed dramas, and providing award-winning coverage of local issues and affairs of the day, WGBH produces nearly a third of the network's shows, including *Frontline, Nova, American Experience, Antiques Roadshow,* and *This Old House.* In the Boston area, WGBH also operates WGBX, Springfield's WGBY, and the radio stations WGBH and WCRB.

WHDH CHANNEL 7
7 Bullfinch Place
Boston, MA 02114
(800) 280-8477
whdh.com

This NBC affiliate has its studios near Boston's Government Center, giving the station great access to Boston City Hall and the state house. Its sister cable station, WLVI, produces a popular 10 p.m. newscast.

Cable Service

Cable is available in nearly every Massachusetts community through one or more providers depending on where you live. There are currently 11 cable providers in the state; the largest by far is Comcast (comcast.com).

Radio

The Massachusetts radio market includes several high-profile radio stations of almost every format that cater to every kind of listener. WXKS, better known as KISS 108 (FM 108), has been a mainstay of Boston's urban radio scene for decades and features a Top 40 format that appeals across generations. The local rock station is WAAF (FM 97.7 and FM 107.3), which specializes in modern album rock but also plays alternative and indie rock. WJMN or "Jam'n" (FM 94.5) is Boston's hip hop station and focuses on mainstream artists with some R&B. Massachusetts may be far north of the Mason-Dixon line, but country music has a loyal listener base here, particularly in the suburbs. Fans can get their country music fix at WKLB (FM 102.5). Locally, several student-run college radio stations still occupy the FM dial, most notably Emerson College's WERS (FM 88.9), which is perennially ranked as one of the top college radio stations in the country.

Non-music radio options include WEEI (FM 93.7), which is the voice of the Boston sports fan and the radio home of the Boston Red Sox. It also streams worldwide online so you will never miss a game. If you're stuck in a rush-hour gridlock, Boston's local all-news radio station is WBZ radio (AM 1030) and is the place for traffic, weather, and breaking news updates.

Broadcasting from its Brighton studios over the Mass Pike, WCRB (FM 99.5) is a listener-supported, NPR member station with a 24-hour all-classical format. *Drive Time Live* on weekday afternoons features in-studio performances by internationally known and New England–based musicians and ensembles. Concerts of the Boston Symphony at Symphony Hall (or Tanglewood in the summer) are broadcast live on Saturday evening.

Boston has not one, but two all-talk public radio stations, WGBH (FM 89.7) and WBUR (FM 90.9). WBUR is known for its local news from its own team of award-winning journalists and for its nationally syndicated content, too, producing *On Point* and *Here and Now.* WGBH mostly broadcasts NPR news programming along with some shows special to the station, including *A Celtic Sojourn.*

INDEX

INSIDERS' GUIDE ®

The acclaimed travel series that has sold more than 2 million copies!

Discover: Your Travel Destination.
Your Home. Your Home-to-Be.

Albuquerque

Anchorage & Southcentral Alaska

Atlanta

Austin

Baltimore

Baton Rouge

Boulder & Rocky Mountain National Park

Branson & the Ozark Mountains

California's Wine Country

Cape Cod & the Islands

Charleston

Charlotte

Chicago

Cincinnati

Civil War Sites in the Eastern Theater

Civil War Sites in the South

Colorado's Mountains

Dallas & Fort Worth

Denver

El Paso

Florida Keys & Key West

Gettysburg

Glacier National Park

Great Smoky Mountains

Greater Fort Lauderdale

Greater Tampa Bay Area

Hampton Roads

Houston

Hudson River Valley

Indianapolis

Jacksonville

Kansas City

Long Island

Louisville

Madison

Maine Coast

Memphis

Myrtle Beach & the Grand Strand

Nashville

New Orleans

New York City

North Carolina's Mountains

North Carolina's Outer Banks

North Carolina's Piedmont Triad

Oklahoma City

Orange County, CA

Oregon Coast

Palm Beach County

Palm Springs

Philadelphia & Pennsylvania Dutch Country

Phoenix

Portland, Maine

Portland, Oregon

Raleigh, Durham & Chapel Hill

Richmond, VA

Reno and Lake Tahoe

St. Louis

San Antonio

Santa Fe

Savannah & Hilton Head

Seattle

Shreveport

South Dakota's Black Hills Badlands

Southwest Florida

Tucson

Tulsa

Twin Cities

Washington, D.C.

Williamsburg & Virginia's Historic Triangle

Yellowstone & Grand Teton

Yosemite

**To order call 800-243-0495
or visit www.Insiders.com**